Canadian

CONTENT

Canadian
CONTENT
Sixth edition

Sarah Norton
Nell Waldman

THOMSON
NELSON

ustralia Canada Mexico Singapore Spain United Kingdom United States

Canadian Content, Sixth Edition

by Sarah Norton and Nell Waldman

Associate Vice President, Editorial Director:
Evelyn Veitch

Editor-in-Chief, Higher Education:
Anne Williams

Executive Editor:
Laura Macleod

Marketing Manager:
Sandra Green

Developmental Editor:
Beth Lariviere

Permissions Coordinator:
Nicola Winstanley

Senior Content Production Manager:
Natalia Denesiuk

Copy Editor:
June Trusty

Proofreader:
Joyce Grant

Manufacturing Coordinator:
Ferial Suleman

Design Director:
Ken Phipps

Interior Design:
Sonya V. Thursby, Opus House Incorporated

Cover Design:
Ken Phipps

Cover Image:
Anne Bradley

Compositor:
Nelson Gonzalez

Printer:
Maracle Press Limited

Library and Archives Canada Cataloguing in Publication Data

Canadian content / [edited by] Sarah Norton, Nell Waldman. — 6th ed.

Includes index.
ISBN-13: 978-0-17-610362-0
ISBN-10: 0-17-610362-7

1. College readers. 2. English language—Rhetoric—Textbooks. I. Norton, Sarah, date II. Waldman, Nell Kozak, date

PE1417.C25 2007   808'.0427
C2006-906068-1

To the Instructor

Canadian Content, Sixth Edition, is a reader intended for Canadian college and university students who are studying English composition. Fifteen of the twenty-seven new selections are by Canadians, including some of our country's best and most thoughtful writers (e.g., Wayson Choy, Erica Ritter, Mark Kingwell, and Ken Wiwa), as well as two new student writers (Trina Rys and Armin Kumarshellah). New selections by British and American writers supplement the international essays retained from previous editions.

Our title, *Canadian Content*, is a play on the title of the mandate of the Canadian Radio-television and Telecommunications Commission (CRTC), the federal broadcasting regulatory agency whose guidelines require that broadcasters provide a minimum of two-thirds Canadian content in their programming. Although print materials are not governed by the CRTC, we thought that the agency's minimum requirement was a worthy goal for a college text.

This edition features some significant changes. In response to reviewers' requests, we have included more light-hearted, upbeat selections. In the Introduction, the "How to Read with Understanding" and "How to Write to Be Understood" sections have been revised in an attempt to provide a short, non-technical overview of the complex tasks of reading and writing. "How to Write a Documented Essay" concludes with a research paper that has been updated for this edition. (A comprehensive treatment of researching, writing, and documenting papers, using both the Modern Language Association (MLA) and the American Psychological Association (APA) documentation methods, is available on our new Web site—www.cancon6e.nelson.com—along with a review of grammar basics and ESL tips.) The unit introductions offer concise explanations of the rhetorical patterns on which the units focus, and each introduction is liberally supported by references to the selections in that unit.

In Unit 1, we introduce, explain, and illustrate narration, description, and example—three strategies that are basic to all writing. Units 2 through 6 focus on traditional expository patterns: process analysis, classification and division, comparison and contrast, causal analysis, and definition. Unit 7 is devoted to argument and persuasion. The essays in each unit are arranged from simplest to most complex, so instructors can either assign readings appropriate to the level of the class or lead the class through progressively challenging readings based on a single rhetorical pattern. Many instructors prefer to organize their courses around themes rather than structural patterns; for their convenience, we have included a thematic table of contents.

Each unit introduction concludes with a short model essay illustrating the organizational pattern that is the focus of the unit. Together, these model essays demonstrate how a single topic—in this case, communication—can be approached from different points of view and supported in different ways. The model essays also exemplify the introductory and concluding strategies explained in the "Glossary" section at the back of the book. Terms that appear in small capital letters throughout the text (AUDIENCE, DICTION, METAPHOR, and THESIS, for example) are defined in this glossary.

Within the units, each essay is preceded by a short biographical note and followed by a "Words and Meanings" section—contextual definitions of words and phrases with which students may not be familiar. As in previous editions, the remaining pedagogical apparatus consists of two sets of questions ("Structure and Strategy," "Content and Purpose") and "Suggestions for Writing." Each unit concludes with "Additional Suggestions for Writing."

ADDITIONAL RESOURCES

The following table outlines the contents of our new Web site (www.cancon6e.nelson.com), which supports teachers and students as they work their way through *Canadian Content*, Sixth Edition.

Instructor Page	Student Page
How to Use *Canadian Content*	How to Research Your Topic
Preventing Plagiarism: Why? What? How?	Summarizing, Paraphrasing, and Quoting
Answers to Questions in the Text	Format and Documentation: MLA
Alternate Set of Model Essays	APA
Test Bank	How to Revise your Paper
	Grammar Basics:
	Sentences: Kinds and Parts
	Parts of Speech
	ESL Tips
	Writing Essay Exams
	Writing Critical Evaluations

A separate *Instructor's Manual* includes suggestions for using the textbook, sample assignments, an alternate set of model essays, suggested answers to questions in the text, and a test bank of questions on the essays.

ABOUT THE COVER ART

The photograph on our cover depicts a tower of books, most of them represented in *Canadian Content*, Sixth Edition, in the shape of an inukshuk (pronounced "in-ook-shook," and meaning "human image"). Inukshuks are massive rock figures erected by the Inuit centuries ago as signposts for travellers seeking their way across the Arctic tundra. These monuments showed what lay ahead: their orientation indicated direction—north–south or east–west—and their structure often indicated what travellers could expect to find: good hunting or fishing, a valley, or a community. What appear to be rough stone images are actually sophisticated communication devices that guided travellers efficiently and safely to their destination.

A good piece of writing does the same thing: it tells the reader where he or she is going and what lies ahead. It guides the reader firmly and safely to the end of the journey. And, just as the rocks of an inukshuk must be perfectly balanced or the structure will collapse, an essay needs to be precisely and logically organized if it is to be meaningful to those who read it. Any superfluous parts, whether an extra rock or a redundant paragraph, will muddle the meaning and confuse rather than enlighten the traveller or reader.

Our goal in preparing this book was to present a selection of readings, each as carefully crafted as an inukshuk, and, by means of the questions that follow the readings, to help the reader identify the component parts of the essay's structure and how each part contributes to the meaning of the whole. Similarly, our guidelines to essay writing break that complex task into its component parts and show you how and why each part is an essential part of the whole.

The inukshuk is a symbol of human connectedness. Communication depends on our willingness and ability to share our thoughts and feelings with others; mutual sharing forms the basis of community. We no longer need to build huge stone structures to connect with others: we can, if we care about what really matters in life, use the written word to connect with thousands of people we are unlikely ever to meet.

ACKNOWLEDGMENTS

We thank the students and teachers across Canada whose feedback has encouraged and helped us to keep refining this text. We are particularly grateful to our reviewers—Derek Hanebury (North Island College), Marcela Jonas (University College Fraser Valley), Peter Miller (Seneca College), JoAnne Soper-Cook (Memorial University), and Valerie Spink (Grant MacEwan College)—whose comments, criticisms, and suggestions have made the book more useful and enjoyable than it otherwise might have been. The authors also thank Natalia Denesiuk, senior content production manager, Thomson Nelson, and June Trusty, copy editor, for their invaluable contributions to this book.

As part of the annual *Thomson Nelson Writing Prize*, student essay submissions are eligible for cash prizes, book giveaways, and the opportunity to become published in our textbooks. For information about this opportunity, please contact the Humanities Marketing Manager at Thomson Nelson.

CONTENTS

By Unit

> "Let me tell you what I think of bicycling," Miss Anthony said. . . .
> "I think it has done more to emancipate women than anything
> else in the world."

> "I could see tears rolling down my oldest sister's cheek as she
> held my other sister close to her shivering body. Mostly, it was the
> horrific look pasted on my mother's face that led me to believe
> how scary this was."

> "And let's be clear: I am not picky. Prior to Toronto, I lived in
> Manhattan, sleeping on a lawn chair in a closet."

> "I had better things to do than hang around with Baba. Back then,
> I didn't know the word 'ashamed.'"

UNIT 2: PROCESS ANALYSIS

UNIT 3: CLASSIFICATION AND DIVISION

UNIT 4: COMPARISON AND CONTRAST

> "Canadians believe that happiness is living in a just society;
> they will not sing the Yankee song that capitalism is happiness;
> capitalism is freedom."

> "Every social environment has its own lingua franca, and the one
> on these sites has been shaped by *American Pie*, spring break, and
> *Girls Gone Wild*."

> "Left-handedness and homosexuality both tend to run in
> families."

> "Men have outgrown many of the traditional sports, while
> women have been growing into them."

> "A film adaptation that is deemed 'faithful' to the novel is not
> necessarily a compliment. The most successful adaptations have
> actually been adulterous. . . ."

UNIT 5: CAUSAL ANALYSIS

> "How do young women become so obsessed with being thin
> that they develop anorexia nervosa?"

> "It is hard to avoid feeling vulnerable to this invisible enemy
> who does not play by known or explicit rules. Of course, that is
> precisely the anxiety that terrorists seek to produce."

> "In time, I learned to smother the rage I felt at so often being
> taken for a criminal."

UNIT 6: DEFINITION

UNIT 7: ARGUMENT AND PERSUASION

UNIT 8: POTLUCK

"Another word for generalization ... is "stereotype," and stereotypes are usually not considered desirable dimensions for our decision-making lives."

"We need literature on the page because it allows us to experience more fully, to imagine more deeply, enabling us to live more freely."

"Hardly anyone . . . believes any longer that literature serves any great purpose beyond alleviating boredom on the bus or the underground, or has any higher ambition beyond being transformed into television or movie scripts. Literature has gone light."

"Are we all one? Is there a power of one? What is the meaning of one, anyway?"

CONTENTS

By Theme

ON CANADA

ON COMMUNICATION AND WRITING

ON THE CONTEMPORARY SCENE

ON THE CULTURAL MOSAIC

ON ETHICS AND MORALITY

ON MEDIA AND THE ARTS

ON NATURE, SCIENCE, AND TECHNOLOGY

ON RELATIONSHIPS, FAMILY, AND GENDER

ON POLITICS

ON SPORTS

INTRODUCTION

How to Read with Understanding

Every college student knows how to read—sort of. The trouble is that many of us don't read very efficiently. We don't know how to adapt our reading style to the reason we are reading (our reading purpose). Most people aren't even aware that there are different ways to read for different purposes.

Basically, there are two kinds of reading: **surface reading,** which is casual reading for pleasure or for easy-to-find facts. This is the type of reading we do when we enjoy a novel or read a newspaper. The second kind of reading is **deep reading.** This is the kind required in college and university courses and on the job: reading to acquire the facts and ideas we need in order to understand a topic. Deep reading has practical rather than recreational purposes. Both kinds of reading can be satisfying, but deep reading takes more time and also brings greater rewards. Good readers (and writers) tend to do well not only in college but also in their careers.

Learning to read analytically is a skill you can master. To begin, follow these general guidelines every time you read for understanding:

- Figure out as much about the piece as you can *before* reading it.
- Identify what you don't understand *while* reading it.
- Review the piece *after* reading it.

There are seven steps to reading and understanding the selections in this text. These same steps will help you read and understand any piece of academic or professional prose.

1. Remove distractions.
2. Preview before you read.
3. Read the selection all the way through.
4. Look up the meaning of words you don't understand.
5. Read the questions that follow the selection.
6. Read the selection a second time—slowly and carefully.
7. Answer the questions following the selection.

STEP 1: REMOVE DISTRACTIONS

Students new to college or university often claim that they can read perfectly well while listening to music, watching television, or talking on the phone. These students are partly right: they can read under those circumstances, but they can't read for understanding. Unlike watching TV, which uses less mental energy than eating, reading for understanding is an *active* process. It requires your full concentration and participation.

Here's what you need before you begin to work:

- A quiet place
- A good reading light
- A pencil
- A current, comprehensive dictionary[1]

STEP 2: PREVIEW BEFORE YOU READ

You cannot learn facts, ideas, or even words in isolation. Learning requires CONTEXT,[2] a sense of the whole into which each new piece of information fits. The more familiar you are with the context and content of an article before you begin it, the better you will understand what you read.

To find out as much as you can before you start reading, look through the essay to get a quick sense of the following:

- *How long is the piece?* You'll want to estimate how much time you'll need to complete it.

---

[1] The *Gage Canadian Dictionary* is convenient, portable, and available in an inexpensive paperback edition. For your desk, we recommend either *The Canadian Oxford Dictionary* (1998) or Nelson's *Canadian Dictionary of the English Language* (1997). ESL students will find the *Oxford Advanced Learner's Dictionary of Current English* (2000) a useful reference.

[2] Definitions of all words that appear in SMALL CAPITAL LETTERS are in the Glossary section at the back of this book.

- *What is the title?* The title often points to something significant about the content.
- *Who wrote the essay?* Knowing something about the author may help you predict the kind of essay you're dealing with. Is the author dead or alive? Is the author a humorist or a social critic? A journalist or an academic? A student or a specialist? What is his or her nationality?
- *What about the* BODY *of the piece?* Are there subheadings or other visual cues that indicate the division of the topic into KEY IDEAS?

In this textbook, first read each unit's introduction for essential information on essay organization and development. Many of the essays in a unit are discussed in the introduction as examples of the unit's key points.

STEP 3: READ THE SELECTION ALL THE WAY THROUGH

For many people, Step 3 is not easy. Most inexperienced readers have a fairly short attention span—eight to ten minutes, roughly the time between TV commercials—and they need to train themselves to increase it. You need to read a piece all the way through in order to get a sense of the whole; otherwise, you cannot fully understand either the essay or its parts. Here's how to approach your first reading of an essay or article:

- *Withhold judgment.* Don't allow your prejudices—in the root sense of the word: "prejudgments"—to affect your response at this stage. If you decide in advance that the topic is boring ("Who cares about toothpaste?") or the style is too demanding ("I couldn't possibly understand anything entitled 'The Pleasures of the Text'"), you cheat yourself out of a potentially rewarding experience. Give the writer a chance. Part of an author's responsibility is to make the writing interesting and accessible to the reader.
- *Use your pencil.* Make notes, underline, and jot questions in the margin. Try to identify the THESIS of the essay as you read. When you come across a sentence or passage you don't understand, put a question mark in the margin.
- *Note the words that are marked with the symbol* °. This symbol indicates that the meaning of the word or phrase is given in the "Words and Meanings" section following the essay. If you're unfamiliar with the term, check the definition we've provided and keep reading. Mark any other words whose meaning you can't figure out from the context. You can look them up later.

Good writers set up their material for you: they usually identify their topic early and indicate the scope of their essay. Your first reading of an essay or article should be a read-through. The goal of a first reading is to get a good idea of what the piece is about: its informational content. You need to read the piece a second or even a third time before you can analyze its structure and the strategies the author has used to convey the content effectively.

STEP 4: LOOK UP THE MEANING OF WORDS YOU DON'T UNDERSTAND

If you can't figure out the meaning of a word from its context, and if you need to know the meaning to understand a sentence or paragraph, it's time to turn to your dictionary. For every word you look up, your dictionary will provide you with more information than you need. Don't assume that the first definition listed is the meaning your author intended. Some words can be used both as nouns and as verbs. Only one meaning will be appropriate in the context you are reading. When you're satisfied that you've located the appropriate definition, write it in the margin.

STEP 5: READ THE QUESTIONS THAT FOLLOW THE SELECTION

After you've answered your own questions about an essay, go through the questions that follow the selection. These questions are divided into two parts. The "Structure and Strategy" questions will help you understand the **form** and STYLE of the essay—the techniques the writer has used to accomplish his or her PURPOSE. The "Content and Purpose" questions will help you understand the **meaning** of the essay—what the writer wanted to communicate and why. Together, these two sets of questions will guide you to a thorough understanding of the selection.

At this point, you won't be able to answer all the questions we've provided, but don't panic. The purpose of going through these questions now is to prepare yourself for a second, closer reading of the essay. All you need to know at this stage is the kind of questions you'll be considering after your second reading.

STEP 6: READ THE SELECTION A SECOND TIME— SLOWLY AND CAREFULLY

Got your pencil ready? The physical act of writing as you read helps keep your attention focused on the essay and serves to deepen your understanding of its content and structure. Here are some guidelines to follow as you read the essay a second time:

1. Analyze the INTRODUCTION of the essay. What strategy has the writer used to establish the topic, the limits of the topic, and the TONE?

2. Underline the author's THESIS (if you haven't already done so during your first reading).

3. Make notes in the margins. Use the margins to jot down, in point form, an outline of the piece, to add supplementary (or contradictory) EVIDENCE, or to call attention to especially significant or eloquently expressed ideas.

4. Identify the writer's main PURPOSE. Is it to explain, to persuade, to entertain? Some combination of these?

5. Identify the writer's target AUDIENCE. Are you included in this group? If not, remember that your reactions to and interpretations of the piece may differ from those of the writer's intended readers.

6. Notice how the writer develops the KEY IDEAS. Be sure you can distinguish between main ideas and supporting details—the examples, definitions, ANALOGIES, and so on—that the writer has used to make key points clear to the reader.

7. Circle key TRANSITIONS (linking words and phrases). Transitions signal to the reader that the writer has concluded one idea and is moving on to another.

8. What is the TONE of the piece? Is it humorous or serious, impassioned or objective, formal or informal? Good writers choose their tone carefully, since it affects the reader's response probably more than any other technical aspect of writing.

9. Consider the CONCLUSION. Does it restate the thesis or expand on it in some way? Are you left with a sense of the essay's completeness, a feeling that all questions raised in the piece have been satisfactorily answered? Or do you feel that you've been left dangling, that some of the loose ends have yet to be tied up?

At this point, you have a decision to make. Are you satisfied that you understand the essay? Are the writer's purpose, thesis, key ideas, and method of development all clear to you? If so, move on to Step 7. If not—as often happens when you are learning to read analytically or when you encounter a particularly challenging piece—go back and read the essay a third time.

STEP 7: ANSWER THE QUESTIONS FOLLOWING THE SELECTION

Consider the questions carefully, one by one, and think about possible answers. Refer to the selection often to keep yourself on the right track. Most of the questions do not have simple or single answers. Some of them ask for your opinion. Write the answers to them in full if that is your assignment. Otherwise, jot down your answers in point form or in short phrases in a notebook or in the margins of the text.

The purpose of the questions is to engage you as deeply as possible in the structure and meaning of each piece. As you analyze *what* the writer has said (the content and purpose) and *how* he or she has said it (the structure and strategies), you will come as close as you can to full understanding. At this point, you are ready to test your understanding in classroom discussion or through writing a paper of your own.

How to Write to Be Understood

Learning to read for understanding will help you to write clear, well-organized prose. As you practise the techniques readers use to make sense of a piece of writing, you will become increasingly skilled at meeting your own readers' needs when you write. For years, you've probably been told to keep your AUDIENCE in mind as you write. By itself, this is not a particularly helpful piece of advice. You need to know not only *who your audience is,* including how much they know and how they feel about your topic, but also *how readers read.* These two pieces of information are the keys to understandable writing. (We are assuming here that you have a firm grasp of your topic. You can't write clearly or convincingly about something you don't understand.)

Once you have decided who your audience is, there are five steps to ensuring that your readers will understand what you say. Writing a paper is like going on a journey: it makes sense—and it's certainly more efficient—to choose your destination and plan your route before you begin. Your THESIS is your destination. Your KEY IDEAS are signposts on the route to your destination. Together, your thesis and key ideas determine the kind of paper you are going to write.

We begin this book by discussing three basic writing strategies—narration, description, and example—that are useful in every kind of writing. Then we explain and illustrate six different ways to approach a topic. Please note: there is *no one way* to explain any topic. Like a geographical destination, a topic can be approached via several routes.

Take a broad, general topic like communication skills, for example. If you flip through the introductions to Units 1 through 7, you will see that each contains a model essay illustrating the kind(s) of writing explained in that unit. The model essays all discuss communication skills, but they are all different. Read these model essays carefully to discover how the organizational pattern discussed in each unit gives COHERENCE and UNITY to a topic.

As you have already discovered, people who are reading analytically don't like surprises: they don't want to encounter sudden shifts in direction or dead ends. They need a smooth, well-marked path through the writer's prose. Your responsibility to your readers is to identify the destination, set them on the path to that destination, and guide them through to the end. If you can keep them interested on their journey, so much the better. As you read through the selections in this book, you will encounter a variety of stylistic devices that you can use to add interest and impact to your own writing.

Rhetoric is the art of using language effectively. The RHETORICAL MODES[3] are four classic kinds of non-fiction writing: NARRATION, DESCRIPTION, EXPOSITION, and ARGUMENT/PERSUASION. Good writers choose whichever mode is best suited to their topic and purpose.

RHETORICAL MODE	PURPOSE	UNIT
• NARRATION	Tell a story	1
• DESCRIPTION	Create a sensory picture	1
• EXPOSITION	Explain or inform	2–6
• ARGUMENT/PERSUASION	Convince	7

Most non-fiction writing falls into the category of exposition, which includes the organizational patterns of *process analysis, classification/division, comparison/contrast, causal analysis,* and *definition.* Units 2 through 6 explain and illustrate these patterns. (A sixth pattern of exposition, *example,* is explained in Unit 1.) Practising each mode in isolation is helpful when you are learning to identify and use basic writing techniques, but you should be aware that most writing is a blend of modes and purposes. Unit 8 contains a selection of "mixed mode" readings.

Here are the five steps to clear, well-organized writing:

1. Clarify your topic.

2. Discover your thesis.

3. Develop a thesis statement, including a preview of your key ideas.

4. Write your first draft.

5. Revise your paper (as many times as necessary), edit, and proofread.

---

[3] Classifying writing into categories is useful for those who are learning how to arrange and develop their ideas effectively, in the same way that practising scales, tempo, and modulation is helpful to people who want to learn how to play a musical instrument. It is necessary to master the basics before attempting to create an original composition.

The first three steps are the *preparation* stage of the writing process. Be warned: these steps will take you as long as—if not longer than—Steps 4 and 5, which involve the actual *writing*. In academic and professional writing, the more time you spend on preparation, the less time the actual writing will take—and the better your paper will be.

STEP 1: CLARIFY YOUR TOPIC

If you have been assigned a topic for your paper or report, don't grumble—be grateful! A large part of the work has already been done for you. You have been handed a limited topic along with a hint as to how to approach it. **Direction words** are reliable clues to the kind of paper/report your instructor/supervisor is looking for:

DIRECTION WORD	WHAT IT MEANS
Compare/Contrast	Show similarities/differences between things, events, concepts, etc. (see Unit 4).
Define	Give the formal meaning of a term, with examples (see Unit 6).
Describe	Give specific details of what the topic looks like if it's a physical object (see Unit 1) or, if the topic is an event, how it happened (see Unit 2).
Discuss/Explain	These direction words do not provide specific clues; they may well leave you wondering what you're supposed to do. However, the vagueness of the direction allows you the freedom to respond to the question using any of the four rhetorical modes, singly or in combination. Give details and, if relevant, the pros and cons of the topic, supported by EVIDENCE (Units 1 through 7).
Evaluate	Give the positive and negative points of the topic; identify which position is stronger and why (Units 3 and 7).
Illustrate	Explain by giving detailed examples (Unit 1).
Justify	Give reasons, supported by evidence (Unit 7).

What should you do if you are asked to come up with a topic of your own? Choosing a satisfactory topic is critical to producing a paper your readers will understand. Inexperienced writers often choose a topic that is far larger than either their knowledge or the assignment can accommodate.

A satisfactory topic is one that is *significant, specific,* and *supportable.*

- A *significant* topic is one that is worth the time and attention you expect your readers to give to your work. You must have something original and interesting to say if you hope to capture and keep a reader's attention. There's a world of difference, for example, between the essay "Toothpaste" by David Bodanis (page 110) and a paper on "How I Brush My Teeth" by an inexperienced writer.
- A detailed discussion of a *specific* topic is always more satisfying to read than a superficial treatment of a broad one. This is why, in "The End of the Wild" (page 48), Wade Davis chooses to discuss three particular examples rather than generalize about ecological disasters.

  You can narrow a broad topic to a specific one by applying one or more limiting factors to it. Think of your topic in terms of a particular *kind,* or *time,* or *place,* or *number,* or *person* associated with it. Davis, for example, limits his topic in terms of *kinds* (passenger pigeon, buffalo, and rainforest), and *place* (North American continent).
- A topic is *supportable* if you can develop it with examples, facts, quotations, descriptions, ANECDOTES, comparisons, definitions, and other supporting details. These supporting details are called EVIDENCE. Evidence, combined with good organization, is what makes your explanation of a topic clear and convincing.

STEP 2: DISCOVER YOUR THESIS

Once you've chosen a suitable topic, you need to decide what you want to say about it. A THESIS is *an idea about a limited topic*; it is a viewpoint that needs to be explained or proved. There are three ways to go about discovering a thesis. The first two are **freewriting** and **brainstorming,** techniques with which most college students are already familiar.

A more structured strategy, **questioning,** involves asking lead-in questions about your topic. A **lead-in question** is one that guides you and your reader into your topic by pointing to an angle or viewpoint that you intend to explore in your paper.

Traditionally, professional writers have relied on six lead-in questions—*when, where, who, how, what,* and *why*—to help them discover what they can say about a topic.

ANSWERING THE QUESTIONS *WHEN, WHERE,* AND *WHO*
The answers to the questions *when, where,* and *who* are basic to every kind of writing. In Unit 1, you will learn how to answer the question *when* by locating a topic in time (NARRATION); the question *where* by locating a topic in space (DESCRIPTION); and the question *who* (or sometimes *what*) by providing examples to help your reader understand your point.

ANSWERING THE QUESTION *HOW*
To answer the question *how* (how something works, or how to do or make something), write a process ANALYSIS. Unit 2 explains how to go about it.

ANSWERING THE QUESTION *WHAT*
The question *what* can be answered in different ways, depending on the angle or viewpoint you want to explore in your paper. Here are your four main choices:

1. If you want to explain the *kinds* or *parts* or *important features* of your topic, write a classification or division paper (see Unit 3).

2. If you want to explain the *similarities* or *differences* between your topic and something else, write a comparison or contrast paper (see Unit 4).

3. If you want to explain what *caused* some event or circumstance, or what the *consequences* were (or will be), write a causal ANALYSIS (see Unit 5).

4. If you want to explain precisely what your topic *means,* write an extended definition (see Unit 6).

ANSWERING THE QUESTION *WHY*
To answer the question *why,* you need to develop an ARGUMENT. There are two kinds of argument: one is intended to convince the reader that your opinion is valid; the other is intended to change the reader's behaviour in some way. Unit 7 explains how to go about this challenging but rewarding task.

STEP 3: DEVELOP YOUR THESIS STATEMENT

A thesis statement is the most efficient way to organize a short paper. It plans your paper for you and it tells your reader what he or she is going to read about. To continue the analogy between reading an essay and taking a trip, the thesis statement is a kind of map: it identifies your destination and the route you are going to take. Like a map, it keeps your reader (and you) on the right track. To be specific, a thesis statement does two things:

A. It states the THESIS of your paper.
B. It previews the KEY IDEAS of your paper.[4]

A. STATING YOUR THESIS

As concisely as possible, identify the topic of your paper and what you intend to explain or prove about that topic (your THESIS). Here are two examples:

> Men and women talk differently. (Thesis of "She Said, He Said," page 136)

> Despite what many people think, marriage is good for everyone involved. (Thesis of "The Case for Marriage," page 246)

Be sure to state an *idea* or *opinion* about your topic; don't just announce it and leave the reader to wonder how you intend to approach it. *Do not write*, for example, "I'm going to discuss how men and women talk" or "This paper is about marriage." These are bald (and boring) topic statements, not thesis statements.

Once you've stated your thesis, look at it carefully. Is it appropriate for the length of your assignment and the amount of time you've been given to write it? Beware of a thesis that is too broad ("Men and women are different in many ways") or too narrow ("I can hardly wait to go shopping for my wedding dress").

B. PREVIEWING YOUR KEY IDEAS

The second part of a thesis statement identifies the KEY IDEAS you will discuss in your paper and the ORDER in which you will discuss them. Go back to your prewriting activity (brainstorming, freewriting, or questioning) and find the three or four best points you came up with. These points are your key ideas.

Next, list your points in as many different arrangements as you can (three points will produce six lists). Choose the arrangement that is most likely to achieve your writing PURPOSE, then write out your points in grammatically parallel form (see PARALLELISM in the Glossary section).

Now you are ready to combine your THESIS and your key ideas into an *expanded thesis statement*. Compare the following exam-

---

[4] Sometimes the order of parts A and B is reversed. For example, the following thesis statement about the topic "body language" states the key ideas before the thesis: "Your head, hands, and feet signal your feelings by sending strong non-verbal messages."

ples with the *simple thesis statements* we provided under "Stating Your Thesis," above. To highlight the difference, we've underlined the key ideas in each statement:

> When men and women engage in that intrinsically human activity called "talking," there is much that is different in <u>why they talk</u>, <u>the way they talk</u>, and <u>what they talk about</u>." ("She Said, He Said," page 136)

> Contrary to what many Americans now believe, getting and staying married is good for men, women, and children. Marriage, it turns out, is by far <u>the best bet for ensuring a healthier</u>, <u>wealthier</u>, and <u>sexier life</u>. ("The Case for Marriage," page 246)

Note that the key ideas in a thesis statement are written in the same grammatical form: all nouns, all phrases, or all clauses.

Not all essays contain full thesis statements. In many of the selections in this book, for example, you will find a statement of thesis but not a preview of the key ideas. Why? Because professional writers don't need the organizational apparatus that non-professionals do. Through experience, they have learned less visible techniques to help their readers follow them through their writing. We recommend, however, that you include a full thesis statement in the papers you write. (The best place to put it is at the end of your introduction.) There is probably no writing strategy you can use that is more helpful to your readers' understanding of the content of your paper.

STEP 4: WRITE A FIRST DRAFT: PARAGRAPH DEVELOPMENT, TRANSITIONS, AND TONE

Before any paper is ready for submission, writers draft and revise, draft and revise—sometimes sequentially, sometimes simultaneously. The purpose of writing a first draft is to get something down on paper that you can work with until you have created a well-organized paper with solid PARAGRAPHS, effective TRANSITIONS, and an appropriate TONE.

A. DEVELOPING YOUR PARAGRAPHS

Every KEY IDEA should be developed in one or more paragraphs, each of which contains a TOPIC SENTENCE that states its main point. The topic sentence often starts the paragraph, so that the reader knows at the outset what to expect. All sentences that follow the topic sentence should support and develop it. Your paragraph will be unified (see UNITY in the Glossary section) if every supporting sentence relates directly to the topic sentence. An adequately developed paragraph includes enough EVIDENCE to make its main idea clear to your readers.

How do you decide the best way to develop a particular paragraph? How much evidence should you include? What kind of support should it be? To make these decisions, put yourself in your reader's place. What does he or she need to know in order to understand your point? If you ask yourself the questions listed below, you'll be able to decide how much and what kind of evidence you need to develop a good paragraph.

1. Would **narrating a story** be an effective way of getting your idea across? Everyone likes to read a story if it's well told and relevant to what's being discussed. Using a personal ANECDOTE to illustrate an idea can be a powerful way of helping readers understand and remember your point. The introduction to Unit 1 provides guidelines to follow when using NARRATION to develop a key idea.

2. Would **specific details** be useful? Providing readers with descriptive details can be effective in developing your key idea and in establishing the mood you are trying to convey. In some paragraphs, facts or statistics are the best way to support your point. See the introduction to Unit 1 for instructions on writing effective DESCRIPTION.

3. Would **examples** help to explain or prove your point? Providing examples is probably the most common method of developing a key idea. The introduction to Unit 1 will show you how to use examples effectively.

4. Is a **series of steps or stages** involved? Sometimes the most logical way to explain a key idea is to outline how to do or make something, or how something is done or works—that is, to relate, in order, the steps involved. The introduction to Unit 2 will give you detailed directions for this kind of development.

5. Would a **comparison** or **contrast** help you communicate your key idea? A *comparison* points out similarities between objects, people, or ideas; a *contrast* shows how the objects, people, or ideas are different. The introduction to Unit 4 explains and illustrates how to do both.

6. Do your readers need a **definition?** If you're using a term that your readers may not know, you should define it. Use your own words; don't quote from a dictionary. See the introduction to Unit 6.

7. Would a **quotation** or a **paraphrase** lend convincing support or emphasis to the point you are explaining? Whenever you use information from an outside source, you must acknowledge that source appropriately in your paper. See our Web site (www.cancon6e.nelson.com) for detailed documentation instructions and examples.

You can, of course, use more than one kind of evidence to develop a paragraph. A definition is often complemented by one or more examples; sometimes an anecdote can be combined with a quotation or PARAPHRASE. There is no fixed rule that governs the kind or number of development strategies you can use. Your responsibility is to provide your readers with everything they need to know to understand your THESIS.

Once you have drafted your key ideas, you have two more paragraphs to write: the INTRODUCTION and the CONCLUSION. All too often, these parts of a paper are dull, clumsy, or repetitive. But they don't have to be. Carefully constructed, these paragraphs can catch your reader's attention and clinch your discussion. The Glossary section contains a number of ideas you can choose from when crafting a beginning and ending for your paper.

B. SUPPLYING TRANSITIONS

As you write and revise, keep in mind that you want to make it as easy as possible for your reader to follow you through your paper. TRANSITIONS are words or phrases that show the logical relationship between one point and the next, causing a paragraph or a paper to hang together and read smoothly. Like the turn signals on a car, transitions such as *first, next, therefore, however,* and *finally* tell the person following you where you're going. The Glossary section will give you suggestions for appropriate transitional phrases, depending on the kind of relationship between ideas that you want to signal.

C. ESTABLISHING AND MAINTAINING AN APPROPRIATE TONE

TONE is the term used to describe a writer's attitude toward a topic as it is revealed through his or her language. A writer may feel angry, amused, nostalgic, or passionate, and this attitude is reflected in the words, examples, quotations, and other supporting details with which he or she develops the thesis. Good writing is usually modulated in tone; the writer addresses the reader with respect, in a calm, reasonable way. Highly emotional writing is often not convincing to readers—what gets communicated is the strength of the writer's feelings rather than depth of knowledge or validity of opinion.

Tone is a complex idea to understand, and control of it is a difficult skill to master. As you read the selections in this book, observe how skilled writers convey a range of emotions. For example, Danny Irvine's "A Tree-Planting Primer" is humorous, yet readers can sense frustration and the occasional flash of anger beneath his language. He accomplishes this combination of wit and outrage through his careful choice of words and manipulation of sentence structure. David Bodanis's "Toothpaste" appears at first to be a straightforward analysis of the ingredients of a product we use every day. The essay could have been as dry and humorless as a chapter from a chemistry text, but Bodanis manages to make it both bizarre and funny.[5]

STEP 5: REVISE, EDIT, AND PROOFREAD YOUR PAPER[6]

At last you've reached the final stage of the writing process. Even though you are probably sick of your assignment by now and eager to be done with it, *do not* omit this step. Revising is essential before your paper is ready to be sent into the world. Ideally, you should revise your paper several days after writing it. After a cooling-off period, you'll be able to view your work more objectively.

A. REVISING

Thorough revision requires at least two reviews of your paper. The first time you go over it, read it aloud, slowly, from beginning to end, keeping your AUDIENCE in mind as you read. Is your THESIS clear? Are the KEY IDEAS arranged in an appropriate ORDER? Are all points adequately explained? Has anything been left out? Are the PARAGRAPHS unified and coherent? Are there any awkward sentences that should be rephrased?

---

[5] Marking the text as you read can help you understand how writers manipulate tone. In "Toothpaste," for example, when you come to a descriptive phrase that makes you respond "Yecchh!," mark it. Similarly, underline or note in the margin any phrases you find funny. When you've finished reading, you can go back over the essay and consider how the author caught your attention: through a change in DICTION, perhaps? Unusual SYNTAX? A surprising example?

[6] For a detailed guide to revising, editing, and proofreading, see "The Three Steps to Revision" on our Web site: www.cancon6e.nelson.com.

B. EDITING

Begin editing by running your essay through the grammar- and spell-check functions of your computer. Don't just go through the document replacing your words with the computer's suggestions, however. Computers are programmed to question, not to decide, the appropriateness of a writer's choices. You must decide for yourself if the questions are useful and if any of the suggestions are suitable.

The second time you read through your paper, read it with the Editing Checklist (on the inside of the front cover) in front of you for easy reference. Pay special attention to the points that tend to give you trouble: for example, sentence fragments, verb errors, misplaced apostrophes, or dangling modifiers. (For help with basic writing skills, go to www.englishresources.nelson.com. In the menu on the right-hand side of the screen, click on "Thomson Nelson English Composition Resource Centre.") Most writers know their weaknesses; unfortunately, it's human nature to ignore these and to focus on our strengths. That is why editing your work can be a painful process. Nevertheless, it is an absolutely essential task. You owe it to yourself and to your reader to find and correct any errors in your writing.

C. PROOFREADING

If your spelling, punctuation, or keyboarding skills are not strong, you will need to read your paper a third time. Grammar- and spell-check it again. Then read it through from the end to the beginning to check every sentence. When reading from back to front, you're forced to look at each sentence individually rather than in CONTEXT, and thus you are more likely to spot your mistakes. It's also a good idea to ask someone else to go over your paper and identify any errors you've missed.

A final word of advice: whether you are writing for a teacher or an employer, **ALWAYS KEEP A COPY OF YOUR PAPER FOR YOUR FILES.**

If you follow these five steps carefully, you and your reader will arrive at your destination without any accident, mishap, or wrong turns. And if, as we have suggested, you keep your audience in focus throughout the process, you can make their journey informative and enjoyable. No reader can ask for more.

How to Write a Documented Essay

This section provides a quick overview of the process of writing research papers. If you need a detailed explanation of how to write and document a research paper, go to our Web site (www.cancon6e.nelson.com) and consult "Researching Your Topic," "Summarizing, Paraphrasing, and Quoting," and "Formatting and Documenting a Research Paper."

For some essays or research assignments, you will be required to locate and integrate other people's ideas, knowledge, or expert opinion into your paper. You will use the written (or, occasionally, spoken) words of external sources to develop your KEY IDEAS and prove your THESIS. As any good lawyer knows, proving your point depends on the effective presentation of quality EVIDENCE. The evidence you assemble and the way you incorporate it into your own writing will determine the success or failure of your documented essay.

Keep in mind that the reason most instructors assign research papers is to give you an opportunity to demonstrate how well you can find, analyze, and evaluate source material, synthesize it, and use it to support your own conclusions about a topic. Very few research assignments require you simply to report other people's findings on a topic. Normally, you are expected to use source material as evidence to support your thesis. Writing a documented essay requires the use of high-order thinking skills: interpreting, summarizing, analyzing, and evaluating. That is why a research paper or term paper so often serves as the culminating test of learning in university and college courses. Such papers are good practice for the world of work, too. The critical thinking skills that a documented essay requires are the same skills that professionals must demonstrate on the job.

STEP 1: GATHERING THE EVIDENCE

Your first task is to find, evaluate, and make notes on source material that supports your thesis. Usually, you do this work in the library, using computer-based research tools, books, periodicals, and academic or professional journals as your sources. Your librarian will help you search for relevant, up-to-date information.

After you have found a number of promising-looking sources, your next task is to evaluate the material to see if it is appropriate for your paper. Inexperienced writers often get bogged down at this point, spending days or even weeks reading each potential source in detail. A more efficient approach is to scan each work quickly and ignore anything that is not current, relevant, or reliable.[7] Once you have identified a number of potentially useful sources, read them carefully, using the reading and note-taking suggestions provided in "How to Read with Understanding" (page xxi). Whenever you make notes from a source, be careful to record the publishing information about it, because whether you are summarizing, paraphrasing, or quoting, you must always identify your source. This process is called **documentation**. Following are the basic guidelines for documenting print and electronic sources:

- **For print sources**: Name(s) of author(s) or editor(s); title; place of publication, publisher's name, and date of publication; page number(s) on which you found the information you are using.
- **For electronic sources**: Name(s) of author(s) or editor(s) (if given); document title; title of the database or site; date of publication or last revision; name of the institution or organization sponsoring the site (if given); date you accessed the source; URL.

Keeping detailed and accurate bibliographical records as you read your sources will save you hours of time and frustration when you come to document your paper and can't remember where you found a crucial piece of information. Accurate bibliographical records will also help to keep you from falling into the trap of unintended plagiarism (more on this later).

STEP 2: PRESENTING THE EVIDENCE

Once your research notes are complete and you have begun your first draft, you need to know how to integrate the information you have found into your own writing. There are three methods you can choose from: summary, paraphrase, or direct quotation. A SUMMARY is a highly condensed version of another person's ideas or observations. A PARAPHRASE is a longer summary. It could include, for

---

[7] Be wary of Internet sources, especially if the source's URL does not end with a recognized domain such as ".gov" (government) or ".edu" (educational institution). You often can check the credibility of an author, company, organization, or institution by using an online search engine such as Google.

example, the KEY IDEA and several supporting details, whereas a summary would present only the key idea. Whether you are summarizing or paraphrasing, you must put *the source information into your own words.* If you use the actual words or phrases of the original, you are *quoting,* and you must signal that fact to the reader by using quotation marks or—for a quotation that runs more than four typed lines in your paper—by indenting the quoted passage 2.5 cm from the left margin and identifying the source either in the preceding text or at the end of the quotation.

A word about **plagiarism:** Most students know that plagiarism is using someone else's ideas and presenting them as your own. Submitting someone else's term paper or collecting material from various articles and passing it off as your own original thinking are clear examples of academic dishonesty. Not everyone realizes, however, that neglecting to identify your sources, even if the omission is unintentional, is also plagiarism. Whenever you use another writer's ideas in an essay, you need to let your reader know whose ideas they are and where you found them. Careful documentation will not only ensure that you avoid plagiarism, it will also ensure that you are given credit for the reading and research you have done.

To document the books, articles, and other information you have used in your paper, you need to follow an approved system of documentation. Two basic styles are used in most colleges and universities: the Modern Language Association (MLA) format, usually required in humanities courses, and the American Psychological Association (APA) format, commonly used in the social sciences. Both formats have abandoned the old-fashioned and cumbersome footnote system in favour of in-text parenthetical referencing, which means indicating the source in parentheses immediately following the summary, paraphrase, or quotation. (You'll find detailed instructions and examples of in-text citations on this book's Web site: www.cancon6e.nelson.com).

The natural and physical sciences require a wide variety of documentation formats, and many colleges and universities publish their own style manuals. If your instructor requires a specific format, use the appropriate handbook to guide you through the task of acknowledging source material. Most systems of documentation require, in addition to parenthetical citations, that you list your sources for the paper in a separate section at the end, called either "Works Cited" (MLA) or "References" (APA). The format of this list—including spacing, order of information, capitalization, and punctuation—must be followed *exactly,* down to the last comma, for your paper and your list of references.[8] If your instructor leaves the choice of format up to you, choose one of the following style guides:

- Gibaldi, Joseph. *MLA Handbook for Writers of Research Papers*. 6th ed. New York: Modern Language Association, 2003. (Online: www.mla.org/store)
- American Psychological Association. *Publication Manual of the American Psychological Association*. 5th ed. Washington, DC: APA, 2001. (Online: www.apastyle.org/pubmanual.html)

Detailed information about the MLA and APA documentation styles is available on the Web site for this book: www.cancon6e. nelson.com. For further information and periodic updates, go to the Web sites of the MLA (www.mla.org) and the APA (www.apa.org). The MLA documentation style has been used in this book; for an example of an essay documented in the APA style, see Trina Rys's "The Slender Trap," on page 165.

The essay that follows, by Katherine Murtha,[9] has been revised and updated for this edition of *Canadian Content*. Documented in MLA style, this paper demonstrates (1) how to incorporate summaries, paraphrases, and short and long quotations into your writing; and (2) how to indicate that you have altered a quotation, either by leaving something out (use ellipses) or by adding or changing a word or phrase (use square brackets).

---

[8] We know this requirement sounds incredibly picky, and it is. However, the format of a documentation entry tells a professional reader just as much as the content of the entry (author's name, title, etc.) does. A documentation entry is like a line of computer code: those who know the language of the symbols can read the message. Your instructors know the code and expect to find it in your "Works Cited" or "References" list.

[9] A native of Lindsay, Ontario, Katherine Murtha holds an M.A. in history and theology from the University of Toronto. She is director of the Retreat Centre for the Scarboro Missions, where she organizes retreats and facilitates workshops, many of them designed for young people. She has written a screenplay about women and bicycles entitled *Wheel Women*, which she plans to produce as a documentary film. The original version of "Cycling in the 1890s: An Orgasmic Experience?" was published in York University's *Canadian Woman Studies* (21.3 (2001–02): 119–21).

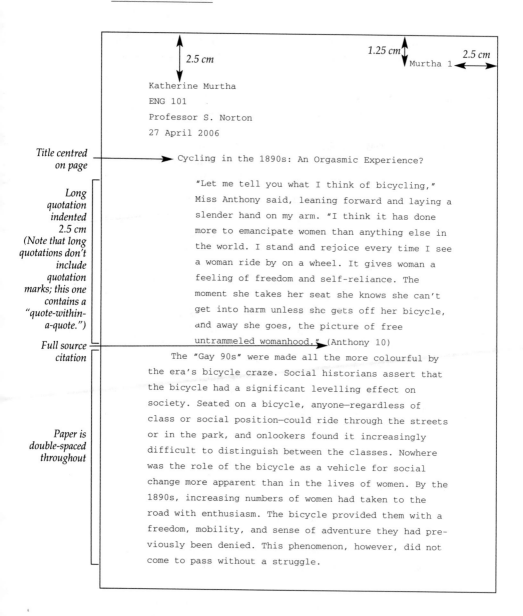

2.5 cm

1.25 cm   2.5 cm

Murtha 1

Katherine Murtha

ENG 101

Professor S. Norton

27 April 2006

Title centred on page →

Cycling in the 1890s: An Orgasmic Experience?

Long quotation indented 2.5 cm (Note that long quotations don't include quotation marks; this one contains a "quote-within-a-quote.")

"Let me tell you what I think of bicycling,"
Miss Anthony said, leaning forward and laying a
slender hand on my arm. "I think it has done
more to emancipate women than anything else in
the world. I stand and rejoice every time I see
a woman ride by on a wheel. It gives woman a
feeling of freedom and self-reliance. The
moment she takes her seat she knows she can't
get into harm unless she gets off her bicycle,
and away she goes, the picture of free
untrammeled womanhood." (Anthony 10)

Full source citation

Paper is double-spaced throughout

The "Gay 90s" were made all the more colourful by
the era's bicycle craze. Social historians assert that
the bicycle had a significant levelling effect on
society. Seated on a bicycle, anyone—regardless of
class or social position—could ride through the streets
or in the park, and onlookers found it increasingly
difficult to distinguish between the classes. Nowhere
was the role of the bicycle as a vehicle for social
change more apparent than in the lives of women. By the
1890s, increasing numbers of women had taken to the
road with enthusiasm. The bicycle provided them with a
freedom, mobility, and sense of adventure they had previously been denied. This phenomenon, however, did not
come to pass without a struggle.

Murtha 2

The newspapers of the time devote a surprising amount of space to bicycle news. Writers dedicated hundreds of column inches to women's relationship with the bicycle, a symbol of modernity. The advent of the bicycle led to passionate debates about women's "proper" nature, role, and attire. Women's new-found freedom to move about in public, unchaperoned, threatened the traditional moral order. Taking direct aim at men's vulnerability, the editor of the *Dominion Medical Monthly* warned, "Bicycle riding produces in the female a distinct orgasm." A little further on, he charged that "Toronto's scorching thoroughfares" made the streets of Sodom and Gomorrah look "as pure as Salvation Army shelters" (qtd. in Roberts 16).

More tentatively, if not more tactfully, *The British Medical Journal* reported in 1895 that the friction produced by cycling "may lead . . . in women of certain temperaments, to other effects on the sexual system, which we need not particularize" (qtd. in Cochrane 7). In the same year, citizens of Sydney, Australia, were treated to a demonstration of the worrisome consequences of bicycle riding. At a public lecture entitled "Cycling for Ladies," local physician Dr. Hodgson mounted a female skeleton upon a bicycle. "Observe the objectionable results," he said, as he jerked the skeleton back and forth on the saddle. A self-styled expert on women's anatomy and health, Dr. Hodgson also purported to be an authority on women's attire. In the same lecture, he declared, "As for style, ladies should remember they have to maintain their grace and dignity, their good figures, and due

Short quotation incorporated into text

Abbreviation qtd. in ("quoted in") used for indirect sources

Paraphrase and quotation from Internet source

proportions. This can hardly be accomplished by too
short a skirt" (Cochrane 6-7).

    Men were not the only ones to express revulsion and
ridicule of women on wheels. Canada's first woman journalist, Kit Coleman, argued as follows:

Author of newspaper source

> No girl over 39 should be allowed to wheel. It
> is immoral. Unfortunately, it is older girls
> who are ardent wheelers. They love to cavort
> and careen above the spokes, twirling and
> twisting in a manner that must remind them of
> long dead dancing days. They have descended
> from the shelves in myriads and in a burst of
> Indian summer are disporting themselves on the
> highways and byways. (5)

Abbreviated source citation (author's name in text)

Similar sentiments were expressed worldwide. The terms
loose (meaning without a corset), *town bike*, and *ride*
all come from this period. These derogatory expressions
were used to keep women in their "proper" place—immobile and at home (Petty 127).

Full source citation (author's name not in text)

    That countless anonymous women persisted in riding
in the face of such opposition is remarkable. In
keeping with the egalitarian spirit of the bicycle
movement, it is interesting to note that it was the
"sisters, sweethearts, and wives of the young chaps
about town, the clerks, the mechanics and such like"
(Denison 281) who broke through convention and took to
the road without waiting for the example or approval of
upper-class women. The mobility provided by the bicycle
also inspired working-class women to fight for the
right to wear comfortable, pant-like bloomers and the
right not to wear wire-and-whalebone corsets. What was

Murtha 4

the use of having a bicycle, they argued, if heavy,
constricting clothing made it virtually impossible to
move? The daring and courageous spirit of these nameless individuals helped to free women from the physical
and social restrictions that had long kept them earth-
bound.

By the summer of 1895, what had previously been
deemed unacceptable became fashionable. The tide of
opinion was turned by the sudden and dramatic appearance of society's upper echelons on wheels. Once the
bicycle had received the stamp of approval from the
upper classes, the fad became a frenzy. Toronto's
trend-setting society women rode the streets and parks
en masse, parading the latest, most exquisite cycling
costumes before amazed spectators. The papers were full
of information about Toronto's fashion show on wheels.
They took note of the latest "cultured" woman to take
to the wheel or the most recent fashionable circle to
host a bicycle party. These sought-after invitations to
bicycle parties often ended with BYOB—bring your own
bicycle (Ritchie 161).

Summary of information from book source

The enterprising men of the bicycle industry were
eager to tap into the new female market. To counteract
the testimony of medical professionals who opposed
women's cycling, the bicycle industry sponsored other
doctors who publicly attested to the health benefits
that were to be derived from bicycle riding. With a
little oiling, some doctors were even known to change
their opinions. Whereas once the evidence was thought
to prove that cycling damaged "the feminine organs of
matrimonial necessity" (Larrabee 86) and caused

Summary of information from three sources, with full citation

skeletal deformations, hernias, varicose veins, weak
hearts, nervous disorders, insomnia, and epilepsy, now
it was thought to prove the contrary (Petty 127; Smith
64).

The bicycle fad faded before the turn of the century, but the craze lasted long enough to silence most
of the critical voices and create a consensus that
cycling was not just acceptable but even beneficial.
The ensuing respectability did not come without setbacks to women's quest for mobility and freedom. A
spirit of boldness and independence marked the initial
entry of cycling women into the public sphere; once the
activity became respectable, however, efforts were
renewed to tame women's spirit and restrict their movement. Although by the mid-1890s it was deemed acceptable for women to ride, cycling had to be performed in
a manner that was considered appropriate for the female
sex. Hence, the controversy surrounding women and the
bicycle continued to rage long after bicycles had
become commonplace.

One controversy was particularly inflammatory: what
could status-conscious female cyclists wear while
riding? "Rational dress" reformers hoped that the
social acceptance of women's cycling would lead to
acceptance of "bloomers," which were far more practical
than long skirts. Many women's hopes were dashed when
bloomers were rejected as being "too masculine."
Eventually, a compromise was reached between the tradi-
tionalists and the reformers: women's skirts were
raised two inches, and elastic undergarments became
acceptable alternatives to punishing whalebone corsets.

*Paraphrase
of informa-
tion from
book source,
with full
citation*

Understandably, the corset industry took an interest in the discussions of the time. Fearing extinction, many companies rallied to the cause by not only loosening the grip of their product, but also by offering incentives such as bicycle insurance with purchases (Smith 66-67).

By the latter half of the 1890s, it was generally agreed that a little exercise was good for the female sex, if done in moderation. The public nature of bicycling provoked extensive discussions on the subject of women and athletics. In the end, the traditional view that women did not benefit from strenuous exercise was upheld, and any attempt by women to exert themselves athletically was viewed as immoral, if not dangerous. The following passage, which appeared in *Cycling* in 1893, expresses the view that came to dominate public opinion:

> A woman can best show what little exertion is required in propelling her cycle by riding with modest ease and moderate pace. For feats of speed and protracted endurance she is . . . [morally] bound, if she respects her sex, to avoid anything in the nature of deleterious excess of exertion. (Qtd. in Ritchie 158)

Women were discouraged from participating in athletics not only by moral strictures, but also by fear of physical harm. Those who persisted in racing and competition were threatened with the phenomenon of "bicycle eyes" or "bicycle face," which, doctors warned, would result from the strain of cycling. It was believed that once "wild eyes" were developed, the con-

Quoted phrases incorporated into text; full source citations

Murtha 7

dition was impossible to cure; the victim would be marked for life (Smith 69-70; Petty 127).

These restrictions blunted the aspirations of women who longed to excel in athletics. During the latter half of the nineteenth century, women had achieved some success and fame in racing and long-distance riding. Now, as the consensus around "exercise in moderation" solidified, the opportunities and recognition that had been available to women began to disappear. France, which had witnessed the beginnings of women's bicycle racing, did not endorse women's events until the 1930s. The League of American Wheelmen, the organization that sanctioned bicycle races, blacklisted women. Cycling magazines refused to print the results of women's rallies. Not until 1958 did the Union Cycliste Internationale re-establish recognition of women cyclists and resume recording their achievements (Browerman 78).

Despite public opposition, a few determined women persisted in entering racing events. In the early 1900s, for example, Mrs. Alice Andrews, Mrs. Clara Grace, Miss Maggie Foster, and Miss M. Harwood formed "a small band of pioneering women cyclists . . . who participated in women's races or, independently of each other, attempted track and road records on men's machines" (Andrews 54). A few who refused to be bound by the dictates of moderation found an outlet for their skills in the circus, where women could take their place alongside men, not as assistants, but as equals. Unfortunately, the compromises forced by public opinion meant that the potential of many women remained unde-

Summary of information from article and full source citation

Summary and quotation from Internet source

Murtha 8

veloped. While men's athletic prowess continued to be
celebrated, women had to be content with awards for
"Most Attractive Lady Cyclist" (Browerman 78).

Although the bicycle boom died before the new century unfolded, reform movements in which the bicycle
had played a part endured. While the bicycle faded from
the pages of newspapers and magazines, it did not disappear from women's lives. In the wake of the bicycle
craze, women gained access to cheaper and better vehicles. For many, the bicycle became a practical means of
transportation. It even facilitated political reform:
as Elizabeth Cady Stanton noted, "Many a woman is
riding to the suffrage on a bicycle" (qtd. in Petty
125).

Murtha 9

Works Cited

Andrews, V. J. "Mrs. Andrews: A Woman Before Her Time."
    The Sports Historian 15 (1995): 54-59. 27 April
    2006 <www.aafla.org./SportsLibrary/
    SportsHistorian/1995/sh15i.pdf>.

Anthony, Susan B. "Champion of Her Sex." Interview with
    Nelly Bly. *New York World* 2 Feb. 1896: 10.

Browerman, Les. "Some Steps in the Long March of the
    'Bloomer Brigade.'" *Cycle History: Proceedings of
    the 8th International Cycle History Conference.* Ed.
    Rob van der Plas. San Francisco: Bicycle Books,
    1998. 78-82.

Cochrane, Peter. "The Bicycle, Fashion and Foreboding."
    ozhistorybytes 8 (2002): 1-14. The National Centre
    for History Education Science and Training.
    Australian Government Department of Education. 23
    April 2006 <http://www.hyperhistory.org/
    index.php?option=displaypage&Itemid=742&op=page>.

Coleman, Kit. "Women's Kingdom." *Mail and Empire* 17
    Aug. 1985, Toronto: 5.

Denison, G. E. "The Evolution of the Lady Cyclist."
    Massey's Magazine Apr. 1897.

Larrabee, Lisa. "Women and Cycling: The Early Years."
    *How I Learned to Ride the Bicycle: Reflections of
    an Influential 19th Century Woman*, by Frances E.
    Willard. Ed. Carol O'Hare. California: Fair Oaks
    Publishing Company, 1991. 81-97.

Petty, Ross. "Women and the Wheel." *Cycle History:
    Proceedings of the 7th International Cycle History
    Conference.* Ed. Rob van der Plas. San Francisco:
    Bicycle Books, 1997. 112-33.

Hanging indents for reference entries, arranged alphabetically

Murtha 10

Ritchie, Andrew. *King of the Road: An Illustrated
    History of Cycling.* Berkeley, CA: Ten Speed Press,
    1975.

Roberts, Wayne. "Rocking the Cradle for the World: The
    New Woman and Maternal Feminism, Toronto, 1877-
    1914." *A Not Unreasonable Claim.* Ed. Linda Kealey.
    Toronto: The Women's Press, 1979. 15-45.

Smith, Robert A. *A Social History of the Bicycle: Its
    Early Life and Times in America.* New York: American
    Heritage Press, 1972.

Three Basic Strategies: Narration, Description, and Example

Narration, description, and example are basic to all writing. Indeed, it would be difficult to write any essay or report without using at least one of these strategies. In this introduction, we use examples from essays in this collection to illustrate what the three strategies are, why we use them, and how to write them.

NARRATION

WHAT IS NARRATION?

Narrative writing tells a story; it relates a sequence of events. Novels and short fiction are narratives, but they are based on imaginary events. In this book, we are concerned with non-fiction—writing that is based on fact. When an essay includes a story (often called an ANECDOTE) to illustrate a KEY IDEA, the reader trusts that the story actually happened. For instance, Douglas Coupland's essay "The Yukon" (page 22) focuses on a trip Coupland took with his father:

> When I was young, trips with Dad in the plane often felt like torture, but with hindsight I can see them as an exotic and

charmed way to have spent a part of my youth. When I was around thirteen, my father flew my younger brother and me in the Twin Otter up to the Yukon.

WHY DO WE USE NARRATION?

Providing a narrative is often a good way to develop a key idea. For example, in the passage below from "Escape to Paradise," Armin Kumarshellah begins his narrative by telling the story of his family's decision to come to Canada.

> We had been suffering through a vicious war between Iran and Iraq for six years, and my parents were fed up. One day, my father began selling our assets and belongings so we could begin our journey to Canada. Throughout the years, my sisters and I were told many fairy tales of how wonderful and magical this land called Canada was. My sisters and I were very anxious to get there. We didn't know about the many obstacles that stood in our way.

This anecdote movingly illustrates the mingled hope and anxiety the children experienced as the parents prepared to emigrate.

Focusing on the lead-in question *when*, a writer may use narration as the sole organizing principle of an essay: When did the first event happen? And then what happened? And then . . .? "Escape to Paradise" is one example of a narrative essay. Another is Shandi Mitchell's "Baba and Me" (page 18), which tells how the author's grandmother worked to build a life for herself and her children in Canada.

More often, however, writers use narration to develop a key idea in an essay that is structured as a classification, comparison, causal analysis, or some other pattern. For example, the following anecdote from Brent Staples's causal analysis, "Just Walk On By" (page 173), supports a key idea about the racist assumptions he encountered:

> Another time I was on assignment for a local paper and killing time before an interview. I entered a jewelry store on the city's affluent Near North Side. The proprietor excused herself and returned with an enormous red Doberman pinscher straining at the end of a leash. She stood, the dog extended toward me, silent to my questions, her eyes bulging nearly out of her head. I took a cursory look around, nodded, and bade her good night.

HOW DO WE WRITE NARRATION?

Narration is based on the principles of storytelling. A good story tells a sequence of events in a way that captures the reader's interest and imagination. Good narration re-creates an experience so that readers can see and hear and feel it as if it had happened to them.

Here are five guidelines for writing effective narration:

1. Decide on your THESIS. Every narrative you use should contribute to your thesis by developing one of your key ideas.

2. Select details that are clearly and directly related to your thesis. What you leave out is as important as what you put in. Put yourself in the reader's position and tell enough of the story to make it both clear and vivid, but do not include so many details that the story wanders away from its point. You'll lose your reader's attention if you go on and on. Stay focused on the PURPOSE of your story—the key idea it supports.

3. Arrange the events in the most effective time order. Usually, a story moves in CHRONOLOGICAL (time) ORDER: first this happened, then this, and finally that. But sometimes a narrative is more effective if the writer begins at the end and then goes back to tell how the story began (this technique is called a **flashback**). It's even possible to begin in the middle of the chronological sequence, introduce a flashback to fill in details that occurred before the point at which the story began, and then proceed to the end. Michael Ignatieff uses this complex sequence in "Deficits" (page 41), an essay about the devastating effects of Alzheimer's disease on his mother. Whatever time order you use, it is important to adhere to the next guideline.

4. Use TRANSITIONS to help your reader follow you as you proceed through the narrative. Provide time-markers (not in every sentence, of course) to indicate the sequence of events: *after, suddenly, next, as soon as,* and *finally* are the kinds of useful transition signals that keep your readers on track.

5. Maintain a consistent POINT OF VIEW. Point of view means the angle of narration: Who is telling the story? If you begin your anecdote with yourself as first-person narrator ("I"), continue telling the story yourself. Don't shift to a different narrator, such as a "you" or a "he" or "she." Readers need to experience a story from a single, consistent narrative perspective.

DESCRIPTION

WHAT IS DESCRIPTION?

Descriptive writing creates a picture in words. It tells readers what a person, a place, or a thing looks like. Effective description appeals not only to the reader's visual sense but also to other senses: hearing, taste, smell, and touch. For example, in "Finding a Flatmate" (page 13), Hilary Doyle creates a vivid picture of an apartment and its occupants.

> I couldn't find the front door, and the stairs up to the third level had compacted themselves, giving way to a sort of precarious slide. There was no doorbell, no living room, no furniture. My new room was locked and empty, save for a yellowed futon mattress, a discarded pine frame and a winter jacket. Lee's current roommate, Rambo, a welfare deserter who could no longer make the rent, had not yet been informed that he was leaving. Lee's fiancée was catatonic. She was also, I suspect, a man. Their cat was black, the air was green and the kitchen was a poetic ensemble of mould, shards of plaster, cat hair and roaches (both crawling and smouldering).

Based on this description, it's easy to see why Doyle didn't stay long in this place.

WHY DO WE USE DESCRIPTION?

Description creates a sensory image of a topic. Concrete descriptive details help clarify abstract ideas; they also appeal to the reader on many levels, including the emotional. Description is an excellent way to make a point in a powerful way. Take, for example, Michael Ignatieff's poignant descriptions of his mother when she was young and as she is now:

> She always loved to swim. When she dived into the water, she never made a splash. I remember her lifting herself out of the pool, as sleek as a seal in a black swimsuit, the water pearling off her back. Now she says the water is too cold. . . .
>
> I bathe her when she wakes. Her body is white, soft, and withered. I remember how, in the changing-huts, she would bend over as she slipped out of her bathing suit. Her body was young. Now I see her skeleton through her skin. When I wash her hair, I feel her skull. I help her from the bath, dry her legs, swathe her in towels, sit her on the edge

of the bath and cut her nails: they are horny and yellow. Her feet are gnarled. She has walked a long way. ("Deficits")

Things—inanimate objects—can also be described in convincing detail. Consider the following passage and see if you can figure out what common substance David Bodanis is describing:

> To keep the glop from drying out, a mixture including glycerine glycol—related to the most common car anti-freeze ingredient—is whipped in with the chalk and water, and to give *that* concoction a bit of substance . . . a large helping is added of gummy molecules from the seaweed *Chrondus crispus*. This seaweed ooze spreads in among the chalk, paint, and anti-freeze, then stretches itself in all directions to hold the whole mass together. A bit of paraffin oil (the fuel that flickers in camping lamps) is pumped in with it to help the moss ooze keep the whole substance smooth. . . .
>
> The only problem is that by itself this ingredient tastes, well, too like detergent. It's horribly bitter and harsh. . . . It's to get around that gustatory discomfort that the manufacturers put in the ingredient they tout perhaps the most of all. This is the flavoring, and it has to be strong. Double rectified peppermint oil is used—a flavorer so powerful that chemists know better than to sniff it in the raw state in the laboratory.

Did you guess that this disgusting-sounding substance is toothpaste? (See Bodanis's essay on page 110.)

Some pieces of writing are entirely descriptive. However, description is most often used to support KEY IDEAS within another organizational pattern. "Toothpaste" is a division essay and "Deficits" is primarily a narrative, yet both are enhanced by strong description. Short passages of description—a sentence or two, or just a phrase—can help you ensure that your ideas are clear to the reader. Consider, for example, Jeffrey Moussaieff Masson's description of a penguin's egg in "Dear Dad," a process analysis essay, (page 80): "Weighing almost a pound [.45 kilograms], and measuring up to 131 millimetres long and 86 millimetres wide, this is one of the largest eggs of any bird."

HOW DO WE WRITE DESCRIPTION?

Description provides details of what your reader needs to visualize in order to understand your point. Good description communicates the writer's attitude to a topic as well as the objective details. Your goal should to be to convey, through the details you choose, a dominant impression that reflects your feelings about the person, place, or thing you are describing. Take another look at the descriptive examples above: Ignatieff's description of his mother, Doyle's description of the flat, and Bodanis's description of toothpaste ingredients. These passages all clearly convey the writers' attitudes toward their topics.

Here are four guidelines for writing good description:

1. Determine your PURPOSE. Are you writing a purely descriptive essay? Or are you using description to develop a KEY IDEA in an expository or persuasive essay? Decide whether you want to present a factual, objective picture (Masson's penguin egg, for example) or if you need to create a dominant impression that reflects your feelings.

2. Select the most important physical details. You cannot describe every detail about a topic without losing your focus (and your reader).

3. Arrange your selected details so that your picture emerges coherently. Usually, you will choose a spatial order (from top to bottom, left to right), but sometimes a psychological order (from external features to internal character) is appropriate. Use the arrangement most likely to accomplish your purpose.

4. Use sensory words in your description. What does the topic look, sound, feel, smell, and taste like? Choose words that contribute to the dominant impression you want to convey.

EXAMPLE

WHAT IS AN EXAMPLE?

An example is something selected from a class of things that is used to show the character of all of them. Examples give concrete form to abstract ideas. In "What I Have Lived For" (page 122), Bertrand Russell writes that he feels "unbearable pity for the suffering of mankind." What does he mean by "the suffering of mankind"? Before we can fully understand Russell's idea, we need examples: "Children in famine, victims tortured by oppressors, helpless old people a hated burden to their sons, and the whole world of loneliness, poverty, and pain make a mockery of what human life should be." In one sentence, Russell gives us three concrete examples that enable us to picture what he means by human suffering.

WHY DO WE USE EXAMPLES?

Good writing is a blend of ABSTRACT and CONCRETE, of GENERAL statements and SPECIFIC examples. It's difficult to imagine *any* kind of writing that doesn't need examples to communicate its KEY IDEAS clearly and effectively.

Examples help to clarify complex ideas so that readers can understand them. In "Altruism" (page 234), Lewis Thomas writes about the instinct that some animals have to surrender their own lives to save the group. He provides several examples to illustrate the mysterious behaviour known as altruism:

> . . . Birds risk their lives, sometimes lose them, in efforts to distract the attention of predators from the nest. Among baboons, zebras, moose, wildebeests, and wild dogs there are always stubbornly fated guardians, prepared to be done in first in order to buy time for the herd to escape.

Writers also use examples to support or back up their generalizations. In "Bonding Online" (page 142), David Brooks includes three examples of online sites where he sees young people forming a community.

> Companionship isn't dead. Go to MySpace.com or Facebook or Xanga or any of the other online sites where people leave messages on the home pages of their friends and you'll see great waves of praise and encouragement. There's scarcely a critical word in the whole social network. It's just fervent declarations of friendship, vows to get together soon and memories of great times.

Examples are used to support key ideas in all kinds of essays. Bertrand Russell's essay, for instance, is organized according to the principle of **division;** the organizing principle of Thomas's essay is **definition;** and Brooks's is **comparison/contrast**.

It is also possible to use examples as the organizing principle of an essay. In this case, the examples are usually described at some length and are called **illustrations.** In "The End of the Wild" (page 48), for example, Wade Davis organizes his plea for the environment around three key ideas, each of which is developed as a long example: an animal extinguished by human greed (the passenger pigeon), an animal greatly diminished by human short-sightedness (the buffalo), and a species of tree that is threatened by the logging industry (the rainforest conifers of British Columbia). Davis supports his THESIS with other examples, description, and several narratives, but the main organizing principle of his essay is three carefully arranged illustrations.

HOW DO WE USE EXAMPLES?

Writers use examples taken from research sources, their personal experience, or the experiences of others. Here are three guidelines for choosing good examples:

1. Be sure that any example you use is representative of your topic. Choose typical examples, not unusual or wacky ones.

2. Use examples that are relevant to your topic. There is a good reason why Wade Davis, in "The End of the Wild," did not include species—such as the dinosaurs—that were extinct before humans appeared on Earth. Davis's thesis is that human beings are recklessly destroying the natural world, and he has chosen examples that directly support this thesis.

3. Limit the number and range of your examples. Include only those examples that directly and effectively support your key ideas. If you include too many examples, you will reduce their effectiveness. Readers need the highlights, not the whole catalogue.

Mastering the three basic strategies we have outlined above is well worth your time and effort. Because they answer the fundamental questions readers ask—What happened? What does it look like? Who (or what) is involved?—narration, description, and example are three of the most useful tools a writer can use to communicate meaning.

The essay below illustrates how narration, description, and example can be used together to help convey a thesis.

A Cultural Exchange

Introduction (provides descriptive details)

The French bar-café is an institution, a unique national treasure. Its patrons are an eclectic mix of blue-clad workmen in cloth caps or berets; lawyers and stockbrokers in business suits; scruffy individuals who could be students, artists, anarchists, or all three; elderly retired gentlemen in tweeds and moustaches; and farmers in rubber boots. The haze of blue smoke that gives the interior such a warm aura is the most distinctive characteristic of a French bar: the unique smell of French tobacco. The harsh Gauloise produces a tangy, dark aroma that is unforgettable.

Narrative begins by describing the situation: a birthday celebration

I had entered this tiny bar on the ground floor of a country hotel in a small village in central France on a mission. My wife and I were staying in the hotel overnight, celebrating her fortieth birthday and recovering from lunch. Valerie's celebratory meal had taken place in nearby Roanne at Restaurant Troisgros, one of the gastronomic wonders of the world. "Lunch" had begun at noon and ended nearly

Description developed by examples

four hours later when we staggered out to our car, stuffed with *foie gras,* lobster *breton poché, noisettes* of lamb, a profusion of French cheeses, and a mind-boggling array of rich desserts. Now, some hours later and a few kilometres away, we were ready to cap the big day with a bottle of champagne on the balcony of our room. Unwilling to guzzle the expensive nectar from bathroom tumblers, I had tottered

General statement about communication; specific example concerning writer's grasp of French

down three flights of stairs to the bar to borrow a pair of proper champagne glasses.

We take communication for granted—so much so that only when it goes awry do we stop to think about what a complex process it is. My French is adequate, I'm told, so far as accent is concerned, but pathetically weak in grammar and vocabulary. Even the simplest conversation requires extensive rehearsal, so it was

Narrative resumes here

with some trepidation that I entered the crowded, smoky bar, muttering to myself the request I was about to make.

"*Oui, monsieur?*" The bartender was a friendly sort, but possessed of one of those voices that, when pitched just right, can be heard in the next province. Conversation gradually died as everyone turned to watch me struggle through my request.

Narrative developed by descriptive details and dialogue

I must have done well enough in my broken French accompanied by expressive hand gestures—shaping the glasses in the air and sipping imaginary bubbly—because the bartender grinned, reached under the bar, and produced two large flutes, polishing them elaborately with his apron.

"*Et pour quelle grande célébration désirez-vous deux verres de champagne, monsieur?*" he boomed as he set the glasses in front of me, winking theatrically. By now the entire bar was concentrating on our conversation, eager to hear what great celebration it was that required champagne glasses.

Confident that I was up to the task, I grinned and told the entire company, *"C'est aujourd'hui le quatorzième anniversaire de ma femme!"*

Topic sentence

The bar erupted in cries of congratulation and admiration. Blue-clad, Gauloise-smoking workmen

Examples enhanced by descriptive details

toasted me, hoisting their glasses overhead and shouting their approval. Others, apparently helpless with laughter, sagged against the bar. Several tried to shake my hand, though I was encumbered by the champagne glasses, and more than one slapped my back resoundingly. One older gentleman, nattily dressed in a blue beret and sporting magnificent waxed moustaches, wept with laughter as he tried to pour some of his *pastis* into my precious glasses. The hilarity seemed a bit overdone, I thought, for such a simple announcement . . . until I replayed the conversation in my head and realized that I had given my

Climactic incident: the "punch line"

wife's age not as *quarante*, forty, but as *quatorze*— fourteen.

Conclusion reinforces thesis: the complexity of communication

Joining the laughter, I bowed deeply, gave my best imitation of a Gallic shrug, and, flourishing my glasses overhead, made my red-faced exit.

Escape to Paradise

ARMIN KUMARSHELLAH

Born in Ahwaz, Iran, Armin Kumarshellah came to Canada when he was nearly seven, via the tortuous route he details in this story. With the exception of the name of "Dr. Nabbi," he says, "the whole thing is true." In 2005, Kumarshellah completed three years at York University's Atkinson Faculty of Liberal and Professional Studies, majoring in marketing.

1 "Everybody hurry to the basement, it's the safest place!" my mother cried. I waddled as fast as I could, with my mother behind me and my two older sisters forming a close train behind her. It was dark and we could hardly see. I was scared but didn't know why. My mother picked me up in her arms trying to comfort me, so that I wouldn't realize the magnitude of what was happening around the house. I could see tears rolling down my

oldest sister's cheek as she held my other sister close to her shivering body. Mostly, it was the horrific look pasted on my mother's face that led me to believe how scary this was. Mother would repeatedly pray for us and for my father, who was at work at the time. The loud sirens were howling across the city followed by the frequent sounds of blasting and explosions, which caused the house to tremble. Of course, being three years old, I didn't know what made the noises; all I knew was that I didn't like it.

We had been suffering through a vicious war between Iran and Iraq for six years, and my parents were fed up. One day, my father began selling our assets and belongings so we could begin our journey to Canada. Throughout the years, my sisters and I were told many fairy tales of how wonderful and magical this land called Canada was. My sisters and I were very anxious to get there. We didn't know about the many obstacles that stood in our way.

Our journey began after we had sold almost everything. We were not permitted to cross the Iranian border while the country was at war with Iraq; therefore, our escape was not only hard but extremely dangerous. If the authorities had realized that our passports were fake, they would have arrested us and executed us. Luckily we arrived safely in India. At this point we were stuck, not knowing what route to take out of India. It took nearly a year for a gentleman named Dr. Nabbi and his crooked associates to forge illegal documents for my father so that he could escape once again. They suggested to my parents that it would be wiser for my father to go by himself to Canada and work so that he could send money to finalize our documents. My father had no complications at the airport and landed in Canada safely. I remember we were ecstatic when we got the long distance call from my dad. We thought that we would be reunited soon.

My father dutifully sent all the money he earned to Dr. Nabbi. After months of negotiations, Dr. Nabbi and his associates were ready to send us to Canada with a stopover at Bangkok airport. Our fake passports said that we were Italian, so my mother continuously reminded us not to speak Farsi while near any authorities at the airport. Before we could board the next plane in Bangkok that was supposed to take us to Canada, the customs officer became suspicious of our documents, so an Italian translator was brought out to expose us. When my mother didn't respond in Italian, they quickly realized that we were illegal refugees and threatened to throw all of us in a Bangkok prison. The thought of having to be separated from her children was unbearable for her. She pleaded with the authorities to let her speak to the Canadian embassy.

5   After several excruciating hours in the terminal we were informed we could go to the embassy. My mother explained our situation to the powerful gentleman behind the desk. She said that we were too young to be placed in jail and that we needed her to survive in Thailand; she begged for mercy. He recognized our plight and helped us stay out of jail but said we would have to stay in Thailand to apply for refugee status. My mother explained to us that this arrangement would only be temporary and we needed to stay there until my father could bring us to Canada.

6   During those years in Thailand, my family and I made frequent trips to the immigration offices. It had been almost three years, and we were beginning to lose hope of ever seeing our father again. So finally, in desperation, my mother packed our bags and took us to the immigration office, threatening to stay there with her three kids until they gave us some sort of answer. For the first few hours they tried to ignore us but later a woman with a white folder in her hand came out and told us she had our visas in the folder and we would be leaving for Canada in a month. And so it was. Soon we were on a plane heading toward Canada.

7   The anticipation of seeing my father made the plane ride seem twice as long as it was. It had been so long since I last saw him, I had forgotten what he looked like. As the plane flew over Toronto I smiled, knowing that this was my new home. As we walked through the maze of people and luggage, I saw two men walking towards us at the end of the hallway. My mother, in her wonderful whispering voice, turned towards me and said, "That's Daddy." I ran as fast as I could toward the two gentlemen, leaped up and hugged my father as hard as I could. But my mother walked to the other gentleman and hugged him. "Armin, this is Daddy," she said with a giggle. My life in Canada had begun.

Structure and Strategy

1. Study the attention-getter (paragraph 1) of this essay. The author grabs the reader's attention by vividly describing the experience that finally prompted his parents' decision to leave their homeland. Identify five or six phrases that contribute to the sense of fear and urgency that this paragraph communicates.
2. What specific details in paragraph 1 make the reader feel immediately sympathetic for the author of this narrative?
3. What is the THESIS of this essay? Is it stated or implied?
4. Do you think the CONCLUSION of the essay is effective? Why or why not?

Content and Purpose

1. What is the political background of the narrative?
2. How many people are in Kumarshellah's family?
3. What happens to the family between the time they leave their home in Iran and finally arrive in Canada? Which paragraphs deal with each stage of the narrative?
4. How old is the author when his narrative begins? How old do you think he is when it concludes?
5. How would you characterize Dr. Nabbi?
6. How would you characterize the Canadian immigration officials as they deal with the Kumarshellah family?
7. What is the IRONY at the conclusion of the essay?

Suggestions for Writing

1. If you or someone you know has come to Canada as a refugee, write a narrative essay about that experience.
2. Write an essay about the effects of a long separation between a parent and child.
3. Write an essay speculating how someone with an experience like Armin's is likely to feel about his or her family, the family's journey to Canada, and about Canada itself.

Finding a Flatmate

HILARY DOYLE

After earning her B.Sc. from Northwestern University in Illinois, Hilary Doyle returned to Canada and began her career as writer and actor. She has written for the *Toronto Star* and *Maisonneuve* magazine, and worked as an investigative reporter, feature writer, and humorist in San Miguel de Allende, Mexico. She has edited for the Ontario government, Canada 25, Care Canada, Ashoka, WWF Russia, and TV Ontario. As an actor, Doyle has worked with the Canadian Film Centre, macIDeas, Crows Theatre, the SOHO Rep, and the Second City National Touring Company. She now works as a freelance journalist and editor in Toronto.

John described his Spadina Avenue apartment as a two-bedroom   1
with lots of light and very high ceilings. He neglected to mention it was a subterranean hovel with tiled floors, one stripped-

wire cot and tiny barred window evocative° of Alcatraz.° He also failed to note that his place was an open studio, which he and his three-legged cat hoped to share, sans wall or curtain, with a hand-picked stranger. When I asked John where he slept, he curled back his upper lip, cackled with glee and said, "Sleep?"

2   That was July 2001, when my hunt for a Toronto apartment was in its nascency°. Know this: when it comes to finding an apartment in Hogtown, nothing (and no one) can be trusted—not rumours, not Craigslist°, not your fellow man. My three-year apartment-hunting nightmare can attest to that.

3   And let's be clear: I am not picky. Prior to Toronto, I lived in Manhattan, sleeping on a lawn chair in a closet. For US$800 a month, I shared a one-bedroom "convert" with a metrosexual exhibitionist and a 250-pound woman from the Bronx who attended registered orgies with sick regularity. At some point during that New York year of "personal development," the tawdriness of my D-list modelling career became unbearable, and [my employer] fired me for being too Canadian. Life was not going according to plan; it was time to make a move. If nothing else, Toronto would improve the status of my personal habitat—certainly, there was nowhere to go but up.

4   Apartment postings, I now know, are expressions of the creative soul. Beware the euphemisms°:

comfortable = miniscule
cozy = dark
charming = mice
vegan = vegan.

5   Dirk carried delusions of Libeskind°-calibre grandeur. Dirk's online photograph showed a pristine white living room with minimalist design and über-chic black lacquered furniture. In 14-point caps, he promised "hip roommates, big rooms, cool vibe." It is one of life's grave injustices that those truly in possession of "hip roommates" or, God help me, "cool vibes" never advertise. When Dirk opened the door, I was surprised but not shocked to come face to face with a tall, forty-three-year-old man swathed in heavy silver insect jewellery. Tattooed, with thinning, dyed-black hair turned white at the roots, Dirk was channelling Marilyn Manson on the Axl Rose decline.

6   He was after a roommate who could gel harmoniously with his chosen ménagerie: Cher (an unapologetically bland treasure), Cher's mute boyfriend (arm in plaster, trial pending), a twentynothing goth (unpronounceable name), Dirk's life-sized plush gorilla and a wily, ill-tempered iguana. For $500 a month (utilities

included), Dirk offered cramped quarters, crumbling walls and a cavernous hole in the kitchen—the result, he said, of a "minor toilet incident." It is fitting to mention that Dirk worked in Toronto as a motivational speaker. . . .

Lee was a wise man. He'd mentioned his fiancée in his posting, which made him sound harmless, smitten and very desirable. Lee lived aboveground, in his own room, and his apartment straddled the best independent video store in Toronto. All this for $475 a month (utilities extra). Lee was sounding good until I stood three storeys below his postage-stamp-sized window, waiting for a workman's sock to be dropped from above. Lee's key. 7

I couldn't find the front door, and the stairs up to the third level had compacted themselves, giving way to a sort of precarious slide. There was no doorbell, no living room, no furniture. My new room was locked and empty, save for a yellowed futon mattress, a discarded pine frame and a winter jacket. Lee's current roommate, Rambo, a welfare deserter who could no longer make the rent, had not yet been informed that he was leaving. Lee's fiancée was catatonic°. She was also, I suspect, a man. Their cat was black, the air was green and the kitchen was a poetic ensemble of mould, shards of plaster, cat hair and roaches (both crawling and smouldering). Lee was baking pies. Lee had the munchies. 8

My years of fieldwork further revealed this: the difference in quality, comfort and privacy between a $550-a-month Toronto apartment and an $800-a-month one is astronomical—not unlike the difference between the Bates Motel° and the Ritz. Post-Lee, I shunned Craigslist; I shunned the Internet altogether. Maybe these frightening people were just cyber-geeks bent on driving me out of town. I needed a fresh approach. I turned off my computer and opened the newspaper. And this is how I met Eve. Eve lived in a Kensington Market duplex. When she came to the door wearing horns and a dog collar, desertion didn't enter my mind. Desperation makes fools of us all. Eve was offering a room for $425 in a house with three roommates. I spotted her ad in *Now*, a popular, free weekly that carries a diverse selection of apartments to suit an alternative, relatively boho° readership. At the time, it cost $44.68 to purchase a headline and two lines of text. Eve's ad read: 9

comfortable room, minutes from streetcar,
large house, laid-back roommates.

The house was indeed large—though my room was small, had exposed sockets, an industrial sink and no door. The centrepiece was actually the backyard's communal compost mound, next to the outdoor fireplace and a diseased orange tree. There were rules, Eve 10 assured me. No partners at the house for more than 40 percent of the week. No spilling over onto other people's refrigerator shelves. No talking shit about the music. Ah yes, the other two roommates were rockers. In abject defiance of the house rules, one of the musicians was Eve's live-in boyfriend. The rules didn't apply to her because she was afraid to sleep alone.

11   I explained that I was a writer. Would it be a problem for me to write during the day, while Eve worked at a guitar shop and the guys tried to get their band off the ground? Eve didn't know if things could get loud, because she'd never been around during the day. "Steve! STEVE! Wake the fuck up!" It was 3 p.m. Steve emerged, droopy-eyed, with hair that looked like a fright wig. "This chick's our new roommate, if we want her. She's a writer." I interjected, "I'm just wondering if it would be a problem for me to write during the day." Steve thought. Hard. "Well, I don't have a problem if you write during the day."

12   By May of 2004, in the gloom of despondence, I settled for a mid-sized dining room in an apartment with Margaret. She was thirtysomething, on the heels of a terrible breakup and reminded me vaguely of an anorexic Medea°.

13   "Hey, Margaret," I'd say, as she merrily chopped up another photograph, cracked into his e-mail account or stared longingly at a 2003 calendar that was, apparently, his favourite. "Where do you keep the green bin?"

14   "Oh, we . . . [eyes welling, voice shaking, body crumpling] I mean I . . . [choking, rocking] I keep the green bin on the porch."

15   Margaret was the last straw. After three years, what I needed more than an apartment was perspective. And respite. I fled to Mexico. A World Values Survey declared Mexico the second happiest country in the world, just behind Nigeria. Obviously this happiness springs from the fact that Mexicans aren't obsessed with hip apartments. I hoped Mexico could show me something more. I took a freelance job as a news reporter for the local paper and prepared to do interviews in fledgling Spanish° for the duration of my five-week break.

16   As papers do, mine had classifieds. In San Miguel de Allende, for less than US$300 a month, it's possible to rent a one-bedroom apartment with a private rooftop patio, a full kitchen, a shower and bath, a weekly maid service and a borrowed wireless signal (utilities included).

17   Adios, Toronto.

Words and Meanings

Paragraph

evocative	suggestive, reminiscent	1
Alcatraz	a famous (though now closed) prison	
nascency	early stages	2
Craigslist	a Web site that lists apartments for rent, community events, discussion forums, personal ads, and much more for hundreds of communities around the world	
euphemisms	the use of positive, pleasant terms for unpleasant realities	4
Libeskind	internationally renowned architect Daniel Libeskind	5
catatonic	in a "frozen" state: unmoving, unspeaking	8
Bates Motel	scene of Hitchcock's horror movie *Psycho*	9
boho	bohemian, unconventional	
Medea	character in a classic Greek tragedy who goes mad when her husband abandons her	12
fledgling Spanish	beginner's Spanish	15

Structure and Strategy

1. How many examples of Toronto apartments does Doyle describe in her essay? Could she have omitted any and still have achieved the same effect?
2. This essay relies primarily on DESCRIPTION to convey Doyle's THESIS. Identify five or six details of the apartments she describes that seem especially disgusting to you.
3. Select six or more details that you think are particularly effective in describing the people Doyle meets during her hunt for an apartment. Which of these people do you think is most vividly described? Why?
4. Does the essay have a thesis statement?
5. What is unusual about the introductory and concluding paragraphs of this essay? (See the Glossary section for definitions and examples of traditional INTRODUCTIONS and CONCLUSIONS.)
6. Doyle uses a number of ALLUSIONS in the essay: Libeskind, Marilyn Manson (paragraph 5); Bates Motel (paragraph 9). Do these allusions help the reader understand Doyle's thesis? Why or why not?

Content and Purpose

1. Where did Doyle live before she began apartment hunting in Toronto? Why did she leave?
2. Where does Doyle look first for apartment listings? When that source proves fruitless, where does she look next? (See paragraph 9.) What difference is there in the results of the two strategies?
3. Where does Doyle eventually end up in Toronto? What's wrong with the roommate described as "the last straw" (paragraph 15)?
4. Where does Doyle go at the end of the essay?
5. What is the IRONY in paragraphs 15 and 16?
6. How would you describe the TONE of this essay?

Suggestions for Writing

1. Have you ever searched for a rental space (apartment or house)? Write a descriptive essay about the places you rejected before you found what you were looking for.
2. Have you ever lived with one or more roommates? Describe the experience.
3. Write an essay that explains how strangers who have little or nothing in common can successfully share living space.

Baba and Me

SHANDI MITCHELL

A native of Nova Scotia who was raised in Alberta, author and screenwriter Shandi Mitchell (b. 1964) co-wrote the short film *Gasoline Puddles* and wrote and directed the television drama *Baba's House*. Her other films include *Beefcake* (1999), *Touch the Moon* (2001), and *Tell Me* (2005). She received the 2001 Anna Pidruchney Award for New Writers for this essay. Mitchell currently lives in Nova Scotia.

1   In 1922, my father, at the age of two, came to Canada with his parents and five brothers and sisters from the Ukraine. They landed at Pier 21 in Halifax and headed west to homestead in northern Alberta. They lived in a sod-and-log house and suffered the prejudice of the times and the poverty of a barren existence.

story

Forty years later, I was born into a lower-middle-class Canadian existence.

In that short span, the Ukrainian culture had been lost to me. My Baba (grandmother) never learned to speak English and I knew no Ukrainian. She was as much a stranger to me as were her customs, foods, thoughts, and life. As a child, I was frightened of her. 2

I knew nothing of her past and none of her secrets. No one spoke of my grandfather. I remember the family visiting a weed-infested lot set aside from the main cemetery. It wasn't until many years later that I was told he had killed himself. 3

It was then 1938: the prairies were choking on dust and Baba was newly widowed, with six children to support. In the next town over, Old Man Kurik's wife had died in childbirth. And so began Baba's next marriage. The old man used the kids as field hands and boxing bags, excepting his own son, whom he schooled to become a "gentleman." Then World War II exploded. One by one all of Baba's children left for the cities. They ran from the wheat fields and their rich, decaying earth. 4

They ran to the plastic, shiny chrome worlds filled with starched sailors and armed forces personnel. They ran to heroes' deaths and cowards' retreats. They fell in love and became "Canadians" or "Americans." They changed their names and became Marshalls, Smiths, and Longs. They travelled the world and sent postcards back home to Baba. She saved the exotic images in a cookie tin under her bed. Eventually, even Baba and Old Man Kurik moved to town. Baba became a grandmother and was asked not to speak Ukrainian around her grandchildren. 5

Baba wrote letters in Ukrainian to the old country, but they remained unanswered. Undaunted by political barriers, she continued to save her pennies, quarters, and nickels for her visit home. She didn't believe that she wouldn't be let in. Her children shushed her when she spoke of her Communist brother. It was as if the world grew up around Baba. Then one day, she found herself a widow again. That morning, she opened every window and door in the house and breathed deeply. It was January. 6

My Baba got old in the seventies. Sometimes, she babysat my brother and me. My parents would drop us off for the weekend. I hated going there. She didn't speak any English, and I blocked out her Ukrainian. She dressed funny, she cooked funny, and she smelled of garlic. She tried to teach me about Ukrainian things. I didn't want to know. My friends were outside playing, the first McDonald's in town was opening down the street, and the Bay City Rollers had a new record. . . . I had better things to do than hang around with Baba. Back then, I didn't know the word "ashamed." 7

8   Baba didn't need English in the town where she lived. There were Ukrainian newspapers, TV and radio stations, stores, neighbours, churches and all the essentials in this weed of a town poking up out of nowhere in northern Alberta. The town of 1600 was divided neatly into French in the north, Ukrainians in the south, Cree in the east, English in the centre, and everyone else crammed into the west. It was in Baba's town that I first learned about poverty, alcoholism, domestic abuse, and racism.

9   When the old man next door died, his house was boarded up, and it became a popular place to sniff glue and drink aftershave. The neighbours pretended not to see. In the safety of daylight, we kids would venture in and gather up the few bottles amongst the cans and then cash them in at the confectionery for nickel candy. Once, we thought we'd found a dead body, but he had only passed out. Baba tended her garden, seemingly oblivious to the world next door, and kept on planning her trip home to the old country.

10   When the neighbourhood began to gentrify° with condos and supermarkets and it was decided that Baba's best friend, Mrs. Westavich, couldn't keep her chickens anymore, Baba rallied to help her and used her precious savings in the process. When the two old women lost their battle, they took the chickens out to the front yard. Baba swung the axe while Mrs. Westavich held the birds down. They chopped their heads off one by one and let the birds' bodies flail and flop over the manicured lawns.

11   When the family decided it was best for Baba to go into a Home, there was no one left to fight for her. The first place was called Sunnyvale. The kids pulled her out from there when they found that she hadn't been bathed in a month and was covered in bed sores; also, her bank account was unaccountably low. Baba liked the new place better. She had a window box there, and grew tomatoes. I went to visit her, once. I called out, "Hi Baba!" and twenty wizened babas turned expectantly to me.

12   I hear Baba's house rents cheap now. The garden is filled with three cars up on blocks. I don't know what happened to her belongings. Her body is buried in Edmonton. I think the family felt it was a greater tribute to be buried in a city lot.

13   So here I sit in front of my computer with cell phone in hand and a coffeemaker brewing, and wonder about my grandmother. I have only one black and white photograph of her. She is squat and round, with huge breasts. She wears a cotton shift dress. Her nylon stockings are bunched at her ankles. A babushka° covers her head. She stands shyly beside a shiny late-model 1950s car. Next to her is my mother, with dark glasses, over-sized sun hat, and wasp waist, posed very much like Greta Garbo. I stand at the edge of the frame, a skinny kid looking as if I'm about to run.

Words and Meanings

gentrify   to transform an aging neighbourhood into a   10
                            more prosperous one through remodelling
                            buildings or houses

babushka   a head scarf folded and tied under the chin   13

Structure and Strategy

1. What kind of INTRODUCTION does Mitchell use in this essay? Is it effective? Why or why not?
2. Identify at least three descriptive details in paragraph 7. How many senses does the DESCRIPTION appeal to? What is the dominant impression that the reader gets from this description?
3. Identify the TRANSITIONS the author uses to link paragraphs 1 to 2, 4 to 5, and 7 to 8. How do they contribute to the effectiveness of the piece?
4. Mitchell develops her THESIS primarily through the use of examples. Choose three that you think are particularly effective and explain how they contribute to the thesis.

Content and Purpose

1. What are the main events of this story? Identify the ORDER in which these events are arranged. Then, in point form, put them in CHRONOLOGICAL ORDER.
2. Baba marries two times. What do you think these marriages were like? Use details from the essay to support your opinions.
3. The northern Alberta town Baba and "Old Man Kurik" move to is described in paragraphs 8 and 9. What kind of place is it? Who lives there? What does Mitchell learn in this town?
4. Why do you think Baba and Mrs. Westavich killed the chickens in the front yard (see paragraph 10)? What is the point of this ANECDOTE?
5. In paragraph 13, the author describes a photograph of her grandmother, her mother, and herself as a child. What do the descriptive details tell you about these people? What does Mitchell imply about the relationships between them?
6. What is Mitchell's PURPOSE in this essay, other than chronicling the life of her grandmother? State in one sentence what you think the "lesson" of the story is. How did the essay affect you?

Suggestions for Writing

1. Write an essay describing an older relative or other person you know (or knew) well. Include physical details, but also describe

the kind of life the person has (or had), as well as your own feelings about him or her.

2. Write an essay explaining the difficulties of being a new immigrant. What does it mean to leave the world one was born into and move to a different country to establish a life for oneself and one's descendants?

3. Read Ken Wiwa's "Nature or Nurture—What's the Real Test of 'Home'?" on page 210. How are Wiwa's experiences of "home" different from Baba's? Write an essay contrasting the two views of "home." You might conclude by suggesting some of the reasons for the difference between Baba's and Wiwa's attitudes to the changes they experienced moving from one place to another.

The Yukon

DOUGLAS COUPLAND

Douglas Coupland (b. 1961), novelist, short-story writer, journalist, sculptor, and winner of two Canadian National Awards for Excellence in Industrial Design, is perhaps most famous for coining the term "Generation X." His novels include *Generation X* (1991), *City of Glass* (2000), *Hey Nostradamus!* (2003), *Eleanor Rigby* (2004), and *jPod* (2006). "The Yukon" is taken from *Souvenir of Canada* (2002), a collection of photographs and essays.

1 When my father went civilian in 1966, one of the first things he did, once he could, was to buy a twin-engine de Havilland Otter floatplane. I think he did this to recreate what were the happiest days of his life, paying for his medical school tuition by flying bush planes during the summer in the wilds of northern Quebec and Labrador, into areas then still marked UNMAPPED. He ferried the inhabitants of remote outposts to and from hospitals, as well as Canadian and American military and mining engineers invading Labrador, part of what was then a brand-new Canadian province (Newfoundland) only a few years old.

2 [When I was young], trips with Dad in the plane often felt like torture, but with hindsight I can see them as an exotic and charmed way to have spent a part of my youth. When I was around thirteen, my father flew my younger brother and me in the Twin Otter up to

the Yukon. First, we overnighted in Whitehorse, a city of diesel fumes, hamburgers, beige dusty roads and people getting really *really* drunk at the local bars. The Klondike fulfills many expectations. The next day we headed off into Kluane *(kloo-awn-ay)* National Park—a place I never even knew existed, but to fly over it was to apprehend God or the next world or something altogether richer than the suburbs of home. Glaciers drape like mink over feldspar ridges like broken backs, and the twenty-four-hour midnight sun somehow burns paler and whiter than the sun in the south—and the horizon seems to come from a bigger planet. To see a wild landscape like this is to crack open your soul and see larger landscapes inside yourself. Or so I believe. Raw nature must be preserved, so that we never forget the grandeur it can inspire.

Anyway, as we landed at a fishing camp on Tincup Lake, my younger brother and I, a bit young for soul-cracking, were intent on panning for gold, having boned up on the subject the week before, becoming experts along the way and doubtlessly destined to tap the mother lode the locals had missed in all of their adult ignorance. We'd barely docked before we hit the nearest stream, our pans verily frisbeeing ahead of us. 3

Several hours later, we were goldless, but as consolation, we played the ancient game of trying to convince each other that the thin, triangular rocks just found were indeed, *no I swear it, man,* arrowheads. 4

The next day boredom set in, and Floyd, the boat boy working for the summer as part of a juvenile rehabilitation program, suggested we ride down to the end of the lake to check out a trapper's cabin that had only ever been sighted from the air. The thing about Floyd was that, well, I wasn't sure if he was a living person or the ghost of a dead boat boy like in a Stephen King novel. Everything about him was white, and he smoked too much and his breath didn't steam the morning air like everybody else's. However, boredom being boredom, we went, with a canoe lying criss-crossed over the twelve-foot aluminum heap powered by an Evinrude 50. We set out around four in the afternoon for the 16-kilometre trip to the end of the lake. Once there, we beached the boat on a gravel bar and paddled downstream. Maybe 3 kilometres down, we came to the cabin, not much to speak of, like the Unabomber's shack after a hundred years of rot. 5

We parked the canoe and went "inside," quotation marks used because half the roof was gone. At the very least, I expected to find a skeleton wrapped in mummified beaver pelts, because after all, I'd canoed to this place with Floyd the Undead. Instead, we found an old coffee can, the top of a tobacco tin and lots of animal bones in a pile out behind. None of this was very exciting, but at least 6 we'd been the first to visit the cabin in probably fifty years, and I felt what visitors to Shackleton's° Antarctic home must feel.

7   Fine.

8   Then we portaged up the river's edge maybe ten paces before Floyd the Undead said, "I guess I was wrong. Doug—we can't portage because there's no path."

9   *Moron.*

10   So we ended up wading 3 kilometres upstream in water only a degree above freezing, three steps ahead, two steps back, and it was past midnight when we finally reached the aluminum boat, which ran out of gas after three putt-putts. But it was bright outside and we were young (at least I was—Floyd, being undead, had no age) so we canoed back down the lake, arriving at 4:00 a.m. and expecting a search party in high anxiety. Instead, we found a poker game at the peak of its action.

11   "Hi guys. Have a good trip down the lake?"

12   Mutter mutter.

13   And that is the Yukon. Or a slice of it. Everyone I've ever met from the Yukon is successful: couture designers, actors, builders and private investigators. Something about the place makes people think and act big—the slightly larger horizon makes them look ahead slightly farther. It's a place that delivers the dream.

Words and Meanings

Paragraph

6   Shackleton

Sir Ernest Henry Shackleton (1874–1922), Irish explorer best known for the perilous journey he undertook to seek help for his stranded crew after his ship, the *Endurance*, was crushed in ice during his third Antarctic expedition, in 1914–16

Structure and Strategy

1. How does the first paragraph set up both the narrative and the TONE of this piece? How would you describe the tone?

2. Paragraph 2 is full of descriptive details. Identify three or four that you think are particularly effective and explain why.

3. In the narrative section of this essay (paragraphs 3 to 12), Coupland tells an ANECDOTE. Several of the paragraphs are one or two words. Why? Are these words intended to represent dialogue or something else? Where does Coupland make clear the point of the anecdote?

Content and Purpose

1. How did Coupland feel about the Yukon wilderness when he was thirteen years old? How does he feel about it as an adult? Where are the two contrasting perspectives highlighted in the essay?
2. Summarize the events of the trip to and from the trapper's cabin (paragraphs 5 to 12). What is the connection between the trip and Coupland's concluding remarks (paragraph 13)?
3. Who is Floyd, and why does Coupland call him "the Undead"? Floyd is the only person in this essay who is described in any detail. What is the similarity between Floyd and the setting in which he lives?
4. What does Coupland think of the Yukon and its people? What connection is there between the landscape and the people?
5. What does Coupland mean by his concluding statement, "It's a place that delivers the dream"?
6. Would Coupland be likely to favour intensive exploration of the Arctic for oil, diamonds, and other natural resources? Why or why not?

Suggestions for Writing

1. Write an essay about a personal experience from your past that seemed difficult, boring, or agonizing at the time but is now a fond memory. Why do you think your feelings about the experience changed?
2. Describe a natural setting you enjoy visiting. What is it about the place that appeals to you?

My Life as a Cleaner

NOREEN SHANAHAN

Noreen Shanahan is a Toronto freelance writer-*cum*-housecleaner. She is at work on a book of her experiences, entitled *Mess: A Housecleaner's Odyssey.*

It was a bright spring afternoon when Suzanne* told me she wouldn't need me anymore. I had just finished my four-hour cleaning shift—tearing up and down the stairs of her three-   1

---

*Some names and details have been changed.

relationship

evidence of

trust.

storey Parkdale home, scraping crayon goo from broadloom and freeing Cheerios snagged in the kitchen sink. She was wearing jeans and a fluffy Gap sweatshirt, sitting at the pine table I had recently polished, a pile of papers scattered around her. "My husband is expecting a 30 per cent pay cut," she said. "We're trying to live as if it's already happened." I felt sorry for her—how could I not? But I also felt a piercing sense of loss. I almost started to cry.

2   I had been cleaning Suzanne's house for five years and had developed an unexpected attachment to her, her husband and their two girls, a 10-year-old and a seven-year-old. It wasn't just that I had become an expert on every dirt-attracting crack in their hardwood floor. Or that I knew the most tedious job in the house was wiping down a thin ledge in the bathroom where seashells and sand dollars perched precariously. Or that I had learned exactly how to position stuffed teddy bears, dogs, dolls, whales and frogs on the girls' beds. It was more than that. I felt I had become a part of the fabric of their lives.

3   Suzanne stayed home with the kids, so in the morning I'd often see her taking them through the alley behind the church to school. And I'd be there when they came home at lunch for grilled cheese sandwiches and piano practice. I had watched them grow up. Now I was being fired, and the weird thing was I really wanted to keep scraping away at the dirt and dusting the girls' rooms. I also felt a little wounded: didn't I deserve some small token of appreciation? A plate of Girl Guides cookies? A hand-drawn card from one of her daughters?

4   I left Suzanne's house that day wondering about the nature of my relationship with my clients. Who am I to them? On one level, I'm merely an employee—the lowest kind of employee, actually. The toilet bowl scrubber, the garbage taker-outer, the mirror Windex-er. But I'm also a trusted member of the household. I work inside people's homes, the place where they sleep, make love; the place where they become the person they rarely show any other person; the place where they lounge in their dressing gowns, picking popcorn kernels out of their teeth. I am the person who vacuums up those kernels. Stains are removed, pillows are fluffed. I appear and disappear. But while washing, dusting, polishing, lifting, sweating—and sometimes cursing—I can't help but be drawn into the dramas unfolding around me.

5   I made the decision to become a cleaner five years ago, when I was a 40-year-old child-care worker and a single mother of a bright and hungry seven-year-old boy. When I found out that my friend Gloria, who cleaned houses, earned more money than I did taking

care of young children in my house, I invited her out for coffee and quizzed her: How much did she charge? Did she declare the income or collect it under the table? How flexible can you be with your hours? (I wanted more time to work on my writing during the day.) Over the years, I'd had many different jobs—as a union organizer, as an activist with feminist collectives and as a teacher—and to my surprise, cleaning started to sound pretty good. It would allow me close proximity to my son, the freedom to dress casually and listen all morning to Shelagh Rogers° and, most important, lots of time on my own.

The only problem was that I didn't know much about the job. My mother didn't have time to teach me housekeeping skills: she was busy raising five daughters and three sons on one unpredictable income. (My father, who usually wore his bathrobe till noon, had a million entrepreneurial schemes, some successful and others less so. Today, he earns a living as a locator of missing heirs.) The last time I had given cleaning serious thought, I was a seven-year-old Brownie, leaning over Tawny Owl's bathtub with Mr. Clean, trying to earn my housekeeping badges while Tawny Owl herself perched on the ledge, inspecting my work. 6

Gloria gave me tips: always work from top to bottom; remember to dust between venetian blinds. Prepared to learn the rest on the job, I thumbtacked a sign to the notice board at Alternative Grounds coffee shop on Roncesvalles. It read "Strong-like-bull dyke: lesbian poet-cum-cleaner wants to dust your books and valuables." I used a pseudonym in my ad, unsure of what I was getting into, a little ashamed to be offering my services as a washerwoman. 7

Suzanne was my first client. On the phone, we agreed to four-hour shifts every second Wednesday for $75. When she first opened her front door, we recognized each other immediately. We'd seen each other around the neighbourhood and at the park. We had even stood next to each other, pushing our kids on the swings. There was an initial awkwardness, partly because it was my first cleaning job—I didn't yet know how to relax and just be professional—but also because of our past association. She knew me as a neighbourhood mom. Now I was her cleaning lady. It didn't take long, however, before I was given my list of tasks and sent on my way. 8

Cleaning proved to be harder than I expected. I sweated, groaned and, at times, regretted my decision. I also made mistakes. On my first day, I accidentally flushed a sodden pile of cleaning rags down the toilet, clogging it. Suzanne's husband—who happened to be home—rescued me with a plunger. Still, despite the mishap, I felt oddly elated at the end of my shift, pleased to have 9 survived my first day. The instant cash also came in handy. I owed $20 to the corner greengrocer and paid him on my walk home.

10   My business grew, partly through word of mouth, partly through ad postings. Within a year, I had 10 clients for whom I worked every other week—all from Parkdale, along the Roncesvalles strip—which added up to a 20-hour workweek. In a good year, my total income would be roughly $20,000, no benefits or sick pay. (I always declare my earnings, which is unusual in my trade.) On any given day, I juggle 15 keys securely strapped to my knapsack and almost as many burglar alarm codes in my head. But my clients aren't wealthy. They tend to be the IKEA crowd, perhaps just one rung up the income ladder from me (I'm more the pick-IKEA-from-the-trash type). They drink $12 chardonnay and leave the dregs in bottles perched on top of the refrigerator, glasses by the side of the bed. Most of them are good about payment (only one cheque ever bounced), and one client even gave me a $10 raise unbidden. I learned pretty quickly that I was a luxury in the economy of these households—and, as such, I was vulnerable to the ups and downs of a family's financial life. When one couple I was working for had a second child, faced with the additional strain on their budget, they got rid of me.

11   After a while, I got into a routine. I'd arrive, peel off my street clothes and slip into my cleaning garb: purple Adidas shorts, with pockets large enough to stuff fistfuls of garbage or vacuum attachments, and a grey T-shirt. While I'd get ready, my client and I would chat about things like how the kids are doing at school, plans for Halloween, whether to get a new puppy. Then I'd be left alone.

12   There is great emotional complexity in the dusty kingdoms my clients entrust to me. When I posted my sign, I had no idea I would be so drawn into their lives. But I see everything when I clean. I watch seasons pass through shoes and boots, coats and umbrellas. I watch holidays come and go through children's artwork spread across surfaces: hearts, wreaths, shamrocks, marigold seedlings in egg cartons, which leave bits of dirt that I wipe away. I know when birthdays happen, when relatives visit. As I dust family photos, I watch children grow beneath the glass.

13   Sometimes, however, I see more than I'd like. I can detect when marriages are in trouble: an overnight bag waiting by the front door, a half-empty box of tissues by the bed. There's a kind of barometer to every home. One day, at the apartment of a client named Rachel, who is roughly my age, I discovered a bag bulging with books on women and depression at the bottom of the stairs.

Rachel has twin toddlers and two puppies. On her bedroom wall, in her wedding pictures, she wears a huge smile. I worried about her, but I never found out why she had those books. Nor could I ever ask.

Another woman I worked for on the same street was going 14 through a divorce and had just returned to work. One morning as I was mopping the floor, I found a sleeping bag unceremoniously stuffed behind the sofa. I imagined late-night arguments, rages while the children huddled in their rooms. Her bedside books were about spirituality, as if she was trying to find calm in the chaos.

Clients sometimes open up to me, confessing stuff they can't 15 easily tell anybody else. The first time it happened, I was shocked. I had been on the job for about a year and was halfway through my shift in a lovely semi-detached Parkdale house. I asked my client where the vacuum bags were kept, but instead of directing me to them, he burst into a tirade against his wife. Only she knew where the bags were kept, but she hadn't yet returned home from a date with her new boyfriend. "How the hell am I expected to keep it all together, get the kids to school and remember to make their damned lunches while she's still out with this guy?" he howled.

Standing by the stove, he refilled his coffee cup, describing the 16 sordid details of his troubled life. I awkwardly mumbled something about how this too shall pass, then hightailed it out of the room in search of a sink to scour. But I never saw the man again. Two weeks later, his wife told me that he had moved out. I revealed nothing to her about our conversation.

Once, a client told me about her pregnancy scare. She was in 17 her mid-30s, already the mother of three children under 10, and was re-entering the workforce after years away. "My period's late," she told me in a shaky voice, a look of horror on her face. I listened sympathetically—what else could I do? Then I pretended the conversation never took place. I don't whether she was pregnant and, if so, what she did about it. I could hardly ask. When you're a cleaner, you're sucked into other people's plot lines and, just as quickly, you're ejected from them. You rarely get closure.

Another time, an exhausted new mother, who'd been up all 18 night with a croupy baby, greeted me at the door at nine a.m. in her wildflower-patterned flannel nightgown and immediately burst into tears. I sat beside her on the couch for a few minutes, wanting nothing more than to hold her hand or draw her soothingly into my arms. "Tell me it's gonna get better," she said in a desperate whisper. I assured her it would, sharing early-motherhood stories of my own. Then I encouraged her to crawl back into bed while the baby slept, knowing how much easier it would feel when she got up, less exhausted, to a clean house.

19 There are things I love about cleaning: the satisfying shoosh and clink as a sizable something slides up the vacuum hose; digging up loose change beneath sofa cushions (which I place in a visible spot for my client to find); discovering a new cleaning product that finally erases grease smeared across the kitchen range. I'm often the only person at a house when a courier pulls up; I'll sign for the package. Or if Grocery Gateway drops off its crates, I'll put the perishables away and add the waybill to the growing mountain of little slips of paper gathered while tidying up. I'm the cleaner; these others are the deliverers. Together, we keep this family functional, well fed, sane, organized and clean. I don't usually do windows, but on a bright day, I might leap into action and wash the window upstairs in the baby's room, so my nursing client can look outside and watch the trees turn, the leaves fall, the snow arrive. I like to imagine she notices my little gift to her.

20 Most of my clients have children—curious, bright little things that jump over my cleaning bucket or obligingly run to the third-floor bathroom if I'm working on the second-floor one. Lifting my head out of the toilet bowl, I'll hand them their toothbrushes and send them on their way. I sometimes wonder what these children make of me, watching me fly by with my feather duster, sudsy red bucket and yellow gloves. I settle stuffed animals on their beds and dust under kid-made clay figurines their parent can't bear to throw out.

21 One five-year-old girl named Claire leaves me notes under her pillow, and the occasional drawing—a dog in the park, her baby brother eating breakfast, a stick-people sketch of the whole family. I write little messages back, describing an exchange I've had with her dolls or suggesting a costume change for Barbie. In a recent note, I thanked Claire for letting me use the new toilet bowl brush she had helped her mom pick out from Wal-Mart.

22 In a Tudor-style house I clean, there's a 10-year-old boy named Ethan, the youngest of five. When he was about seven, he dug out his art supplies and sketched me while I worked. He sat before me with his legs crossed, eyes fixed on my every gesture. I remember the purposeful way he watched me scoop up the plastic bones of Crayola markers and felt stickers, placing them in their proper boxes or drawers. I kept his sketch on my fridge for weeks.

23 I crossed a line once and told a client to get rid of the puzzle under her daughter Emily's bed. For months, I had been pulling out this abandoned puzzle, dusting it off, then sliding it back under. Emily also has no fewer than six dollhouses of varying sizes, equipped with tiny plates, beds, chairs and pets. Some days, when the pieces crunched underfoot, I hated them all. My client commis-

erated and agreed, but the next time I cleaned, the puzzle was still there, tugging at the end of my mop.

There's an unspoken agreement in the client-cleaner partnership 24
that I'll pretend to know nothing about them. My job is to erase, scrape up and brush away all signs of messy life. I've thrown out used condoms, scrubbed down shit-streaked toilets (I privately refer to one house as belonging to the "diarrhea family"), but we all observe a distant decorum. I am not to know these people have sex in the sheets, which I straighten, making sure all four corners are even along the stitching; that they drool on the pillows I shake out and plump up. I certainly feign ignorance when I run into a client at the IGA, Granowska's deli or the High Park library. Usually, the client will barely recognize me, then stumble and stammer awkwardly past, avoiding eye contact. It reminds me of how I felt, in my early 20s, running into one-night stands.

I used to see Suzanne frequently at Alternative Grounds café. 25
We'd sit at different tables. I'd usually be alone, writing, and she'd be somewhere near the back with a gathering of other at-home moms. Or if the café was crowded, we'd end up at tables beside each other. We'd smile but keep our distance.

One of the things you sacrifice when you become a housekeeper 26
is the cleanliness of your own home. The last thing I want to do is return from scrubbing someone else's house to clean mine. What I really want to do is soak in a lavender bath and eat chocolate. So, too often I shut the door to the glistening splendour of one of my clients' homes, then open the door to my dusty rented bungalow.

Friends and acquaintances ask advice on dealing with their 27
cleaners: how to get them to vacuum dog hair from the sofa ("Just talk to them," I counsel), whether to tip at Christmas and, if so, how much ("Sure," I say, "why not?"). Sometimes I imagine running workshops on how to negotiate life with cleaners. Here's what I'd instruct: De-clutter the house the night before, so the cleaner can scrub the cupboards and dust the picture frames instead of wasting your time and money putting away dishes. Keep supplies well stocked. Trade in your upright vacuum for a canister one. Leave clear instructions on the priority of tasks. Offer her a cup of tea once in a while. And, most important, remember to raise her pay from time to time, because a pound of butter costs the same for your cleaner as it does for you.

First clients, like first lovers, are hard to part with. But Suzanne, 28
of course, was not my lover. She wasn't even a friend. I saw her, as I see all my clients, in the raw—their smatterings of scattered things, their detritus, their leftover signs of life. But because they are usu-

ally absent in the flesh, they don't see me. I am, in many ways, an invisible presence in their lives—part of what it takes to have a sparkly clean kitchen sink and all the toys finally, finally put away. At the same time, my existence triggers associations with grunge and grime and the endlessness of wiping counters. I remind them of the shame of having a messy house. And I trigger their middle-class guilt about getting someone else to do their dirty work.

Words and Meanings

Paragraph
5

Shelagh Rogers	Canadian writer and radio broadcaster, host of CBC One's *Sounds Like Canada*

Structure and Strategy

1. Paragraphs 1–3 serve as the INTRODUCTION to the essay. What strategy does Shanahan use to engage readers' interest? How does it set up the essay's CONCLUSION?
2. Which paragraphs of the essay explain how Shanahan got into cleaning as a career?
3. Choose a paragraph that you think is effective because of its DESCRIPTION. Identify several details that you think are particularly striking. What is the dominant impression that these details leave with the reader?
4. Paragraph 27 is a short process ANALYSIS. What is its purpose?
5. What is the THESIS of this essay? Is it implied or stated?

Content and Purpose

1. The names given to Shanahan's clients are presumably false. How do you know this? Why do you think the author changes the names of people she works for?
2. Why did the writer decide to become a housecleaner? How did she set up her business?
3. What do we learn about Shanahan's personal life?
4. What details in the narrative suggest that Shanahan is a fundamentally honest person?
5. What income class do Shanahan's clients belong to: wealthy, upper-middle class, or middle class? Where do we learn about their financial lives?
6. How does Shanahan learn about the emotional ups and downs in her clients' lives?
7. What does the writer like about her career?
8. What is the "unspoken agreement" (paragraph 24) between cleaner and client? Why does it exist?

9. What is the IRONY in paragraph 26?
10. What is the "middle-class guilt" that Shanahan refers to in the final paragraph? Why does it exist?

Suggestions for Writing

1. Have you ever worked in someone's home as a cleaner, handyperson, baby-sitter, or other job? Write an essay describing what you learned about the people for whom you were working.
2. Have you or would you ever hire a person to clean up after you or perform another kind of personal service job (e.g., driver, maid, cook, nanny, trainer, shopper)? Write an essay about the nature of the relationship between you and the hired person.
3. Read Hal Niedzviecki's "Stupid Jobs Are Good to Relax With" on page 274. Then compare Shanahan's and Niedzviecki's views of working at jobs that do not require the level of education they have achieved. What points would they agree on? Disagree on?

Dispatches from the Poverty Line

PAT CAPPONI

Pat Capponi (b. 1949) is the author of *Upstairs in the Crazy House*, *Dispatches from the Poverty Line*, *The War at Home: An Intimate Portrait of Canada's Poor*, and *Bound by Duty: Walking the Beat with Canada's Cops*. A survivor of psychiatric illness and long periods of unemployment, Capponi is familiar with the world of the sick and the poor, and has served on numerous agency and hospital boards. She is a recipient of the Order of Ontario and the C. M. Hincks Award by the Canadian Mental Health Association.

We live in a time when manipulation of public opinion has been elevated to a science, when stereotypes are accepted as true representatives of their segment of the population. And, as always, stereotypes cause a great deal of pain to those tarred with the same brush. . . . 1

I am not innocent as far as taking refuge in stereotypes goes. As much as I try to catch myself at it, on occasion I'm forced to 2 admit to myself, and sometimes to others, that I've fallen prey to its comforting lure.

3   I've served on many committees, task forces, working groups and boards in my seventeen years of mental health advocacy°. Before consumer involvement became more widely accepted, I was often the only ex-patient at the table, trying to deal with hospital administrators, bureaucrats, psychiatrists, nurses and family groups. I didn't think any board could scare me again, or silence me through intimidation.

4   I was, however, being forced to admit that one hospital board in particular was giving me a great deal of angst°. It left me feeling as though I'd been flung back through time. . . . I used to tell audiences of consumers and mental health staff that one of our biggest problems was that there was no consensus in the system concerning the value of involving clients in the management and delivery of services. One day I'd be working with an agency that possessed the equivalent of New York sophistication around the issues, and the next I'd feel as though I were in Alabama before the civil rights movement got under way. It wasn't unusual for these opposites to be within a few city blocks of each other.

5   That was part of my problem with this board, that it was Alabama-like while believing itself to be cutting edge. But there was more. There were deep and obvious class distinctions, and even though I was, at the time, gainfully employed, a published author, someone who possessed the respect of my community, I felt intimidated, looked down on, stereotyped and all the rest. It got so that I had to force myself to attend.

6   The board was a status board, composed of high-powered bankers, lawyers, publishers and consultants, as well as hospital executives. I was the only one in jeans, in a hat. I was the only one from my particular class and background. I was the only voice expressing criticism of the liberal establishment we were running. . . . Meetings were corporate°; when I would leave for a cigarette I felt I should be bowing and backing up to the door. Nobody laughed, it seemed, ever. Nobody talked out of turn.

7   Then, one afternoon when I had screwed up my courage to attend, I bumped into the "fat cat" lawyer in the hallway. He made a joke, and I made one back before I had time to think about it. We both laughed, and . . . we both stared at each other, surprised at the unlikely evidence of a sense of humour beneath the stereotype. Ice got broken. Then the banker who had offered me lifts home before, which I'd declined—what would I have to talk to him about in the car?—offered again, and I accepted. I even teased him about his brand new BMW and the pervasive smell of leather from the seats.

IIe demonstrated how his car phone responded to voice orders to dial numbers, and I confess I got a kick out of the gimmickry. . . .

I remember another kind of breakthrough event at that board. I was trying once again to explain why I needed more people like me (from my class and experience) around the table. How easy it was to get intimidated in the setting we were in if you didn't find the corporate air invigorating. How easy it was to dismiss the views I was putting forward because it was only me they were hearing them from. How our class differences, our life experiences, created gulfs between us.   8

My banker friend took umbrage°. He was sure, he said, that he was quite capable of relating to me as a person, as another human being. He felt we were operating on a level playing field°, and that I wasn't giving them enough credit.   9

My lawyer friend then made a remarkable statement.   10

"That's not true," he said. "Pat didn't start out on a level playing field with me. I took one look at her and summed her up. It wasn't until later that I started to see her differently."   11

"And I," I said, "did the same thing, summed up you guys at a glance, and what I felt was your attitude towards me. It got easier to walk around with a chip on my shoulder than to try and relate to you."   12

Even the publisher chimed in: 13

"I understand what you mean about intimidation. I never saw myself as intimidating, I like to think I'm an easygoing, friendly guy. But some of my staff have been pointing out to me that people who work for me don't have that same picture, because I have power over them. It's not easy or comfortable to realize that you may scare people, but a lot of times it's true."

Only the banker held out for the level playing field precept, but of course the conversation was ruled out of order and we were on to the next item on the agenda°.   14

A month or two later, I decided to transfer my bank account to a branch nearer my residence. To get an account in the first place had been a challenge. I don't have credit cards, or a driver's licence: therefore, I don't have a system-recognized identity. This is a very common dilemma for those who make up the underclass, and it accounts for the prevalence° and huge success of Money Mart cheque-cashing services in poor areas. As long as I've been an advocate, various groups of workers have tried to break through the banking system, to work out generally acceptable ways of identifying clients to tellers through letters of introduction, or special cards, with no real success. . . .   15

In order for me to get an account in the first place, my publisher, Cynthia Good, had to take me into her branch, where we met   16 with her "personal banking representative," and on the basis of Cynthia's knowledge of me, I got an account in time to deposit the cheque I'd received for the movie rights to my book.

17   I confess I felt quite mainstream for a while, with my PIN number and cheques and account book, as though I'd arrived. It was enough to make me overconfident. I decided it was silly to travel forty minutes to that branch when there was one a few blocks from me. I still had a balance of a little over $5,000, so I didn't antic-ipate any problems. I walked into my local branch and was soon seated across from yet another "personal banking representative."

18   "What I can do for you today?" she asked, pleasantly.

19   "I'd like to transfer my account to here, please," I responded, handing over my account book and bank card.

20   "I see, um, would you have some identification?"

21   I was puzzled.

22   "Nothing you guys seem to accept. But I only want to transfer, not open, an account."

23   She persists:
"A major credit card? A driver's licence?"

24   I have a birth certificate. I remember trying to rent a video using it, and the owner of the store turning the card over and saying, "Your signature's not on it."

25   I shake my head. I give her the card of the other personal banking representative, the one in whose presence I had been vali-dated. She phones. She shakes her head. That person is on vacation. She purses her lips, not liking to create difficulties for me, but there are rules.

26   "I'm sorry, we really do need identification."

27   I'm getting angry, and I suspect she feels it, which accounts for her visible nervousness. It won't help to get snippy with her. I could just pack it in and leave—it wouldn't be the end of the world, after all. But the battle for reason is under way. It would feel too much like defeat to withdraw now.

28   I try for a reasoned, measured tone.

29   "I don't want to withdraw anything. I have $5,000 in my account. You have my card, my cheques, my account book."

30   I hear steps behind me, I'm sure the security guard is getting ready to pounce.

31   "It's a different branch of the same bank. C'mon, be reasonable."

32   "Don't you even have your Indian Status Card?"

33   "I'm not Indian!"

34   Ordinarily, I would take it as a compliment, being mistaken for one of the First People, but in this context, I know there's some heavy stereotyping, and quite possibly some heavy attitude, going on.

I get a flash. I'm terrible about names, remembering names. I   35
can recall the most minute° details of conversations, mannerisms,
backgrounds and clothing but not names. But I do remember the
division my BMW banker is president of. And I do remember it's
this same corporation.

I ask her to look up the name of the guy in charge of ———.   36

"Why?" she asks, immediately suspicious.   37

"I know him, he can tell you I exist."   38

Perhaps to humour me, she flips open a book and recites some   39
names.

"That's him," I cry, vindicated°. "Give him a call, will you?"   40

I suppose it's like telling a private to ring up a general at the   41
request of a possible lunatic, an aboriginal impersonator: it's not
done.

She excuses herself to consult with a superior. Long minutes   42
pass. I feel myself being examined from the glassed-in cubicles
where the decision-makers sit. I feel the breath of the security
officer. I feel renewed determination.

She's back.   43

"I'm sorry for the delay. His secretary had some difficulty   44
reaching him, he's in a meeting. But he is available now."

My understanding smile is as false and strained as her apology.   45

She picks up the phone and annoyingly turns her chair away   46
from me while she speaks in low tones into the receiver. A few
heartbeats, then she passes the phone to me.

Not waiting for his voice, I say: 47

"I told you there's no level playing field."

He laughs, loudly and honestly.   48

In under ten minutes, I have my new account, my new card,   49
cheques and a small degree of satisfaction.

Chalk up one for the good guys.   50

I take refuge in a nearby park, liking and needing the sun and a   51
place to enjoy it. I've checked out the four or five in my neighbourhood, and on days when I need to walk, I go up to the one opposite
the Dufferin Mall. I love the solitude, the birds, the green—a perfect
setting for reading and tanning. Picking an empty bench, away
from small clumps of people dotting the large park, I open my
paperback and disappear into it.

It doesn't seem very long (my watch died a few months ago)   52
before an old fellow, tottering on his cane, shuffles towards me. I look
up at his approach, smile briefly and dive back into P. D. James. I am
dismayed when he chooses to perch on the other end of my bench,
and I try to ignore his presence while my conscience starts bothering

me. Now, I only smiled at him because I am aware that some folks think I look a bit tough, and I didn't want him worrying, but he might have mistaken the gesture for a come-chat-with-me invitation. He's probably lonely, isolated, this is probably his big daily outing. Would it kill me to spend a couple of minutes talking to him? Damn.

53   I close my book, look over at him looking over at me expectantly.

54   "Beautiful day, isn't it?"

55   I can barely make out his reply, cloaked in a thick accent, but his head bobbing up and down is pretty clear. I'm stuck for the next sentence, but he keeps going enthusiastically. I make out his name, repeating it triumphantly: "Victor! Hi, I'm Pat."

56   One arthritic hand grasps mine briefly, then goes back to rest on his cane with the other one.

57   "I'm retired." He's getting better at speaking clearly, maybe it was just a lack of opportunity that made him rusty. "I was an engineer."

58   "You live around here?"

59   He turns painfully, pointing vaguely over his shoulder.

60   "Right over there, a beautiful place. Very beautiful place."

61   "Good for you."

62   I offer him a cigarette, which he accepts, and we sit in companionable silence in the sun. I'm thinking after the smoke I will move on, find another park, maybe nearer my home.

63   He's talking again, and when I realize what he's saying my jaw drops open.

64   "If you come see my place, I will give you twenty dollars."

65   "Jesus Christ! Are you crazy?" I'm so annoyed, and shocked, and thrown off balance by his offer, that I'm blustering. I want to whack him, except he'd probably fall over, like the dirty-old-man character on *Laugh-In*.

66   "Listen to me," I lecture, as I shake my finger in his face. "First off, you're committing a crime. Secondly, it's stupid and dangerous for you. You can't go around offering money to people you don't know for things I don't want to think about. You've insulted me. I could have you arrested! Do you understand?"

67   Now I'm pretty sure what his daily tour of the park is about, and I worry about the school-age girls that hang out at lunch time.

68   "If I see you doing this to anyone else, I will report you, do you get that? I'll be watching you!"

69   He's stuttering out an apology, which I don't believe, and I refrain from kicking his cane, though I really want to.

70   On my way home, in between feeling outraged and feeling dirtied, I start to laugh at my own stereotyping of a lonely old man in need of conversation in juxtaposition° with his own stereotyping of me.

People ought to wear summing-up signs sometimes, just so you'd know what to expect. 71

Words and Meanings

		Paragraph
mental health advocacy	working for improvement in the lives of people with mental illnesses	3
angst	anxiety	4
corporate	formal, businesslike	6
took umbrage	objected	9
operating on a level playing field	business jargon for "equal"	
agenda	list of topics to be discussed at a meeting	14
prevalence	widespread existence	15
minute	tiny, insignificant	35
vindicated	justified, cleared of suspicion	40
in juxtaposition	occurring close together	70

Structure and Strategy

1. This piece consists of two distinct narrative ILLUSTRATIONS. The first takes place in paragraphs 1 to 50, the second in paragraphs 51 to 71. What links the two examples?
2. Identify the author's thesis statement.
3. Why does Capponi introduce her discussion of stereotyping with a CLICHÉ ("tarred with the same brush," paragraph 1)? What does this cliché mean?
4. Why do you think the author describes her experience as a mental health advocate in Canada in terms of a contrast between "New York sophistication" and "Alabama before the civil rights movement" (paragraph 4)? Are these comparisons meaningful to the Canadian audience she is writing for? Are they original or are they STEREOTYPES?
5. Capponi relies primarily on dialogue to tell her story. Why do you think she chooses to re-create her experiences for the reader through dialogue rather than to summarize them through DESCRIPTION and NARRATION?

Content and Purpose

1. Based on the hints given in the essay, what do you think Capponi looks like? How does she dress? Given her appearance and behaviour, how might people STEREOTYPE her?
2. Paragraph 7 contains two examples of stereotyping. What are they, and who is responsible for them? What succeeds in breaking through these stereotypes? What other "breakthrough events" does Capponi relate in this essay?
3. How does Capponi succeed in opening her first bank account? Why is banking a problem for her? Does she think it is a problem for others? If so, why and for whom?
4. Why does the "personal banking representative" not want to transfer Capponi's account to her branch? In what ways does this woman stereotype Capponi?
5. How is the standoff with the banking representative resolved? How does Capponi feel about the resolution? What solutions do you think might be available to other victims of stereotyping?
6. In the second ILLUSTRATION (paragraphs 51 to 71), what does Capponi think the old man in the park is looking for? What is he really looking for? How does Capponi react to the misunderstanding? Does she learn anything from this experience?

Suggestions for Writing

1. Have you ever experienced stereotyping because of the way you look? Write an essay that recounts your experience and your response to it.
2. Have you ever wrongly stereotyped someone based on his or her appearance or behaviour? Write an essay that tells the story of your experience and indicates what you learned from it.
3. Read Brent Staples' "Just Walk On By: A Black Man Ponders His Power to Alter Public Space" on page 173 and Malcolm Gladwell's "Troublemakers: What Pit Bulls Can Teach Us About Profiling" on page 349. Choose one of these essays and compare and contrast its treatment of stereotyping with that of "Dispatches from the Poverty Line."

Deficits

MICHAEL IGNATIEFF

Michael Ignatieff (b. 1947) is a scholar, writer, and journalist who was born and raised in Toronto, the son of a Russian émigré diplomat and a Canadian mother. He holds degrees from or has taught at a number of distinguished universities, including the University of Toronto, Oxford, and Harvard. Ignatieff is considered to be one of the world's leading experts on democracy, human rights, and international affairs. Along with his scholarly work and broadcasting, he is an important writer of both fiction and non-fiction. His latest work is *The Lesser Evil: Political Ethics in an Age of Terror* (2004). In February 2006, Ignatieff was elected as the member of Parliament for the Toronto riding of Etobicoke Lakeshore. "Deficits" is a personal essay that deals with his mother's struggle against Alzheimer's disease.

It begins the minute Dad leaves the house.   1
"Where is George?"   2
"He is out now, but he'll be back soon."   3
"That's wonderful," she says.   4
About three minutes later she'll look puzzled: "But George . . ."   5
"He's away at work, but he'll be back later."   6
"I see."   7
"And what are you doing here? I mean it's nice, but . . ."   8
"We'll do things together."   9
"I see."   10

Sometimes I try to count the number of times she asks me these   11
questions but I lose track.

I remember how it began, five or six years ago. She was 66   12
then. She would leave a pot to boil on the stove. I would discover it
and find her tearing through the house, muttering, "My glasses, my
glasses, where the hell are my glasses?"

I took her to buy a chain so that she could wear her glasses   13
around her neck. She hated it because her mother used to wear *her*
glasses on a chain. As we drove home, she shook her fist at the
windscreen.

"I swore I'd never wear one of these damned things."   14

I date the beginning to the purchase of the chain, to the silence   15
that descended over her as I drove her home from the store.

The deficits, as the neurologists call them, are localized. She can   16
tell you what it felt like when the Model T Ford ran over her at the
school gates when she was a girl of seven. She can tell you what her
grandmother used to say, "A genteel° sufficiency will suffice°,"
when turning down another helping at dinner. She remembers the

Canadian summer nights when her father used to wrap her in a blanket and take her out to the lake's edge to see the stars.

17   But she can't dice an onion. She can't set the table. She can't play cards. Her grandson is five, and when they play pairs with his animal cards, he knows where the second penguin will be. She just turns up cards at random.

18   He hits her because she can't remember anything, because she keeps telling him not to run around quite so much.

19   Then I punish him. I tell him he has to understand.

20   He goes down on the floor, kisses her feet, and promises not to hit her again.

21   She smiles at him, as if for the first time, and says, "Oh, your kiss is so full of sugar."

22   After a week with him, she looks puzzled and says, "He's a nice little boy. Where does he sleep? I mean, who does he belong to?"

23   "He's your grandson."

24   "I see." She looks away and puts her hand to her face.

25   My brother usually stays with her when Dad is out of town. Once or twice a year, it's my turn. I put her to bed at night. I hand her the pills—small green ones that are supposed to control her moods—and she swallows them. I help her out of her bra and slip, roll down her tights, and lift the nightie over her head. I get into the bed next to hers. Before she sleeps she picks up a Len Deighton and reads a few paragraphs, always the same paragraphs, at the place where she has folded down the page. When she falls asleep, I pick the book off her chest and I pull her down in the bed so that her head isn't leaning against the wall. Otherwise she wakes up with a crick in her neck.

26   Often when I wake in the night, I see her lying next to me, staring into the dark. She stares and then she wanders. I used to try to stop her, but now I let her go. She is trying to hold on to what is left. There is a method in this. She goes to the bathroom every time she wakes, no matter if it is five times a night. Up and down the stairs silently, in her bare feet, trying not to wake me. She turns the lights on and off. Smooths a child's sock and puts it on the bed. Sometimes she gets dressed, after a fashion, and sits on the downstairs couch in the dark, clutching her handbag.

27   When we have guests to dinner, she sits beside me at the table, holding my hand, bent forward slightly to catch everything that is said. Her face lights up when people smile, when there is laughter. She doesn't say much any more; she is worried she will forget a name and we won't be able to help her in time. She doesn't want anything to show. The guests always say how well she does. Sometimes they say, "You'd never know, really." When I put her to bed afterward I can see the effort has left her so tired she barely knows

her own name.

She could make it easier on herself. She could give up asking questions.   28

"Where we are now, is this our house?"

"Yes."   29

"Where is our house?"   30

"In France."   31

I tell her: "Hold my hand, I'm here. I'm your son."   32

"I know."   33

But she keeps asking where she is. The questions are her way of trying to orient° herself, of refusing and resisting the future that is being prepared for her.   34
                                                                                                                                                                   35

She always loved to swim. When she dived into the water, she never made a splash. I remember her lifting herself out of the pool, as sleek as a seal in a black swimsuit, the water pearling off her back. Now she says the water is too cold and taking off her clothes too much of a bother. She paces up and down the poolside, watching her grandson swim, stroking his towel with her hand, endlessly smoothing out the wrinkles.   36

I bathe her when she wakes. Her body is white, soft, and withered. I remember how, in the changing-huts, she would bend over as she slipped out of her bathing suit. Her body was young. Now I see her skeleton through her skin. When I wash her hair, I feel her skull. I help her from the bath, dry her legs, swathe her in towels, sit her on the edge of the bath and cut her nails: they are horny and yellow. Her feet are gnarled°. She has walked a long way.   37

When I was as old as my son is now I used to sit beside her at the bedroom mirror watching her apply hot depilatory° wax to her legs and upper lip. She would pull her skirt up to her knees, stretch her legs out on the dresser, and sip beer from the bottle, while waiting for the wax to dry. "Have a sip," she would say. It tasted bitter. She used to laugh at the faces I made. When the wax had set, she would begin to peel it off, and curse and wince, and let me collect the strips, with fine black hairs embedded in them. When it was over, her legs were smooth, silky to touch.   38

Now I shave her. I soap her face and legs with my shaving brush. She sits perfectly still; as my razor comes around her chin we are as close as when I was a boy.   39

She never complains. When we walk up the hill behind the house, I feel her going slower and slower, but she does not stop until I do. If you ask her whether she is sad, she shakes her head. But she did say once, "It's strange. It was supposed to be more fun than this."   40

41   I try to imagine what the world is like for her. Memory is what reconciles° us to the future. Because she has no past, her future rushes toward her, a bat's wing brushing against her face in the dark.

42   "I told you. George returns on Monday."

43   "Could you write that down?"

44   So I do. I write it down in large letters, and she folds it in her white cardigan pocket and pats it and says she feels much less worried.

45   In half an hour, she has the paper in her hand and is showing it to me.

46   "What do I do about this?"

47   "Nothing. It just tells you what is going to happen."

48   "But I didn't know anything of this."

49   "Now you do," I say and I take the paper away and tear it up.

50   It makes no sense to get angry at her, but I do.

51   She is afraid Dad will not come back. She is afraid she has been abandoned. She is afraid she will get lost and never be able to find her way home. Beneath the fears that have come with the forgetting, there lie anxieties for which she no longer has any names.

52   She paces the floor, waiting for lunch. When it is set before her, she downs it before anyone else, and then gets up to clear the plates.

53   "What's the hurry?" I ask her.

54   She is puzzled. "I don't know," she says. She is in a hurry, and she does not know why. She drinks whatever I put before her. The wine goes quickly.

55   "You'll enjoy it more if you sip it gently."

56   "What a good idea," she says and then empties the glass with a gulp.

57   I wish I knew the history of this anxiety. But I don't. All she will tell me is about being sprawled in the middle of Regent Street° amid the blood and shop glass during an air raid, watching a mother sheltering a child, and thinking: I am alone.

58   In the middle of all of us, she remained alone. We didn't see it. She was the youngest girl in her family, the straggler in the pack, born cross-eyed till they straightened her eyes out with an operation. Her father was a teacher and she was dyslexic°, the one left behind.

59   In her wedding photo, she is wearing her white dress and holding her bouquet. They are side by side. Dad looks excited. Her eyes are wide open with alarm. Fear gleams from its hiding place. It was her secret and she kept it well hidden. When I was a child, I thought she was faultless, amusing, regal. My mother.

She thinks of it as a happy family, and it was. I remember them
sitting on the couch together, singing along to Fats Waller records.
She still remembers the crazy lyrics they used to sing:

There's no disputin'
That's Rasputin
The high-falutin loving man.

I don't know how she became so dependent on him, how she lost
so many of the wishes she once had for herself, and how all her
wishes came to be wishes for him.

She is afraid of his moods, his silences, his departures, and his
returns. He has become the weather of her life. But he never lets her
down. He is the one who sits with her in the upstairs room,
watching television, night after night, holding her hand.

People say: it's worse for you, she doesn't know what is happening. She used to say the same thing herself. Five years ago,
when she began to forget little things, she knew what was in store,
and she said to me once, "Don't worry. I'll make a cheerful old nut.
It's you who'll have the hard time." But that is not true. She feels
everything. She has had time to count up every loss. Every night,
when she lies awake, she stares at desolation.

What is a person? That is what she makes you wonder. What
kind of a person are you if you only have your habits left? She can't
remember her grandson's name, but she does remember to shake
out her tights at night and she never lets a dish pass her by without
trying to clean it, wipe it, clear it up, or put it away. The house is littered with dishes she is putting away in every conceivable cup-
board. What kind of a person is this?

It runs in the family. Her mother had it. I remember going to see
her in the house with old carpets and dark furniture on Prince Arthur
Avenue. The windows were covered with the tendrils of plants
growing in enormous Atlas battery jars, and the parquet° floors shone
with wax. She took down the giraffe, the water buffalo, and the
leopard—carved in wood—that her father had brought back from
Africa in the 1880s. She sat in a chair by the fire and silently watched
me play with them. Then—and it seems only a week later—I came to
have Sunday lunch with her and she was old and diminished and
vacant, and when she looked at me she had no idea who I was.

I am afraid of getting it myself. I do ridiculous things: I stand
on my head every morning so that the blood will irrigate my brain;
I compose suicide notes, always some variant of Captain Oates's: "I
may be gone for some time." I never stop thinking about what it
would be like for this thing to steal over me.

66   She has taught me something. There are moments when her pacing ceases, when her hunted look is conjured° away by the stillness of dusk, when she sits in the garden, watching the sunlight stream through all the trees they planted together over 25 years in this place, and I see something pass over her face which might be serenity°.

67   And then she gets up and comes toward me looking for a glass to wash, a napkin to pick up, a child's toy to rearrange.

68   I know how the story has to end. One day I return home to see her and she puts out her hand and says: "How nice to meet you." She's always charming to strangers.

69   People say I'm already beginning to say my farewells. No, she is still here. I am not ready yet. Nor is she. She paces the floor, she still searches for what has been lost and can never be found again.

70   She wakes in the night and lies in the dark by my side. Her face, in profile, against the pillow has become like her mother's, the eye sockets deep in shadow, the cheeks furrowed° and drawn, the gaze ancient and disabused°. Everything she once knew is still inside her, trapped in the ruined circuits—how I was when I was little, how she was when I was a baby. But it is too late to ask her now. She turns and notices I am awake too. We lie side by side. The darkness is still. I want to say her name. She turns away from me and stares into the night. Her nightie is buttoned at the neck like a little girl's.

Words and Meanings

Paragraph

16	genteel	polite, well-bred
	suffice	be enough, satisfy
35	orient	find her bearings; figure out where she is in time and space
37	gnarled	knobby, crooked
38	depilatory	hair remover
41	reconciles	makes us able to accept; resigns us
57	Regent Street	street in central London, England
58	dyslexic	having a reading disability
64	parquet	wood floor laid out in square design
66	conjured	made to disappear magically
	serenity	inner peace
70	furrowed	deeply wrinkled
	disabused	undeceived, under no illusion

Structure and Strategy

1. Look up the word "deficits" in a good general dictionary. What meanings of the word apply to Ignatieff's title?
2. Using both NARRATION and DESCRIPTION, Ignatieff describes the effects of Alzheimer's disease on its victims, and on those who care for them. What function does the opening dialogue (paragraphs 1 to 11) serve?
3. This essay contains several passages of dialogue. Each is included because it supports Ignatieff's THESIS in some way. Consider how each of the following passages contributes to the PURPOSE or intended effect of the essay: paragraphs 28 to 35; paragraphs 42 to 49; paragraphs 52 to 56.
4. Paragraphs 37 to 39 present the ironic contrast between Ignatieff's boyhood relationship with his mother and their current relationship. Identify the specific details that you think are most effective in conveying this contrast.
5. How does the author's own fear of contracting Alzheimer's disease affect the TONE of the essay?
6. The THESIS of Ignatieff's essay is implied rather than explicitly stated. Sum up the thesis in a one-sentence thesis statement.

Content and Purpose

1. What was the initial reaction of the mother when the first signs of the disease appeared? Does she maintain this feeling as her confusion and loss of memory increase?
2. Ignatieff includes a number of poignant descriptive details: the toenails, the gnarled feet, the depilatory wax, the bath. Why does he include these intimate aspects of his mother's life and condition? What emotional effect do they have on the reader?
3. What is the fundamental IRONY underlying the relationship between mother and son? Reread paragraphs 25, 27, and 70 for clues.
4. What experiences in the mother's life may be responsible for the "fear [that] gleams from its hiding place" in her eyes?
5. Is Ignatieff comfortable with the task of caring for his mother? Identify specific passages in the essay that point to the writer's personal conflict.

Suggestions for Writing

1. Modelling your essay on the combination of descriptive and narrative techniques that Ignatieff uses in "Deficits," write a paper on the physical and psychological impact of a serious illness on someone you know and on his or her immediate family.

2. Using "Deficits" and "Baba and Me" as background material, write an essay explaining how society can and must enable older people to live in dignity, despite physical or psychological limitations.

3. Traditional societies such as the Chinese respect and venerate the old, but progressive Western societies increasingly see the aged as an unwelcome burden. Write an essay in which you identify and explain two or three significant reasons why our society excludes or rejects the elderly.

The End of the Wild

WADE DAVIS

A native of British Columbia, Wade Davis (b. 1953) has worked as a logger, park ranger, forestry engineer, researcher, writer, and environmental activist. He holds a degree in ethnobotany from Harvard. He is an anthropologist, biologist, botanical explorer, and photographer whose books include *The Serpent and the Rainbow* (1985), *Passage of Darkness* (1988), *Shadows in the Sun* (1993), *Nomads of the Dawn* (1995), *One River* (1996), *The Clouded Leopard* (1998), *Rainforest* (1998), and *Light at the End of the World* (2002). Davis's television credits include *Earthguide*, a series on the environment.

1   Some time ago at a symposium° in Barbados, I was fortunate to share the podium with two extraordinary scientists. The first to speak was Richard Leakey, the renowned anthropologist who with his mother and father drew from the dust and ashes of Africa the story of the birth of our species. The meeting concluded with astronaut Story Musgrave, the first physician to walk in space. It was an odd and moving juxtaposition of the endpoints of the human experience. Dr. Musgrave recognized the irony and it saddened him. He told of what it had been like to know the beauty of the earth as seen from the heavens. There he was, suspended 200 miles above the earth, travelling 18,000 miles per hour with the golden visor of his helmet illuminated by a single sight, a small and fragile blue planet enveloped in a veil of clouds, floating, as he recalled, "in the velvet void of space." To have experienced that vision, he said, a sight made possible only by the brilliance of human technology, and to remember the blindness with which we

as a species abuse our only home, was to know the purest sensation of horror.

Many believe that this image of the earth, first brought home to   2
us but a generation ago, will have a more profound impact on human thought than did the Copernican revolution of the 16th century, which transformed the philosophical foundations of the western world by revealing that the planet was not the center of the universe. From space, we see not a limitless frontier nor the stunning products of man, but a single interactive sphere of life, a living organism composed of air, water, and earth. It is this transcendent vision which, more than any amount of scientific data, teaches us the earth is a finite place that can endure our foolish ways for only so long.

In light of this new perspective, this new hope, the past and   3
present deeds of human beings often appear inconceivably cruel and sordid. Shortly after leaving Barbados, while lecturing in the midwest of the United States, I visited two places that in a different, more sensitive world would surely be enshrined as memorials to the victims of the ecological catastrophes that occurred there. The first locality was the site of the last great nesting flock of passenger pigeons, a small stretch of woodland on the banks of the Green River near Mammoth Cave, Ohio. This story of extinction is well known. Yet until I stood in that cold, dark forest, I had never sensed the full weight of the disaster, the scale and horror of it.

At one time passenger pigeons accounted for 40% of the entire   4
bird population of North America. In 1870, at a time when their numbers were already greatly diminished, a single flock a mile wide and 320 miles long containing an estimated 2 billion birds passed over Cincinnati on the Ohio River. Imagine such a sight. Assuming that each bird ate half a pint of seeds a day, a flock that size must have consumed each day over 17 million bushels of grain. Such sightings were not unusual. In 1813, James Audubon° was travelling in a wagon from his home on the Ohio River to Louisville, some sixty miles away, when a flock of passenger pigeons filled the sky so that the "light of noonday sun was obscured as by an eclipse." He reached Louisville at sunset and the birds still came. He estimated that the flock contained over 1 billion birds, and it was but one of several columns of pigeons that blackened the sky that day.

Audubon visited roosting and nesting sites to find trees two   5
feet in diameter broken off at the ground by the weight of birds. He found dung so deep on the forest floor that he mistook it for snow. He once stood in the midst of a flock when the birds took flight and

then landed. He compared the noise and confusion to that of a gale, the sound of their landing to thunder.

6 It is difficult now to imagine the ravages of man that over the course of half a century destroyed this creature. Throughout the 19th century, pigeon meat was a mainstay of the American diet and merchants in the eastern cities sold as many as 18,000 birds a day. Pigeon hunting was a full time job for thousands of men. The term "stool pigeon" derives from a standard killing technique of the era. A hunter would sew shut the eyes of a living bird, bind its feet to a pole driven into the ground, and wait in the surrounding grass for the flocks to respond to its cry. When the birds came, they arrived in such numbers that the hunter could simply bat them out of the air with a club. The more affluent classes slaughtered birds for recreation. It was not unusual for shooting clubs to go through 50,000 birds in a weekend competition; hundreds of thousands of live birds were catapulted to their death before the diminishing supply forced skeet shooters to turn to clay pigeons.

7 By 1896, a mere 50 years after the first serious impact of man, there were only some 250,000 birds left. In April of that year, the birds came together for one last nesting flock in the forest outside of Bowling Green, Ohio. The telegraph wires hummed with the news and the hunters converged. In a final orgy of slaughter over 200,000 pigeons were killed, 40,000 mutilated, 100,000 chicks destroyed. A mere 5,000 birds survived. The entire kill was to be shipped east but there was a derailment on the line and the dead birds rotted in their crates. On March 24, 1900 the last passenger pigeon in the wild was shot by a young boy. On September 1, 1914, as the Battle of the Marne consumed the flower of European youth, the last passenger pigeon died in captivity.

8 When I left the scene of this final and impossible slaughter, I travelled west to Sioux City, Iowa to speak at Buena Vista College. There I was fortunate to visit a remnant patch of tall grass prairie, a 180-acre preserve that represents one of the largest remaining vestiges of an ecosystem that once carpeted North America from southern Canada to Texas. Again it was winter, and the cold wind blew through the coneflowers and the dozens of species of grass. The young biology student who was with me was familiar with every species in that extraordinary mosaic—they were like old friends to him. Yet as we walked through that tired field my thoughts drifted from the plants to the horizon. I tried to imagine buffalo moving through the grass, the physics of waves as millions of animals crossed that prairie.

9 As late as 1871 buffalo outnumbered people in North America. In that year one could stand on a bluff in the Dakotas and see

nothing but buffalo in every direction for thirty miles. Herds were so large that it took days for them to pass a single point. Wyatt Earp described one herd of a million animals stretched across a grazing area the size of Rhode Island. Within nine years of that sighting, buffalo had vanished from the Plains.

The destruction of the buffalo resulted from a campaign of bio-   10
logical terrorism unparalleled in the history of the Americas. U.S. government policy was explicit. As General Philip Sheridan wrote at the time, "The buffalo hunters have done in the past two years more to settle the vexed Indian Question than the regular army has accomplished in the last 30 years. They are destroying the Indians' commissary°. Send them powder and lead, and let them kill until they have exterminated the buffalo." Between 1850 and 1880 more than 75 million hides were sold to American dealers. No one knows how many more animals were slaughtered and left on the prairie. A decade after native resistance had collapsed, Sheridan advised Congress to mint a commemorative medal, with a dead buffalo on one side, a dead Indian on the other.

I thought of this history as I stood in that tall grass prairie near   11
Sioux City. What disturbed me the most was to realize how effortlessly we have removed ourselves from this ecological tragedy. Today the people of Iowa, good and decent folk, live contentedly in a landscape of cornfields that is claustrophobic in its monotony. For them the time of the tall grass prairie, like the time of the buffalo, is as distant from their immediate lives as the fall of Rome or the battle of Troy. Yet the destruction occurred but a century ago, well within the lifetime of their grandfathers.

This capacity to forget, this fluidity of memory, is a frightening   12
human trait. Several years ago I spent many months in Haiti, a country that as recently as the 1920s was 80% forested. Today less than 5% of the forest cover remains. I remember standing with a Vodoun priest on a barren ridge, peering across a wasteland, a desolate valley of scrub and half-hearted trees. He waxed eloquent as if words alone might have squeezed beauty from that wretched sight. He could only think of angels, I of locusts. It was amazing. Though witness to an ecological holocaust that within this century had devastated his entire country, this man had managed to endure without losing his human dignity. Faced with nothing, he adorned his life with his imagination. This was inspiring but also terrifying. People appear to be able to tolerate and adapt to almost any degree of environmental degradation. As the farmers of Iowa today live without wild things, the people of Haiti scratch a living from soil that will never again know the comfort of shade.

13   From a distance, both in time and space, we can perceive these terrible and poignant events as what they were—unmitigated ecological disasters that robbed the future of something unimaginably precious in order to satisfy the immediate and often mundane needs of the present. The luxury of hindsight, however, does nothing to cure the blindness with which today we overlook deeds of equal magnitude and folly.

14   As a younger man in Canada I spent a long winter in a logging camp on the west coast of Haida Gwaii, or the Queen Charlotte Islands as they were then commonly known. It was a good life and it put me through school. I was a surveyor, which meant that I spent all of my time far ahead of the loggers in the dense uncut forest, laying out the roads and the falling boundaries, determining the pattern in which the trees would come down. At the time I had already spent more than a year in the Amazon and I can tell you that those distant forests, however immense and mysterious, are dwarfed by the scale and wonder of the ancient temperate rainforests of British Columbia. In the valleys and around the lakes, and along the shore of the inlet where the soil was rich and deep, we walked through red cedar and sitka spruce, some as tall as a 25-storey building, many with over 70 million needles capturing the light of the sun. Miracles of biological engineering, their trunks stored thousands of gallons of water and could be twenty feet or more across at the base. Many of them had been standing in the forest for more than a thousand years, the anchors of an extraordinarily complex ecosystem° of mountains and rain, salmon and eagles, of squirrels that fly, fungi that crawl, and creatures that live on dew and never touch the forest floor. It is a world that is far older, far richer in its capacity to produce the raw material of life, and far more endangered than almost any region of the Amazon.

15   To walk through these forests in the depths of winter, when the rain turns to mist and settles softly on the moss, is to step back in time. Two hundred million years ago vast coniferous° forests formed a mantle across the entire world. Then evolution took a great leap and the flowers were born. The difference between the two groups of plants involves a mechanism of pollination and fertilization that changed the course of life on earth. In the case of the more primitive conifers, the plant must produce the basic food for the seed with no certainty that it will be fertilized. In the flowering plants, by contrast, fertilization itself sparks the creation of the seed's food reserves. In other words, unlike the conifers, the flowering plants make no investment without the assurance that a viable seed will be produced. As a result of this and other evolutionary advances, the flowering plants came to dominate the earth in an astonishingly

short period of time. Most conifers went extinct and those that survived retreated to the margins of the world, where a small number of species managed to maintain a foothold by adapting to particularly harsh conditions. Today, at a conservative estimate, there are over 250,000 species of flowering plants. The conifers have been reduced to a mere 700 species and in the tropics, the hotbed of evolution, they have been almost completely displaced.

On all the earth, there is only one region of any size and significance where, because of unique climatic conditions, the conifers retain their former glory. Along the northwest coast of North America the summers are hot and dry, the winters cold and wet. Plants need water and light to create food. Here in the summer there is ample light for photosynthesis, but not enough water. In the winter, when both water and light are sufficient, the low temperatures cause the flowering plants to lose their leaves and become dormant. The evergreen conifers, by contrast, are able to grow throughout the long winters and since they use water more efficiently than broad-leafed plants, they also thrive during the dry summer months. The result is an ecosystem so rich, so productive, that the biomass° in the best sites is easily four times as great as that of any comparable area of the tropics. 16

Inevitably there was, at least for me, an almost surrealistic quality to life in our remote camp where men lived away from their families and made a living cutting down in minutes trees that had taken a thousand years to grow. The constant grinding of machinery, the disintegration of the forest into burnt slash and mud, the wind and sleet that froze on the rigging and whipped across the frozen bay, etched patterns into the lives of the men. Still, no one in our camp had any illusions about what we were doing. All the talk of sustained yield and overmature timber, decadent and normal forests we left to the government bureaucrats and the company PR hacks. We used to laugh at the little yellow signs stuck on the sides of roads that only we would ever travel, that announced that twenty acres had been replanted, as if it mattered in a clearcut that stretched to the horizon. . . . 17

Everyone knew, of course, that the ancient forests would never come back. One of my mates used to say that the tangle of half-hearted trees that grew up in the slash° no more resembled the forest he'd cut down, than an Alberta wheatfield resembled a wild prairie meadow. But nobody was worried about what they were doing. It was work, and living on the edge of that immense forest, they simply believed that it would go on forever. 18

If anyone in the government had a broader perspective, we never heard about it. Our camp was nineteen miles by water across 19 an inlet from a backroad that ran forty miles to the nearest forestry office. The government had cut back on overtime pay, and, what with the statutory coffee and lunch breaks, the forestry fellows couldn't figure out how to get to our camp and back in less than seven and a half hours. So they didn't try. The bureaucracy within the company wasn't much better. The mills down south kept complaining that our camp was sending them inferior grades of Douglas fir, which was surprising since the species doesn't grow on the Charlottes.

20   There were, of course, vague murmurs of ecological concern that filtered through to our camp. One morning in the cookhouse I ran into a friend of mine, a rock blaster named Archie whose voice had been dusted by ten thousand cigarettes and the dirt from a dozen mine failures. Archie was in a particularly cantankerous mood. Clutching a donut he'd been marinating in caffeine, he flung a three-day-old newspaper onto the table. The headline said something about Greenpeace.

21   "Fucking assholes," he critiqued.

22   "What's wrong, Arch?" I asked.

23   "Sons of bitches don't know a damn thing about pollution," he said. Archie then proceeded to tell me about working conditions in the hard rock uranium mines of the Northwest Territories shortly after the Second World War. The companies, concerned about the impact of radioactivity, used to put the workers, including Archie, into large sealed chambers and release a gas with suspended particles of aluminum in it. The idea being that the aluminum would coat the lungs and, at the end of the shift, the men would gag it up, together with any radioactive dust.

24   "Now that," growled Archie, "was environmental pollution."

25   In truth, it is difficult to know how much the forest destruction actually affected the men. Some clearly believed blindly in the process and were hardened by that faith. Others were so transient, moving from camp to camp, sometimes on a monthly basis, that they never registered the full measure of the impact of any one logging show. Some just didn't care. The entire industry was so itinerant° that no one ever developed a sense of belonging to a place. There was no attachment to the land, nor could there be given what we were doing. In the slash of the clearcuts, there was little room for sentiment.

26   I knew of a veteran faller who, having cut down thousands of trees, finally came upon one giant cedar that was simply too magnificent to be felled. When he refused to bring it down, the bullbucker° threatened to fire him. The faller felt he had no choice. He brought it down and then, realizing what he had done, he sat on

the stump and began to weep. He quit that afternoon and never cut another tree.

Like everyone else in our camp, I was there to make money. On weekends, when our survey crew was down, I picked up overtime pay by working in the slash as a chokerman°, wrapping the cables around the fallen logs so the yarders° could drag them to the landings° where they were loaded onto the trucks. Setting beads° is the most miserable job in a logging show, the bottom rung of the camp hierarchy. 27

One Saturday I was working in a setting high up on the mountain that rose above the camp. It had been raining all day and the winds were blowing from the southeast, dragging clouds across the bay and up the slope, where they hung up in the tops of giant hemlocks and cedars that rose above the clearcut. We were working the edge of the opening, but the landing was unusually close by. It took no time at all for the mainline to drag the logs in, and for the haulback° to fling the chokers° back to us. We'd been highballing° all day and both my partner and I were a mess of mud, grease and tree sap. He was a native boy, a Nisga'a from New Aiyansh on the Nass River, but that's all I knew about him. 28

Late in the afternoon, something got fouled up on the landing, and the yarder shut down. Suddenly it was quiet and you could hear the wind that had been driving the sleet into our faces all day. My partner and I abandoned the slash for the shelter of the forest. We found a dry spot out of the wind in a hollow at the base of an enormous cedar and waited for the yarder to start up. We didn't speak. He kept staring off into the forest. All hunched up with the cold, we looked the same—orange hardhats, green-black rain gear, rubber corkboots. We shared a cigarette. I was watching his face as he smoked. It struck me as strange that here we were, huddled in the forest in silence, two young men from totally different worlds. I tried to imagine what it might have been like had we met but a century before, I perhaps a trader, he a shadow in the wet woods. His people had made a home in the forest for thousands of years. I thought of what this country must have been like when my own grandfather arrived. I saw in the forest around us a world that my own children might never know, that Nisga'a children would never know. I turned to my partner. The whistle blew on the landing. 29

"What the hell are we doing?" I asked. 30

"Working," he said. I watched him as he stepped back into the clearcut, and then I followed. We finished the shift and, in the falling darkness, rode back to camp together in the back of the company crummy. That was the last I saw of him. 31

32   Fifteen years have passed since I left that camp and I've often wondered what became of the Nisga'a boy. It's a good bet he's no longer working as a logger. Natives rarely get promoted beyond the landing and, what's more, over the last decade a third of all logging jobs have been lost. The industry keeps saying that environmentalists are to blame, but in reality all the conservation initiatives of the last ten years in B.C. have not cost the union more than a few hundred jobs, if that. Automation and dwindling timber supplies have put almost 20,000 people out of work in this province alone. And still we keep cutting. In Oregon, Washington and California only 10% of the original coastal rainforest remains. In British Columbia roughly 60% has been logged, largely since 1950. In the mere 15 years since I stood in the forest with that Nisga'a boy, over half of all timber ever extracted from the public forests of British Columbia has been taken. At current rates of harvest, the next 20 years will see the destruction of every valley of ancient rainforest in the province.

33   We are living in the midst of an ecological catastrophe every bit as tragic as that of the slaughter of the buffalo and the passenger pigeon. Our government policies are equally blind, our economic rationales equally compelling. Until just recently, forestry policy in British Columbia explicitly called for the complete eradication of the old growth forests. The rotation cycle, the rate at which the forests were to be cut across the province, and thus the foundation of sustained yield forestry, was based on the assumption that all of these forests would be eliminated and replaced with tree farms. In other words, consideration of the intrinsic value of these ancient rainforests had no place in the calculus of forestry planning. Like the buffalo and the passenger pigeon, these magnificent forests were considered expendable°.

34   But while the passenger pigeons are extinct, and the buffalo reduced to a curiosity, these forests still stand. They are as rare and spectacular as any natural feature on the face of the earth, as biologically significant as any terrestrial ecosystem that has ever existed. If, knowing this, we still allow them to fall, what will it say about us as a people? What will be the legacy of our times?

35   The truth is, in an increasingly complex and fragmented world we need these ancient forests, alive and intact. For the children of the Nisga'a they are an image of the dawn of time, a memory of an era when raven emerged from the shadow of the cedar and young boys went in search of spirits at the north end of the world. For my own two young girls these forests echo with a shallow history, but one that is nevertheless rich in the struggles of their great grandparents, men and women who travelled halfway around the world to live in this

place. Today all peoples in this land are drawn together by a single thread of destiny. We live at the edge of the clearcut, our hands will determine the fate of these forests. If we do nothing, they will be lost within our lifetimes and we will be left to explain our inaction. If we preserve these ancient forests they will stand apart for all generations and for all time as symbols of the geography of hope.

Words and Meanings

Paragraph

symposium	academic conference	1
Audubon	Haitian-born U.S. scientist and artist who painted all the species of birds known in North America in the early nineteenth century	4
commissary	food supply	10
ecosystem	interdependent network of all living things	14
coniferous	pertaining to cone-bearing evergreen trees	15
biomass	weight (density) of all living things in a given area	16
slash	an open space in a forest resulting from logging	18
itinerant	travelling from place to place	25
	The terms in these paragraphs are loggers' jargon to describe the act of getting trees out of the slash. The foreman (bullbucker) supervises the workers who hook the logs onto a cable (choker) that is operated by a machine (yarder). Once the logs reach the "landing," the site from which they are loaded onto trucks, another line (the haulback) returns the empty chokers (or beads) to the site to be reset. Performing these activities at top speed to ensure maximum production is "highballing."	26 to 28
expendable	something we can use up for short-term gain without serious consequences	33

Structure and Strategy

1. Davis introduces his essay with examples of two scientists who spoke, along with the author, at an international conference. Why did he choose to begin with Leakey and Musgrave? What is the "odd and moving juxtaposition" these two men represent?
2. What is the THESIS of this essay? Which sentence in paragraph 3 most clearly expresses it?

3. Which paragraphs detail the extinction of the passenger pigeon? Which deal with the decimation of the plains buffalo herds? What is the third ILLUSTRATION of Davis's point? In what ORDER has he arranged these three main sections of his essay?
4. Identify vivid descriptive details in paragraphs 5, 14, and 17. What is the purpose of the ANECDOTE in paragraph 26?
5. Identify the TOPIC SENTENCES in paragraphs 6, 10, 12, and 16; then determine what kind of support the author uses to develop his topic in each of these paragraphs.
6. How is the topic of paragraph 7 developed? Find another paragraph in the essay that uses the same kind of support to develop the topic. What effect do these paragraphs have on the reader?
7. What is the TONE of paragraph 19? How does the tone contribute to your understanding of the author's opinion of the government?
8. Why does Davis elaborate his third point in such detail, including dialogue and characterization?
9. Besides EXPOSITION, what other RHETORICAL MODE does Davis employ in "The End of the Wild"?
10. Who is the intended AUDIENCE for this piece? What is its overall tone?

Content and Purpose

1. According to the essay, what does the earth look like from space? (See paragraph 2.) What IRONY is explored in paragraphs 2 and 3? According to Davis, what should we have learned from the image of earth as seen by space travellers?
2. What was the passenger pigeon population in North America in 1870? What happened to them? How? Why?
3. What is a "stool pigeon" (paragraph 6)? What is the meaning of the idiom today?
4. What has North America lost along with the buffalo? (See paragraphs 8, 10, and 11.) How do these paragraphs reinforce Davis's THESIS?
5. Explain in your own words the political purpose of the U.S. government in promoting the slaughter of the buffalo that makes this "biological terrorism" (paragraph 10) so horrific.
6. According to Davis, why are the rainforests of British Columbia even more remarkable and more endangered than those of the Amazon? (See paragraphs 14 through 16.)
7. According to the essay, what are the attitudes of the loggers, the logging companies, the government, and the Native peoples to clearcutting the rainforest?

8. Why do you think Davis includes the narrative involving "a rock blaster named Archie" (paragraphs 20 through 24) and "a native boy, a Nisga'a from New Aiyansh" (paragraphs 28 through 33)? What effect do these narratives have on the reader?
9. Summarize what has happened in the years since the author worked in the logging industry (see paragraph 32).
10. How does Davis unify his essay in the CONCLUSION (paragraphs 33 through 35)? How does he connect his three examples? Why does he want to preserve the rainforests?

Suggestion for Writing

Using an example from the natural environment (avoid pigeons, buffaloes, and rainforests), write an essay illustrating the interdependence of humanity and the rest of the ecosystem. What, for example, is happening to ice and glaciers in polar regions? To fish stocks all over the world? What has caused the changes, and how has it affected those who have traditionally relied on these resources?

Additional Suggestions for Writing

Choose one of the topics below and write a thesis statement based on it. Expand your thesis statement into an essay by selecting specific narrative details, descriptions, and/or examples from your own experience to develop the KEY IDEAS.

1. A dangerous spot that you have explored
2. A humorous family story
3. A vacation or holiday you would like to forget
4. An experience that led to success
5. An experience that led to failure
6. A journey that taught you something
7. A place that was special to you when you were a child
8. The birth of a child
9. A sacred place
10. Blogs
11. The stupidest thing you ever did

12. The death of someone close to you
13. People are not always what they appear to be.
14. Travel teaches us about ourselves as well as others.
15. Services offered by your college that help (or don't help) students
16. Movies reveal some important things about our culture.
17. You are (or are not) what you wear.
18. The effects of prolonged exposure to violence on people
19. You are optimistic (pessimistic) about the world as we move through the first decade of the twenty-first century.
20. "Good fences make good neighbours." (Robert Frost)
21. "All happy families resemble one another, but each unhappy family is unhappy in its own way." (Leo Tolstoy)
22. "Beauty in things exists in the mind which contemplates them." (David Hume)
23. "We are all immigrants to this place, even if we were born here." (Margaret Atwood)
24. "The truths of the past are the clichés of the present." (Ned Rorem)
25. "It is always easier to draw on the storehouse of memory than to find something original to say." (Michel de Montaigne)

UNIT 2

Process Analysis

WHAT IS PROCESS ANALYSIS?

Process analysis is writing that explains *how* something happens. It explains the steps or phases of a particular process. For example, the model essay in this unit, "Metamorphosis," explains how a baby learns to talk. It charts the course of a baby named Jeanie from birth to eighteen months of age, explaining the stages that she goes through as she develops from a crying infant to a talking toddler.

WHY DO WE USE PROCESS ANALYSIS?

Process analysis answers the lead-in question *how*. It is a familiar pattern of writing. Just think of the magazines you read and the how-to books that people rush to buy. They are full of instructions for improving your looks, your game, your house, your relationship with your spouse, children, parents, boss, pet—or anything else you can think of.

Process analysis is used for two purposes that lead to two different kinds of essays or reports. A **directional process analysis**—the "how-to-do-it" essay—gives readers the directions they need to perform the process themselves, whether it's building a Web site or training a dog. One example of a directional process analysis in this unit is Paul Quarrington's "Home Brew," which tells you how to make beer.

The second kind of process analysis provides information about how something happens (or happened). Readers of an **informational process analysis** do not want to perform the process they are reading about; they just want to learn how it is (or was) performed. For example, Jeffrey Moussaieff Masson's "Dear Dad" (page 80) describes the fascinating role played by male penguins in the reproductive cycle. Information (not directions) is the goal of this kind of process analysis.

Some writers use process analysis as a vehicle for humour or social commentary. The conventional how-to-do-it essay can be funny if a writer provides instructions for something no one wants to do, such as become obese or fail in school. A more serious social purpose underlies Danny Irvine's "A Tree-Planting Primer" (page 85)—a directional process analysis—and Jessica Mitford's "Behind the Formaldehyde Curtain" (page 92)—(an informational process analysis).

HOW DO WE WRITE PROCESS ANALYSIS?

Here are five guidelines for writing an effective process analysis:

1. Think through the whole process carefully and write an outline detailing all the steps involved. If you are writing a directional process analysis, be sure to include any preparatory steps or special equipment the reader should know about.

2. Put the steps of the process into CHRONOLOGICAL ORDER.

3. Write a clear thesis statement. (You need not include a preview of the main steps unless your topic is complex or your instructor specifically requires it.)

4. Write your first draft. Define any specialized or technical terms that may be unfamiliar to your reader. Use TRANSITIONS, or time-markers, to indicate the progression through the steps or stages (*first, next, after,* and so on).

5. Revise your draft carefully. Clarify any steps that cause confusion and revise until the whole paper is both clear and interesting.

The model essay that follows is an informational process analysis.

Metamorphosis

Meet newborn Jeanie. Weak and helpless as a caterpillar, Jeanie's only defence against hunger and pain is
the one sound she can make at will: crying. Eighteen
months later, Jeanie will be a busy toddler who asks
questions, expresses opinions, and even makes jokes.
From helplessness to assertiveness: how does this
wondrous transformation take place? To discover how
we learn to speak, let's follow Jeanie as she develops
from infant to toddler, from caterpillar to butterfly.

Infancy, the first stage of language development,
literally means "not able to speak." For the first six
months of her life, Jeanie isn't able to talk, but she can
respond to speech. Shortly after birth, she'll turn her
head toward the sound of a voice. By two weeks of
age, she will prefer the sound of a human voice to
non-human sounds. Between two and four months,
she will learn to distinguish the voices of her care-
givers from those of strangers, and she knows
whether those voices are speaking soothingly or
angrily. By the time she is two months old, Jeanie will
have learned to coo as well as cry, and she coos happily when people smile and talk to her. Now she can
express contentment as well as discomfort. At around
four months of age, Jeanie's happy sounds become
more varied and sophisticated: she registers delight on
a scale ranging from throaty chuckles to belly laughs.
All this vocal activity is actually a rehearsal for speech.
As Jeanie cries and coos and laughs, her vocal cords,
tongue, lips, and brain are developing the coordination
required for her to speak her first words.

At six or seven months of age, Jeanie is no longer
an infant; she's moved on to the *baby* stage of language development. Like a pupa in its cocoon, Jeanie
is undergoing a dramatic but (to all but her closest
observers) invisible change. She looks at her mother
when someone says "Mama." She responds to simple
directions: she'll clap her hands or wave "bye-bye" on
request. By the time she is a year old, Jeanie will recognize at least twenty words. The sounds Jeanie produces at this stage are called *babbling*, a word that
technically describes a series of reduplicated single
consonant and vowel sounds and probably derives its

name from a common example: "ba-ba-ba-ba." About halfway through this stage of her development, Jeanie progresses to *variegated babbling*, in which sounds change between syllables. "Da-dee, da-dee, da-dee," she burbles, to the delight of her father (who doesn't know that Jeanie cannot yet connect the sounds she makes to the meaning they represent to others). But by the time Jeanie celebrates her first birthday, the variety, rhythm, and tone of her babbling have become more varied, and her family begins to sense consistent meaning in the sounds she makes. "Go bye-bye!" is as clearly meant as it is spoken—Jeanie wants to get going!

Third stage (developed with description, examples, dialogue)

Jeanie's recognition of the link between sounds and meanings signals her entry into the *toddler* stage—twelve to eighteen months. At eighteen months, Jeanie will understand approximately 250 words—more than ten times the number she understood at twelve months. Most of what she says are single-word utterances: "kitty" for a cat in her picture book, "nana" for the bananas she loves to squish and eat. But even single words now function as complex communications depending on the intonation Jeanie gives them. "Kitty?" she inquires, looking at a picture of a tiger. She demands a "nana!" for lunch. About halfway through the toddler stage, Jeanie begins to link words together to make sentences. "Mama gone," she cries when her mother leaves for work. "Me no go bed," she tells her father. Though it marks the beginning of trouble for her parents, this development marks a triumph for Jeanie. She has broken out of the cocoon of passive comprehension into the world of active participation.

Reference to metamorphosis analogy contributes to unity

Conclusion (refers back to introduction and completes analogy)

In less than two years, Jeanie has metamorphosed from wailing newborn to babbling baby to talking toddler. Through language, she is becoming her own woman in the world. Now she can fly.

The Magic of Moviegoing

RICK GROEN

Rick Groen (b. 1947) holds an M.A. in English literature from the University of Toronto. He has been an arts critic, reviewing both television and film, at *The Globe and Mail* since the early 1980s.

What movies to watch; whom to watch; where, when and why   1
to watch. Oh, we got it covered, and so does everyone else.
Turn to your favourite newspaper or magazine and, on any
given week, these cinematic five Ws will all be lined up and duly
addressed. In the arts no less than the news, they're the standard
quintet of queries, forming the foundation for most critical commentary. But there's another question, equally interesting, that seldom gets
examined or even asked. It's not the What but the How of the matter:
How do we behave during this pop rite of going to the picture show?

Let's confine our little inquiry to theatres proper, and exclude   2
living rooms. Obviously, it's a very different experience viewing a
film in the bright confines of your home and through the tiny frame
of a TV set. There, we tend to watch more forgivingly, more toler-
antly. For every majestic opus, every *Lawrence of Arabia*, that suffers
when removed from the big screen, there are a myriad humdrum
flicks—tepid thrillers, formula comedies—that actually seem more
palatable° on the tube. They get better because our expectations get
lowered—our investment (of time and money) is just smaller.

Clearly, the stakes are raised when the setting shifts to a real   3
movie house. So how do we watch there? Well, indulge me for a
second while I pick up a popular line of thought about film theatres, the one that insists on a connection between Where and
What. This theory suggests that the architecture of the movie theatre is somehow intrinsically linked to the makeup of the movies.
Back in the era of the single-screen theatre, the films neatly fit their
abodes—a charming Fred Astaire musical felt right at home in an
art-deco palace°. And now, with the switch from unique local cin-
emas to multiplex malls, these vast generic structures are attracting
the product they deserve—loud, look-alike films for loud, look-
alike boxes. There, the argument continues, the patrons pick out a
movie as they would a channel, and with about as much optimism—18 screens yet nothing to watch.

I don't think so. Although no fan of the multiplex, I'm leery of   4
such rear-view mirror reasoning, the nostalgic yearning for an illu-
sory past where every screen was silver and every movie golden.
Anyway, nostalgia just keeps getting updated. No doubt, a few
decades from now, some savage modernist will be tearing down

some vintage multiplex, and today's 20-year-olds will be penning tearful odes to the passing of an aesthetic landmark. And they'll be doing so for a good reason. Although where we watch and what we watch have changed radically over time, how we watch has stayed relatively constant. Indeed, for many, the ritual of moviegoing is a large part of the allure, every bit as appealing as the movies themselves.

5   That ritual begins at the box office. Movies were invented as a form of mass entertainment, and there's a nicely democratic quality to the very act of entering a theatre. What you buy is a general admission ticket, not an assigned seat, which invariably leads to that through-the-foyer-into-the-aisle scramble for your preferred location—way up front where actors look like giant celluloid idols, mid-range for a less infantilizing perspective, deep in the far reaches for those with extracinematic pursuits° in mind.

6   Yes, *that* part of the ritual. Moviegoing is a social experience. People tend to go in couples or groups. Always, they want to sit together. Too often, they want to talk together. And usually, they want to eat and drink together. In fact, given the wider variety of fare—the hot dogs, the nachos, the pastries—available at the multiplex, "dinner and a movie" has been replaced by "dinner at the movie." (Thanks to the concessions' inflated prices, the hit to the wallet is about the same.) Last, but hardly least, don't forget to add sex to the social equation. A movie is frequently a date; it's foreplay.

7   But now the picture starts, and a tension immediately develops between two competing interests—between moviegoing, which is primarily a social experience, and movie-watching, which is essentially an individual experience. A film projected onto a screen in a darkened theatre approximates the state of dreaming, and is intensely personal. So when the lights go down, these duelling impulses—to socialize or to watch, to talk with others or to dream alone—begin to meld. As they do, the theatre becomes simultaneously a public and a private space, with people striving to get the balance right and to keep the boundaries straight.

8   We strive for a similar balance inside our automobiles—another hybrid of public and private space. Of course, the car and the motion picture enjoy a shared history. Both came of age through the early part of the last century; both are transporting devices in their separate fashions; and both serve as havens for our sexual desires, either symbolically or otherwise. Inevitably, their twin paths intersected in the steamy atmosphere of the drive-in theatre, a place that typically specialized in showing B-pictures—the kind that weren't too distracting, that prevented the private experience of movie-watching from infringing on the social experience of moviegoing.

Which brings us to a conclusion less obvious than it might seem at first glance: How we behave at a movie is directly influenced by what we're viewing. The more engrossing the film, the more that moviegoing gives way to movie-watching. We've all observed, even felt this transition—it's almost palpable. Suddenly, popcorn stops being munched, words stop being exchanged, passes stop being made. As we get lost in the movie, we get lost to our companions. But there's a paradox at work here too. This convergence of disparate people turns into an audience, becomes one, only when the various social groupings have disintegrated and its members have splintered off into their private selves. The irony is bald but delicious: When we are most truly alone, we are most truly an audience.

That's how we watch movies at our best. And, for me, that's the recurring magic of movies, the alchemical° wizardry that can break down a buzzing crowd into islands of attentive individuals, then re-assemble those islands into the archipelago° of a rapt audience. Funny thing about this wizardry. Disdainful of borders and blind to class, the stuff can pop up anywhere folks gather to find it—at a sprawling multiplex in Dolby surround-sound, or on a white sheet strung between tent poles in the thin open air. The magic may come, or not, but one thing is sure—it's always worth the wait.

Words and Meanings

Paragraph

palatable	pleasant, acceptable, or satisfactory	2
art-deco palace	a movie theatre constructed in a decorative art and architectural style—characterized by bold lines, geometric shapes, and strong colours—that was popular in the 1920s and 1930s	3
extracinematic pursuits	interests lying outside of cinema	5
alchemical	miraculously transforming; adjective form of *alchemy*, the medieval pseudo-science that sought to turn base metals into gold and silver	10
archipelago	a large group of islands in the sea; metaphorically, a large group of individuals	

Structure and Strategy

1. In his INTRODUCTION, the author refers to the "five Ws"—the questions that make up "the foundation for most critical commentary." What are the five Ws? What is the other question around which Groen has chosen to structure his KEY POINTS?
2. What stages in the ritual of moviegoing does Groen identify? Which paragraphs describe each stage? Have any stages been left out?
3. Paragraphs 7 and 8 are developed by means of comparison. What two things are compared in paragraph 7? In paragraph 8? Do you agree with the comparisons? Why or why not?
4. Identify the METAPHOR in the last paragraph. Do you think it is effective? Why or why not?

Content and Purpose

1. According to Groen, what is the difference between watching a movie at home and watching a movie in a theatre?
2. Paragraph 3 presents an ARGUMENT about the architecture of theatres and the kinds of movies that are shown in them. Summarize this argument. Does Groen agree with it? Do you? Why or why not?
3. According to the author, how do people choose a seat in a movie theatre?
4. Identify the elements of the "social experience" (paragraph 6) of going to a movie.
5. According to paragraph 9, what is the connection between people's behaviour at a movie and the movie itself?
6. What is the central IRONY expressed in paragraph 9? How is it essential to the "recurring magic of movies" (paragraph 10)? Do you agree with this idea? Why or why not?

Suggestions for Writing

1. Write an essay describing the kinds of movies you like to watch. Why do you find them entertaining?
2. Write an essay on the ritual involved in another form of entertainment (for example, a sports or cultural event, a nightclub, or live theatre).

Put What Where? 2,000 Years of Bizarre Sex Advice

JOHN NAISH

John Naish is a health journalist for *The Times* (London). He is a tai chi-practising vegetarian who loves rock music and rides fast motorcycles.

Mating. Reproduction. Nothing is more crucial to humanity's survival, so it would be logical to expect us to have got it sussed° early in our evolution. But since the start of civilisation, the fundamentals of human sex—where to put it, how and when—have been absurdly confused by a parade of moralists, pundits and visionaries all claiming to know the magic secrets and only too happy to pass them on at a very reasonable price. Just as every generation thinks that it invented sex, we also think we invented lovemaking manuals, or at least based them on a few prototypes such as the *Kamasutra* and Marie Stopes's 1918 *Married Love*. But today's maelstrom of books, videos and DVDs has a far richer, more twisted heritage than that.   1

The tradition of bestselling love guides goes back to the Ancient Chinese. Our earliest known manuals were first written in 300 BC and buried in a family tomb at Mawangdui, in Hunan province. Recent translation reveals the timeless nature of the subjects they tackled. Written as *Cosmo* coverlines, they would look like this: Four Seasons of Sex—and Why Autumn Is Hot, Hot, Hot; Wild New Positions; Tiger Roving, Gibbon Grabbing and Fish Gobbling; Aphrodisiacs to Keep You Up All Night! Plus Exclusive! Your Love Route to Immortality. As ever, it was all nonsense: home-made Viagra recipes involved ingredients such as beetle larvae, wasps and dried snails. The books also promised that any man who had sex with a different virgin every night for 100 nights without ejaculating would live forever (albeit rather uncomfortably).   2

These odd beginnings set a trend: weird tips from strange authors, many of whom became manual martyrs. Ovid, the Roman poet, advised women on the best positions to suit their bodies in his poem *Ars Amatoria*. For example: "If you are short, go on top/If you're conspicuously tall, kneel with your head turned slightly sideways." The prudish Emperor Augustus banished poor Ovid to a chilly outpost of empire (a small town on the Black Sea in modern Romania).   3

Medieval European sex advice followed the strait-laced trend: most of it said "don't". Pleasure paved Hell's roads and misogynistic manuals such as *De Secretis Mulierum* (*The Secrets of Women*)   4 claimed that females used sex to drain men of their power and that some hid sharp shards of iron inside themselves to injure innocent lovers.

5   A technological breakthrough in the Renaissance put us back on our lascivious° tracks. The printing press enabled publishers to churn out dodgy books faster than the Church authorities could ban them. Readers were treated to gems such as Mrs Isabella Cortes's handy hint from 1561 that a mixture of quail testicles, large-winged ants, musk and amber was perfect for straightening bent penises. The era also brought us the earliest recorded recommendation of slippers as a sex aid ("Cold feet are a powerful hindrance to coition," warned Giovanni Sinibaldi in his 1658 book *Rare Verities*.)

6   But to find history's oddest advisers, we must look to the Victorians and Edwardians°. William Chidley, for example, believed that he could best promote his ideas by walking around in a toga. Chidley, an Australian, advised readers in his 1911 pamphlet *The Answer* that heavy clothing caused erections, which would lead to sexual overexcitement, illness and death, as well as being "ugly things" of which "we are all ashamed". He urged people to live on fruit and nuts and to practise a method of flaccid intercourse apparently based on horses' sex lives. Yet it wasn't his ideas that got him repeatedly arrested, but his silk toga, which the authorities thought indecent. After his death, supporters continued propounding his theories into the 1920s.

7   For the ultimate proof that you don't need relevant qualifications to become a world expert, we turn to Marie Stopes. She was married and in her late thirties when she wrote one of Britain's most enduring sex guides, *Married Love*. But she was also a virgin. Stopes was inspired by her betrothal to Reginald "Ruggles" Gates, who, she told a divorce court, had failed ever to become "effectively rigid". When *Married Love* hit the shelves early in 1918 it outsold the bestselling contemporary novels by a huge margin. By 1925, sales had passed the half-million mark. Stopes was a fan of Hitler's eugenics and arrogant enough to offer Rudyard Kipling and George Bernard Shaw advice on writing. Her main sex-manual innovation was a theory that women have a "sex tide" of passion that ebbs and flows on a fortnightly basis—and woe betide the man who didn't understand this. In case her second husband, the manufacturing magnate Humphrey Verdon Roe, got it wrong, she made him sign a contract releasing her to have sex with other men.

8   So that's our sexual forebears, a weird lot with funny ideas. Compared with them we might appear at the zenith of sexual enlightenment. Our age is remarkable for the sheer volume of sex

advice being consumed: one woman in four now owns a sex manual, says a survey by the publishers Dorling Kindersley. Everyone from porn stars to the car-manual firm Haynes has one out. Well, I wonder. In 50 years' time, I foresee the students at a university faculty of sexual semiotics° studying the early Twenty-Ohs with the same mirth, incredulity and horror that shake us when we consider our ancestors' obsessions. Perhaps they will wonder why we bought so many manuals, videos and DVDs but seemed to have so little time or energy left for sex. Maybe they will link our obsession with orgasms to our endless need to go shopping. They might also connect our avid consumption of sex advice to our growing terror of personal embarrassment and "getting it wrong". They may even have a name for us; perhaps the erotic neurotics.

Words and Meanings

		Paragraph
sussed	figured out	1
lascivious	lustful, sex-obsessed	5
Victorians and Edwardians	those who lived in England (and its colonies) during the reign of Queen Victoria (1837–1901) and King Edward VII (1901–1910)	6
semiotics	the study of the meaning of signs and symbols such as language, clothing, behaviour	8

Structure and Strategy

1. This article provides several examples of ANALYSIS: how-to guides to better sex. Identify the examples the writer discusses.
2. In what ORDER are the examples organized?
3. What is the TOPIC SENTENCE of paragraph 8?

Content and Purpose

1. Which sentence contains the THESIS of this article?
2. Do you agree or disagree with Naish's contention that "every generation thinks that it invented sex" (paragraph 1)? Why?
3. Which of the historic periods Naish discusses had the most negative attitude toward sex? Why do you think this is so?
4. Who does Naish describe as "history's oddest advisers"? Is there any IRONY in this characterization?
5. How does Naish think people in the future will look back at our era in terms of sexual enlightenment? Do you agree or disagree?

Suggestions for Writing

1. Write an essay exploring the impact on adults and/or children of the increasingly explicit sexual content of TV, DVDs, the Internet, and print sources.
2. Write an essay that explains the process through which you learned about sex.
3. Write an essay that compares your parents' generation's attitude toward sexual behaviour with your generation's view of it.
4. Write a brief, tongue-in-cheek "how-to" guide to sex for a visitor from another planet. How do humans make love?

Home Brew

PAUL QUARRINGTON

Novelist, playwright, screenwriter, journalist, and critic, Paul Quarrington (b. 1953) is one of Canada's most versatile writers. A former rock musician, he writes song lyrics as well as fiction, non-fiction, plays, and films. His works include *Whale Music* (1989), *Civilization (and Its Part in My Downfall)* (1994), *The Boy on the Back of the Turtle* (1997), and *Galveston* (2004).

1   The first thing I must explain is that my brother helped me with this project. We share certain traits my brother and I, and chief among them is a fondness, nay an *over*-fondness for beer. We have even developed a Trivial Pursuit-type game featuring questions about beer. Indeed, every question can be answered by bellowing, "Beer!" My brother and I take a foolish delight in ordering drinks in the same fashion, screaming out "Beer!" at helpful bartenders and waiters, deviating from this only to the extent of making it "More beer!" as the evening progresses.

2   At any rate, when asked by this fine journal if I would look into the making of beer—home brewing—my brother stepped into the breach (I could not stop him), and his presence shall make itself known. For example, at one point during the procedure, I took to ruminating aloud. "Making beer," I mused, "is as natural as childbirth."

3   "True," agreed my brother, "but the child could be a homicidal maniac."

4   By which my brother made oblique° reference to the truly vile bogswill that people had forced upon us in days long gone by, bottles filled half with a dull, cloudy liquid, half with some other-

worldly sludge. It used to be that no words filled me with as much dread as "homemade beer." But I have learned much—the afore-mentioned bogswill was likely the doing of "the wild yeasties"— and, while learning, have tasted many exceptional beers. My brother and I are very pleased with our own batch and have spent several lovely evenings in his living room, occasionally glancing up at the other and bellowing, "Beer!"

But let us get down to basics; let us make sure we all know 5
exactly what is going on here. Beer is a beverage that is fermented from cereals and malt and flavoured with hops. From this single statement, all else shall follow, so it is good to fix in your mind, to repeat it inwardly a couple times. (Or, put as a question in our game: What beverage is fermented from cereals and malt and flavoured with hops? Answer: Beer!)

The first significance arising from the statement is that beer is 6
made with cereals rather than with fruit as in, say, wine. The process of fermentation occurs when a molecule of sugar splits, cre-ating two molecules of carbon dioxide (CO_2) and two molecules of ethyl alcohol (C_2H_5OH). Starch, such as that found in those cereals, cannot be converted into alcohol. This would be extremely bad news for us beer lovers, except for a vegetable enzyme called amy-lase. You see, starch is, chemically speaking, a long chain of mole-cules ($C_6H_{10}O_5$, et cetera, et cetera). Amylase breaks up the chain, pairs the molecules and adds a water molecule, thus creating $C_{12}H_{22}O_{11}$, which is a maltose sugar molecule that can thence undergo fermentation, praise the Lord. It is this process that is car-ried out at malting houses, which is why we begin our beer-making with a large can of malt extract (usually hopped malt extract) rather than with a bucket of barley.

I will abandon the pseudoscientific° tone now. It is bound to go 7
down in flames right around the time I try to throw in the scientific name for the yeast used to make lager beers, *Saccharomyces carlsber-gensis*. That yeast, you see, was named for the place it was discov-ered, and do not be embarrassed if you, too, failed to realize that there are all sorts of different yeasts with all sorts of fancy names— not to mention those unruly thugs and hooligans, the wild yeasties. Yeast is what does the actual work of fermentation. It is a plant organism, a living thing; and when it dies, it sinks to the bottom and forms sludge.

Malt and yeast are all you truly need to make beer, and 8
humankind has been making it for something like 8,000 years. (Q: What has humankind been making for 8,000 years? A: Beer!) Hops did not appear on the European scene until the 12th century, and even at that time, there was a resistance in the form of laws forbid-

ding their use. Hops are the flowers of the female hop vine (an aggressive spreader, it has earned the lovely nomenclature *Humulus lupulus* and is also known as the "wolf of the willows"), and their resins and oils impart flavour of a slightly bitter nature to the beer.

9   There are many different kinds of hops; they all have different names (Cluster, Fuggles, Tetenang), and they come in either pellet or leaf form. It really is quite mind-boggling. That is why it is important to have a firm grasp on the basics. (Q: Combine malt, hops, yeast and water, and in time, you will have what? A: Beer!) This is no more mysterious than, say, the baking of bread. Not coincidentally, the Old English *breowan* gives us both "brew" and "bread."

10   The first step in making beer at home is to leave it—your home, that is—and hie down to a specialty shop. We chose a Wine-Art/Brewers-Art store (in Toronto) because it happened to be closest, but Wine-Art/Brewers-Art stores also have a reputation for helpfulness, and many of the home brewers I spoke with steered me in that direction. And indeed, we were greeted by a friendly sort, Martin Jordan (manager), who spent a long time explaining things. The process detailed below is, in fact, Martin's Improved Method.

11   You need to acquire some basic equipment: a primary fermenter, a secondary fermenter and a siphoning hose. This should run you somewhere between $30 and $40. Allow me a moment to deal with the financial advantages of home brewing. Clearly, home brewing is a lot less expensive than buying beer at the beer store. This seems to me, however, to be one of the least noble reasons for undertaking the endeavour. You will encounter people who brew because it is cheap, and they usually give themselves away by saying something like, "And the beer is just as good as the stuff you buy."

12   These people are missing the point, I think. The great thing about home brewing is that you can make some really wonderful beers, you can alter recipes to suit your individual taste and if it ends up being economical, that is a fact to be savoured rather than gloated over. Besides, it may not be all that economical: although the three items listed above are really all you need, they are not all you will end up carting out of the store.

13   You will want a hydrometer to measure specific gravity (I will explain in a moment). You will want a vapour lock, and you will want a plastic J-tube which is crooked at the bottom so that you don't have to stand there holding the siphoning hose. You will want a hose clamp for when you are bottling, which reminds me— you need some bottles. And caps. And a capper. And you will want

some potassium metabisulphite crystals to cleanse and disinfect all that stuff.

The primary fermenter is typically a large plastic pail—prefer- 14
ably a food-grade pail, but nothing used for oils or vinegars—with a tight-fitting lid. The secondary fermenter is typically a large glass bottle (such as might contain a genie). These are called, for reasons that have not been explained to my satisfaction, carboys. They come in two sizes, 19 and 23 litres. Those are the two quantities you make beer in, 19 and 23 litres. We are going to be making 23 litres.

Now that you have your basic equipment, you need to pur- 15
chase the ingredients for the wort. The wort is the combination of malt, grains and hops whence flows your batch of beer. My brother and I chose to make an English-style bitter and purchased a can of hopped malt extract with the word BITTER printed on it. You could purchase Brown Ale, American Light, Stout, Pale Ale, et cetera. Each can contains 1.5 kilograms of hopped malt extract, yeast and instructions, and costs around $15. One could make a batch of beer just by using the stuff in the can (actually, you need some corn sugar), but Martin Jordan suggested that we also purchase some roasted barley and bittering hops. This we did, because he said the resulting beer would taste like Smithwick's, a statement that had my brother and me leaping about the store like puppies.

So now you are all loaded up, and it cost approximately $75, of 16
which perhaps $55 was a one-time investment. Therefore, for about $20, you are going to get 23 litres of beer. (I find it hard not to get excited.)

The first step takes place in the kitchen, where you cook up the 17
wort in a huge pot. To begin, you bring four to six litres of water to a boil. You add the bittering hops. The hops look like rabbit pellets, which is a bit off-putting. Martin Jordan suggested that in the course of cooking the wort, you occasionally take a single hop and fling it with certain élan° into the mixture. I think this is sage advice. I doubt a single hop affects the flavour much, but it does help the novice brewmaster to relax.

At any rate, you let the hops boil for 15 to 20 minutes, at which 18
point you add the sugar. Let that boil for another five minutes, then add the crushed malt grains. (Take a pinch and eat them; you'll be surprised how good they taste.) Let that simmer for five minutes, then add the malt extract, which you will discover is a thick, gluti-nous syrup with the consistency of molasses. Return the mixture to a low simmer.

While the wort is cooking (and whenever you are not flinging 19
hop pellets into it) it is a good time to clean and disinfect your pri-mary fermenter—or, in my case, a good time to discover that your

brother has an obsessive-compulsive personality disorder. I counsel thoroughness rather than monomania°. For instance, if, having disinfected your primary fermenter, you then pick it up and move it closer to the stove, it is not necessary—although my brother found it so—to redisinfect where the offending fingers were placed. It is a good idea to mark the 23-litre level on the inside of the container.

20   Now put some cold water in that primary fermenter. (A tip from Mr. Jordan: You might draw the water the day before and let it sit overnight, which helps get rid of the chlorine taste.) You now strain the wort into it. You stir and then add more water until you reach the 23-litre mark. You pitch the yeast, which is less strenuous than it sounds, adding it when the mixture is between 70 and 80 degrees F. (Warning: If it is too hot, you will kill the yeast.)

21   Now, ahem, allow me to get a little scholarly here. The specific gravity of water is 1.000. Liquids containing sugar have a higher specific gravity because they are denser. Alcohol is lighter than water. Therefore, during fermentation, the specific gravity of your brew will drop as more and more of the sugar is converted into alcohol. Some of the malt will not convert (which is what gives beer its taste), so although the final specific gravity will approach 1.000 again, it will never truly arrive.

22   A rule of thumb is that when the specific gravity stops dropping, fermentation is complete. Got it? For this reason, we now take our hydrometer, which looks like a futuristic fishing float°, and place it in our beer-to-be. It might read, say, 1.046. The higher the figure, the more potential alcohol, and some recipes will even say, "At this point, your starting s.g. should be at 1.048," in which case you would add more malt and/or sugar until that level is attained.

23   All right now. Fermentation splits a molecule of sugar into ethanol and carbon dioxide. The latter is gas, gas that is exuded with a series of very satisfying mulching galoomps. So we need to let the gas escape. But if we leave the container uncovered, guess what's going to get into it? The wild yeasties! For even though many yeasts are civilized and gentrified, there are unruly yeasts floating about in the air, little gangs of them just looking to mess up somebody's beer. To get into it and produce *off flavours*. That is Martin Jordan's way of saying the wild yeasties will make, you know, bogswill. You therefore cover your primary fermenter very securely, having purchased a lid for that purpose. You will notice that the lid has a largish hole dead centre, which seems foolish until you see that your fermentation lock's rubber stopper will plug it admirably. The fermentation lock is a twisted piece of tubing, half-filled with water, which will let out the CO_2, and vent the last gasps of expiring yeast without admitting the dreaded hordes.

You then move down to the basement, especially if you are attempting to make lager. Lager, derived from the German for "storage," cannot be properly made when the weather is too warm, so if you are doing this in the summer, you had best make an ale. Ale is fermented at higher temperatures, which causes most of the yeast to rise to the top. Ale is thus a top-fermenting brew, lager a bottom-fermenting brew. And there, at last, we know the difference between the two. 24

You can relax now for approximately five days. It should be easy to determine whether fermentation is taking place (bubbles in the vapour lock), although our brew appeared strangely inactive. Martin Jordan suggested that the gas was probably escaping from somewhere else, perhaps from around the lid rather than through the vapour lock, and by taking a series of readings with the carefully sterilized hydrometer, we were able to determine that all was as it should be. 25

On day five, you siphon into the secondary fermenter. Your primary fermenter will have developed a sludgy bottom layer made up of yeast corpses, and although the siphoning tube has a crook at the bottom, hopefully raising it above it all, great care should be taken not to transfer the sludge. By the way, you realize I am assuming that all of this stuff has been cleansed and sterilized. Any slip-up on the sanitation front could result in *off flavours,* so never let down your guard. (While we were making our beer, a number of bad batches were reported to Martin Jordan at his store, as if wild germs and yeasties had gone on a citywide rampage. Beware.) 26

On day 15, you add the "finings," commonly isinglass, which is made from the scrapings of sturgeons' swim bladders. This makes your beer less cloudy. Don't ask how, just do it. 27

On day 20, you bottle. Beer's effervescence is created from extra fermentation at the end of the process, so you now add a little more corn sugar or finishing malt. You could add about half a teaspoon of sugar per bottle, although the sensible thing to do is add 1-1/4 cups to the 23-litre carboy. Siphon off some beer, dissolve the sugar in it, then reintroduce it to the brew. Don't start stirring in your carboy, lest you disturb the sludge. 28

My brother and I bottled in plastic litre bottles with screw-on plastic caps, which I realize is cheating, but I thought it worked wonderfully. A potential downside is that you need to drink a litre whenever you want a beer, but my brother and I conceived of this as *no big problem.* You might choose to bottle the standard 341-millilitre size, which you would then cap in the traditional manner. My big tip here is to purchase a clamp for the end of your siphoning 29 tube, a simple device that stops the flow momentarily as you move from bottle to bottle.

30   If you are still in the basement at this point, it might be an idea to move your lot upstairs where it is warmer to sort of kick-start this last bit of fermentation. Five days later, you should return your beer to a cool place, and five days after that, you could drink one. Which is to say, it is the earliest you should drink one, but time will only improve your beer. Many claim it is best in three months.

31   Perhaps the diciest aspect of home brew comes with the actual drinking. That final bit of fermentation produced bubbles, a little more alcohol and some dead yeast cells, which are now lying on the bottom of the bottle. When pouring the beer, it is best to hold the bottle in front of a light so that you can view the sludge's advent toward the neck. The trick is to avoid dead yeast without leaving behind half a bottle of beer. And once you have poured the beer, rinse out the bottle immediately, because as the remaining liquid evaporates, the sludge will adhere to the inside and render it useless as a beer receptacle.

32   So there you have it. The procedure is simple, virtually idiot-proof—nothing can stop those yeasts from splitting up sugar molecules—and also educational.

33   Q: What beverage contains pelletized wolf of the willows and sturgeon swim bladder scrapings?

34   A: You got it.

Words and Meanings

Paragraph

4   oblique   indirect

7   pseudoscientific   scientific-sounding, not based on genuine science

17 élan   careless flair

19 monomania   obsession

22 fishing float   a cork or other buoyant material used to keep a fishing net or line on top of the water

Structure and Strategy

1. Quarrington's INTRODUCTION involves another character. What does he have in common with the author? Where else does he appear in the essay? What purpose does this character serve?

2. Where does the essay provide a definition of beer? What is it contrasted with?
3. Where does Quarrington begin his process ANALYSIS? Is he writing an informational or a directional analysis? What are the first two things he explains?
4. Quarrington provides "documentation" of a sort for his beer-making process. Who is the source of his recipe? Where else does this person appear in the essay?
5. Compare the DICTION of paragraphs 1 and 6.
6. Quarrington uses a SIMILE (see also FIGURES OF SPEECH in the Glossary section) near the end of paragraph 15. How does it contribute to the TONE of the essay?
7. Identify at least four descriptive details in paragraph 23. What purpose do they serve?
8. Some of the TRANSITIONS in the essay are single words or short phrases; for example, "Got it?" (paragraph 22) and "All right now" (paragraph 23). Identify other examples and explain why Quarrington uses them in his essay.
9. What is the connection between the INTRODUCTION and CONCLUSION of this essay?

Content and Purpose

1. What basic equipment and ingredients are required to make beer? Why does Quarrington not begin his essay with this information?
2. Identify the stages of beer-making. How long does the process take?
3. Why, according to Quarrington, should beer drinkers consider making their own beer? To save money?
4. What is "vile bogswill" (paragraph 4)? What are "wild yeasties"?
5. Paragraph 8 is a digression from the process analysis. What is its purpose?
6. What is the difference between ale and lager?
7. What is the most peculiar and unexpected ingredient that goes into beer?
8. What is the "diciest aspect" of home brewing?
9. Do you think Quarrington's beer-making instructions are "simple, virtually idiot-proof" (paragraph 32)? Could you make beer by following his instructions?

Suggestions for Writing

1. Write a process analysis essay that explains how to make your own wine, yogurt, sourdough bread, or any other fermented product.

2. Write a process analysis that describes the process of preparing a special meal for and with family members. Try to communicate the emotional links between the people who are sharing the food and its preparation.
3. Compare "Home Brew" with "A Tree-Planting Primer" (page 85). Obviously, the essays have dissimilar topics, but how do they compare in terms of PURPOSE and STYLE?

Dear Dad

JEFFREY MOUSSAIEFF MASSON

Jeffrey Moussaieff Masson (b. 1941) taught Sanskrit and Indian Studies at the University of Toronto from 1969 to 1980. After graduating from the Toronto Institute of Psychoanalysis in 1978, he served as projects director of the Sigmund Freud Archives. He has demonstrated his fascination with animal psychology in such books as *When Elephants Weep* (1994), *Dogs Never Lie About Love* (1997), *The Nine Emotional Lives of Cats* (2002), and *The Pig Who Sang to the Moon: The Emotional World of Farm Animals* (2003).

1   One reason that so many of us are fascinated by penguins is that they resemble us. They walk upright, the way we do, and, like us, they are notoriously curious creatures. No doubt this accounts for our fondness for cartoon images of penguins dressed up at crowded parties, but as fathers, penguins are our superiors.

2   Unlike mammals, male birds can experience pregnancy as an intimate matter, with the father in many species helping to sit (brood) the egg. After all, a male can brood an egg as well as a female can. But in no other species does it reach this extreme.

3   The emperors usually wait for good weather to copulate, any time between April 10 and June 6. They separate themselves somewhat from the rest of the colony and face each other, remaining still for a time. Then the male bends his head, contracts his abdomen, and shows the female the spot on his belly where he has a flap of skin that serves as a kind of pouch for the egg and baby chick. This stimulates the female to do the same. Their heads touch, and the male bends his head down to touch the female's pouch. Both begin to tremble visibly. Then the female lies face down on the ice, partially spreads her wings and opens her legs. The male climbs onto her back and they mate for 10 to 30 seconds.

They stay together afterward constantly, leaning against one 4
another when they are standing up, or if they lie down, the female
will glide her head under that of her mate. About a month later,
between May 1 and June 12, the female lays a single greenish-white
egg. French researchers noted that the annual dates on which the
colony's first egg was laid varied by only eight days in 16 years of
observation. Weighing almost a pound [.45 kilograms], and measuring up to 131 millimetres long and 86 millimetres wide, this is
one of the largest eggs of any bird. The male stays by the female's
side, his eyes fixed on her pouch. As soon as he sees the egg, he
sings a variation of what has been called the "ecstatic" display by
early observers, and she too takes up the melody.

She catches the egg with her wings before it touches the ice and 5
places it on her feet. Both penguins then sing in unison, staring at
the egg for up to an hour. The female then slowly walks around the
male, who gently touches the egg on her feet with his beak, making
soft groans, his whole body trembling. He shows the female his
pouch. Gently she puts the egg down on the ice and just as gently
he rolls it with his beak between his large, black, powerfully clawed
feathered feet, and then, with great difficulty, hoists the egg onto
the surface of his feet. He rests back on his heels so that his feet
make the least contact with the ice. The transfer of the egg is a delicate operation. If it falls on the ice and rolls away, it can freeze in
minutes or it might even be stolen. If it is snatched away by a
female penguin who failed to find a mate, its chances of survival
are slight because the intruder will eventually abandon the egg,
since she has no mate to relieve her.

With the egg transfer successfully completed, the happy couple 6
both sing. The male parades about in front of the female, showing
her his pouch with the egg inside. This thick fold, densely feathered
on the outside and bare inside, now completely covers the egg and
keeps it at about 95 degrees Fahrenheit, even when the temperature
falls to 95 degrees below zero.

The female begins to back away, each time a little farther. He 7
tries to follow her, but it is hard, since he is balancing the egg.
Suddenly she is gone, moving purposefully toward the open sea.
She is joined by the other females in the colony, who, by the end of
May or June, have all left for the ocean almost 100 kilometres away.
The females have fasted for nearly a month and a half, and have
lost anywhere between 17 to 30 per cent of their total weight. They
are in urgent need of food.

The female must renew her strength and vitality so that she can 8
return with food for her chick. Going to the sea, she takes the
shortest route to reach a polynya (open water surrounded by ice).

Penguins appear to be able to navigate by the reflection of the clouds on the water, using what has been called a "water sky."

9   The male penguin, who has also been fasting, is now left with the egg balanced on his feet. The first egg was laid on the first of May; a chick will emerge in August. Since the seasons are reversed south of the equator, full winter has arrived, with many violent blizzards and the lowest temperatures of the year. Emperor penguins are well adapted to the almost unimaginable cold of these 24-hour Antarctic nights: Their plumage is waterproof, windproof, flexible and renewed annually. They may not need tents, but as soon as the bad weather starts, generally in June, the males need some protection from the bitter cold, and nearly all of them find it by forming a *tortue*, which is a throng of very densely packed penguins. When the storms come they move in close to one another, shoulder to shoulder, and form a circle. The middle of the tortue is unusually warm and one would think that every penguin fights to be at the epicentre of warmth. But in fact what looks like an immobile mass is really a very slowly revolving spiral. The constantly shifting formation is such that every penguin, all the while balancing that single precious egg on his feet, eventually winds up in the middle of the tortue, only to find himself later at the periphery.

10   What early French explorers noticed during the two- to three-month incubation period is an almost preternatural calm among the males. This is no doubt necessitated by the long fast that is ahead of them. Many of them have already fasted, like the females, for two months or more, and must now face another two months of fasting. And moving about with an egg balanced on one's feet is difficult at the best of times.

11   The only time a father will abandon an egg is if he has reached the maximum limit of his physiological° ability to fast, and would die if he did not seek food. Not a small number of eggs are left for this reason, and it would seem that in each case the female is late in returning.

12   In July or August, after being gone for almost three months, the female emperor returns from the sea, singing as she penetrates various groups of birds, searching for her mate and her chick or egg. The males do not move, but make small peeping noises. When she finds her partner, she sings, she makes little dance steps, then she goes quiet and both birds can remain immobile for up to 10 minutes. Then they begin to move around one another. The female fixes her eyes on the incubatory pouch of her partner, while her excitement grows visibly. Finally, if it is the right bird, the male allows the egg to fall gently to the ice, whereupon the female takes it and then turns her back to the male, to whom, after a final duet, she becomes

completely indifferent. The male becomes increasingly irritated, stares at his empty pouch, pecks at it with his beak, lifts up his head, groans, and then pecks the female. She shows no further interest in him and eventually he leaves for the open sea, to break his long fast. The whole affair has lasted about 80 minutes. . . .

The miracle is that the mothers usually return on the day their 13 chicks hatch. How is it, one wonders, that the female emperor penguin is able to return just in time for the birth of her chick? As Alexander Skutch notes in his wonderful book, *The Minds of Birds*, it is improbable that she has consciously counted the 63 days or whatever the exact number is between the laying of her egg and the hatching of her chick. "Some subconscious process, physiological or mental, was evidently summing the days to prompt the birds to start homeward when the proper number had elapsed."

If the egg has hatched before her arrival and the male already 14 has a chick between his legs, the female is even more excited to hear it peep, and quickly removes it from the male. She immediately regurgitates food to the chick. If she is late in coming, the male, in spite of his near starvation, has a final resource: He regurgitates into the beak of his peeping newborn a substance known as penguin milk, similar to pigeon's milk, or crop milk, which is secreted from the lining of his esophagus. The secretion is remarkably rich, containing essential amino acids, much like the milk of marine mammals such as seals and whales. These feedings allow the young birds to survive for up to two weeks after hatching. Many of these males have now fasted for four and a half months, and have lost up to half of their body weight. It is a sight to see the well-nourished, sleek, brilliantly feathered, healthy-looking females arrive, and the emaciated°, dirty, tired males leave.

How difficult it is for us to understand the emotions involved 15 in these events. Yet it is hard to resist the anthropomorphic urge. Obviously the male emperor is aware of the loss of what has, after all, been almost a part of his body for two to three months. Is he disappointed, bewildered, relieved, or are his feelings so remote from our own (not inferior, mind you, just different) that we cannot imagine them? We would groan, too, under such circumstances, but the meaning of a penguin's groan is still opaque° to us. Yet we, too, are fathers and mothers with babies to protect and comfort, negotiating meals and absences and other obligations, just like our Antarctic cousins. Sometimes, when we are overwhelmed by an emotion, we are hard-pressed to express ourselves. If penguin fathers could speak about this moment in their lives, perhaps they would be at a similar loss for words. Perhaps the songs and groans of the male penguin are all the expression they need.

Words and Meanings

11 physiological — having to do with the physical functioning of a living creature

14 emaciated — thin, starved

15 opaque — not transparent; difficult to figure out

Structure and Strategy

1. What kind of attention-getter does Masson use in the INTRODUC-TION (paragraphs 1 and 2)?
2. What is Masson's THESIS? Is it implied or stated in the essay?
3. Which paragraphs are developed primarily by means of numerical facts and statistics? Why is this a useful strategy for explaining the KEY IDEAS of these paragraphs? Are there any factual details the essay doesn't provide that you would have been interested to learn about?
4. How is the key idea of paragraph 13 developed?
5. The DICTION of this essay combines scientific terms with words and phrases more commonly associated with human emotion, such as "happy couple" in paragraph 6 and "increasingly irritated" in paragraph 12. Find other examples of diction that Masson uses to support the ANALOGY he draws between penguins and humans. Why do you think he uses the penguin–human analogy to develop his process analysis? Do you find this analogy interesting or off-putting? Why?

Content and Purpose

1. In two or three sentences, summarize Masson's PURPOSE in this essay.
2. In this analysis of the emperor penguins' reproductive cycle, which parts of the process are described in paragraphs 3 to 8, 9 through 11, and 12 through 14?
3. How do emperor penguins mate? What physical characteristic makes it possible for the male to "experience pregnancy as an intimate matter" (paragraph 2)?
4. Why do the female penguins temporarily abandon their eggs and mates? What happens when the females return?

5. What kind of "male bonding" takes place among the males during the females' absence? What purpose is served by the *tortue*?
6. Identify three reproductive behaviours that penguins have in common with humans. Identify three behaviours that are significantly different.
7. What is the mystery at the core of the essay's CONCLUSION (paragraph 15)? What do you think is the source of "the songs and groans of the male penguin"?
8. What is the author's attitude toward the creatures he writes about? Identify three or four examples to support your opinion.
9. From an evolutionary perspective, how is the emperor penguin's mating and chick-rearing process adaptive? (See Helena Cronin's "The Evolution of Evolution," on page 191, for an explanation of this concept.)

Suggestions for Writing

1. Write an essay about the role of a father in his child's life. What are the essential tasks of fatherhood?
2. Write an essay about being a caregiver. Describe a situation in which you have cared for someone on an ongoing basis. What does this narrative reveal about you, the caregiver?
3. When people attribute human characteristics and feelings to gods, animals, or things, they are engaging in *anthropomorphism*. Write an essay that provides one or more examples of anthropomorphism. Why do you suppose people anthropomorphize? Are there any dangers in attributing human feelings to animal behaviours? If so, what are they?

A Tree-Planting Primer

DANNY IRVINE

Danny Irvine was born in southern Ontario in 1980, and graduated with a degree in English and Theatre from Redeemer University College, in Ancaster, Ontario, in 2004. He abandoned tree planting after university and moved to Asia, living first in Taiwan and now in Japan, where he teaches English. Irvine's "Primer" won third prize in the 2002 Conference on Christianity and Literature Non-Fiction Contest.

INTRODUCTION

1   Welcome to the wonderful world of tree planting. You are about to embark on an adventure of awesome proportions, fending for yourself in the coniferous° Klondike—the very heartland of Canada. Are you intimidated? Don't be. You can rest assured that any stories you may have heard about the gruelling savagery of the tree-planting experience, about inhospitable landscapes, maimed bodies, and inhuman exhaustion are wild exaggerations, nothing more than hallucinations of former planters who are suffering the residual effects of some obscure psychological trauma.

2   The wilderness is a nurturing, healing place, and it is well known that physical labour can be a contemplative, therapeutic activity. You can see its effects in the euphoria° of the planters at the end of the season. Nevertheless, you may still be a little apprehensive about the planting contract and may feel somewhat alien in your new environment, so far away from the familiar comfort of the city, with its paved roads and snowless summers, its docile elements and herbivorous° wildlife. We encourage you to think of the North as your "home away from home": the trees and rocks your walls and floors, the darkening clouds your vaulted ceiling, the bears and wolves your friendly neighbours. What's more, you have this primer, which is designed to help you to survive and to profit from your silvicultural° experience.

EQUIPMENT

3   By this time, you will have been given your tree-planting equipment. Your planting bags—three pouches of high-tensile nylon, suspended from a padded, ergonomic belt and adjustable shoulder straps—are the first order of business. You will wear this set of bags all day, every day, for the duration of the contract. They will be your uniform, the armour of the noble tree planter; they will adorn and distinguish you; they will soak up your sweat and bear your scent. Think of them as indispensable articles of clothing, a sort of "second underwear," which you put on as soon as you awake and without which you never leave home. Do not get caught without your planting bags. Since this second underwear will be weighted with more than 20 kg of trees, you will want to adjust the belt and shoulder straps to the position most closely approximating comfort. Ignore any uncomfortable chafing you may experience; this abrasion will soon become too familiar to be troublesome.

4   The second piece of equipment: your shovel. Hold it in your hand. Grip it. Swing it. Can you feel the earth part before you? No? Swing it again. Hit something with it. This is no ordinary shovel;

this is your livelihood. This is your weapon. This steel-spaded, wood-shafted, D-handled shovel is the instrument with which you will split the earth and subdue the forests. It will be your trusty machete when you encounter obstructive branches and brush. It will be your means of carving yourself bathroom facilities when you are miles from civilization. It will be your sure defence in the event of an encounter with squirrels, raccoons, or small, sickly black bears. For these reasons, it is important that you respect your shovel. Never let it out of your sight. Take care of it. Name it. Talk to it. It will be your best and only friend in the long days of solitude out on the clear cut. At first, your shovel may feel awkward and heavy, but after several weeks of continuously gripping it, you will feel as if it were a fifth limb. You and your shovel will form such a bond that you will find it almost unbearably painful to unclench your grip at night.

GETTING STARTED

Once you have familiarized yourself with your equipment, you are ready to plant. To begin, put your planting bags around your waist. If the belt slips, readjust it. If it continues to slip, duct-tape the straps together. If even duct tape fails to maintain a fit, the problem is probably faulty belt buckles. Find a fellow planter with undamaged bags and inconspicuously swap your bag for hers. Write your name on your new bag with a waterproof magic-marker and avoid that planter for a few days.   5

Next, decide how many trees you are willing to carry in one trip, and load up your bags. This is not a casual decision. On the one hand, since you are being paid per tree, there is financial reward in carrying as many trees as you can squeeze into your bags. On the other hand, a heavy load will weigh and slow you down. You will tire quickly, and you will not be able to stop for a rest until your bags are fully unloaded. What's that? You don't plan on taking any breaks? That's the attitude! Heavy or light: you must find a middle road. Forestry is, after all, fundamentally a matter of balance: harvesting lumber without decimating° the sustainable forests, planting new growth without destabilizing the ecosystem, working harder than a machine without destroying your body, keeping the bugs away without developing cancer from insect repellent.   6

Once you have packed up your trees, scan the area and pick up any trees you may have inadvertently dropped. The forestry company has paid a good deal of money for these trees, and you will find that they become a little testy if they discover any lying on the ground. Throw any fallen trees into your bag, or, alternatively, onto the ground where another planter has been working.   7

8   Packing up your trees, or "bagging up," as you will become conditioned to call it, can, admittedly, be a time-consuming procedure. Having to sit in one place to perform it can be particularly irritating if it happens to be raining or snowing; if it happens to be in the frigid early months or the scorching later months of the season; or if the blackflies, mosquitoes, horseflies, or deerflies happen to be out. But never mind. Having packed up your bags, knowing precisely how many trees you are carrying, you are ready to go. What? You didn't keep track of how many you put in? Well, you'd better take them all out and count again.

9   Once you have confirmed your count, take your shovel in your right or left hand, whichever is the stronger. This will be your "shovel hand"; your weaker hand will be your "bag hand." Your bag hand is the hand that will pick up and plant each tree; that is why you have put the trees into the pouch on that same side. What? You didn't know this, and put the trees into the pouch on the side of your stronger hand? Well, you'd better take them all out and start again.

10   Your bags strapped and loaded, your shovel firmly gripped, you are at long last ready to plant your first tree. Make your way to the piece of land, "the block," that has been allotted to you. The block may be a short, convenient distance from your tree depot. More often, however, you will have a long hike to get to the entrance to your land. You may be compensated if this travel time is unusually lengthy or particularly gruelling. But don't count on it. Your employer is more likely to consider this trek an opportunity for you to explore the untamed wilderness and reflect on your contribution to the development of our country's sustainable resources.

PLANTING A TREE

11   Planting a tree is an art that requires control and precision and, for many individuals, takes years to learn. In Japan, for instance, bonsai-tree planters are chosen while they are still infants and taken to mountain pagodas, where they spend their youth in rigorous training under the tutelage of revered masters. Each day they spend hours in the forest, learning respect for the trees; they participate in disciplined physical exercises, developing scrupulous control of their bodies; and only after seven years of barehanded labour in the stony Japanese soil are they permitted to handle a shovel.

12   You, on the other hand, have the good fortune to live in a much less demanding culture. With this guide to help you, you can easily learn to plant a tree without years of arduous training. To be a successful tree planter, you need to learn two things. First, you must

understand and accept the essential, organic, and spiritual union of body and land—a dynamic, beautiful marriage of arms, legs, back, and shovel with tree and soil. Second, you must learn to harness and relentlessly exploit this union for your own purposes.

Begin by retrieving a tree from your bag with (you guessed it) your bag hand. At the same time, step forward with the corresponding leg, pinpoint the spot where you wish to plant a tree, and, with your shovel hand, raise your shovel.   13

This is probably a good point at which to discuss generating and maintaining motivation and morale while out on the clear cut. As everyone knows, a certain degree of mental fortitude is helpful when you are repeatedly performing even the simplest of tasks. The oppressive, dark, and forbidding clouds that perpetually crowd the skies this far north may already have suggested to you that not every planting day will be a sunny outing in the woods. Some planters have even experienced moments of mild discouragement at their work.   14

If ever you should feel a twinge of despair over your ability to fulfill the planting contract, to meet the quota of trees that you have set as a standard for yourself; if ever you are worried that you will not earn enough money to pay off your student debts and will have to sell the family heirlooms to pay your tuition; if you have been planting in a swamp for three weeks and have not spoken to another soul for days; if you notice the extremities of your body turning numb from the cold, from insect bites, or from the pesticides on the trees; if the zipper on your tent has torn and your boots have holes in them and your leg is broken and infected and your girlfriend or boyfriend has stopped writing letters and your mother has forgotten about you and rented out your room to a new son or daughter and you are on the verge of impaling yourself on your own planting shovel, do not be dismayed. Stop. Look about you at the miles of muddied and overturned land, at the endless expanse of barren clear cut, at the infinitely distant and uncompromising sky, and reflect on your relative insignificance. Remember that compared to the immensity and mysterious purposefulness of the universe, your life and worries are inconsequential. Then, your mind cleared and reinvigorated, take a deep breath, and get back to work.   15

So, with your shovel aloft in your shovel hand, and with a tree in your tree hand, take a second step forward—this time with your other leg, the one that corresponds to your shovel hand. Bring down your shovel with a swift, heavy stroke, stabbing the blade into the earth as deeply as possible. If your shovel doesn't penetrate the surface, it is likely that you have struck a rock or some sort of impervious sun-fired clay. Nevertheless, you must plant a tree as close to   16 this spot as you can. Move to the next nearest planting spot. If the soil in this location visibly leeches water when you step on it, it is too wet and will drown your tree. Move to the next closest location. If this one is within two metres of a tree that has somehow miraculously survived the clear-cutting, bulldozing, and chemical spraying that has otherwise sterilized the land, keep moving. Eventually, you will find a patch of acceptable soil, a sufficiently rotten stump, or a sizable pile of bear droppings in which to plant your tree.

17   With your shovel plunged in the earth, take the third and final step, again with the leg that corresponds to your bag hand. Twist the D-handle of your shovel away from you in a wide outward arc, laying open a hole in the ground, and, with the tree still in your bag hand, bend down over your shovel. Poke the roots of the tree into the freshly dug hole and hold the seedling in place while pulling your shovel from the soil. As you straighten your back, slide your fingers up the length of the tree until they gently grip the tip. Remember, the needles of the trees are laced with pesticides, so avoid pricking your fingers. Once you are upright, close the hole by lightly stomping on the ground immediately beside the tree. Finally, give the seedling a small tug to ensure that it is snug in the soil.

18   Congratulations! You have planted your first tree. Know that you are following in a great human tradition, one that began when agricultural man first informed the flora and fauna° of the world that he knew better than they did how and where they should grow. Since then, humankind has been proudly asserting its place in the natural world and now you, too, are a part of this noble history. Your father and mother are every farmer who ever pressed a seed into the soil, every gardener who ever ripped a weed from its bed, every farm hand who ever forced a bit into a horse's mouth.

19   All that stands between you and fortune are three easy steps, a swift bend, and a few fluid motions with your shovel—repeated three or four thousand times a day. You have planted your standard. Eventually, one tree at a time, you will own the North.

20   Unless, of course, your tree is not within the two- or three-millimetre margin of depth; unless it is leaning; unless it is crooked, or its roots are not straight; unless it is less or more than the permitted distance from any other tree, natural or planted; unless the tree is unhealthy, diseased, smothered by loose dirt or missing its tip; or if, as you filled the hole, it got stepped on, or . . .

Words and Meanings

coniferous	relating to cone-bearing evergreen trees	1
euphoria	a feeling of extreme happiness, ecstasy	2
herbivorous	plant-eating	
silvicultural	adjective form of *silviculture,* the branch of forestry dealing with the growing and cultivation of trees	
decimating	destroying	6
flora and fauna	plant and animal life	18

Structure and Strategy

1. What is a "primer"? Is this essay a good example of a primer? Why or why not?
2. List, in order, the steps in planting a tree.
3. Identify at least three places in the essay that make it clear the author is addressing a specific listener. Who is this imagined listener? Do you think that this person is the actual AUDIENCE for the essay? If not, what audience did Irvine really have in mind when he wrote "A Tree-Planting Primer"?
4. Consider the DICTION of the essay. The author frequently uses sophisticated vocabulary in long sentences. (See, for example, paragraph 2: "docile elements . . . herbivorous wildlife . . . vaulted ceiling . . . silvicultural experience.") What is the effect of the contrast between the stated topic—a simple process—and the formal, complex style in which the topic is explained?
5. The first sentence in paragraph 15 is a monster run-on that goes on for many lines. The author stops punctuating the clauses about two-thirds of the way through the sentence. How does the structure of the sentence reflect its meaning?
6. Consider the last two paragraphs of this essay. Identify Irvine's SUMMARY of his KEY IDEAS. In the final paragraph, he presents no real CONCLUSION; the last sentence just trails off into silence. Why? Is this ending effective? Why or why not?
7. How does the TONE of the essay communicate Irvine's attitude toward tree planting and the companies that sponsor it? (See especially paragraphs 6, 16, and 18.)

Content and Purpose

1. Is this essay a directional process analysis? In other words, does Irvine set out to teach readers how to succeed as tree planters? If not, what is his real PURPOSE? (See IRONY.)

2. What are the two required pieces of tree-planting equipment? According to the author, how should a tree planter regard this equipment?

3. Paragraphs 11 and 12 are based on a contrast between two cultures. What are the two cultures, and what are the differences between them? What is the point of this contrast? Is Irvine serious about the point he makes here?

4. After thirteen paragraphs of instruction that bring us to the point of actually planting a tree, the author suddenly breaks off and begins discussing how to maintain "motivation and morale while out on the clear cut." Why? What are the effects of this digression?

5. In one or two sentences, summarize the message that Irvine communicates to the intended (not the pretend) AUDIENCE in this essay.

Suggestions for Writing

1. Write a directional process analysis about an outdoor task that you know well, such as fishing, camping, skiing, gardening, or jogging. Use the second-person POINT OF VIEW, as Irvine does in his essay.

2. Write a directional process analysis that is ostensibly about a particular job or task, but use the ironic tone that Irvine and Mitford ("Behind the Formaldehyde Curtain") use in their essays. In other words, tell someone how to do something that you really think they shouldn't be doing.

Behind the Formaldehyde° Curtain

JESSICA MITFORD

Essayist Jessica Mitford (1917–1996) was born to a prominent family at Batsford Mansion, England, and settled in the United States in 1939. Mitford began her writing career in the 1950s. Among her best-known works are *Hons and Rebels*, *The Trial of Dr. Spock*, and *The American Way of Death*.

1   The drama begins to unfold with the arrival of the corpse at the mortuary.

Alas, poor Yorick°! How surprised he would be to see how his 2
counterpart of today is whisked off to a funeral parlor and is in short
order sprayed, sliced, pierced, pickled, trussed, trimmed, creamed,
waxed, painted, rouged and neatly dressed—transformed from a
common corpse into a Beautiful Memory Picture. This process is
known in the trade as embalming and restorative art, and is so universally employed in the United States and Canada that the funeral
director does it routinely, without consulting corpse or kin. He
regards as eccentric those few who are hardy enough to suggest that it
might be dispensed with. Yet no law requires embalming, no religious
doctrine commends it, nor is it dictated by considerations of health,
sanitation, or even of personal daintiness. In no part of the world but
North America is it widely used. The purpose of embalming is to
make the corpse presentable for viewing in a suitably costly container;
and here too the funeral director routinely, without first consulting the
family, prepares the body for public display.

Is all this legal? The processes to which a dead body may be 3
subjected are after all to some extent circumscribed by law. In most
states, for instance, the signature of next of kin must be obtained
before an autopsy may be performed, before the deceased may be
cremated, before the body may be turned over to a medical school
for research purposes; or such provision must be made in the dece-
dent's° will. In the case of embalming, no such permission is
required nor is it ever sought. A textbook, *The Principles and
Practices of Embalming*, comments on this: "There is some question
regarding the legality of much that is done within the preparation
room." The author points out that it would be most unusual for a
responsible member of a bereaved family to instruct the mortician,
in so many words, to "*embalm*" the body of a deceased relative. The
very term "embalming" is so seldom used that the mortician must
rely upon custom in the matter. The author concludes that unless
the family specifies otherwise, the act of entrusting the body to the
care of a funeral establishment carries with it an implied permission to go ahead and embalm.

Embalming is indeed a most extraordinary procedure, and one 4
must wonder at the docility° of Americans who each year pay hundreds of millions of dollars for its perpetuation, blissfully ignorant
of what it is all about, what is done, how it is done. Not one in ten
thousand has any idea of what actually takes place. Books on the
subject are extremely hard to come by. They are not to be found in
most libraries or bookshops.

In an era when huge television audiences watch surgical opera- 5
tions in the comfort of their living rooms, when, thanks to the animated cartoon, the geography of the digestive system has become

familiar territory even to the nursery school set, in a land where the satisfaction of curiosity about almost all matters is a national pastime, the secrecy surrounding embalming can, surely, hardly be attributed to the inherent gruesomeness of the subject. Custom in this regard has within this century suffered a complete reversal. In the early days of American embalming, when it was performed in the home of the deceased, it was almost mandatory° for some relative to stay by the embalmer's side and witness the procedure. Today, family members who might wish to be in attendance would certainly be dissuaded° by the funeral director. All others, except apprentices, are excluded by law from the preparation room.

6   A close look at what does actually take place may explain in large measure the undertaker's intractable reticence° concerning a procedure that has become his major *raison d'être*°. Is it possible he fears that public information about embalming might lead patrons to wonder if they really want this service? If the funeral men are loath to discuss the subject outside the trade, the reader may, understandably, be equally loath to go on reading at this point. For those who have the stomach for it, let us part the formaldehyde curtain. . . .

7   The body is first laid out in the undertaker's morgue—or rather, Mr. Jones is reposing in the preparation room—to be readied to bid the world farewell.

8   The preparation room in any of the better funeral establishments has the tiled and sterile look of a surgery, and indeed the embalmer-restorative artist who does his chores there is beginning to adopt the term "dermasurgeon" (appropriately corrupted by some mortician-writers as "demi-surgeon") to describe his calling. His equipment, consisting of scalpels, scissors, augers, forceps, clamps, needles, pumps, tubes, bowls and basins, is crudely imitative of the surgeon's, as is his technique, acquired in a nine- or twelve-month post-high-school course in an embalming school. He is supplied by an advanced chemical industry with a bewildering array of fluids, sprays, pastes, oils, powders, creams, to fix or soften tissue, shrink or distend it as needed, dry it here, restore the moisture there. There are cosmetics, waxes and paints to fill and cover features, even plaster of Paris to replace entire limbs. There are ingenious aids to prop and stabilize the cadaver: a Vari-Pose Head Rest, the Edwards Arm and Hand Positioner, the Repose Block (to support the shoulders during the embalming), and the Throop Foot Positioner, which resembles an old-fashioned stocks°.

9   Mr. John H. Eckels, president of the Eckels College of Mortuary Science, thus describes the first part of the embalming procedure: "In the hands of a skilled practitioner, this work may be done in a comparatively short time and without mutilating the body other

than by slight incision—so slight that it scarcely would cause serious inconvenience if made upon a living person. It is necessary to remove the blood, and doing this not only helps in the disinfecting, but removes the principal cause of disfigurements due to discoloration."

Another textbook discusses the all-important time element: "The earlier this is done, the better, for every hour that elapses between death and embalming will add to the problems and complications encountered. . . ." Just how soon should one get going on the embalming? The author tells us, "On the basis of such scanty information made available to this profession through its rudimentary and haphazard system of technical research, we must conclude that the best results are to be obtained if the subject is embalmed before life is completely extinct—that is, before cellular death has occurred. In the average case, this would mean within an hour after somatic° death." For those who feel that there is something a little rudimentary°, not to say haphazard, about his advice, a comforting thought is offered by another writer. Speaking of fears entertained in early days of premature burial, he points out, "One of the effects of embalming by chemical injection, however, has been to dispel fears of live burial." How true; once the blood is removed, chances of live burial are indeed remote.

To return to Mr. Jones, the blood is drained out through the veins and replaced by embalming fluid pumped in through the arteries. As noted in *The Principles and Practices of Embalming,* "every operator has a favorite injection and drainage point—a fact which becomes a handicap only if he fails or refuses to forsake his favorites when conditions demand it." Typical favorites are the carotid artery, femoral artery, jugular vein, subclavian vein. There are various choices of embalming fluid. If Flextone is used, it will produce "mild, flexible rigidity. The skin retains a velvety softness, the tissues are rubbery and pliable. Ideal for women and children." It may be blended with B. and G. Products Company's Lyf-Lyk tint, which is guaranteed to reproduce "nature's own skin texture . . . the velvety appearance of living tissue." Suntone comes in three separate tints: Suntan; Special Cosmetic Tint, a pink shade "especially indicated for young female subjects"; and Regular Cosmetic Tint, moderately pink.

About three to six gallons of a dyed and perfumed solution of formaldehyde, glycerin, borax, phenol, alcohol and water is soon circulating through Mr. Jones, whose mouth has been sewn together with a "needle directed upward between the upper lip and gum and brought out through the left nostril," with the corners raised slightly "for a more pleasant expression." If he should be buck-toothed, his teeth are cleaned with Bon Ami and coated with colorless nail polish. His eyes, meanwhile, are closed with flesh-tinted eye caps and eye cement.

13   The next step is to have at Mr. Jones with a thing called a trocar. This is a long, hollow needle attached to a tube. It is jabbed into the abdomen, poked around the entrails and chest cavity, the contents of which are pumped out and replaced with "cavity fluid." This done, and the hole in the abdomen sewn up, Mr. Jones's face is heavily creamed (to protect the skin from burns which may be caused by leakage of the chemicals), and he is covered with a sheet and left unmolested for a while. But not for long—there is more, much more, in store for him. He has been embalmed, but not yet restored, and the best time to start the restorative work is eight to ten hours after embalming, when the tissues have become firm and dry.

14   The object of all this attention to the corpse, it must be remembered, is to make it presentable for viewing in an attitude of healthy repose. "Our customs require the presentation of our dead in the semblance of normality . . . unmarred by the ravages of illness, disease or mutilation," says Mr. J. Sheridan Mayer in his *Restorative Art*. This is rather a large order since few people die in the full bloom of health, unravaged by illness and unmarked by some disfigurement. The funeral industry is equal to the challenge: "In some cases the gruesome appearance of a mutilated or disease-ridden subject may be quite discouraging. The task of restoration may seem impossible and shake the confidence of the embalmer. This is the time for intestinal fortitude° and determination. Once the formative work is begun and affected tissues are cleaned or removed, all doubts of success vanish. It is surprising and gratifying to discover the results which may be obtained."

15   The embalmer, having allowed an appropriate interval to elapse, returns to the attack, but now he brings into play the skill and equipment of sculptor and cosmetician. Is a hand missing? Casting one in plaster of Paris is a simple matter. "For replacement purposes, only a cast of the back of the hand is necessary; this is within the ability of the average operator and is quite adequate." If a lip or two, a nose or an ear should be missing, the embalmer has at hand a variety of restorative waxes with which to model replacements. Pores and skin texture are simulated by stippling with a little brush, and over this cosmetics are laid on. Head off? Decapitation cases are rather routinely handled. Ragged edges are trimmed, and head joined to torso with a series of splints, wires and sutures. It is a good idea to have a little something at the neck—a scarf or a high collar—when time for viewing comes.

Swollen mouth? Cut out tissue as needed from inside the lips. If too much is removed, the surface contour can easily be restored by padding with cotton. Swollen necks and cheeks are reduced by removing tissue through vertical incisions made down each side of the neck. "When the deceased is casketed, the pillow will hide the suture incisions . . . as an extra precaution against leakage, the suture may be painted with liquid sealer."

The opposite condition is more likely to present itself—that of 16 emaciation. His hypodermic syringe now loaded with massage cream, the embalmer seeks out and fills the hollowed and sunken areas by injection. In this procedure the backs of the hands and fingers and the under-chin area should not be neglected.

Positioning the lips is a problem that recurrently challenges the 17 ingenuity of the embalmer. Closed too tightly, they tend to give a stern, even disapproving expression. Ideally, embalmers feel, the lips should give the impression of being ever so slightly parted, the upper lip protruding slightly for a more youthful appearance. This takes some engineering, however, as the lips tend to drift apart. Lip drift can sometimes be remedied by pushing one or two straight pins through the inner margin of the lower lip and then inserting them between the two front upper teeth. If Mr. Jones happens to have no teeth, the pins can just as easily be anchored in his Armstrong Face Former and Denture Replacer. Another method to maintain lip closure is to dislocate the lower jaw, which is then held in its new position by a wire run through holes which have been drilled through the upper and lower jaws at the midline. As the French are fond of saying, *il faut souffrir pour être belle°*.

If Mr. Jones has died of jaundice, the embalming fluid will very 18 likely turn him green. Does this deter the embalmer? Not if he has intestinal fortitude. Masking pastes and cosmetics are heavily laid on, burial garments and casket interiors are color-correlated with particular care, and Jones is displayed beneath rose-colored lights. Friends will say "How *well* he looks." Death by carbon monoxide, on the other hand, can be rather a good thing from the embalmer's viewpoint: "One advantage is the fact that this type of discoloration is an exaggerated form of a natural pink coloration." This is nice because the healthy glow is already present and needs but little attention.

The patching and filling completed, Mr. Jones is now shaved, 19 washed and dressed. Cream-based cosmetic, available in pink, flesh, suntan, brunette and blond, is applied to his hands and face, his hair is shampooed and combed (and, in the case of Mrs. Jones, set), his hands manicured. For the horny-handed son of toil° special care must be taken; cream should be applied to remove ingrained grime, and the nails cleaned. "If he were not in the habit of having them manicured in life, trimming and shaping is advised for better appearance—never questioned by kin."

20   Jones is now ready for casketing (this is the present participle of the verb "to casket"). In this operation his right shoulder should be depressed slightly "to turn the body a bit to the right and soften the appearance of lying flat on the back." Positioning the hands is a matter of importance, and special rubber positioning blocks may be used. The hands should be cupped slightly for a more lifelike, relaxed appearance. Proper placement of the body requires a delicate sense of balance. It should lie as high as possible in the casket, yet not so high that the lid, when lowered, will hit the nose. On the other hand, we are cautioned, placing the body too low "creates the impression that the body is in a box."

21   Jones is next wheeled into the appointed slumber room where a few last touches may be added—his favorite pipe placed in his hand or, if he was a great reader, a book propped into position. (In the case of little Master Jones a Teddy bear may be clutched.) Here he will hold open house for a few days, visiting hours 10 a.m. to 9 p.m.

22   All now being in readiness, the funeral director calls a staff conference to make sure that each assistant knows his precise duties. Mr. Wilber Kriege writes: "This makes your staff feel that they are a part of the team, with a definite assignment that must be properly carried out if the whole plan is to succeed. You never heard of a football coach who failed to talk to his entire team before they go on the field. They have drilled on the plays they are to execute for hours and days, and yet the successful coach knows the importance of making even the bench-warming third-string substitute feel that he is important if the game is to be won." The winning of *this* game is predicated upon glass-smooth handling of the logistics°. The funeral director has notified the pallbearers whose names were furnished by the family, has arranged for the presence of clergyman, organist, and soloist, has provided transportation for everybody, has organized and listed the flowers sent by friends. In *Psychology of Funeral Service* Mr. Edward A. Martin points out: "He may not always do as much as the family thinks he is doing, but it is his helpful guidance that they appreciate in knowing they are proceeding as they should. . . . The important thing is how well his services can be used to make the family believe they are giving unlimited expression to their own sentiment."

23   The religious service may be held in a church or in the chapel of the funeral home; the funeral director vastly prefers the latter arrangement, for not only is it more convenient for him but it affords him the opportunity to show off his beautiful facilities to the gathered mourners. After the clergyman has had his say, the mourners

queue up to file past the casket for a last look at the deceased. The family is *never* asked whether they want an open-casket ceremony; in the absence of their instruction to the contrary, this is taken for granted. Consequently well over 90 per cent of all American funerals feature the open casket—a custom unknown in other parts of the world. Foreigners are astonished by it. An English woman living in San Francisco described her reaction in a letter to the writer:

> I myself have attended only one funeral here—that of an elderly fellow worker of mine. After the service I could not understand why everyone was walking towards the coffin (sorry, I mean casket), but thought I had better follow the crowd. It shook me rigid to get there and find the casket open and poor old Oscar lying there in his brown tweed suit, wearing a suntan makeup and just the wrong shade of lipstick. If I had not been extremely fond of the old boy, I have a horrible feeling that I might have giggled. Then and there I decided that I could never face another American funeral—even dead.

The casket (which has been resting throughout the service on a 24
Classic Beauty Ultra Metal Casket Bier) is now transferred by a hydraulically operated device called Porto-Lift to a balloon-tired, Glide Easy casket carriage which will wheel it to yet another conveyance, the Cadillac Funeral Coach. This may be lavender, cream, light green—anything but black. Interiors, of course, are color-correlated, "for the man who cannot stop short of perfection."

At graveside, the casket is lowered into the earth. This office, 25
once the prerogative° of friends of the deceased, is now performed by a patented mechanical lowering device. A "Lifetime Green" artificial grass mat is at the ready to conceal the sere° earth, and overhead, to conceal the sky, is a portable Steril Chapel Tent ("resists the intense heat and humidity of summer and the terrific storms of winter . . . available in Silver Grey, Rose or Evergreen"). Now is the time for the ritual scattering of earth over the coffin, as the solemn words "earth to earth, ashes to ashes, dust to dust" are pronounced by the officiating cleric. This can today be accomplished "with a mere flick of the wrist with the Gordon Leak-Proof Earth Dispenser. No grasping of a handful of dirt, no soiled fingers. Simple, dignified, beautiful, reverent! The modern way!" The Gordon Earth Dispenser (at $45) is of nickel-plated brass construction. It is not only "attractive to the eye and long wearing"; it is also "one of the 'tools' for building better public relations" if presented as "an appropriate non-commercial gift" to the clergyman. It is shaped something like a saltshaker.

26   Untouched by human hand, the coffin and the earth are now united.

27   It is in the function of directing the participants through this maze of gadgetry that the funeral director has assigned to himself his relatively new role of "grief therapist." He has relieved the family of every detail, he has revamped° the corpse to look like a living doll, he has arranged for it to nap for a few days in a slumber room, he has put on a well-oiled performance in which the concept of *death* has played no part whatsoever—unless it was inconsiderately mentioned by the clergyman who conducted the religious service. He has done everything in his power to make the funeral a real pleasure for everybody concerned. He and his team have given their all to score an upset victory over death.

Words and Meanings

Title	formaldehyde	chemical used to embalm bodies
Paragraph 2	Alas, poor Yorick	famous line from Shakespeare's *Hamlet*, addressed to a skull
3	decedent	dead person
4	docility	lamblike trust and willingness
5	mandatory	necessary
	dissuaded	persuaded against
6	intractable reticence	stubborn unwillingness to discuss
	raison d'être	reason for existing [French]
8	stocks	wooden shackles used to punish offenders
10	somatic	bodily
	rudimentary	basic
14	intestinal fortitude	"guts," courage
17	*il faut souffrir pour être belle*	you have to suffer to be beautiful [French]
19	horny-handed son of toil	cliché for a labourer
22	logistics	complex arrangements
25	prerogative	privilege
	sere	dry
27	revamped	altered

Structure and Strategy

1. Consider the title and first paragraph of this essay. What ANALOGY is introduced? How does the analogy help establish Mitford's TONE?
2. Look at the last paragraph. How is the analogy introduced in paragraph 1 reinforced in the CONCLUSION? What words specifically contribute to the analogy?
3. The process of preparing a corpse for burial involves two main procedures: embalming and restoration. Identify the paragraphs in which Mitford explains these two procedures.
4. Identify the substeps that make up the final stage In the burial process (paragraphs 20 through 25).

Content and Purpose

1. In paragraphs 2 and 8, without saying so directly, how does Mitford imply that she disapproves of embalming? Can you find other examples of her implied disapproval?
2. What justification for embalming is offered in paragraph 10? How does Mitford undercut this argument?
3. Why does Mitford refer to the corpse as "Mr. Jones"?
4. What reason does Mitford suggest is behind the "secrecy surrounding embalming"? If the details of the procedure were common knowledge, what do you think the effect would be on the mortuary business?
5. What was your reaction to Mitford's essay? Do you think your response was what the author intended?

Suggestions for Writing

1. Mitford's essay explains the funeral director's job as a process. Write an informational process analysis explaining a task or procedure with which you are familiar.
2. Research another means of disposing of the dead, such as cremation (burning a dead body) or cryonics (freezing a dead, diseased body in the hope of restoring it to life when a cure has been found). Write an informational process paper explaining it.
3. Research the relatively new field of "grief therapy," particularly the kind of industry that springs up in reaction to a public tragedy. Write an essay on the methods and effectiveness of "grief therapy."
4. Write an informational process analysis explaining the ceremony or ritual behaviour associated with the birth of a baby, a

child's birthday, or the initiation of a child into the religious community (such as a bar mitzvah or confirmation).

Additional Suggestions for Writing: Process Analysis

I. Choose one of the topics below and develop it into an informational process ANALYSIS.
1. How a cellphone (or any other electronic device) works
2. How an animal is born or hatched
3. How a particular rock group, sports personality, or political figure appeals to the crowd
4. How to save Canada's universal health-care system (medicare)
5. How a company plans the marketing of a new product
6. How alcohol (or any other drug) affects the body
7. How a star is born
8. How the Internet has changed dating
9. How a particular process in nature occurs—for example, how coral grows, a spider spins a web, salmon spawn, lightning happens, a snowflake forms, a specific crop is grown and harvested

II. Choose one of the topics below and develop it into a directional process analysis.
1. How to buy (or sell) something—for example, a used car, a home, a piece of sports equipment, a computer, or a work of art
2. How to get into a good college
3. How to play roulette, blackjack, poker, or some other game of chance
4. How to get your driver's licence
5. How to create a scrapbook, newsletter, or digital record commemorating an event, a person, or a family
6. How to use search engines effectively
7. How to make or build something—for example, wine, bread, a kite, or a radio transmitter
8. How to survive English (or any other subject that you are studying)
9. How to get your own way
10. How to talk your way out of a traffic ticket, a failing grade, a date, a conversation with a bore, a threatened punishment, or keeping a promise

UNIT 3

Classification and Division

WHAT ARE CLASSIFICATION AND DIVISION?

ANALYSIS is the process of separating something into its parts in order to understand the whole better. In Unit 2, we used the term "process analysis" to refer to a writing pattern in which a process (planting a tree, for example) is described in terms of the steps or stages involved in accomplishing it. All forms of analysis involve sorting or dividing—breaking a complex whole into its stages, parts, or categories in order to understand it better.

In the rhetorical pattern called *classification,* the writer sorts a group of things or people into classes or categories on the basis of some shared characteristic. For example, in "The World Is Phat," Martin Edlund classifies different kinds of hip-hop according to the countries in which they originated. Dennis Dermody, in "Sit Down and Shut Up or Don't Sit by Me," classifies moviegoers on the basis of their behaviour in the movie theatre.

In *division*, on the other hand, a single thing (not a group of things) is divided into its component parts. For example, the model essay "Listen Up" divides the skill of listening into its three separate parts. In "Toothpaste," David Bodanis breaks down the everyday substance of toothpaste into its constituent ingredients and surprises us with the odd stuff that we put into our mouths every morning.

WHY DO WE USE CLASSIFICATION AND DIVISION?

Classification and division answer the lead-in question *what.* (What are the different kinds? What are the various parts?) Classifying or dividing a topic organizes it into logically related units that a reader can understand. These two strategies are essential ways of making sense of the world around us.

A **classification essay** uses a sorting mechanism to examine a group of similar things that have meaningful differences among them. A **division essay** looks at a topic in terms of its constituent parts; it examines each part to discover its distinctive features and its function within the whole. Sometimes writers use both strategies. For example, in "What I Have Lived For," Bertrand Russell divides his life's purpose—his reason for living—into what he calls "three passions": the longing for love, the search for knowledge, and pity for the suffering of mankind. Then he classifies his search for knowledge into the three kinds of knowledge he sought: the social sciences, the natural sciences, and mathematics.

Besides giving form and focus to unorganized chunks of information, division and classification are useful for evaluation purposes. When a writer's purpose is to evaluate the relative merits of several items or ideas, classification and division can help to ensure a clear, coherent piece of communication.

HOW DO WE WRITE CLASSIFICATION AND DIVISION?

Here are three guidelines for writing a good classification paper:

1. Be sure that your classifying principle is logical and consistent. For example, Edlund classifies hip-hop music geographically. It wouldn't be logical, then, to include the artists' earnings as part of the classification.

2. Make sure that your categories do not overlap. Dennis Dermody's humorous classification of annoying moviegoers includes *latecomers, chatterers, krinklers,* and *popcorn people.* The addition of the category *talkers* would overlap with "the *chatterers* [who] comment blithely on everything that is happening on the screen" (108).

3. Include a clear thesis statement. For example: "The recent influx of three international styles—reggaeton from Puerto Rico, grime from Britain, and baile funk from Brazil—suggests that this situation may finally be changing" (Edlund, 114).

Here are three guidelines for writing a good division paper:

1. Identify the principle of division. Bertrand Russell's division essay, "What I Have Lived For," divides the complex idea of his reasons for living into three passions that have ruled his life.

2. Clearly explain the KEY IDEAS of your topic. In "The Dimensions of a Complete Life," Martin Luther King, Jr., develops his key ideas with numerous and varied kinds of support; in fact, he draws on *all* types of support in this selection.

3. Construct a clear division thesis statement. For example: "Active listening results from the interaction of three related components: questioning, paraphrasing, and empathizing." ("Listen Up", 105).

Classification and division are two of the most effective strategies you can use to explain a complex topic to your readers. The ability to analyze through classification and division is a valuable skill that every writer should acquire.

The model essay that follows divides the skill of *listening* into its component parts.

Listen Up

Introduction (a striking fact)

As surprising as it is to most of us, listening—not reading, not writing, not speaking—is the communication skill we use most frequently. Perhaps equally surprising is that listening is a skill that can be learned and improved. In other words, we can all become better, more effective listeners: *active* listeners, listeners who not only "hear" but also "understand."

Thesis statement

Active listening results from the interaction of three related components: questioning, paraphrasing, and empathizing.

First component of listening process (developed with an illustration)

One of the easiest ways to check whether you've "heard right" is to ask. By asking questions, you not only show interest, but also get additional details and clarification. For example, if your friend Cindy says she has to cancel the plans the two of you had made for Saturday night, you would be wise to ask why she is cancelling before you assume that she is angry with you.

Second component (supported by definition and one example)

Paraphrasing is another way to ensure that you "got it right." It is actually a form of feedback: restating in your own words in a summarized form what you think the speaker said. Perhaps Cindy cancelled by saying, "I've had a terrible week at work, and I don't think I'll be good company on Saturday. I'm really not in much of a mood to sit in a crowded theatre and watch a three-hour movie I haven't heard anything good about." It would be in both your and Cindy's best interests if you "checked" her message by paraphrasing it to make sure you understood her correctly; for example, "You're tired, so you don't feel up to the movie on Saturday. Would you like to get together for a movie or a game of tennis on Sunday?"

Third component (defines term and further develops the example)

Empathizing—putting yourself in the other person's shoes, so to speak—involves a sincere interest in the speaker and his or her perceptions. If you empathize with Cindy, you will respect her feelings although you may not necessarily agree with what she says. You may think that Cindy doesn't have a particularly exhausting job, and you may know that the movie you had planned to see got rave reviews. But what matters is that Cindy isn't feeling up to going out on Saturday night as the two of you had originally planned. Whether you share Cindy's perspective or not isn't the point. The point is to understand what Cindy is saying. Empathizing means listening to the story through the speaker's ears.

Conclusion (restates the thesis and asks a rhetorical question)

As you can see, in any conversation, questioning, paraphrasing, and empathizing are intertwined. It is not easy to separate them because they all stem from the same motive: a genuine concern for the speaker that inspires the listener to *want* to hear the message the way it was intended. Active listening improves not only your communication skills but also your ability to get along with the people around you. Are you listening?

Sit Down and Shut Up
or Don't Sit by Me

DENNIS DERMODY

Dennis Dermody lives in New York, where he is a film critic for *Paper Magazine*. He appeared as himself in a 2004 *Biography* television production about director John Waters.

A ll right, I admit it: I'm a tad neurotic when it comes to making it to the movies on time. I have to be there at least a half hour before the feature begins. Not that I'm worried about long lines at the box office, either. The movies I rush off to see are generally so sparsely attended you can hear crickets in the audience. It's just a thing I do.

Of course, sitting for 30 minutes watching a theater fill up is pretty boring, but through the years I've amused myself with a Margaret Mead°–like study of the way people come in and take their seats and their antics during a movie. I felt I should share my impressions lest you find yourself succumbing to these annoying traits.

Right off the bat: Leave the kids at home. We're not talking about *Aladdin* or *Home Alone 2*—that I understand—but recently I went to see *Body of Evidence*, and it looked like a day-care center in the theater. Strollers were flying down the aisle, children were whining for candy, restless and audibly bored (especially during the hot-wax-dripping sequence), and eventually the day-care atmosphere caused fights among the adults. "Shut your kid up!" prompted a proud parent to slug a fellow patron, and before you knew it there were angry skirmishes all over the theater and the police had to be brought in. So either leave them at home with a sitter or tie them up to a fire hydrant outside the theater.

For some people, choosing a seat takes on moral and philosophical implications. Sometimes they stand in the middle of the aisle juggling coats, popcorn, and Cokes, seemingly overwhelmed by the prospect of choice. Should I sit down front, or will that be too close? Is this too far back? That man seems awfully tall, I bet I couldn't see the movie if I sat behind him. I'd love to sit somewhere in the middle but would I be too close to that group of teenagers shooting heroin into their necks? If I sit on this side, will the angle be too weird to watch the movie? Is that seat unoccupied because it's broken? Good Lord, the lights are dimming and I haven't made up my mind and now I won't be able to see where I'm going.

5   Many, upon choosing their seats, find they are unsatisfied and have to move. I've watched many couples go from one spot to another more than a dozen times before settling down—it's like watching a bird testing different spots to build a nest.

6   As the lights begin to dim and the annoying theater-chain logo streaks across the screen, lo and behold, here come the *latecomers!* Their eyes unaccustomed to the dark, in a panic they search for friends, for assistance, for a lonely seat. Just the other day, I watched an elderly woman come into the darkened theater 10 minutes after the movie had begun and say out loud, "I can't see anything!" She then proceeded to inch her way down the aisle, grabbing onto what she thought were seats but were actually people's heads. I saw her sit down right in the lap of someone who shrieked in shock. After the woman stumbled back into the aisle, chattering wildly, someone mercifully directed her to an empty seat. Then, after a great flourish of getting out of her bulky coat, she asked spiritedly of the grumbling souls around her, "What did I miss?"

7   I also must address the behavior of people *during* the movie. The *chatterers* comment blithely on everything that is happening on the screen. Like Tourette's syndrome° sufferers unable to control what they blurt out, these people say anything that comes into their heads. "What a cute puppy," they say when they spy an animal ambling off to the side of the frame. "I have that lamp at home," they exclaim. And add, five minutes later, "But mine is red."

8   The *krinklers* wander down the aisle with a million shopping bags and wait for a key sequence, then begin to forage° in their bags for the perfect and most annoying plastic wrap, which they use to make noise with sadistic relish. You try to focus on the screen but the racket starts up again with a wild flourish. I've seen grown men leap to their feet with tears streaming down their face and scream, "Will you stop shaking that motherfucking bag!"

9   The *unending box of popcorn* people sit directly behind you and start masticating during the opening credits. It's bad enough having the smell of cooked corn wafting around you, but the sound is enough to drive you mad. You tell yourself that eventually they'll finish, but they never do. They keep chewing and chewing and chewing and you're deathly afraid that next they'll start on a four-pound box of malted milk balls.

10   So in summary: Get to the movie theater early and scout out the territory. It's a jungle in there, filled with a lot of really stupid animals. Know the telltale signs and act accordingly. And then sit down and shut up.

Words and Meanings

Margaret Mead	U.S. anthropologist famous for her studies of people's behaviour in various "exotic" cultures	2
Tourette's syndrome	hereditary disease that causes uncontrollable physical twitching and bursts of speech in its sufferers	7
forage	search for food	8

Structure and Strategy

1. What is the function of paragraph 3? After all, not all moviegoers bring their children to the theatre.
2. Identify three SIMILES in paragraphs 3, 5, and 7. How would the impact of this essay be lessened if the author had not included these figures of speech?
3. When Dermody uses phrases such as "tie them up to a fire hydrant" (paragraph 3) or "teenagers shooting heroin into their necks" (paragraph 4), he obviously does not mean to be taken seriously. Identify two or three other examples of this kind of exaggeration and consider how it affects the TONE of the essay.
4. What METAPHOR does Dermody use in the CONCLUSION of this piece? How does it contribute to the UNITY of the essay?

Content and Purpose

1. What does Dermody mean when he admits, in his opening sentence, that he is a "tad neurotic"? How does this confession affect the reader's response to the judgments that follow?
2. What is the author's PURPOSE (see paragraph 2)? Do you think he achieves it?
3. This essay classifies moviegoers according to their pre-movie and during-movie behaviours. Identify the six categories of the author's classification system.
4. Would you like to go to a movie with the author? Why or why not?

Suggestions for Writing

1. Write an essay in which you classify partygoers, friends, relatives, neighbours, children, workers, bosses, students, or any other group of people you choose. Be sure your classification is logical and consistent, and that the purpose of your classification is clear to your reader.

2. How do you spend your time? Write an essay identifying the categories into which you divide your time each week. What do you learn about yourself from this exercise?

Toothpaste

DAVID BODANIS

David Bodanis is an educator, business consultant, and science writer who publishes in both the United States and England, where he now lives. His published books include *The Body Book: A Fantastic Voyage to the World Within* (1984), *The Secret House: The Extraordinary Science of an Ordinary Day* (1986), *E=mc²: A Biography of the World's Most Famous Equation* (2000), *Electric Universe: The Shocking True Story of Electricity* (2005), and *Passionate Minds: The Great Love Affair of the Enlightenment, Featuring the Scientist Emilie du Chatelet, the Poet Voltaire, Sword Fights, Book Burnings, Assorted Kings* (2006).

1   Into the bathroom [we go], and after the most pressing need is satisfied it's time to brush the teeth. The tube of toothpaste is squeezed, its pinched metal seams are splayed, pressure waves are generated inside, and the paste begins to flow. But what's in this toothpaste, so carefully being extruded° out?

2   Water mostly, 30 to 45 per cent in most brands: ordinary, everyday simple tap water. It's there because people like to have a big gob of toothpaste to spread on the brush, and water is the cheapest stuff there is when it comes to making big gobs. Dripping a bit from the tap onto your brush would cost virtually nothing; whipped in with the rest of the toothpaste the manufacturers can sell it at a neat and accountant-pleasing $2 per pound equivalent. Toothpaste manufacture is a very lucrative occupation.

3   Second to water in quantity is chalk: exactly the same material that schoolteachers use to write on blackboards. It is collected from the crushed remains of long-dead ocean creatures. In the Cretaceous° seas chalk particles served as part of the wickedly sharp outer skeleton that these creatures had to wrap around themselves to keep from getting chomped by all the slightly larger other ocean creatures they met. Their massed graves are our present chalk deposits.

The individual chalk particles—the size of the smallest mud   4
particles in your garden—have kept their toughness over the
aeons°, and now on the toothbrush they'll need it. The enamel
outer coating of the tooth they'll have to face is the hardest substance in the body—tougher than skull, or bone, or nail. Only the
chalk particles in toothpaste can successfully grind into the teeth
during brushing, ripping off the surface layers like an abrading
wheel grinding down a boulder in a quarry.

The craters, slashes, and channels that the chalk tears into the   5
teeth will also remove a certain amount of built-up yellow in the
carnage, and it is for that polishing function that it's there. A certain
amount of unduly enlarged extra-abrasive chalk fragments tear
such cavernous pits into the teeth that future decay bacteria will be
able to bunker down there and thrive; the quality control people
find it almost impossible to screen out these errant super-chalk
pieces, and government regulations allow them to stay in.

In case even the gouging doesn't get all the yellow off, another   6
substance is worked into the toothpaste cream. This is titanium
dioxide. It comes in tiny spheres, and it's the stuff bobbing around
in white wall paint to make it come out white. Splashed around
onto your teeth during the brushing it coats much of the yellow
that remains. Being water soluble it leaks off in the next few hours
and is swallowed, but at least for the quick glance up in the mirror
after finishing it will make the user think his teeth are truly white.
Some manufacturers add optical whitening dyes—the stuff more
commonly found in washing machine bleach—to make extra sure
that the glance in the mirror shows reassuring white.

These ingredients alone would not make a very attractive con-   7
coction°. They would stick in the tube like a sloppy white plastic
lump, hard to squeeze out as well as revolting to the touch. Few
consumers would savor rubbing in a mixture of water, ground-up
blackboard chalk and the whitener from latex paint first thing in
the morning. To get around that finicky distaste the manufacturers
have mixed in a host of other goodies.

To keep the glop from drying out, a mixture including glyc-   8
erine glycol—related to the most common car anti-freeze ingredient—is whipped in with the chalk and water, and to give *that*
concoction a bit of substance (all we really have so far is wet colored chalk) a large helping is added of gummy molecules from the
seaweed *Chondrus crispus*. This seaweed ooze spreads in among the
chalk, paint and anti-freeze, then stretches itself in all directions to
hold the whole mass together. A bit of paraffin oil (the fuel that
flickers in camping lamps) is pumped in with it to help the moss
ooze keep the whole substance smooth.

9   With the glycol, ooze and paraffin we're almost there. Only two major chemicals are left to make the refreshing, cleansing substance we know as toothpaste. The ingredients so far are fine for cleaning, but they wouldn't make much of the satisfying foam we have come to expect in the morning brushing.

10   To remedy that, every toothpaste on the market has a big dollop of detergent added, too. You've seen the suds detergent will make in a washing machine. The same substance added here will duplicate that inside the mouth. It's not particularly necessary, but it sells.

11   The only problem is that by itself this ingredient tastes, well, too like detergent. It's horribly bitter and harsh. The chalk put in toothpaste is pretty foul-tasting too for that matter. It's to get around that gustatory° discomfort that the manufacturers put in the ingredient they tout° perhaps the most of all. This is the flavoring, and it has to be strong. Double rectified peppermint oil is used—a flavorer so powerful that chemists know better than to sniff it in the raw state in the laboratory. Menthol crystals and saccharin or other sugar simulators are added to complete the camouflage operation.

12   Is that it? Chalk, water, paint, seaweed, anti-freeze, paraffin oil, detergent and peppermint? Not quite. A mix like that would be irresistible to the hundreds of thousands of individual bacteria lying on the surface of even an immaculately cleaned bathroom sink. They would get in, float in the water bubbles, ingest the ooze and paraffin, maybe even spray out enzymes to break down the chalk. The result would be an uninviting mess. The way manufacturers avoid that final obstacle is by putting something in to kill the bacteria. Something good and strong is needed, something that will zap any accidentally intrudant bacteria into oblivion. And that something is formaldehyde—the disinfectant used in anatomy labs.

13   So it's chalk, water, paint, seaweed, anti-freeze, paraffin oil, detergent, peppermint, formaldehyde and fluoride (which can go some way towards preserving children's teeth)—that's the usual mixture raised to the mouth on the toothbrush for a fresh morning's clean. If it sounds too unfortunate, take heart. Studies show that thorough brushing with just plain water will often do as good a job.

Words and Meanings

Paragraph

1	extruded	pushed
3	Cretaceous	relating to the last period of the Mesozoic era (135 million to 65 million years ago)
4	aeons	ages, an immensely long time

concoction	mixture	7
gustatory	having to do with taste	11
tout	advertise; promote aggressively in order to attract customers	

Structure and Strategy

1. This essay analyzes toothpaste by dividing it into its component parts. Identify each ingredient and the paragraph(s) in which it is described.
2. What is the function of paragraph 7? Paragraph 9? Paragraph 13?
3. Underline six or seven examples of the author's use of vivid DESCRIPTION to help communicate KEY IDEAS.
4. Part of the effect of this essay depends on Bodanis's description of toothpaste. He uses words that are very different from those we are familiar with in television commercials to describe the same product. For example, in paragraph 8 we read, "seaweed ooze spreads in among the chalk, paint and anti-freeze." Find other examples of Bodanis's use of language that you would never hear in a product advertisement. What effect does his DICTION have on the reader?

Content and Purpose

1. What is toothpaste's main ingredient and what is its primary function? What is the purpose of the SIMILE used in paragraph 4 to describe this function?
2. What's the function of glycol in toothpaste? The seaweed and paraffin? The detergent? The formaldehyde?
3. Explain the IRONY in the last paragraph.
4. Did you have any idea what toothpaste was made of before you read this essay? Did any of the ingredients surprise you? Revolt you? Why?

Suggestions for Writing

1. Does Bodanis's ANALYSIS of toothpaste make you wonder about the composition of other familiar products? Do you know what goes into margarine? Lipstick? Kraft Dinner? A hot dog? Write an essay that identifies the surprising elements of a common substance.
2. Write an essay in which you classify the different kinds of grooming aids available to assist us in making ourselves irresistible (or at least attractive) to others.

The World Is Phat

MARTIN EDLUND

Martin Edlund is a writer living in New York. The publications in which his articles have appeared include *The New York Sun, The New York Times, Slate,* and *The New Republic Online.*

1   Hip-hop has always been obsessed with geography. Coming from the streets may give a rapper credibility, but coming from *particular* streets—or, for that matter, a particular hood, side, city, region, or coast—gives him an identity and situates him within the larger hip-hop culture. But this obsession with the local has produced a kind of isolationism: While the world devours American hip-hop, America ignores the hip-hop of the rest of the world. The recent influx of three international styles—reggaeton from Puerto Rico, grime from Britain, and baile funk from Brazil— suggests that this situation may finally be changing. Taken together, they dispel the notion that globalization breeds homogeneity°. Each is the product of a country importing American hip-hop, blending it with native traditions, and refashioning it in its own image.

2   Reggaeton (pronounced reggae-tone) emerged from the barrios° of Puerto Rico (and, to a lesser extent, Latin American countries) back in the mid-1990s. The sound is an amalgam of foreign and domestic styles: hip-hop, reggae, merengue, and the Puerto Rican dance music bomba. It has succeeded in America due to some clever viral marketing: DJs began remixing popular American hip-hop songs with reggaeton beats, interspersing Spanish verses with the original English ones. The songs spread throughout the American mixtape underground and eventually found their way onto the playlists of trendsetting urban radio stations like Hot 97 in New York City.

3   Reggaeton is now in the curious spot of being both ubiquitous° (in New York, Los Angeles, and Miami) and totally unknown (everywhere else). It won't remain that way for long—all the major labels [have] set up Latin urban imprints . . . and P. Diddy . . . threw his hat in the ring, announcing the formation of Bad Boy Latino. Other top American MCs and producers—Lil Jon, 50 Cent, The Game, and Fat Joe among them—are now working with established reggaeton stars, appearing on and remixing *their* tracks.

4   British grime is also enjoying a vogue in America, though of a less mainstream sort. Instead of bubbling up through the streets in America, as reggaeton did, grime was handed down by a community of MP3 bloggers and music tastemakers like the *Fader* magazine and [the Web site] Pitchfork. First came Mercury Prize-winner

Dizzee Rascal, riding a trans-Atlantic wave of adulation in early 2004. Now the rest of the U.K. grime scene is trying to make the leap, targeting a flurry of compilations and solo albums at American listeners. The style grew out of London's mostly black projects, called council estates, sometime around 2002, and spread via pirate radio, which functions in Britain essentially as mixtapes do here. The name originated as an adjective for the sound: a spare, gritty mix of depth-charge bass, pinging synth notes, retro video-game effects, and paper-thin drum beats that owe as much to the British traditions of garage and jungle as to American hip-hop. The lyrics are dense and percussive—so much so that they almost serve as a second drum track to many of the songs.

Brazilian baile funk, perhaps the unlikeliest candidate for   5 import, originated as the sound track for weekend block parties in the *favelas* of Rio de Janeiro—the drug-infested, hillside slums depicted in the film *City of God*. It might never have been heard out-side their walls if not for the American DJ Diplo (aka Wesley Pentz), who, like some kind of postmodern folk-song hunter, traveled to Rio to investigate the music he first heard on a scratchy tape given to him at a party. Composed in makeshift studios on vintage equip-ment with bootlegged computer programs, baile funk is hip-hop as it might sound in the post-apocalyptic wasteland of *Mad Max*. The songs are a choppy bricolage° of hip-hop, electro-funk, Carnival rhythms, Miami bass, and samba. The vocalists—many of whom sound about 12 years old—shout flat, repetitive lines in squeaky Portuguese.

Diplo emerged from Rio with material for his first baile funk   6 mixtape, *Favela On Blast: Rio Baile Funk 04*, which served up 30-plus minutes of jittery, anonymous, booty-shake music. But it was another mix that really broke the sound in America: *Piracy Funds Terrorism*, co-produced with future Internet darling M.I.A. (née Maya Arulpragasam), interspersed and blended baile funk clips with unreleased M.I.A. tracks. The sound suits her sassy, polyglot° hip-pop perfectly, so it's no surprise that baile funk elements and samples also found their way onto her official release, *Arular* (XL).

The success of all three foreign styles in America parallels, in   7 many respects, the emergence of new scenes *within* America. Throughout the 1990s, U.S. hip-hop was all about the East Coast/West Coast divide; everything else was the rap suburbs. But in the last five years, the map has been redrawn to include Atlanta and the Dirty South, St. Louis, Detroit, Chicago, and Houston. Each new locale announced itself with a distinctive sound, slang, and set of personalities.

8   Foreign hip-hop has followed a similar model. Reggaeton, grime, and baile funk—like Jamaican dancehall before them— arrived on America's doorstep as complete packages, with their own identities and sounds. They succeeded simply by innovating, not imitating. The U.K., for instance, has been churning out ersatz° American hip-hop for decades, but it is only now—with a sound as aggressively original as grime—that America has taken notice.

9   The incorporation of new domestic scenes in the last five years has reinvigorated American hip-hop, saving it from the doldrums° of P. Diddy party rap and taking it in startling new directions—Lil Jon's popularization of crunk, and, more recently, the breakthrough of Houston's chopped and screwed sound. In a similar way, the internationalization of hip-hop will continue the rebirth. Consider the creative explosion rock 'n' roll experienced when it collided with Britain's talents beginning in the 1960s, producing the British Invasion, glam, punk rock, shoegazer rock, and other styles.

10   In the case of hip-hop, however, the rate of innovation will likely be far more rapid, and the range of influences far more diverse. MP3 blogging, file-sharing, and home PC music produc- tion software has replicated, on an international scale, the culture of street mixtapes and pirate radio—a culture in which unofficial releases, alternate versions, and remixes are the coin of the realm. Already, we're witnessing a rampant cross-pollination of styles. File-sharing networks and blogs are flooded with grime versions of American hip-hop songs; chopped and screwed versions of reg- gaeton songs; crunk versions of grime songs; beats composed from baile funk bootlegs; and countless reggaeton remixes of American hip-hop and R&B hits.

11   In some cases, America's name-brand producers and artists are leading the way. Lil Jon, the Zelig° of the American pop charts, has crunked-out reggaeton songs by Daddy Yankee ("Gasolina") and the Cuban-American rapper Pitbull ("Toma" and "Culo"), and he attached his name to a new crunk-meets-grime mixtape produced by U.K. DJ Semtex—stamping both styles with his all-important imprimatur. Dizzee Rascal achieved the same thing in reverse when asked by Beck to contribute a grim remix of the song "Hell Yes," called "Fax Machine Anthem," to the deluxe edition of his new album, *Guero*.

12   But whether foreign artists representing these styles—or just their inventive sounds—will succeed here is still an open question. Reggaeton star Daddy Yankee's 2004 album, *Barrio Fiono*, has sold an impressive 560,000 copies to date in the U.S. But Dizzee Rascal, grime's leading light, has sold only 58,000 copies stateside of his much-hyped debut *Boy In Da Corner*. His follow-up, *Showtime*, has

sold less than half that many. Perhaps Dizzee will one day match Jay-Z, but for now at least, the pop-chart-topping status of American hip-hop heavyweights is foreign territory for international acts.

Words and Meanings

Paragraph

homogeneity	sameness	1
barrios	urban neighbourhoods or districts	2
ubiquitous	everywhere	3
bricolage	here, a musical composition made out of bits and pieces of other works	5
polyglot	composed in several languages	6
ersatz	imitation	8
doldrums	stagnation or dead zone: period in which nothing exciting happens	9
Zelig	protagonist of the 1983 Woody Allen mock-documentary of the same name; lacking any identity of his own, Zelig takes on the characteristics of whomever he's with	11

Structure and Strategy

1. Who is the intended AUDIENCE for this essay? How does the DICTION help you identify the readers for whom Edlund wrote this piece?
2. Find the author's definitions of *reggaeton, grime,* and *baile funk.* Then identify and define four or five slang terms with which readers outside the target audience are unlikely to be familiar.
3. What topic does the essay classify? Which paragraphs develop each category?
4. Identify the TOPIC SENTENCES in paragraphs 2, 4, 5, 10, 11, and 12.
5. Paragraphs 8 and 9 are developed by means of COMPARISON. What is being compared in each of them?

Content and Purpose

1. What is the THESIS of this essay?
2. The INTRODUCTION states a commonly held opinion that Edlund challenges. What is it?

3. Where do the three kinds of hip-hop that Edlund writes about come from? What, despite their widely differing geographic origins, do these three types of music have in common?
4. Why does Edlund think that the pace of innovation and globalization in hip-hop music will continue to increase? Does he think this is a good thing?
5. What is the question that Edlund poses at the end of the essay? How would you answer it?

Suggestions for Writing

1. Write an essay classifying the major categories of a style of music (except for hip-hop) with which you are familiar.
2. Do you agree or disagree that international styles of hip-hop are improving the quality of the music? Write an essay explaining your opinion.
3. Are there any Canadian innovations that could be added to the examples in this essay? Write an essay that describes the artists and the kind(s) of music they are creating.
4. Write an essay on hip-hop music using your own principle of division (e.g., the essential characteristics of good hip-hop music) or classification (e.g., the influence of hip-hop on contemporary culture; women hip-hop artists).

Principled Uncertainty

RICHARD FEYNMAN

American physicist Richard Feynman (1918–1988) studied at the Massachusetts Institute of Technology and Princeton University before becoming a professor at Cornell University (1945–50) and the California Institute of Technology, where he remained for the rest of his career. He was a joint winner of the 1965 Nobel Prize in physics for his work on quantum electrodynamics.

1   From time to time, people suggest to me that scientists ought to give more consideration to social problems—especially . . . the impact of science upon society. It seems to be generally believed that if scientists would only look at these very difficult social problems and not spend so much time fooling with the less

vital scientific ones, great success would come of it. Most scientists do think about these problems from time to time, but we don't put full-time effort into them—because we know that social problems are very much harder than scientific ones, and that we usually don't get anywhere when we do think about them. I believe that a scientist looking at non-scientific problems is just as dumb as the next guy—and when he talks about a non-scientific matter, he will sound as naïve as anyone untrained in the matter. Since the question of the value of science is not a scientific subject, this discussion is dedicated to proving my point by example.

The first way in which science is of value is familiar to everyone. 2 Scientific knowledge enables us to do and to make all kinds of things. Of course if we make good things, it is to the credit not only of science but also of the moral choice that led us to do good work. The applied sciences should free men from material problems. Medicine controls diseases, for example, and the record here seems to be good. Yet there are also men patiently working to create great plagues and poisons. Scientific knowledge is an enabling power to do either good or bad; it does not carry instructions on how to use it.

I learned a way of expressing this common human problem on 3 a trip to Honolulu. In a Buddhist temple there, the man in charge explained a little bit about the Buddhist religion and then ended his talk with a proverb: "To every man is given the key to the gates of heaven; the same key opens the gates to hell." What, then, is the value of the key to heaven? It is true that the key may be a dangerous object if we lack clear instructions that help to distinguish between the gate to heaven and the gate to hell, but it obviously has value. How can we enter heaven without it?

Intellectual enjoyment, which some people get from reading and 4 learning and thinking about science and which others get from working in science, is clearly valuable as well. Science has led us to imagine all sorts of things that are infinitely more marvelous than the imaginings of the poets and dreamers of the past. Science teaches us that the imagination of nature is far, far greater than the imagination of man. Consider how much more remarkable it is for us all to be stuck—half of us upside down—by a mysterious attraction to a spinning ball that has been swinging in space for billions of years than to be carried on the back of an elephant supported on a tortoise swimming in a bottomless sea°.

We find that thrill of discovery whenever we look deeply into 5 any scientific problem. Knowledge serves only to deepen the mysteries of nature, which lure us onward to more discoveries. It is true that few unscientific people have this particular type of religious experience. Our poets do not write about it; our artists do not try to portray it. I don't know why. Is nobody inspired by our present picture of the universe? The value of science remains unsung; ours is not yet a scientific age.

6   Perhaps one reason for this is that you have to know how to read the music. A scientific article, for instance, might say something like this: "The radioactive phosphorus content of the cerebrum of the rat decreases to one-half in a period of two weeks." Now, what does that mean? It means that the phosphorus in the brain of a rat (and also in mine and yours) is not the same phosphorus that was there two weeks ago. All the atoms that are in the brain are being replaced, and the ones that were there before have gone away. So what is this mind? What are these atoms with consciousness? Last week's potatoes! Which now can remember what was going on in your mind a year ago—a mind that was long ago replaced. When we discover how long it takes for the atoms of the brain to be replaced by other atoms, we come to realize that the thing I call my individuality is only a pattern or dance. The atoms come into my brain, dance a dance, and then go out, always new atoms but always performing the same dance, remembering what the dance was yesterday.

7   Ultimately, however, the real value of science may lie in uncertainty. The scientist has a lot of experience with ignorance and doubt and uncertainty, and this experience is very important. Scientific knowledge is a body of statements of varying degrees of certainty—about some of them we are mostly unsure, some are nearly certain, none are *absolutely* certain. We scientists are used to this, and we take it for granted that it is perfectly consistent to be unsure, that it is possible to live and not to know. But I don't know whether everyone realizes that this is true.

8   This is not a new idea; it is the central idea of the Age of Reason° and of the philosophy that guided the men who made the democracy under which we live. The idea that no one really knew how to run a government led to the notion that we should arrange a system in which new ideas could be developed, tried, and tossed out—a system of trial and error inspired by the scientific advances of the eighteenth century. Even then it was clear to socially minded people that openness was an opportunity and that doubt and discussion were essential to progress. If we want to solve the problems that face us, we must leave the door to the unknown ajar.

Words and Meanings

Paragraph

on the back . . . sea   an allusion to an ancient image of the world,   4
which was rendered obsolete by the advent
of modern science

Age of Reason   the eighteenth century was the period when   8
rationalism challenged traditional European
political, religious, social, and philosophical
beliefs; also called the Enlightenment

Structure and Strategy

1. The author begins his essay with a premise that he then argues against. Summarize the premise in one sentence. Why does Feynman reject it?
2. Identify the THESIS of the essay. Underline the three KEY IDEAS Feynman explores in this piece. In what ORDER has he arranged these ideas?
3. In paragraph 2, what is the TOPIC SENTENCE? What example does the author use to develop it? Summarize in one sentence the point he makes with this example.
4. What is the function of paragraph 3? How does it support Feynman's first key idea?
5. What words or phrases in paragraphs 4 and 7 are used to show the TRANSITION from one point to the next?
6. Explain the METAPHOR with which Feynman opens and concludes paragraph 6.

Content and Purpose

1. According to Feynman, how valuable is a scientist's view of social or other non-scientific problems? (See paragraph 1.)
2. What is the "mysterious attraction to a spinning ball" described in paragraph 4? What point of Feynman's ARGUMENT does this example support?
3. Summarize the process Feynman describes in paragraph 6. Why do you think he chose the brain of a rat to illustrate this process? How does this paragraph support the second point of his argument?
4. According to Feynman, what may be the most important value of science? (See paragraph 7.) How does he suggest that non-scientists view this particular value?
5. In paragraph 8, what form of government is used to exemplify the value of scientific uncertainty? How does this example support the author's point?

6. After reading this essay, are you more persuaded than you were before about the value of science in the postmodern age? Why or why not?

Suggestion for Writing

Write an essay about a significant concept or lesson that you have learned from science.

What I Have Lived For

BERTRAND RUSSELL

Bertrand Russell (1872–1970), philosopher, mathematician, and social reformer, was awarded the Nobel Prize for Literature in 1950. His progressive views on the liberalization of sexual attitudes and the role of women led to his dismissal from the University of California at Los Angeles in the 1920s. Russell was a leading pacifist and proponent of nuclear disarmament. Among his many books are *Principia Mathematica*, *Why I Am Not a Christian*, and *History of Western Philosophy*.

1   Three passions, simple but overwhelmingly strong, have governed my life: the longing for love, the search for knowledge, and unbearable pity for the suffering of mankind. These passions, like great winds, have blown me hither and thither, in a wayward° course, over a deep ocean of anguish, reaching to the very verge° of despair.

2   I have sought love, first, because it brings ecstasy°—ecstasy so great that I would often have sacrificed all the rest of life for a few hours of this joy. I have sought it, next, because it relieves loneliness—that terrible loneliness in which one shivering consciousness looks over the rim of the world into the cold unfathomable lifeless abyss°. I have sought it, finally, because in the union of love I have seen, in a mystic miniature, the prefiguring° vision of the heaven that saints and poets have imagined. This is what I sought, and though it might seem too good for human life, this is what—at last—I have found.

3   With equal passion I have sought knowledge. I have wished to understand the hearts of men. I have wished to know why the stars shine. And I have tried to apprehend the Pythagorean° power by which number holds sway above the flux°. A little of this, but not much, I have achieved.

Love and knowledge, so far as they were possible, led upward   4
toward the heavens. But always pity brought me back to earth.
Echoes of cries of pain reverberate° in my heart. Children in famine,
victims tortured by oppressors, helpless old people a hated burden
to their sons, and the whole world of loneliness, poverty, and pain
make a mockery of what human life should be. I long to alleviate°
the evil, but I cannot, and I too suffer.

This has been my life. I have found it worth living, and would   5
gladly live it again if the chance were offered me.

Words and Meanings

Paragraph

wayward	unpredictable, wandering	1
verge	edge, brink	
ecstasy	supreme joy	2
abyss	bottomless pit, hell	
prefiguring	picturing to oneself beforehand	
Pythagorean	relating to the Greek philosopher Pythagoras and his theory that through mathematics one can understand the relationship between all things and the principle of harmony in the universe	3
flux	continual motion, change	
reverberate	echo	4
alleviate	relieve, lessen	

Structure and Strategy

1. Identify Russell's thesis statement and the TOPIC SENTENCES of paragraphs 2, 3, and 4.
2. How does the structure of the second sentence in paragraph 1 reinforce its meaning?
3. The number three is the basis for the structure of Russell's essay. Three is an ancient symbol for unity and completeness and for the human life cycle: birth, life, death. Find as many examples as you can of Russell's use of "threes." (Look at paragraph and sentence structure as well as content.)
4. What is the function of the first sentence of paragraph 4?
5. How does Russell's concluding paragraph contribute to the UNITY of the essay?
6. Refer to the introduction to this unit and show how paragraph 1 sets up a division essay and how paragraph 4 is actually a classification.

7. Analyze the ORDER in which Russell explains his three passions. Do you think the order is chronological, logical, climactic, or random? Does the order reflect the relative importance or value that Russell ascribes to each passion? How?

Content and Purpose

1. For Bertrand Russell, love means more than physical passion. What else does he include in his meaning of love (paragraph 2)?
2. What are the three kinds of knowledge Russell spent his life seeking?
3. Which of Russell's three "passions" has he been least successful in achieving? Why?
4. Which passion is most important to Russell? How do you know?

Suggestions for Writing

1. What goals have you set for yourself for the next ten years? Write a short paper in which you identify and explain two or three of your goals.
2. In what ways are you different from other people? Write a short paper in which you identify and explain some of the qualities and characterlstics that make you a unique human being.
3. Imagine that you are seventy-five years old. Write a short paper explaining what you have lived for.

The Dimensions of a Complete Life

MARTIN LUTHER KING, JR.

Dr. Martin Luther King, Jr. (1929–1968), the American civil rights leader, was a Baptist minister who advocated racial equality and non-violent resistance against discriminatory laws and practices. He was awarded the Nobel Prize for Peace in 1964. In 1968, he was assassinated in Memphis, Tennessee.

1   Many, many centuries ago, out on a lonely, obscure island called Patmos°, a man by the name of John° caught a vision of the new Jerusalem descending out of heaven from God. One of the greatest glories of this new city of God that John saw was its completeness. It was not partial and one-sided,

but it was complete in all three of its dimensions. And so, in describing the city in the twenty-first chapter of the book of Revelation, John says this: "The length and the breadth and the height of it are equal." In other words, this new city of God, this city of ideal humanity, is not an unbalanced entity but it is complete on all sides.

Now John is saying something quite significant here. For so 2 many of us the book of Revelation° is a very difficult book, puzzling to decode. We look upon it as something of a great enigma° wrapped in mystery. And certainly if we accept the book of Revelation as a record of actual historical occurrences it is a difficult book, shrouded with impenetrable mysteries. But if we will look beneath the peculiar jargon of its author and the prevailing apocalyptic° symbolism, we will find in this book many eternal truths which continue to challenge us. One such truth is that of this text. What John is really saying is this: that life as it should be and life at its best is the life that is complete on all sides.

There are three dimensions of any complete life to which we 3 can fitly give the words of this text: length, breadth, and height. The length of life as we shall think of it here is not its duration or its longevity, but it is the push of a life forward to achieve its personal ends and ambitions. It is the inward concern for one's own welfare. The breadth of life is the outward concern for the welfare of others. The height of life is the upward reach for God.

These are the three dimensions of life, and without the three 4 being correlated, working harmoniously together, life is incomplete. Life is something of a great triangle. At one angle stands the individual person, at the other angle stand other persons, and at the top stands the Supreme, Infinite Person, God. These three must meet in every individual life if that life is to be complete.

Now let us notice first the length of life. I have said that this is 5 the dimension of life in which the individual is concerned with developing his inner powers. It is that dimension of life in which the individual pursues personal ends and ambitions. This is perhaps the selfish dimension of life, and there is such a thing as moral and rational self-interest. If one is not concerned about himself he cannot be totally concerned about other selves.

Some years ago a learned rabbi, the late Joshua Liebman, wrote 6 a book entitled *Peace of Mind*. He has a chapter in the book entitled "Love Thyself Properly." In this chapter he says in substance that it is impossible to love other selves adequately unless you love your own self properly. Many people have been plunged into the abyss° of emotional fatalism° because they did not love themselves properly. So every individual has a responsibility to be concerned about himself enough to discover what he is made for. After he discovers his calling he should set out to do it with all of the strength and power in his being. He should do it as if God Almighty called him at this particular moment in history to do it. He should seek to do his job so well that the living, the dead, or the unborn could not do it better. No matter how small one thinks his life's work is in terms of the norms of the world and the so-called big jobs, he must realize that it has cosmic significance if he is serving humanity and doing the will of God.

7   To carry this to one extreme, if it falls your lot to be a street-sweeper, sweep streets as Raphael painted pictures, sweep streets as Michelangelo carved marble, sweep streets as Beethoven com-posed music, sweep streets as Shakespeare wrote poetry. Sweep streets so well that all the hosts of heaven and earth will have to pause and say, "Here lived a great street-sweeper who swept his job well." In the words of Douglas Mallock:

> If you can't be a highway, just be a trail;
> If you can't be the sun, be a star
> For it isn't by size that you win or you fail—
> Be the best of whatever you are.

When you do this, you have mastered the first dimension of life—the length of life.

8   But don't stop here; it is dangerous to stop here. There are some people who never get beyond this first dimension. They are bril-liant people; often they do an excellent job in developing their inner powers; but they live as if nobody else lived in the world but them-selves. There is nothing more tragic than to find an individual bogged down in the length of life, devoid of the breadth.

9   The breadth of life is that dimension of life in which we are concerned about others. An individual has not started living until he can rise above the narrow confines of his individualistic con-cerns to the broader concerns of all humanity.

10   You remember one day a man came to Jesus and he raised some significant questions. Finally he got around to the question, "Who is my neighbor?" This could easily have been a very abstract question left in mid-air. But Jesus immediately pulled that question out of mid-air and placed it on a dangerous curve between Jerusalem and Jericho. He talked about a certain man who fell among thieves. Three men passed; two of them on the other side. And finally another man came and helped the injured man on the ground. He is known to us as the good Samaritan. Jesus says in substance that this is a great man. He was great because he could project the "I" into the "thou."

So often we say that the priest and the Levite were in a big   11
hurry to get to some ecclesiastical meeting and so they did not have
time. They were concerned about that. I would rather think of it
another way. I can well imagine that they were quite afraid. You
see, the Jericho road is a dangerous road, and the same thing that
happened to the man who was robbed and beaten could have happened to them. So I imagine the first question that the priest and
the Levite asked was this: "If I stop to help this man, what will
happen to me?" Then the good Samaritan came by, and by the very
nature of his concern reversed the question: "If I do not stop to help
this man, what will happen to him?" And so this man was great
because he had the mental equipment for a dangerous altruism°.
He was great because he could surround the length of his life with
the breadth of life. He was great not only because he had ascended
to certain heights of economic security, but because he could conde-
scend° to the depths of human need.

All this has a great deal of bearing in our situation in the world   12
today. So often racial groups are concerned about the length of life,
their economic privileged position, their social status. So often
nations of the world are concerned about the length of life, perpetu-
ating their nationalistic concerns, and their economic ends. May it
not be that the problem in the world today is that individuals as
well as nations have been overly concerned with the length of life,
devoid of the breadth? But there is still something to remind us that
we are interdependent°, that we are all involved in a single process,
that we are all somehow caught in an inescapable network of mutuality. Therefore whatever affects one directly affects all indirectly.

As long as there is poverty in the world I can never be rich,   13
even if I have a billion dollars. As long as diseases are rampant and
millions of people in this world cannot expect to live more than
twenty-eight or thirty years, I can never be totally healthy even if I
just got a good check-up at Mayo Clinic. I can never be what I
ought to be until you are what you ought to be. This is the way our
world is made. No individual or nation can stand out boasting of
being independent. We are interdependent. So John Donne placed it
in graphic terms when he affirmed, "No man is an island entire of
itself. Every man is a piece of the continent, a part of the main."
Then he goes on to say, "Any man's death diminishes me because I
am involved in mankind, and therefore never send to know for
whom the bell tolls; it tolls for thee." When we discover this, we
master the second dimension of life.

Finally, there is a third dimension. Some people never get   14
beyond the first two dimensions of life. They master the first two.
They develop their inner powers; they love humanity, but they stop

right here. They end up with the feeling that man is the end of all things and that humanity is God. Philosophically or theologically, many of them would call themselves humanists°. They seek to live life without a sky. They find themselves bogged down on the horizontal plane without being integrated on the vertical plane. But if we are to live the complete life we must reach up and discover God. H.G. Wells was right: "The man who is not religious begins at nowhere and ends at nothing." Religion is like a mighty wind that breaks down doors and makes that possible and even easy which seems difficult and impossible.

15   In our modern world it is easy for us to forget this. We so often find ourselves unconsciously neglecting this third dimension of life. Not that we go up and say, "Good-by, God, we are going to leave you now." But we become so involved in the things of this world that we are unconsciously carried away by the rushing tide of materialism° which leaves us treading in the confused waters of secularism°. We find ourselves living in what Professor Sorokin of Harvard called a sensate° civilization, believing that only those things which we can see and touch and to which we can apply our five senses have existence.

16   Something should remind us once more that the great things in this universe are things that we never see. You walk out at night and look up at the beautiful stars as they bedeck the heavens like swinging lanterns of eternity, and you think you can see all. Oh, no. You can never see the law of gravitation that holds them there. You walk around this vast campus and you probably have a great esthetic experience as I have had walking about and looking at the beautiful buildings, and you think you see all. Oh, no. You can never see the mind of the architect who drew the blueprint. You can never see the love and the faith and the hope of the individuals who made it so. You look at me and you think you see Martin Luther King. You don't see Martin Luther King; you see my body, but, you must understand, my body can't think, my body can't reason. You don't see the me that makes me me. You can never see my personality.

17   In a real sense everything that we see is a shadow cast by that which we do not see. Plato° was right: "The visible is a shadow cast by the invisible." And so God is still around. All of our new knowledge, all of our new developments, cannot diminish his being one iota°. These new advances have banished God neither from the microcosmic compass of the atom nor from the vast, unfathomable ranges of interstellar space. The more we learn about this universe, the more mysterious and awesome it becomes. God is still here.

So I say to you, seek God and discover him and make him a   18
power in your life. Without him all our efforts turn to ashes and our
sunrises into darkest nights. Without him, life is a meaningless
drama with the decisive scenes missing. But with him we are able
to rise from the fatigue of despair to the buoyancy of hope. With
him we are able to rise from the midnight of desperation to the day-
break of joy. St. Augustine was right—we were made for God and
we will be restless until we find rest in him.

Love yourself, if that means rational, healthy, and moral self-   19
interest. You are commanded to do that. That is the length of life.
Love your neighbor as you love yourself. You are commanded to
do that. That is the breadth of life. But never forget that there is a
first and even greater commandment, "Love the Lord thy God with
all thy heart and all thy soul and all thy mind." This is the height of
life. And when you do this you live the complete life.

Thank God for John who, centuries ago, caught a vision of the   20
new Jerusalem. God grant that those of us who still walk the road
of life will catch this vision and decide to move forward to that city
of complete life in which the length and the breadth and the height
are equal.

Words and Meanings

		Paragraph
John of Patmos	Christian saint, author of the book of Revelation	1
the book of Revelation	last book of the New Testament, concerned with the end of the world and other mysteries	2
enigma	puzzle, mystery	
apocalyptic	concerned with the Apocalypse, the last day	
abyss	bottomless pit, hell	6
fatalism	belief that a predetermined fate rules our lives	
altruism	selfless concern for others	11
condescend	stoop, bend down to	
interdependent	dependent on each other	12
humanists	people interested in human nature and concerns	14
materialism	concern only for the goods of this world	15
secularism	social and non-religious concern for the world	
sensate	perceived by the senses	
Plato	ancient Greek philosopher, idealist	17
iota	smallest particle	18

Structure and Strategy

1. What ANALOGY are paragraphs 1 and 2 based on? What analogy is introduced in paragraph 4?
2. Identify King's thesis statement. What question of division does it answer? (See the introduction to this unit.)
3. What is the function of paragraph 3? How does King begin to develop his three points in this paragraph?
4. Identify the paragraphs that develop each of the three dimensions of life. In what ORDER has King arranged his points?
5. How does paragraph 8 contribute to COHERENCE? Paragraphs 9 and 14?
6. Paragraphs 19 and 20 form the CONCLUSION of this piece. What is the function of paragraph 20? How does it round off or conclude the essay effectively?
7. Writers and speakers often use parallel structure to emphasize KEY IDEAS. King's thesis statement is, of course, an example of PARALLELISM, but there are other examples. Identify parallel structures in paragraphs 7 and 16. What do they emphasize? How effective are they? (Hint: Read the paragraphs aloud.)

Content and Purpose

1. King originally wrote "Dimensions" as a speech. As you read through the piece, what clues can you find that indicate it was designed to be heard rather than read?
2. King regards the length of life as "selfish," but, nevertheless, the basis of the other dimensions of life. How does King convince the reader that this "selfishness" is a positive rather than a negative quality?
3. What is a parable? What is the purpose of the parable in paragraphs 10 and 11?
4. King's purpose in this piece is to demonstrate that the complete life is one in which the personal, social, and spiritual dimensions are integrated. Study King's development of one of these dimensions and show how he has carefully selected his examples to reinforce his THESIS.

Suggestions for Writing

1. Write an essay of division in which you analyze your own vision of the complete life. What will bring you happiness and satisfaction?

2. Though it lasted only 39 years, King's own life fulfilled the dimensions of a "complete life." After doing some research, write a short paper describing his accomplishments.
3. Think of someone you know or have read about and write a paper explaining how that person's life satisfies King's criteria for completeness.

Additional Suggestions for Writing: Classification and Division

Use classification or division, whichever is appropriate, to analyze one of the topics below into its component parts, or characteristics, or kinds. Write a thesis statement based on your analysis and then develop it into an essay that will interest a reader who doesn't necessarily share your point of view.

1. part-time jobs
2. marriage
3. films
4. media celebrities, such as movie stars, pop stars, politicians, environmental advocates
5. computer games
6. popular novels
7. sitcoms
8. a family or families
9. dreams
10. college students
11. commercials
12. drivers
13. activists
14. friendship or friends
15. an unforgettable event
16. teachers
17. reality TV shows
18. a short story, poem, or play
19. shoppers
20. a religious or social ritual (such as a wedding, funeral, baptism, bar/bat mitzvah, birthday celebration)

UNIT 4

Comparison and Contrast

WHAT ARE COMPARISON AND CONTRAST?

Technically, to *compare* two things is to point out the similarities between them, and to *contrast* them is to point out their differences. When we look at both similarities and differences, we are engaging in *comparison and contrast*. Often, however, people use the term "comparison" to describe all three processes. "Comparison shopping," for example, means to discover significant differences among similar items. Therefore, while the purpose of the model essay "She Said, He Said" is to explore the differences between men's and women's conversation, few people would notice or object if you called the essay a comparison.

WHY DO WE USE COMPARISON AND CONTRAST?

Comparison and contrast answer the lead-in question *what*. In what ways are two things alike? In what ways are they different? Comparing and contrasting things is a common mental process; it's something we do, consciously or unconsciously, all the time. Using such a pattern in written communication can be useful in two specific ways.

First, an essay or report structured to compare various items can provide a reader with helpful information. It can offer new insight into two topics by looking at them side by side. For example, Jay Teitel's "Shorter, Slower, Weaker: And That's a Good Thing" contrasts men's and women's performances in a number of sports in order to make an interesting point about the changing physical characteristics of athletes and their games.

Second, a comparison paper can evaluate as well as inform. It can assess the relative merits of two topics and explain the writer's preference for one over the other. In "Ottawa vs. New York," for example, Germaine Greer not only contrasts the two cities but also argues strongly for the quality of life in Canada versus that in the United States.

HOW DO WE WRITE COMPARISON AND CONTRAST?

Here are four guidelines for organizing a paper according to the principles of comparison and contrast:

1. Make sure that your two topics are in fact comparable; they must have something significant in common even if you want to focus on differences.

2. Select terms of comparison that apply to both topics. For example, don't compare the hair, eyes, and figure of one person with the intelligence, ambition, and personality of another. Use the same terms of comparison for both topics.

3. Decide on the most appropriate pattern of organization to use: block or point-by-point (see below).

4. Write a thesis statement that clearly identifies your topic, states or implies your lead-in question, and indicates your organizational pattern.

Organizing a comparison according to the **block pattern** involves separating the two topics and discussing them one at a time, under the headings or categories you've chosen as your KEY IDEAS. If you were asked, for example, to compare the play and the movie versions of William Shakespeare's *Romeo and Juliet,* you might decide to focus your analysis on the characters, the setting, and the plot of the two versions. You would first discuss the play in terms of these three key ideas, and then you would do the same for the film. Here is a sample block outline for such an essay:

Paragraph 1   Introduction and thesis statement
Paragraph 2   The play

    a. characters in the play

    b. setting of the play

    c. plot of the play

Paragraph 3   The film

                   a. characters in the film

                   b. setting of the film

                   c. plot of the film

Paragraph 4   Conclusion summarizing the similarities and differences and possibly stating your preference

The block pattern does not rule out discussing the two topics in the same paragraph. In this example, particularly in your analysis of the film, some mention of the play might be necessary. However, the overall structure of a block comparison should communicate the essentials about Topic 1 and then communicate the essentials about Topic 2. The block style works best with fairly short papers (essay questions on exams, for instance) in which the reader does not have to remember many intricate details about Topic 1 while trying to understand the details of Topic 2.

Structuring a comparison according to the **point-by-point pattern** involves setting out the terms or categories of comparison, then discussing both topics under each category heading. Organized by points, the *Romeo and Juliet* essay could communicate the same information as it does in the block pattern, yet its shape and outline would be quite different:

Paragraph 1   Introduction and thesis statement

Paragraph 2   Characters

                   a. in the play

                   b. in the film

Paragraph 3   Setting

                   a. in the play

                   b. in the film

Paragraph 4   Plot

                   a. in the play

                   b. in the film

Paragraph 5   Conclusion summarizing the similarities and differences and possibly stating your preference

A point-by-point structure makes the resemblances and differences between your two topics more readily apparent to the reader. This structure is ideally suited to longer reports and papers in which the terms of comparison are complex and demand high reader recall.

The model essay that follows illustrates the point-by-point pattern of organization.

She Said, He Said

Introduction
(a scenario)

It's Friday night. You and some friends have met at your favourite bar for a little relaxation. You all place your orders, and the conversation begins. If you watch and listen carefully, you'll notice patterns in this conversation, and, depending on whether you are a male in an all-male group or a female in an all-female one,

Thesis
statement

the patterns you observe will not be the same. When men and women engage in that intrinsically human activity called "talking," there is much that is different in why they talk, the way they talk, and what they talk about.

First key idea
(specific
details
highlight
differences)

Men talk mainly to exchange information, accomplish a task, offer advice, or enhance their status. In other words, they see conversation as a tool and consequently tend to talk for a reason, often with a specific purpose in mind. Women, on the other hand, talk in order to nurture and support and empathize. Sometimes accused of "talking for the sake of talking," women in fact talk to establish and maintain relationships. Because conversation is a human connection, women perceive talking as an end in itself rather than as the means to an end.

Second key
idea (developed
by facts and
examples)

The way men and women talk also differs. Men more readily take charge of a conversation, and they are more assertive in expressing their opinions. They are more likely to interrupt another speaker or to argue with what someone else says. Men tend to make declarative statements—unlike women, who inject their conversation with numerous questions, often ending even their assertions with an uplift of the voice as if their statements were questions. Men tend to state their opinions straight out: "The problem is . . ." Women tend to soften their opinion statements with "I think that . . ." Women also tend to preface their opinions with an apology: "Perhaps I don't understand what's at issue here, but I think that . . ." The pronouns men use most often are *I* and *he;* the pronouns that occur most often in women's speech are *you* and *we*. Men tend to listen in silence, giving non-verbal signals of consent or disagreement; women tend to make positive sounds of encouragement as they listen ("Uh-huh," "Mm-hm"), even when they disagree with the speaker. Women are more willing to defer, are more emotional in their speech, and are more interested in keeping a conversation going than in controlling it.

Note transitional phrase

Third key idea (supported with examples)

Given the differences in why and how men and women talk, it should come as no surprise that what they talk about differs too. If you're a male in a group of males, you'll probably hear discussion of such things as the latest advance in hi-def technology, last night's hockey game, the price of gas, a proposed fishing trip, why Japanese cars continue to outsell North American ones, and who drank the most beer the last time you were all together. The conversation tends to focus on things more than on people. If you're a female in a group of females, chances are you'll hear about quite different topics: a new boyfriend, the latest advance in weight-loss theory, or someone's argument with her mother, fiancé, husband, child, neighbour, boss, or any combination of the above. Female conversations tend to focus less on things than they do on relationships and people.

Conclusion restates the thesis and issues a challenge

Although it is dangerous to stereotype according to gender, research has shown that there are differences in the way men and women converse. Part of what makes male and female relationships so intriguing, if sometimes frustrating, is the divergence in their speech patterns. You're still not convinced? Then conduct your own research. Just listen to your friends: why, how, and what they're saying.

Ottawa vs. New York

GERMAINE GREER

Controversial Australian feminist, author, and lecturer Germaine Greer (b. 1939) holds degrees from the universities of Melbourne, Sydney, and Cambridge. A regular contributor to periodicals and newspapers, she earned international recognition for her first book, *The Female Eunuch* (1970). Her later works include *The Obstacle Race* (1979), *Sex and Destiny* (1984), *The Whole Woman* (1999), and *The Beautiful Boy* (2003).

1   Waking up in Ottawa is not something I expect to do more than two or three times in this lifetime, and two of those times have already happened. This is not solely because Ottawa coffee is perhaps the worst in Canada and Canadian coffee on the whole the bitterest and weakest you will ever encounter, though these truths have some bearing. The badness of the coffee could be directly related to the current weakness of the currency; there was certainly an air of poverty-strickenness about the once great hotel I woke up in. My room was huge; as long as it was lit only by the forty-watt bulbs in the four lamps that cowered by the walls I could not see the dispiriting dun colour of the quarter-acre or so of carpet, but I could smell its depressing cocktail of sixty years of food, drink, smoking, cosmetics and sex, overlaid by a choking amalgam of air-freshener, carpet-deodoriser, -dry cleaner and -shampoo. I slept with the window open as the first line of defence, and then leapt out of bed and into a shower that could not be regulated heatwise or pressurewise, and scooted off to an equally dun, dispiriting and malodorous dining room for breakfast, to wit, one bran muffin and juice made from concentrate. It is sybaritism°, rather than self-discipline, that has reduced me to the semi-sylph-like proportions that I at present display. Mind you, giving interviews and making speeches "over lunch" effectively prevents ingestion of anything solid. The Women of Influence lunches I spoke at in Canada featured cold noodle salad and poly-styrene chicken thighs, suggesting more plainly than words could that Canadian businesswomen have at their command small influence and less money.

2   To escape from Ottawa . . . to New York and the Pierpont Morgan Library, I took a plane to LaGuardia. Air Canada, as desperate to penny-pinch as all other Canadian operations, was sneakily folding the Newark flight into mine, which made me forty-five minutes late, and all the good people who needed to travel to New Jersey a great deal later. In that forty-five minutes the best-run hotel on the planet, or on Fifth Avenue, which comes to the same thing, let some interloper have my room.

3   The yingling at reception was so very, very sorry. Would I endure a night in a suite at the room rate instead of the statutory $3,000 a night, and let them move me to my own room tomorrow? I hummed and hawed and sighed for as long as I thought decent, then leapt at the chance. The yingling took me up himself, and threw open the door. I strode past him into a forty-foot mirrored

salon hung with yellow silk damask; through the French windows
a terrace hedged with clipped yew offered a spectacular view of
aerial New York, as well as serried ranks of terracotta planters in
which green and rose parrot tulips exhibited themselves. The east
end of my salon was crowded with sofas and armchairs, all paying
homage to a state-of-the-art music centre which, if I'd come
equipped, I could have programmed for the whole evening. The
west end featured a baronial fireplace and a ten-seater dining table.
The yingling showed me my kitchen, my two bathrooms, and my
seven-foot-square bed in my twenty-foot bedroom, and swept out
before I could decide whether he should be tipped or not.

The only way to bring such magnificence into perspective was   4
to take off all my clothes and skip about as naked as a jaybird,
opening and shutting my closets, cupboards and drawers, turning
all my appliances off and on, my phones, my faxes, my safe. If I had
been anything more substantial than a nude scholar, I could have
invited forty friends for cocktails, nine friends for dinner and a
hundred for after-dinner drinks, and scribbled my signature on a
room service check somewhere in the high six figures.

The salon soon felt less welcoming than vast, so I took a   5
Roederer from the fridge and a salad into the bedroom, where,
perched amid piles of pillows and bolsters stuffed with goosedown,
I watched the fag-end of the Florida Marlins' batting order knock
the Atlanta Braves' relief pitcher all over the park. The bed was
meant for better things; under the television there was a VCR
player. I could have ordered a selection of video-porn from room
service, and had a cute somebody sent up to watch them with me.

Which is the great thing about New York. Anything, but any-   6
thing, can be had for money, from huge diamonds of the finest
water°, furs of lynx and sable, wines of vintages long said to have
been exhausted, important works of art and rock cocaine, to toy-
boys of the most spontaneous, entertaining and beautifully made,
of any sexual orientation and all colours. Every day, planes land at
JFK freighted with orchids from Malaysia, roses from Istanbul,
mangos gathered that morning from trees in Karnataka, passion-
fruit from Townsville, limes from Barbados, truffles from Perigord,
lobsters brought live from the coldest seas on the planet. Within
twenty-four hours all will have been put on sale and consumed.
The huge prices are no deterrent. The New York elite likes to be
seen to pay them with nonchalance°, on the J. P. Morgan principle
that if you need to know how much something costs you can't
afford it. Nobody looks at the tab; the platinum credit card is
thrown down for the obsequious salesperson to do his worst with.

That is what I don't like about New York. Below the thin upper   7
crust of high rollers there is a dense layer of struggling aspirants° to

elite status, and below them dead-end poverty, which no longer aspires, if it ever did. The vast mass of urban New Yorkers are struggling to get by, in conditions that are truly unbearable, from the helots° who open the hair salons at six in the morning and lock them up at eight at night to the dry-cleaners who have worked twelve hours a day in the steam and fumes ever since they stepped off a boat from Europe sixty or even seventy years ago. It's great that I can get my hair washed at any hour of day or night and my clothes altered or invisibly mended within four hours of dropping them off, but it is also terrible. If I ask these people about their working lives they display no rancour°; they tell me that they cannot afford to retire and are amused at my consternation°. They would rather keep on working, they say. What else would they do? The pain in the hair-dresser's feet and back, the listlessness and pallor of the dry-cleaner, can't be complained of. Everybody has to be up.

8   The power of positive thinking is to persuade people that the narrative of their grim existence is a success story. Though New Yorkers have been telling themselves that story for so long that they have stopped believing it, they cannot permit themselves to stop telling it. Everywhere in New York, wizened ancients are drudging. The lift-driver who takes me up to my hotel room looks ninety if a day. Her bird-body balances on grossly distorted feet; the hands in her white gloves are knobby with arthritis; her skeletal face is gaily painted and her few remaining hairs coloured bright auburn and brushed up into a transparent crest. She opens and shuts the doors of her lift as if her only ambition had ever been to do just that. I want to howl with rage on her behalf. The covers of the bolsters I frolic on have all been laundered, lightly starched and pressed by hand; as I play at being a nabob°, I imagine the terribleness of the hotel laundry-room, all day, every day.

9   Though I love New York, I disapprove of it. Dreary as Ottawa was, it was in the end a better place than New York. Canadians believe that happiness is living in a just society; they will not sing the Yankee song that capitalism is happiness, capitalism is freedom. Canadians have a lively sense of decency and human dignity. Though no Canadian can afford freshly squeezed orange juice, every Canadian can have juice made from concentrate. The lack of luxury is meant to coincide with the absence of misery. It doesn't work altogether, but the idea is worth defending.

Words and Meanings

Paragraph

1   sybaritism   devotion to luxury

water	quality	6
nonchalance	casual lack of concern or indifference	
aspirants	people who seek or hope to attain something (in this case, status)	7
helots	serfs or enslaved people	
rancour	bitter, deep-seated resentment	
consternation	bewilderment and dismay	
nabob	a rich and powerful person	8

Structure and Strategy

1. Greer bases her contrast primarily on DESCRIPTION. Identify details that appeal to four physical senses in paragraph 1. What is the dominant impression created by these details? Now consider Greer's description of her second hotel room, in paragraph 3. What is the dominant impression created by these details?
2. In paragraphs 2 and 3, Greer tells an ANECDOTE to explain her sudden change of surroundings. Where does she go? What happens? Summarize the events.
3. The topic of paragraph 6 is developed by examples. Identify the TOPIC SENTENCE. Which of the examples do you recognize? Which are unfamiliar to you? Do these examples effectively support Greer's KEY IDEA?
4. The THESIS of this essay appears in the CONCLUSION. Summarize it in your own words.

Content and Purpose

1. Why is Greer in Ottawa as the essay begins? How does she feel about the city?
2. Who is "the yingling" in paragraph 3? What does he do? Why do you think she refers to him as a yingling? Define the term in your own words.
3. According to the author, what is "the great thing about New York"?
4. What doesn't Greer like about New York? What contrast is the basis of this dislike? (See paragraph 7.)
5. Summarize Greer's DESCRIPTION of the woman who operates the hotel elevator (paragraph 8). Why do you think this description is so detailed? How does it affect you?
6. How does Greer feel about life in Canada? In New York? Where do you think she would rather live? Do you agree with her? Why or why not?

Suggestions for Writing

1. Write an essay comparing or contrasting two cities that you are familiar with.
2. The contrast Greer draws between Ottawa and New York is based on her assessment of the attitudes toward wealth implicit in those cities. Write an essay that contrasts life in a wealthy family, city, or country with life in a less wealthy counterpart.

Bonding Online: Websites as Substitute Communities

DAVID BROOKS

David Brooks is a senior editor with *The Weekly Standard* (Washington, DC), the Op/Ed page columnist for *The New York Times,* and a contributing editor for *Newsweek* and the *Atlantic Monthly*. He is also a regular commentator on National Public Radio, CNN's *Late Edition*, and *The NewsHour* with Jim Lehrer. He is the author of *Bobos In Paradise: The New Upper Class and How They Got There* (2000) and *On Paradise Drive: How We Live Now (And Always Have) in the Future Tense* (2004). His articles have appeared in *The New Yorker, Forbes, The Washington Post*, the *TLS (The Times Literary Supplement)*, *The Washington Times Commentary*, and many other magazines.

1 "**D**ude, we totally need to hang out. . . . Erin, you're a (great) waitress and friend. We definitely need to hang out sometime. . . . It was awesome seeing you. . . . Where did you go!!! I haven't seen you in a long time and I NEED to see you!!! Cause I love you!!! Happy New Year my sexy friend. I love you sooo much!"

2   Companionship isn't dead. Go to MySpace.com or Facebook or Xanga or any of the other online sites where people leave messages on the home pages of their friends and you'll see great waves of praise and encouragement. There's scarcely a critical word in the whole social network. It's just fervent declarations of friendship, vows to get together soon and memories of great times.

3   Some sociologists worry that we're bowling alone°, but these sites (MySpace has 20 million visitors a month) are all about community. They're commonly used by people in the new stage of life that's been created over the past few decades. They are in their early to mid-20s, out of school but with no expectation of marrying

soon. They're highly mobile, half-teen/half-adult, looking for a life plan and in between the formal networks of school, career and family.

So they bond online with an almost desperate enthusiasm. The Web pages they create are part dorm-room wall, part bulletin board, part society page. They post photos of favorite celebrities, dirty postcards and music videos. And there are tons of chug-and-grins: photos of the gang gripping beers at a bar, the tribe chugging vodka on the beach, the posse doing shots at an apartment.   4

You can see why Rupert Murdoch° . . . spent $580 million to buy the company that owns MySpace. It's become a treasured institution and in many ways, quite a positive one.   5

But, this being youth culture in America, of course there's something to make parents cringe. Every social environment has its own lingua franca°, and the one on these sites has been shaped by *American Pie*, spring break and *Girls Gone Wild*. The sites are smutty. Facebook, restricted to students and alumni of colleges, is rollicking but respectable. But there is a huge class distinction between the people on Facebook and the much larger and less-educated population that uses MySpace, where the atmosphere is much raunchier.   6

To get the attention of fast-clicking Web surfers, many women have posed for their photos in bikinis or their underwear or in *Penthouse*-parody "I clutch my breasts for you" positions. Here's a woman in a jokey sadomasochistic pose. There's one with the caption: "Yes, I make out with girls. Get over it"—with a photo of herself liplocked with a buddy.   7

The girls are the peacocks in this social universe. Their pages are racy, filled with dirty jokes and macha° declarations: "I'm hot and like to party. Why have one boy when there are plenty to go around?!" The boys' pages tend to be passive and unimaginative: a guy posing with a beer or next to a Corvette. In a world in which the girls have been schooled in sexual aggressiveness, the boys sit back and let the action come to them.   8

On most Web pages, there's a chance to list favorite TV shows and books. And though the TV lists are long (*The O.C., Desperate Housewives, Nip/Tuck*, etc.), many of the book lists will make publishers suicidal: "Books! Ha! Me! What a joke! I think reading's ridiculous. . . . I don't finish books very often but I'm attempting *Smart Women Finish Rich*. . . . This is what I have to say about books (next to an icon of Bart Simpson's rear end)."   9

The idea is to show you're a purebred party animal, which leaves us fogies with two ways to see MySpace. The happy view is that this is a generation of wholesome young people building nurturing communities, and the smutty talk is just a harmless way of   10 demarcating° an adult-free social space. The dark view is that these prolonged adolescents are filled with earnest desires for meaningful human contact, but they live in a culture that has provided them with no vocabulary to create such bonds except through cleavage and vodka.

11   Depending on the person, both views are true.

Words and Meanings

Paragraph

3	bowling alone	allusion to an influential 1996 essay by Robert D. Putnam, who argues that a strong democracy requires active involvement of its citizens and that American participation in community and political activities has declined significantly over the past 30 years; Putnam uses bowling as a metaphor for this decline: we used to bowl in leagues, but now we bowl alone
5	Rupert Murdoch	CEO of the global News Corporation empire, the largest and most influential media conglomerate in the world
6	lingua franca	a common language
8	macha	aggressive female behaviour (the feminine form of "macho")
10	demarcating	putting boundaries around

Structure and Strategy

1. Is this essay based on a comparison or a contrast? Support your answer with reference to specific paragraphs.
2. What kind of INTRODUCTION does Brooks use? Where else in the essay do you find this strategy? Why do you think Brooks uses it?
3. What is the THESIS of this essay? Is it stated or implied?
4. Why does Brooks refer to "parents" in paragraph 6? Who do you think is the intended AUDIENCE for this piece?

Content and Purpose

1. What similarities does Brooks identify in online sites such as MySpace and Facebook? See paragraphs 2, 3, and 4.
2. What is the basis of the contrast in paragraph 6? Are you familiar with these sites or similar sites?

3. What is the basis of the contrast in paragraph 8? Do you agree or disagree with the author's observation? Why?
4. What contrasting ways of looking at these Web sites does paragraph 10 offer his readers—"us fogies"? Do you agree or disagree with the author's analysis? Why?

Suggestions for Writing

1. If you use a Web site to communicate or connect with people, write an essay that explores its value in your life.
2. Write an essay comparing/contrasting your physical and your virtual communities. Some factors to consider are availability, trust, intimacy, support, and reliability of feedback. You may want to conclude by explaining to the reader which community is more important to you, and why.
3. Read "The Pleasures of the Text" (page 270) or "Net Gain: A Pollyanna-ish View of Online Personals" (page 257). Compare the view of online communication in one of these essays with that expressed in David Brooks' essay.

For Minorities, Timing Is Everything

OLIVE SKENE JOHNSON

Born in Vancouver in 1929, Johnson is a retired neuropsychologist and writer. The mother of five children, she became interested in the topic of homosexuality when she learned that her two oldest sons were gay. She went back to graduate school in psychology to learn more about human sexuality and diversity. She was awarded a Ph.D. in 1980, and in 2004, she published *The Sexual Spectrum: Exploring Human Diversity*. Johnson's articles have appeared in *Maclean's, Chatelaine*, and *McCall's*.

L eft-handedness and homosexuality both tend to run in fami-   1
lies. As my husband's family and mine have some of each, it
is not surprising that one of our children is left-handed and
another homosexual. Both my left-handed daughter and my homosexual son turned out to be bright, funny, talented people with
loving friends and family. But their experience of growing up in different minority groups was a striking contrast and an interesting
illustration of how societal attitudes change as sufficient knowledge
accumulates to make old beliefs untenable.

2   By the time my daughter was growing up, left-handedness was
no longer regarded as a sign of immorality or mental deficiency.
Almost everybody knew "openly" left-handed friends, teachers
and relatives and viewed them as normal people who wrote differently. Except for a little awkwardness in learning to write at school,
my daughter's hand preference was simply never an issue. If
people noticed it at all, they did so with a shrug. Nobody called her
nasty names or banned school library books about left-handed families, as school trustees in Surrey, B.C., recently banned books about
gay families. Nobody criticized her left-handed "lifestyle" or suggested that she might be an unfit role model for young children.
Nobody claimed that she *chose* to be left-handed and should suffer
the consequences.

3   My gay son did not choose to be different either, but when he
was growing up, homosexuality was still too misunderstood to be
accepted as just another variant of human sexuality. Because gay
people still felt unsafe revealing their sexual orientation, he was
deprived of the opportunity of knowing openly gay teachers,
friends and relatives. He grew up hearing crude jokes and nasty
names for people like him, and he entered adulthood knowing that
being openly gay could prevent you from getting a job or renting
an apartment. It could also get you assaulted.

4   Bigotry has never been reserved for homosexuality, of course. I
am old enough to remember the time when bigotry directed toward
other minorities in Canada was similar to that which is still sometimes aimed at homosexuals. In my Vancouver childhood, Chinese
were regularly called "Chinks" (the boys in my high school wore
black denim "Chink pants" tailored for them in Chinatown). Black
people were "niggers," prohibited from staying in most Vancouver
hotels. Kids in the special class were "retards" or "morons." Jews
were suspected of all sorts of crazy things, and physically disabled
people were often regarded as mental defectives.

5   When I was a child, left-handed children were still being pun-
ished for writing with their left hand, particularly in the more religious parts of Canada. (When I was a graduate psychology student
in Newfoundland doing research on handedness, I discovered that
several of my "right-handed" subjects were actually left-handers; at
school their left hands had been tied behind their backs by zealous
nuns.)

6   The gay children and teachers of my childhood were simply
invisible. Two female teachers could live together without raising
eyebrows, chiefly because women in those days (especially women
teachers) were not generally thought of as sexual persons. Two male
"bachelors" living together did tend to be suspect, and so gay men

brave enough to live together usually kept their living arrangements quiet. "Sissy" boys and "boyish" girls took a lot of teasing,
but most people knew too little about homosexuality to draw any
conclusions. These boys and girls were expected to grow up and
marry people of the opposite sex. Some of them did, divorcing
years later to live with one of their own.

Many of the teachers and parents of my childhood who tried to   7
convert left-handed children into right-handers probably believed
they were helping children avoid the stigma of being left-handed,
just as many misguided therapists tried to "cure" patients of their
homosexuality to enable them to avoid the stigma of being gay in a
heterosexual world.

Thanks to advances in our understanding, left-handedness   8
gradually came to be seen as a natural and innate trait. We know
now that people do not *choose* to be more skillful with one hand
than the other; they simply are. While researchers are still debating
the precise mechanisms that determine hand preference, there is
general agreement that left- and right-handedness are just two different (and valid) ways of being. Left-handers are a minority in
their own right, not "deviants" from normal right-handedness.

The same is true for sexual orientation. Although we do not yet   9
clearly understand the mechanisms that determine sexual orientation, all indicators point to the conclusion that it results from interactions between genetic, hormonal and possibly other factors, all
beyond the individual's control. Like left-handedness, sexual orientation is an innate trait, not a choice or "lifestyle." Like left-handedness, homosexuality is a valid alternative sexuality, not a deviance
from "normal" heterosexuality.

As with other minorities, attitudes toward homosexuality are   10
inevitably becoming more liberal, at least in Canada. A recent poll,
commissioned by the B.C. Teachers' Federation, found that almost
70 per cent of B.C. residents think students should be taught in
school to accept homosexuals and treat them as they would other
people. (Twenty per cent said homosexuality should be discouraged, 9 per cent said they didn't know and 3 per cent refused to
answer.) These results indicate that overt bigotry toward homosexuality is increasingly limited to religious extremists. The Surrey
school trustees who voted against having gay and lesbian resource
materials in schools are probably at about the same stage of cultural
evolution as were the Newfoundland nuns who tied children's left
hands behind their backs 40 years ago.

Even so, I'm grateful that they're further along the path of   11
enlightenment than their predecessors in medieval Europe, who
burned many left-handers and homosexuals at the stake. Being

born in the late 20th century was a wise move on the part of my son and daughter. In some things, timing is everything.

Structure and Strategy

1. What two topics are compared and contrasted in this essay? How is the essay structured—in blocks, or point by point?
2. Is the THESIS of this essay stated or implied?
3. What is the TOPIC SENTENCE of paragraph 4? How is the topic developed?
4. What is the TOPIC SENTENCE of paragraph 10? How is it developed? What sentence in this paragraph is likely to alienate some of Johnson's target AUDIENCE?
5. Look at the final paragraph of this essay. Is it an effective CONCLUSION? Why or why not?

Content and Purpose

1. The title of this essay is a generalization. What do you think it means? Do you agree with the statement it makes?
2. To develop the main points of this essay, Johnson uses her own children as examples. Does the personal connection enhance or detract from the point she is making?
3. What are the points that Johnson uses to contrast the way that her children were treated as they were growing up?
4. Paragraphs 5–7 develop a different contrast. What is it?
5. Summarize the comparison that Johnson makes between "handedness" and homosexuality in paragraphs 8 and 9.
6. What is the main PURPOSE of this piece? How effective do you think the author is in achieving it?

Suggestions for Writing

1. Do you agree or disagree with Johnson's THESIS? Write a clearly organized PERSUASIVE essay based on your opinion. Use a variety of support for your opinion; don't rely on personal ANECDOTES alone.
2. Choose two kinds of discrimination, and write an essay that compares and/or contrasts them.
3. Do some research into "handedness" and write an essay that explains why people are either right- or left-handed. Where does ambidexterity fit into this classification?

4. Have you experienced discrimination or bigotry? Write an essay that explains your experience and explores its effect on you.

Shorter, Slower, Weaker: And That's a Good Thing

JAY TEITEL

Jay Teitel (b. 1949), an award-winning writer and editor, graduated from the University of Toronto in 1973. A frequent contributor to magazines, he writes non-fiction, fiction, humour, and screenplays and is co-inventor of the board game Therapy.

Three years ago I was channel-surfing on a Sunday afternoon in December, bouncing between NFL offerings that were even deadlier than usual, when I flicked to a hockey game that stopped me cold. There was something about the game that was both strange and naggingly familiar. For starters, the play on the ice was shapely and unbroken; teams moved out of their zones in creative wholes, the patterns unclogged by so much of the frantic flukiness of modern NHL play. On top of that, passes were being completed at a rate that wouldn't have been out of place on a basketball court, and that I hadn't seen on a rink since I watched a sixteen-year-old Wayne Gretzky play for the Sault Ste. Marie Greyhounds. In fact I assumed for a second that I was watching a junior game, maybe an all-star match. But a younger age group couldn't possibly have explained the style of play I was seeing. And then it came to me: I was watching something not younger, but older—something historical. I'd stumbled onto a weirdly faithful recreation of the old grainy kinetypes of NHL games from the thirties and forties. I was watching a memory.

At which point one of the more boisterous anachronisms° got a penalty for slashing. A helmet was pulled off in chagrin, and I saw exactly who the creators of this lost and perfect game were: women.

A quick glance through recent issues of *Sports Illustrated*, or TSN's weekend listings, is enough to suggest that there is a small but unprecedented explosion in the popularity of women's sports, both amateur and professional. Part of this movement is probably linked to an increased female fan-base (women are buying more cars than ever, for instance, and car companies traditionally

1

2

3

sponsor sports events), but just as significant is the phenomenon I witnessed that afternoon three years ago on my TV screen: what you might call the Law of the Intersecting Gender Gap. . . . Men have outgrown many of the traditional sports, while women have been growing into them.

4   For anyone who's spent a couple of introspective hours watching TV sports lately, the evidence is tangible. While it's undeniable that male athletes today have elevated the skill level in most of the popular sports—football, basketball, hockey, tennis, golf, even track and field—to a dazzling level, in virtually all these sports the same male players have outstripped in size and speed the confines of the standard playing spaces that define their games. Whether it's on rinks, fields, or courts, they just don't seem to fit any more. Pro football, with 250-pound guided missiles capable of running four-second forty-yard dashes on a 100-yard postage stamp of a field, has turned into a kind of mesomorphic pinball; NHL hockey, as much a game of space as speed, is too often more of the same. NBA basketball, half the time a breathtaking nightly highlight package, for the other half is a pituitary, one-dimensional jamboree, with as many field goals being released above the rim as below, with jump shots clanging off rims, and two guys playing one-on-one the rest of the game. In men's golf, prodigal *Übermen-schen°* like Tiger Woods have made the notion of par fives, and even fours, obsolete with 350-yard drives, and in tennis the 120-mile serve-and-volley game has turned the sport into a live-action Super Mario game that ends every seven seconds.

5   At the same time the female version of every one of the above-mentioned sports has quietly become an oasis of form. Women's hockey is even more fun to watch now than it was [before body-checking was outlawed]; women's tennis features long rallies and good net play; the women's golf tour continues to boast better putters and fine short-iron players, if less monstrous drivers; and as far as round-ball goes, the legendary John Wooden, coach of ten NCAA men's champion teams at UCLA, recently noted that "Some of the best pure basketball I see lately is being played by women." There seems to be a confluence° between playing surface and game in women's sports that is harmonious and satisfying. The men amaze you, you jump out of your chair crying "All right!" at the same time knowing that something is half wrong. The women let you sink back into the sofa with a quieter delight, and reach for the chips. They have the space to play; you have the space to watch.

6   If this yearning seems nostalgic, it's no accident. The fact is that nearly all modern sports were either invented or codified into their present-day form at the same time—[just over 100 years ago]. More

critically, they were designed to be played by men at the turn of the century. And it turns out that men 100 years ago were closer to the women athletes of today, in both size and performance, than they were remotely close to their modern male counterparts. In women's sports today we see not only the original sports recreated, but the original athletes.

Basketball is a classic example. The average height of the [1990s] Toronto Raptors, an "average" NBA team, [was] 6'6⅓"—about nine inches taller than the average for the male population at large. In 1898, though, just seven years after the transplanted Canadian James Naismith nailed his peach baskets ten feet above the floor at a Springfield, Massachusetts, Y, the average height of the Buffalo Germans, one of the first pro teams, was only marginally taller than the lay-population average of the day. "From 1898 to 1915," notes Bill Himmelman, President/Owner of Sports Nostalgia Research in New Jersey and league historian for the NBA, "the 'big men' on pro teams, the centres, were anywhere from 6' to 6'3". The first exceptional big man, John Wendelken of Columbia University, was all of 6'2". The guards of the day, defensive specialists, were in the 5'10" range, while the forwards, the speedy shooters, were about 5'7"." Assuming equal distribution among the players, the average height of a team like the Buffalo Germans would have been in the 5'11" range—precisely the average height of the women playing in one of today's new professional leagues, the ABL.

But maybe more important than the numerical match was the style of the turn-of-the-century game. "The set-shot was the big weapon then, a 24–40 foot shot, compared to a 21-foot three-point shot today," adds Bill Himmelman, "and the only way a short guy could get it off was to back up on the taller players. Your forwards were your best shooters and your best drivers. Coaches actually avoided recruiting tall players; height was considered a handicap, it was thought to make you uncoordinated. As far as dunking went, coaches wouldn't let you do it; it was considered an absolute sham." No dunking, precision outside shooting, an emphasis on the fast break, a foul shooting percentage consistently higher than the NBA's—all these are hallmarks of topflight women's basketball today. Again, the individual manoeuvres aren't nearly as awe-inspiring as in the NBA, but the gestalt° is a whole level higher. The acting's less prodigious, but the story's better. . . .

The pattern in hockey is the same. Although size statistics don't exist from 1893, the year Baron Stanley of Preston donated a cup to the winners of collegiate hockey in Canada (rink size had been standardized by McGill University students about fifteen years earlier), they are available from 1940. In an NHL guide from that year, the first two pages alone list eighteen players under 5'10" in height, including seven at 5'7" and four at 5'6", with an average weight of 166 lbs (compared to the 6'1", 198-pound average in the NHL today). Using historical growth rates, it's reasonable to posit° a men's pro hockey team at the turn of the century with an average height in the 5'6½" range, and an average weight of about 150 lbs. The averages for the first six position players on the 1996/97 Canadian Women's National Hockey team list? 5'6½", 150 lbs.

10   It could be argued that such coincidences still deal mainly with size, and size doesn't necessarily translate to performance. A 150-pound man, for instance, will probably be stronger and faster than a 150-pound woman. (Tiger Woods, at 160 pounds, regularly outdrives not only 160-pound women but 260-pound men.) But it's in the one sport where we have hard historical comparative performance records that the similarity between today's female athletes and males at the dawn of the century is at its eeriest. It turns out that nearly every major track and field record held by women today is almost identical to the records held by men seventy to ninety years ago. . . .

11   Aside from a couple of intriguing future speculations—in about 2085 someone's great-granddaughter should be matching Donovan Bailey's current record time in the 100 metres—the most important implication of all the above is philosophical as opposed to logistic. The match between today's women and yesterday's men is signifi-cant because it gives us a seat at an unexpected remake of a "golden age" of athletics, when sport was less about spectacle and entertainment and more about the game itself. The argument one large camp of veteran sports fans will make in response, that if men's sports were so proportionally deficient today they wouldn't also be so unprecedentedly popular, is as flawed as any cultural argument from popularity. Droves of people go to see pro wrestling and [bad] movies—is that convincing proof of their quality? No, the radical, "dated" notion is that there might be an ideal in sport that actually diverges from the TV ratings. No one denies that male pro sports can be exciting (with the possible exception of NFL football, which without the point spread would be like watching paint dry), but they are a new universe unto themselves that lacks the satisfac-tion of the conventions, the old verities° of shapeliness.

12   As far as shapeliness of "fit" goes, for that matter, the solution for men's sports seems obvious: if the shoe crimps, stretch it. If male athletes have outgrown the physical spaces they play on, enlarge the spaces. Only a combination of greed (having fewer exorbitantly priced seats to sell) and timidity (having to listen to

Don Cherry bray) has prevented the NHL from widening its rinks fifteen feet to Olympic size, and returning the game to its skill players, halting the clutch and grab movement in mid-hook. If the Canadian Football League can produce a superior game with inferior players by dint of a field ten yards longer and fifteen yards wider than the NFL gridiron, how much more superior would the American game be if it stretched its boundaries? As for basketball, if James Naismith had known that a 7'7" Romanian redwood named Gheorghe Muresan would someday bestride his wooden court, would he not have raised the basket a foot or so?

But juggling dimensions is only half the fix, one that on its own   13 evades the deeper lesson that women's sports have to teach us. In a socio-economic coincidence as unerring as the physical one, women athletes today, particularly team sport athletes, are crossing precisely the same threshold between amateurism and professionalism their male counterparts did at the turn of the century. Love of the game is far more likely to be burning in them than love of money or fame, because the latter simply aren't there. Women's pro leagues are in their infancy; big crowds are still largely wishful thinking. Unless they're tennis players or golfers, most female athletes can only dream about six-figure salaries, let alone the millions doled out regularly to journeyman male athletes. As a result they're still refreshingly free of the arrogance that permeates so many pro male locker-rooms these days. . . . Aside from their physical gifts, the ways and means of women athletes tend to be modest. Which is to say, like ours.

And this is the most delicate message of women's sports today: 14 it isn't necessary that our athletic heroes have our physical limitations, but it helps if their aspirations are scaled close enough to ours that the rhythm of our dreams coincides. Size in this context may be just a handy metaphor. In their rudeness, their ego, the unseemly magnitude of their contracts, and their substitution of contempt for sportsmanship, a large percentage of male pro athletes today have become not just physical but emotional misfits. They have burst not just the dimensions of sport, but its spirit. Conversely, in their relative sincerity, their humility, their lack of affect, their newness to professionalism in many cases, women athletes go a long way towards restoring the balance. This too may change, but for the moment they have about them a forgotten scent of something eternally ancient and eternally new, a sense of proportion, an old-fashioned passion for the game well played.

Words and Meanings

Paragraph		
2	anachronisms	persons, things, ideas, or customs that are attributed to a historical period to which they do not belong
4	*Übermenschen*	supermen [German]
5	confluence	a coming together
8	gestalt	an integrated set of elements or experiences which is perceived as a whole that is more than the sum of its parts [German]
9	posit	assume or propose as a fact
11	verities	truths

Structure and Strategy

1. What strategy does Teitel use in his INTRODUCTION? Why is paragraph 2 so short?
2. In paragraph 4, what KEY IDEA is supported by examples? Have any significant examples been omitted?
3. To develop his THESIS, does Teitel rely on comparison or contrast—or a combination of the two? Why do you think he chose this pattern of development to explore his topic?

Content and Purpose

1. What is your opinion of the essay's title? Did it appeal to you? What did it lead you to expect from the essay?
2. What is the "Law of the Intersecting Gender Gap" as Teitel explains it in paragraph 3?
3. While men's sports have been outgrowing their playing surfaces, women's sports have "quietly become an oasis of form." Study the examples Teitel provides in paragraph 5 to explain the phrase "oasis of form." Then define this phrase in your own words.
4. What does the comparative record of men's and women's performance in track and field for the past seventy to ninety years suggest about the validity of Teitel's ARGUMENT? (See paragraph 10.)
5. Teitel would like to see playing fields, courts, rinks, and golf courses enlarged to accommodate the increased size and strength of today's male athletes. Do you agree with him? Why or why not?
6. Why does Teitel think that male professional athletes have become "emotional misfits" (paragraph 14)? Do you agree with him? Why or why not?

7. According to Teitel, who is more likely to harbour a "love of the game": professional male athletes or professional female athletes? What are the reasons behind Teitel's position? Summarize his argument.

Suggestions for Writing

1. Are professional athletes overpaid? How do multimillion-dollar salaries affect the performances of individual athletes and their teams? Write an essay on the dramatic growth in professional sports salaries in recent years.
2. Should male and female athletes play together on the same teams? Why or why not?

Yeah, But the Book Is Better

THANE ROSENBAUM

Thane Rosenbaum is an essayist, a law professor, and the award-winning author of several critically claimed novels, including *Second Hand Smoke* (1999) and *The Golems of Gotham* (2002). His articles, reviews, and essays appear frequently in *The New York Times*, the *Los Angeles Times*, *The Wall Street Journal*, *The Washington Post*, and *The New York Sun*. He is now working on a novel for young adults, *The Stranger Within Sarah Stein*.

Whenever a film is adapted from a favorite novel, serious 1 readers of fiction are prone to say, "Yeah, but the book is better." True partisans° of the written page are always in conflict with those who like their stories cinematically revealed, projected onto wide screens that illuminate the darkness and pierce the quiet with Dolby Surround sound. The magic of movies, for so many in our increasingly visual society, is a far more stimulating and efficient storytelling experience than the labor intensity of reading.

I've had to think about this recently because one of my novels, 2 *Second Hand Smoke*, is being developed into an independent feature film, and I was asked to co-write the screenplay. I had never written dialogue that was naked of narrative, and so I learned a good deal about what goes into a screenplay and what has to be taken out of a novel in adapting it into a film.

3   While certain novelists have successfully written screenplays from their own books—John Irving received an Academy Award for his adaptation of *The Cider House Rules*; Vladimir Nabokov wrote the screenplay for his *Lolita*; Robert Stone co-wrote *Who'll Stop the Rain*, which was adapted from his novel, *Dog Soldiers*; and E. L. Doctorow lifted his fictional Rosenbergs from the page and brought them to the screen in *Daniel* (from *The Book of Daniel*)—I'm not sure that there is, generally, a great advantage to having the author of the novel become part of the filmmaking team. After all, the novelist may know the story best, but perhaps he or she knows it too well.

4   Those who maintain that imitation is the sincerest form of flattery have obviously never been imitated; any ego boost is offset by the nervous laughter from having all those tics, gestures and intonations exaggerated to the point of caricature. The same is true with a film adaptation. Giving art a second life sometimes creates more of a mutant than a clone. This explains the natural impulse to preserve the story in its original form. Any adaptation results in something new, and thereby false when compared with the original.

5   Yet, the film version may offer its own virtues. Indeed, many films have outshone the books that inspired them. *The Godfather* and *Gone With the Wind* come to mind. The fact is, novels and films are entirely different storytelling experiences. When it comes to making a movie based on a book—or ultimately watching the movie—being too invested in the integrity of the novel is probably a bad idea.

6   A film adaptation that is deemed "faithful" to the novel is not necessarily a compliment. The most successful adaptations have actually been adulterous: Liberties are taken; all kinds of cheating ensues. The artistic license enables great leaps of improvisation. There are redesigned endings, compressed time periods and newly invented characters, and often an entirely different storytelling mechanism. Anyone who read *The English Patient* before having seen the Academy Award-winning movie remembers shaking his head, imagining how in the world Michael Ondaatje's superbly interior novel could ever sparkle so majestically on the silver screen.

7   But what films sacrifice in the small window of opportunity of a movie screen they make up in artfulness. Montage effects, slow motion, split screens, close-ups and superimposed images create visual moments that aren't easily described in prose and are even more difficult to re-imagine as a reader. These filmic devices may be manipulative, but they are often emotionally effective.

Films require dispensing with many secondary characters that   8
fit nicely within a novel but tend to overcrowd a movie. Sometimes
several minor characters of a novel are consolidated to form one
great "character actor" for a film. Other times, filmmakers change
the geography of the novel—as in the short film *Bartleby*, based on
Herman Melville's "Bartleby, the Scrivener," in which New York
was replaced by Los Angeles. The novels of Charles Dickens have
undergone all sorts of reworkings, some bearing only a tenuous
connection to the original story. *Great Expectations*, for instance, was
recently adapted into a late 20th-century tale with characters
renamed and foggy London entirely lifted and replaced by the clear
skies of Florida.

As Chekhov famously once instructed, if there is a gun in Act I,   9
it needs to be fired in Act II, and the same holds true with films
(though the aphorism° is tweaked slightly to also make sure that a
gun is never inserted into a scene unless it makes a loud noise).
Certain things have to happen at various markers of a movie, otherwise audiences, expecting such contrivances, will simply walk out.

Yet, in novels, all kinds of props are abandoned on the page.   10
Not everything needs to be resolved, not every loose end must be
tied up for the novel to be satisfying. Ambiguity is tolerated much
more readily; the impulse toward linearity—the beginning, middle
and end of a story—is almost nonexistent in modern fiction.

It is for this reason that Franz Kafka has never received a cine-   11
matically successful treatment of his fiction, even though he has
been arguably the most important literary figure of the past century. Magical realism doesn't translate well into films. Similarly,
dark psychological complexity is not particularly well suited to
cinema, which is why Fyodor Dostoevsky's novels have not been
successfully adapted, either. A strong interior narrative voice
simply doesn't come across in film—even if one allows for
voiceovers.

With all these obstacles and risks, you can see why starting   12
from scratch with an original screenplay makes sense. Other than
studio executives, no one has any great expectations because no one
is guarding the central text, hovering nervously and breathing
down the screenwriter's back.

Ultimately, feature films cannot replicate the experience of   13
reading, nor can everything about a novel end up being adapted—
nor should it be. Filmmaking is about compromise and concession.
It's a miracle they don't toss the book right out the window.

With a novel, the author forms an implicit partnership with his   14
audience. He provides the story and its voice, but the reader adds

the visuals. The power of a novel's description is often tempered by sketchy details. Much is left out in order to leave something to the imagination. The reader is free to conjure the characters in his own way, to picture how they look, because the mind's eye has a way of assembling an image that is quite different from how a character might appear on screen. In the end, the novelist surrenders his book to his readers. Thereafter it becomes theirs, and his proprietary interest° ceases.

15   Movies, by contrast, are more controlled; the director calls the shots, and the camera focuses the point of view. The eyes of the audience are being drawn in a certain direction, but not necessarily from left to right. Which is, after all, what central casting° looks for in a reader.

Words and Meanings

Paragraph

1	partisans	enthusiastic supporters
9	aphorism	a familiar truth
14	proprietary interest	total ownership and control
15	central casting	figurative reference to the agency or studio department responsible for hiring actors for specific parts

Structure and Strategy

1. How does the first paragraph introduce the contrast that is the basis for this essay?
2. How does the personal ANECDOTE included in paragraph 2 contribute to the author's credibility on this topic?
3. Identify the CLICHÉ with which the author begins paragraph 4. Does the author believe this cliché is accurate or true? What connection does he make between the cliché and the adaptation of a novel into a film?
4. Rosenbaum cites a number of writers to support his THESIS. Which ones have you read or heard of? Who do you think is the target AUDIENCE for this essay?
5. What is the ANALOGY that begins paragraph 6? Do you think this analogy is effective in explaining why creative adaptations of a novel to film are often more successful than strict print-to-film translations?

Content and Purpose

1. Does Rosenbaum argue that books are better than movies, or vice versa? What are the specific contrasts developed in the essay?
2. What are two movies, according to Rosenbaum, that have been better than the novels they are based on? Do you agree or disagree? Why?
3. Why does Rosenbaum think that novelists are not necessarily the best adapters of their books to movies?
4. What are some of the technical effects movies can use that novelists cannot? (See paragraph 7.)
5. What are some of the changes to a novel that filmmakers can make to enhance the movie experience? Identify at least three examples.
6. According to the author, which storytelling method—novels or movies—is more tolerant of "ambiguity" (paragraph 10)? Do you agree or disagree? Why?
7. Which novelists and kinds of fiction don't translate well into film, according to Rosenbaum? Why?
8. Summarize the key differences between books and movies that Rosenbaum explains in paragraphs 13–15. Which medium do you think he prefers?

Suggestions for Writing

1. Which method of storytelling do you prefer: novels or movies? Write an essay that explains your preference.
2. Write an essay that compares and/or contrasts the movie version with a novel or play that you've read.
3. Read "With Pens Drawn" by novelist Mario Vargas Llosa on page 361. Compare Rosenbaum's ideas about the relationship of film and fiction with Vargas Llosa's view.

Additional Suggestions for Writing: Comparison and Contrast

Write a comparison and/or contrast paper based on one of the topics below. Make sure that your thesis statement identifies the basis of your comparison or contrast, then develop it by providing relevant examples and details.

1. Contrast two people of your acquaintance whose lifestyles reveal different attitudes toward life.
2. Compare and/or contrast living in Canada with living in another country.
3. Compare and/or contrast two sports, teams, or players.
4. Compare and/or contrast men and women as consumers (or voters, employees, supervisors, friends, roommates, students, etc.).
5. Compare and/or contrast two artists—painters, poets, film directors, musicians, or actors—with whose work you are familiar.
6. Contrast your present career goals with those you dreamed of as a child. How do you account for the differences between the two sets of goals?
7. Compare and/or contrast two types of contemporary music, such as hip-hop, techno, or house.
8. Compare and/or contrast the way in which you and your parents view a particular issue: premarital sex, postsecondary education, raising children, children's obligations to their parents.
9. Compare and/or contrast men's and women's attitudes toward love, children, and family responsibilities.
10. "All happy families resemble one another, but each unhappy family is unhappy in its own way." (Leo Tolstoy)

Causal Analysis

WHAT IS CAUSAL ANALYSIS?

In Unit 3, we defined ANALYSIS as the process of separating something into its parts in order to understand the whole better. The word "causal" (not to be confused with "casual," which means something else entirely) refers to "causes," so *causal analysis* means identifying the causes or reasons for something; the term also refers to analyzing effects.

Causal analysis is a rhetorical pattern based on this kind of thinking. A writer may explain *causes*, the reasons for something. For example, the model essay in this unit, "The Trouble with Readers," explains the reasons for breakdowns in written communication. (Actually, the "cause" isn't readers at all—it's writers.) Or a writer may analyze the *effects* of something. In his funny and sad essay "The Telephone" (page 178), Anwar Accawi describes the effects of the arrival of the first telephone in his small village in Lebanon. Sometimes, a writer explores both causes and effects, which is often a longer, more complex process. In "Just Walk On By" on page 173, Brent Staples looks at some causes of racism and traces its effects on the author.

WHY DO WE USE CAUSAL ANALYSIS?

Causal analysis answers the lead-in question *what*. Our natural human curiosity leads us to ask, "What made this happen?" and "What were the results?" We look for causes and examine effects in an attempt to make sense of the flow of events around us.

Causal analysis can be used to explain complicated connections between ideas. Often, complex historical, political, or scientific phenomena are best understood by looking at their causes. For example, in "The Evolution of Evolution" (on page 191), Helena Cronin makes the difficult concept of Darwinian evolution accessible to readers by asking simple questions about the causes of quite different phenomena: sexual attraction and the craving for fast food.

Causal analysis is also used to get readers to think about new ideas and to argue the merits of a particular point of view. For instance, in "Saving the Songs of Innocence" (on page 186), John Dixon refers to the devastating effects that humans have had on the environment to support his argument that we must respect the natural world.

HOW DO WE WRITE CAUSAL ANALYSIS?

Causal analysis is a challenging pattern of EXPOSITION. It is not easy to write because the thinking behind it must be rigorously logical. During the research and preparation stage, take the time to sort out your ideas before you begin to write. Here are six guidelines for writing a good causal analysis:

1. Be objective in your research. Don't oversimplify. Recognize that an event can be triggered by a number of causes.

2. Don't mistake coincidence for cause. The fact that one event happened before another does not mean the first event caused the second.

3. Analyze complex ideas carefully in order to sort out the *remote* (more distant, not immediately apparent) causes or effects and the *immediate* (direct, readily apparent) causes or effects.

4. Choose your focus and scope with care. In a short essay, you may have to focus on several immediate causes, while omitting more remote or complicated ones.

5. Write a clear thesis statement. Usually, it will contain a preview of the causes or effects you intend to explain as KEY IDEAS.

6. Support your causal analysis with sufficient, interesting, and well-chosen EVIDENCE (e.g., statistical data, examples, facts, definitions where required, and "expert witness" quotations). This supporting material should make the logic of your analysis clear to the reader.

The model essay that follows is a causal analysis of some of the causes of miscommunication between writers and readers.

The Trouble with Readers

Introduction (a set of questions)

Have you ever wondered why a letter you spent a long time composing was misunderstood by the recipient? Or why a report you submitted after careful research didn't have the impact you intended? Written language is vulnerable to misinterpretation, and the trouble with readers is that they read what you write, not what you

Thesis statement

mean. Clarity gives way to confusion if the writer fails to pay attention to the ambiguity of words, the mechanics of writing, or the organization of ideas.

First cause (developed by definition and examples)

English is notorious for its ambiguity—many English words have more than one meaning. The word *fan,* for instance, means a cooling device, an avid sports enthusiast, and a bird's tail. A *bank* may be a place to deposit money, the edge of a river, or the side-to-side slope of a racetrack. In addition to their dictionary meanings, words are subject to personal interpretation, and the more abstract the word, the more personal the interpretation becomes. Most readers can agree on what *cat* means but have different emotional reactions to words such as *abortion* or *euthanasia*, whose meanings resonate more deeply than their dictionary definitions imply. Even *cat* can stir feelings if used in one of its many slang senses or if the reader is allergic to cats.

Second cause (developed by examples)

If a writer has a shaky grasp of the mechanics of writing and cannot spell, punctuate, or construct grammatical sentences, clarity will be further eroded. Correctness goes beyond avoiding such obvious errors as "We could of done better." Even a single punctuation mark can dramatically alter meaning. Leave out the apostrophe in "The instructor called the students' names," and your reader will assume you have a provocateur, not a professor, in the classroom. Sometimes misunderstanding results from faulty word order: "Under the proposed plan, the elderly who now receive free prescription drugs will be abolished." Few readers will make the mistake of thinking that the writer of this sentence intended its dire implications, but most readers will smile. Of all the possible misunderstandings between writer and reader, perhaps the most painful is being laughed at when you didn't intend to be funny.

Third cause (developed by division and examples)

Finally, there is the matter of content: what to include and in what order. You need to include enough detail to give your reader the complete picture—in other words, all the information he or she requires. But different readers require different amounts of information. For example, if you are a computer programmer writing a report, you will not waste your supervisor's time by defining terms such as OOP, MIME, or URL.

Note transition words Finally, For example, Alternatively

Alternatively, if your report is destined for someone who has little familiarity with computers, you will need to explain these terms and probably many more. You don't want to include anything irrelevant or redundant. If you do, you will create confusion, boredom, frustration—or all three. The order in which you present your points makes a difference, too. In writing, as in life, humans need to perceive a sequence to events. When no order is apparent, readers become confused. If you're describing a process, for example, you will probably arrange your points chronologically. But if you are writing to convince, you will want to build to a strong conclusion and will likely arrange your points in climactic order. Never underestimate the importance of logic in writing!

Conclusion (highlights significance of topic; refers back to introduction)

Communicating clearly is not easy, and writing is the most demanding of all forms of communication. As a writer, you must pay close attention to words, mechanics, and organization. If you ignore even one of these obligations, your message may well be misinterpreted—because your readers will read what you wrote, not what you meant.

The Slender Trap*

TRINA RYS

Born in Kirkland Lake, Ontario, in 1980, Trina Rys studied at the University of Guelph and Humber College. She wrote this essay in her first semester at Humber. Trina is currently a stay-at-home mom, living in Mississauga, Ontario, with her husband and daughter.

> Starvation is not a pleasant way to expire. In advanced stages of famine, as the body begins to consume itself, the victim suffers muscle pain, heart disturbances, loss of hair, dizziness, shortness of breath, extreme sensitivity to cold, physical and mental exhaustion. The skin becomes discoloured. In the absence of key nutrients, a severe chemical imbalance develops in the brain, inducing convulsions and hallucinations. (Krakauer, 1996, p. 198)

Every day, millions die of hunger. The symptoms of starvation are so horrific that it seems unthinkable anyone would choose this way of death. How is it possible that in the Western world, one in two hundred young women from upper- and middle-class families practises starvation as a method of weight control? How do young women become so obsessed with being thin that they develop anorexia nervosa? To cause such a fearsome and potentially fatal condition, the influencing factors must be powerful indeed. And they are powerful: the psychological pressures of adolescence, the inescapable expectations of family and peers, and the potent influence of the media.

A tendency to perfectionism, lack of identity, and feelings of helplessness are three aspects of a young woman's psychology that can contribute to the development of anorexia nervosa. Young women who exhibit perfectionism are particularly susceptible to the disease because they often have unrealistic expectations about their physical appearance. These expectations can lead to feelings of helplessness and powerlessness, and some young women with these feelings see starving themselves as a means to empowerment. Their diet is often the only thing they can control, and they control it with a single-mindedness that astonishes and horrifies their families and friends. As well as the need for control, anorexia in young women can be caused by a weak or unformed identity. Confused

---

*This essay is an example of use of the American Psychological Association (APA) documentation method. For information on APA essay formatting and style, go to the Web site for this book at www.cancon6e.nelson.com.

about who they are, many young women define themselves by how closely they approximate our society's notion of the ideal woman. Unfortunately, for the past half-century, Western society's ideal female image has been that of an unrealistically thin young woman. When women focus on this impossible image as the ideal and strive to starve their bodies into submission, they suffer emotional and physical damage.

3   In addition to an unstable psychological state, family and peer pressure can contribute to a fragile young woman's development of anorexia nervosa. By emphasizing physical appearance, by criticizing physical features, and even by restricting junk food, family members can push a young woman over the cliff edge that separates health from illness. A home environment in which physical appearance is overvalued can be destructive for young women. Surrounded by family members and friends who seem to be concerned primarily about appearance, a young woman can begin to feel insecure about how she looks. This uncertainty can produce the desire—and then the need—to look better. And better means thinner. This flawed logic underlies the disease in many young women. A family or peer group that overvalues physical appearance is often also critical of physical flaws. Critical comments about weight and general appearance, even when spoken jokingly, can be instrumental in a young woman's desire to be thin. Ironically, food restrictions imposed by parents can also contribute to anorexia in young women. Restricting the consumption of junk food, for example, has been known to cause bingeing and purging, a condition associated with anorexia.

4   While a young woman's developing psyche and the pressures of those close to her can exert tremendous influence, the root cause of the "thin is beautiful" trap is a media-inspired body image. Television, fashion magazines, and stereotypical Hollywood images of popular stars provide young women with an unrealistic image of the ideal female body. While only 5 percent of North American females are actually underweight, 32 percent of female television and movie personalities are unhealthily thin (ANRED, 2004). The media's unrealistic portrayal of a woman's ideal body can cause a young woman to develop a sense of inadequacy. To be considered attractive, she feels she must be ultra-thin. Television's unrealistic portrayal of the way young women should look is reinforced in the pages of fashion magazines. Magazine ads feature tall, beautiful, *thin* women. Media images also perpetuate the stereotype that a woman must be thin in order to be successful. Thanks to television and movies, when we think of a successful woman, the image that comes to mind is that of a tall, well-dressed, *thin* woman. This

stereotypical image leads impressionable young women to associate success with body weight and image. When internalized by young women, these artificial standards can result in the development of anorexia nervosa.

If the media do not begin to provide young women with a posi- 5
tive and healthy image of femininity, we will see no lessening in the numbers of anorexia victims. If our cultural ideal of female beauty does not change to reflect a range of healthy body types, the pressures to realize idealized and unhealthy physical standards will continue, and young women's feelings of helplessness and inadequacy will persist. In order for anorexia to become less prominent among young women, healthier associations must replace the existing connections among beauty, success, and thinness. Young women must realize that self-inflicted starvation is not a means to empowerment, but a process of self-destruction.

References

ANRED: Anorexia Nervosa and Related Eating Disorders, Inc. (2004). Retrieved June 13, 2004 from http://www.anred.com/causes.html.

Krakauer, J. (1996). *Into the Wild.* New York: Villard Books.

Structure and Strategy

1. What kind of INTRODUCTION does Rys use? Is it effective? Why?
2. How many points are included in the TOPIC SENTENCE of paragraph 2? How many of these points does Rys develop in the paragraph?
3. What development strategy does the author use to support the topic of paragraph 3?
4. Identify the TRANSITION statements with which the author begins paragraphs 3 and 4.
5. Which KEY IDEA is developed by information discovered through research? How does Rys incorporate the results of her research into her essay?
6. Study the concluding paragraph of this essay carefully. The author summarizes her key points in an unusual way. Compare her concluding summary with her introduction of the key points in paragraph 2. Why do you think the author introduced and concluded her key points so differently?

7. For what AUDIENCE do you think Rys wrote this essay? What clues helped you come to this conclusion?

Content and Purpose

1. What is the THESIS of this essay?
2. What, according to Rys, are the causes of anorexia nervosa?
3. According to paragraph 3, what are the three ways in which families can, without meaning to, encourage anorexic behaviour in young women? What role do others—friends, for example—play in unintentionally encouraging the illness?
4. What, according to Rys, is the "root cause" of anorexia nervosa in young women? Do you agree or disagree?
5. What are three different kinds of media that Rys argues promote unrealistic ideals of female bodies? Can you think of any other examples?
6. What does Rys think must happen to decrease the prevalence of anorexia nervosa among young women?
7. Are young men affected by anorexia? Do you think Rys should have included men along with women in her analysis? Why?

Suggestions for Writing

1. Have you or has anyone you know suffered from an eating disorder? Write an essay describing its effects on the sufferer and on that person's family and closest friends. Explain what you think caused the eating disorder.
2. How do the media contribute to our definition of physical beauty? How realistic are these images? Are they healthy images for most people to emulate? Support your views with examples.
3. Anorexia nervosa does not affect only adolescent females. After some research into the topic, determine how this disease affects other populations (e.g., older women or young men). Write an essay explaining the causes and effects of this disease on the population group you choose.

Scaring Us Senseless

NASSIM NICHOLAS TALEB

Essayist, researcher, and financial trader Nassim Nicholas Taleb was born in 1960 in Lebanon. He holds graduate degrees from the Wharton School of Business and the University of Paris, and teaches in the management school at the University of Massachusetts. Taleb studies the philosophy of randomness and the role of uncertainty in society. His most recent book is *Fooled by Randomness: The Hidden Role of Chance in Life and in the Markets*, published in 2005.

I was visiting London when a second wave of attacks hit the city, just two weeks after the traumatic events of July 7 [2005]. It is hard to avoid feeling vulnerable to this invisible enemy who does not play by known or explicit rules. Of course, that is precisely the anxiety that terrorists seek to produce. But its opposite—complacency—is not an option.   1

The truth is that neither human beings nor modern societies are wired to respond rationally to terrorism. Vigilance is easy to muster immediately after an event, but it tends to wane quickly, as the attack vanishes from public discourse. We err twice, first by over-reacting right after the disaster, while we are still in shock, and later by under-reacting, when the memory fades and we become so relaxed as to be vulnerable to further attacks.   2

Terrorism exploits three glitches in human nature, all related to the management and perception of unusual events. The first and key among these has been observed over the last two decades by neurobiologists and behavioral scientists, who have debunked a great fallacy that has marred Western thinking since Aristotle° and most acutely since the Enlightenment°. That is to say that as much as we think of ourselves as rational animals, risk avoidance is not governed by reason, cognition° or intellect. Rather, it comes chiefly from our emotional system.   3

Patients with brain lesions that prevent them from registering feelings even when their cognitive and analytical capacities are intact are incapable of effectively getting out of harm's way. It is largely our emotional toolkit, and not what is called "reason," that governs our capacity for self-preservation.   4

Second, this emotional system can be an extremely naïve statistician, because it was built for a primitive environment with simple dangers. That might work for you the next time you run into a snake or a tiger. But because the emotional system is impressionable and prefers shallow, social and anecdotal information to abstract data, it hinders our ability to cope with the more sophisticated risks that afflict modern life.   5

6   For example, the death of an acquaintance in a motorcycle accident would be more likely to deter you from riding a motorcycle
than would a dispassionate, and undoubtedly far more representative, statistical analysis of motorcycles' dangers. You might avoid
Central Park on the basis of a single comment at a cocktail party,
rather than bothering to read the freely available crime statistics
that provide a more realistic view of the odds that you will be vic-
timized.

7   This primacy of the emotions can distort our decision-making.
Travelers at airports irrationally tend to agree to pay more for terrorism insurance than they would for general insurance, which
includes terrorism coverage. No doubt the word "terrorism" can be
specific enough to evoke an emotional reaction, while the general
insurance offer wouldn't awaken the travelers' anxieties in the
same way.

8   In the modern age, the news media have the power to amplify
such emotional distortions, particularly with their use of images
that go directly to the emotional brain. Consider this: Osama bin
Laden continued killing Americans and Western Europeans in the
aftermath of Sept. 11, though indirectly. How? A large number of
travelers chose to drive rather than fly, and this caused a corresponding rise in casualties from automobile accidents (any time we
drive more than 20 miles, our risk of death exceeds that of flying).
Yet these automobile accidents were not news stories—they are a
mere number. We have pictures of those killed by bombs, not those
killed on the road. As Stalin° supposedly said, "One death is a
tragedy; a million is a statistic."

9   Our emotional system responds to the concrete and proximate°.
Based on anecdotal information, it reacts quickly to remote risks,
then rapidly forgets. And so the televised images from bombings in
London cause the people of Cleveland to be on heightened alert—
but as soon as there is a new tragedy, that vigilance is forgotten.

10   The third human flaw, related to the second, has to do with
how we act on our perceptions, and what sorts of behavior we
choose to reward. We are moved by sensational images of heroes
who leap into action as calamity unfolds before them. But the long
pedestrian slog of prevention is thankless. That is because prevention is nameless and abstract, while a hero's actions are grounded
in an easy-to-understand narrative.

11   How can we act on our knowledge of these human flaws in
order to make our society safer?

12   The audiovisual media, with the ability to push the public's
emotional hot buttons, need to play a more responsible role. Of
course it is the news media's job to inform the public about the risk

and the incidence of terrorism, but they should try to do so without helping terrorists achieve their objective, which is to terrify. Television images, in all their vividness and specificity, have an extraordinary power to do just that and to persuade the viewer that a distant risk is clear and present while a pressing but underreported one is nothing to worry about.

Like pharmaceutical companies the news media should study   13
the side effects of their product, one of which is the distortion of the viewer's mental risk map. Because of the way the brain is built, images and striking narratives may well be necessary to get our attention. But just as it takes a diamond to cut a diamond, the news industry should find ways to use images and stories to bring us closer to the statistical truth.

Words and Meanings

Paragraph

Aristotle	4th-century B.C.E. Greek philosopher, who developed the deductive method of logical reasoning on which much of Western thought was based	3
Enlightenment	18th-century philosophical movement that emphasized the faculty of reason in studying questions of science, doctrine, and tradition	
Cognition	the mental process of knowing (awareness, perception, reasoning, and judgment) based on factual evidence	
Stalin	(1879–1953) Soviet politician who was the top official of the Communist Party between 1922 and 1953, and premier of the U.S.S.R. between 1941 and 1953. Stalin was notorious for his indifference to humanitarian principles	8
proximate	very close in space, time, or order	9

Structure and Strategy

1. Write a sentence that summarizes the THESIS and KEY IDEAS of this essay.
2. How does the INTRODUCTION contribute to the author's credibility?
3. Identify three paragraphs that are developed primarily by means of examples.
4. What TRANSITIONS does Taleb use to move from one key idea to the next?

5. Which point is supported with a quotation? Why is this quotation IRONIC?
6. Why do you think that paragraph 11 consists of a one-sentence question?

Content and Purpose

1. According the author, which of the "three glitches" that "terrorism exploits" (paragraph 3) is most significant?
2. According to Taleb, are human beings essentially rational or emotional creatures when it comes to avoiding danger? How does this predilection affect our behaviour?
3. Why does Taleb consider our emotional reactions more appropriate to a "primitive environment" (paragraph 5)?
4. Why do people tend to buy unnecessary—and expensive—insurance against terrorism at airports, rather than relying on their general insurance, which would cover them if they were attacked on a plane?
5. According to Taleb, how did the attacks of 9/11 continue to kill people indirectly in the weeks and months that followed?
6. Why do people tend to admire heroes who "leap into action" in a crisis more than they respect the people who endure the "long pedestrian slog" of preventing crises?
7. What answer does the author offer to the question he poses in paragraph 11? Do you agree or disagree? Why?
8. What does Taleb do for a living? How do you think this work relates to his essay?

Suggestions for Writing

1. Have you ever experienced or been frightened by terrorist violence? Write an essay that describes the incident or threat and its effects on you.
2. Do people rely too much on emotion and anecdotal information and too little on reason and intellect in dangerous situations (e.g., crime, terrorism, accidents, storms)? Choose a situation, do some research into the chances of being injured or killed in that situation, and write an essay that realistically assesses the risks involved.

Just Walk On By: A Black Man Ponders His Power to Alter Public Space

BRENT STAPLES

Brent Staples (b. 1951) holds a Ph.D. in psychology from the University of Chicago. An editorial writer for *The New York Times*, he wrote the award-winning memoir *Parallel Time: Growing Up in Black and White* (1994). Much of his writing focuses on race relations, education, and the media.

My first victim was a woman—white, well dressed, probably in her early twenties. I came upon her late one evening on a deserted street in Hyde Park, a relatively affluent neighborhood in an otherwise mean, impoverished section of Chicago. As I swung onto the avenue behind her, there seemed to be a discreet, uninflammatory distance between us. Not so. She cast back a worried glance. To her, the youngish black man—a broad six feet two inches with a beard and billowing hair, both hands shoved into the pockets of a bulky military jacket—seemed menacingly close. After a few more quick glimpses, she picked up her pace and was soon running in earnest. Within seconds she disappeared into a cross street. 1

That was more than a decade ago. I was 22 years old, a graduate student newly arrived at the University of Chicago. It was in the echo of that terrified woman's footfalls that I first began to know the unwieldy inheritance I'd come into—the ability to alter public space in ugly ways. It was clear that she thought herself the quarry of a mugger, a rapist, or worse. Suffering a bout of insomnia, however, I was stalking sleep, not defenseless wayfarers. As a softy who is scarcely able to take a knife to a raw chicken—let alone hold it to a person's throat—I was surprised, embarrassed, and dismayed all at once. Her flight made me feel like an accomplice in tyranny. It also made it clear that I was indistinguishable from the muggers who occasionally seeped into the area from the surrounding ghetto. That first encounter, and those that followed, signified that a vast, unnerving gulf lay between nighttime pedestrians—particularly women—and me. And I soon gathered that being perceived as dangerous is a hazard in itself. I only needed to turn a corner into a dicey situation, or crowd some frightened, armed person in a foyer somewhere, or make an errant° move after being pulled over by a policeman. Where fear and weapons meet—and they often do in urban America—there is always the possibility of death. 2

3   In that first year, my first away from my hometown, I was to become thoroughly familiar with the language of fear. At dark, shadowy intersections in Chicago, I could cross in front of a car stopped at a traffic light and elicit° the *thunk, thunk, thunk, thunk* of the driver—black, white, male, or female—hammering down the door locks. On less traveled streets after dark, I grew accustomed to but never comfortable with people who crossed to the other side of the street rather than pass me. Then there were the standard unpleasantries with police, doormen, bouncers, cab drivers, and others whose business it is to screen out troublesome individuals *before* there is any nastiness.

4   I moved to New York nearly two years ago and I have remained an avid° night walker. In central Manhattan, the near-constant crowd cover minimizes tense one-on-one street encounters. Elsewhere—visiting friends in SoHo, where sidewalks are narrow and tightly spaced buildings shut out the sky—things can get very taut indeed.

5   Black men have a firm place in New York mugging literature. Norman Podhoretz in his famed (or infamous) . . . essay, "My Negro Problem—And Ours," recalls growing up in terror of black males; they "were tougher than we were, more ruthless," he writes—and as an adult on the Upper West Side of Manhattan, he continues, he cannot constrain his nervousness when he meets black men on certain streets. Similarly, a decade later, the essayist and novelist Edward Hoagland extols° a New York where once "Negro bitterness bore down mainly on other Negroes." Where some see mere panhandlers, Hoagland sees "a mugger who is clearly screwing up his nerve to do more than just *ask* for money." But Hoagland has "the New Yorker's quick-hunch posture for broken-field maneuvering," and the bad guy swerves away.

6   I often witness that "hunch posture," from women after dark on the warrenlike° streets of Brooklyn where I live. They seem to set their faces on neutral and, with their purse straps strung across their chests bandolier style, they forge ahead as though bracing themselves against being tackled. I understand, of course, that the danger they perceive is not a hallucination. Women are particularly vulnerable to street violence, and young black males are drastically overrepresented among the perpetrators° of that violence. Yet these truths are no solace against the kind of alienation that comes of being ever the suspect, against being set apart, a fearsome entity with whom pedestrians avoid making eye contact.

7   It is not altogether clear to me how I reached the ripe old age of 22 without being conscious of the lethality° nighttime pedestrians attributed to me. Perhaps it was because in Chester, Pennsylvania,

the small, angry industrial town where I came of age in the 1960s, I was scarcely noticeable against a backdrop of gang warfare, street knifings, and murders. I grew up one of the good boys, had perhaps a half-dozen fist fights. In retrospect°, my shyness of combat has clear sources.

Many things go into the making of a young thug. One of those things is the consummation° of the male romance with the power to intimidate. An infant discovers that random flailings send the baby bottle flying out of the crib and crashing to the floor. Delighted, the joyful babe repeats those motions again and again, seeking to duplicate the feat. Just so, I recall the points at which some of my boyhood friends were finally seduced by the perception of themselves as tough guys. When a mark cowered and surrendered his money without resistance, myth and reality merged—and paid off. It is, after all, only manly to embrace the power to frighten and intimidate. We, as men, are not supposed to give an inch of our lane on the highway; we are to seize the fighter's edge in work and in play and even in love; we are to be valiant in the face of hostile forces.   8

Unfortunately, poor and powerless young men seem to take all this nonsense literally. As a boy, I saw countless tough guys locked away; I have since buried several, too. They were babies, really—a teenage cousin, a brother of 22, a childhood friend in his mid-twenties— all gone down in episodes of bravado played out in the streets. I came to doubt the virtues of intimidation early on. I chose, perhaps even unconsciously, to remain a shadow—timid, but a survivor.   9

The fearsomeness mistakenly attributed to me in public places often has a perilous flavor. The most frightening of these confusions occurred in the late 1970s and early 1980s when I worked as a journalist in Chicago. One day, rushing into the office of a magazine I was writing for with a deadline story in hand, I was mistaken for a burglar. The office manager called security and, with an ad hoc posse°, pursued me through the labyrinthine halls, nearly to my editor's door. I had no way of proving who I was. I could only move briskly toward the company of someone who knew me.   10

Another time I was on assignment for a local paper and killing time before an interview. I entered a jewelry store on the city's affluent Near North Side. The proprietor excused herself and returned with an enormous red Doberman pinscher straining at the end of a leash. She stood, the dog extended toward me, silent to my questions, her eyes bulging nearly out of her head. I took a cursory° look around, nodded, and bade her good night. Relatively speaking, however, I never fared as badly as another black male journalist. He went to nearby Waukegan, Illinois, a couple of   11 summers ago to work on a story about a murderer who was born there. Mistaking the reporter for the killer, police hauled him from his car at gunpoint and but for his press credentials would probably have tried to book him. Such episodes are not uncommon. Black men trade tales like this all the time.

12   In "My Negro Problem—And Ours," Podhoretz writes that the hatred he feels for blacks makes itself known to him through a variety of avenues—one being his discomfort with that "special brand of paranoid touchiness" to which he says blacks are prone. No doubt he is speaking here of black men. In time, I learned to smother the rage I felt at so often being taken for a criminal. Not to do so would surely have led to madness—via that special "paranoid touchiness" that so annoyed Podhoretz at the time he wrote the essay.

13   I began to take precautions to make myself less threatening. I move about with care, particularly late in the evening. I give a wide berth to nervous people on subway platforms during the wee hours, particularly when I have exchanged business clothes for jeans. If I happen to be entering a building behind some people who appear skittish°, I may walk by, letting them clear the lobby before I return, so as not to seem to be following them. I have been calm and extremely congenial° on those rare occasions when I've been pulled over by the police.

14   And on late-evening constitutionals° along streets less traveled by, I employ what has proved to be an excellent tension-reducing measure: I whistle melodies from Beethoven and Vivaldi and the more popular classical composers. Even steely New Yorkers hunching toward nighttime destinations seem to relax, and occasionally they even join in the tune. Virtually everybody seems to sense that a mugger wouldn't be warbling bright, sunny selections from Vivaldi's *Four Seasons*. It is my equivalent of the cowbell that hikers wear when they know they are in bear country.

Words and Meanings

Paragraph

2	errant	unexpected
3	elicit	cause to happen
4	avid	keen, enthusiastic
5	extols	praises highly
6	warrenlike	crowded, narrow, dark—like a rabbit warren
	perpetrators	those who perform or commit a criminal action
7	lethality	deadliness
	retrospect	hindsight, thinking about the past

consummation	completion, fulfillment	8
ad hoc posse	group of people quickly assembled to catch a criminal	10
cursory	hasty, superficial	11
skittish	nervous	13
congenial	pleasant, friendly	
constitutionals	walks	14

Structure and Strategy

1. What strategy does Staples use in his INTRODUCTION? Identify the details that help the reader picture the scene described. Explain the IRONY in the first sentence.
2. What is the function of the paragraphs that include quotations from writers Norman Podhoretz and Edward Hoagland (paragraphs 5 and 12)? How would the impact of the essay differ if Staples had not included these supporting examples of racist thinking?
3. How is the TOPIC SENTENCE of paragraph 10 developed?
4. What is the TONE of this essay?

Content and Purpose

1. This essay reflects on the effects that the author, a black man, has on people in the street, merely by his presence. It also deals with the effects that this phenomenon has on him. What are they?
2. Explain what Staples means by his "unwieldy inheritance" and his feeling like "an accomplice in tyranny" (paragraph 2).
3. What does Staples acknowledge in paragraph 6? How does this acknowledgment prepare the reader for the next point he makes about street violence (in paragraphs 7 through 9)?
4. What measures does the author take to minimize his effect on other pedestrians as he walks at night?
5. In paragraph 7, the author observes that his own "shyness of combat has clear sources." What causes does he identify for his dislike of violence?
6. Paragraph 8 deals with the causes of another social tragedy, "the making of a young thug." What are these causes, as Staples sees them? How has this sad reality affected his own life?

Suggestions for Writing

1. It is often suggested that our society is much more violent than it was a few decades ago. Others argue that we are simply more fearful, and that the incidence of violent crimes has actually decreased. Write an essay that explores the causes either for the increase or for the perception of an increase in violence.

2. Write an essay that explores the causes or effects of being an "outsider," someone who is seen not to "belong." Support your thesis from personal experience. How did your experience(s) affect you?

3. Read Pat Capponi's "Dispatches from the Poverty Line" on page 33 and/or Malcolm Gladwell's "Troublemakers: What Pit Bulls Can Teach Us About Profiling" on page 349. Choose one of these essays and compare and contrast the ways that your chosen essay and Staples's essay deal with the issue of stereotyping.

The Telephone

ANWAR F. ACCAWI

Anwar F. Accawi was born in the middle of World War II in a small village in the hills of south Lebanon. He moved to the United States in 1965 when he won a scholarship. Accawi has taught at the English Language Institute at the University of Tennessee since 1979. In 1985, he started writing stories for his children about his childhood home. His book, *The Boy from the Tower of the Moon* (1999), is a personal narrative of his boyhood in Lebanon.

1   When I was growing up in Magdaluna, a small Lebanese village in the terraced, rocky mountains east of Sidon, time didn't mean much to anybody, except maybe to those who were dying, or those waiting to appear in court because they had tampered with the boundary markers on their land. In those days, there was no real need for a calendar or a watch to keep track of the hours, days, months, and years. We knew what to do and when to do it, just as the Iraqi geese knew when to fly north, driven by the hot wind that blew in from the desert, and the ewes knew when to give birth to wet lambs that stood on long, shaky legs in the chilly March wind and baaed hesitantly, because they were small and cold and did not know where they were or what to do now that they were here. The only timepiece we had need of then was the sun. It rose and set, and the seasons rolled by, and we sowed seed and harvested and ate and played and married our cousins and had babies who got whooping cough and chickenpox—and those children who survived grew up and married *their* cousins and had babies who got whooping cough and chick-

enpox. We lived and loved and toiled and died without ever needing to know what year it was, or even the time of day.

It wasn't that we had no system for keeping track of time and of the important events in our lives. But ours was a natural—or, rather, a divine—calendar, because it was framed by acts of God. Allah himself set down the milestones with earthquakes and droughts and floods and locusts and pestilences°. Simple as our calendar was, it worked just fine for us.

Take, for example, the birth date of Teta Im Khalil, the oldest woman in Magdaluna and all the surrounding villages. When I first met her, we had just returned home from Syria at the end of the Big War° and were living with Grandma Mariam. Im Khalil came by to welcome my father home and to take a long, myopic° look at his foreign-born wife, my mother. Im Khalil was so old that the skin of her cheeks looked like my father's grimy tobacco pouch, and when I kissed her (because Grandma insisted that I show her old friend affection), it was like kissing a soft suede glove that had been soaked with sweat and then left in a dark closet for a season. Im Khalil's face got me to wondering how old one had to be to look and taste the way she did. So, as soon as she had hobbled off on her cane, I asked Grandma, "How old is Teta Im Khalil?"

Grandma had to think for a moment; then she said, "I've been told that Teta was born shortly after the big snow that caused the roof on the mayor's house to cave in."

"And when was that?" I asked.

"Oh, about the time we had the big earthquake that cracked the wall in the east room."

Well, that was enough for me. You couldn't be more accurate than that, now, could you? Satisfied with her answer, I went back to playing with a ball made from an old sock stuffed with other, much older socks.

And that's the way it was in our little village for as far back as anybody could remember: people were born so many years before or after an earthquake or a flood; they got married or died so many years before or after a long drought or a big snow or some other disaster. One of the most unusual of these dates was when Antoinette the seamstress and Saeed the barber (and tooth puller) got married. That was the year of the whirlwind during which fish and oranges fell from the sky. Incredible as it may sound, the story of the fish and oranges was true, because men—respectable men, like Abu George the blacksmith and Abu Asaad the mule skinner, men who would not lie even to save their own souls—told and retold that story until it was incorporated° into Magdaluna's calendar, just like the year of the black moon and the year of the locusts before it. My father, too, confirmed the story for me. He told me that he had been a small boy himself when it rained fish and oranges from heaven. He'd gotten up one morning after a stormy night and walked out into the yard to find fish as long as his forearm still flopping here and there among the wet navel oranges.

9   The year of the fish-bearing twister, however, was not the last remarkable year. Many others followed in which strange and wonderful things happened: milestones added by the hand of Allah to Magdaluna's calendar. There was, for instance, the year of the drought, when the heavens were shut for months and the spring from which the entire village got its drinking water slowed to a trickle. The spring was about a mile from the village, in a ravine that opened at one end into a small, flat clearing covered with fine gray dust and hard, marble-sized goat droppings, because every afternoon the goatherds brought their flocks there to water them. In the year of the drought, that little clearing was always packed full of noisy kids with big brown eyes and sticky hands, and their mothers—sinewy°, overworked young women with protruding collarbones and cracked, callused brown heels. The children ran around playing tag or hide-and-seek while the women talked, shooed flies, and awaited their turns to fill up their jars with drinking water to bring home to their napping men and wet babies. There were days when we had to wait from sunup until late afternoon just to fill a small clay jar with precious, cool water.

10   Sometimes, amid the long wait and the heat and the flies and the smell of goat dung, tempers flared, and the younger women, anxious about their babies, argued over whose turn it was to fill up her jar. And sometimes the arguments escalated into full-blown, knockdown-dragout fights; the women would grab each other by the hair and curse and scream and spit and call each other names that made my ears tingle. We little brown boys who went with our mothers to fetch water loved these fights, because we got to see the women's legs and their colored panties as they grappled and rolled around in the dust. Once in a while, we got lucky and saw much more, because some of the women wore nothing at all under their long dresses. God, how I used to look forward to those fights. I remember the rush, the excitement, the sun dancing on the dust clouds as a dress ripped and a young white breast was revealed, then quickly hidden. In my calendar, that year of drought will always be one of the best years of my childhood, because it was then, in a dusty clearing by a trickling mountain spring, I got my first glimpses of the wonders, the mysteries, and the promises hidden beneath the folds of a woman's dress. Fish and oranges from heaven . . . you can get over that.

But, in another way, the year of the drought was also one of the 11
worst of my life, because that was the year that Abu Raja, the
retired cook who used to entertain us kids by cracking walnuts on
his forehead, decided it was time Magdaluna got its own telephone.
Every civilized village needed a telephone, he said, and Magdaluna
was not going to get anywhere until it had one. A telephone would
link us with the outside world. At the time, I was too young to
understand the debate, but a few men—like Shukri, the retired
Turkish-army drill sergeant, and Abu Hanna the vineyard keeper—
did all they could to talk Abu Raja out of having a telephone
brought to the village. But they were outshouted and ignored and
finally shunned by the other villagers for resisting progress and
trying to keep a good thing from coming to Magdaluna.

One warm day in early fall, many of the villagers were out in 12
their fields repairing walls or gathering wood for the winter when
the shout went out that the telephone-company truck had arrived at
Abu Raja's *dikkan*, or country store. There were no roads in those
days, only footpaths and dry streambeds, so it took the telephone-
company truck almost a day to work its way up the rocky terrain
from Sidon—about the same time it took to walk. When the truck
came into view, Abu George, who had a huge voice, and, before the
telephone, was Magdaluna's only long-distance communication
system, bellowed the news from his front porch. Everybody dropped
what they were doing and ran to Abu Raja's house to see what was
happening. Some of the more dignified villagers, however, like Abu
Habeeb and Abu Nazim, who had been to big cities like Beirut and
Damascus and had seen things like telephones and telegraphs, did
not run the way the rest did; they walked with their canes hanging
from the crooks of their arms, as if on a Sunday afternoon stroll.

It did not take long for the whole village to assemble at Abu 13
Raja's *dikkan*. Some of the rich villagers, like the widow Farha and the
gendarme° Abu Nadeem, walked right into the store and stood at the
elbows of the two important-looking men from the telephone company, who proceeded with utmost gravity, like priests at Com-
munion, to wire up the telephone. The poorer villagers stood outside
and listened carefully to the details relayed to them by the not-so-
poor people who stood in the doorway and could see inside.

"The bald man is cutting the blue wire," someone said. 14

"He is sticking the wire into the hole in the bottom of the black 15
box," someone else added.

"The telephone man with the mustache is connecting two 16
pieces of wire. Now he is twisting the ends together," a third voice
chimed in.

17   Because I was small and unaware that I should have stood outside with the other poor folk to give the rich people inside more
room (they seemed to need more of it than poor people did), I wrig-
gled my way through the dense forest of legs to get a first-hand
look at the action. I felt like the barefoot Moses, sandals in hand,
staring at the burning bush on Mount Sinai. Breathless, I watched
as the men in blue, their shirt pockets adorned with fancy lettering
in a foreign language, put together a black machine that supposedly would make it possible to talk with uncles, aunts, and cousins
who lived more than two days' ride away.

18   It was shortly after sunset when the man with the mustache
announced that the telephone was ready to use. He explained that
all Abu Raja had to do was lift the receiver, turn the crank on the
black box a few times, and wait for an operator to take his call. Abu
Raja, who had once lived and worked in Sidon, was impatient with
the telephone man for assuming that he was ignorant. He grabbed
the receiver and turned the crank forcefully, as if trying to start a
Model T Ford. Everybody was impressed that he knew what to do.
He even called the operator by her first name: "Centralist." Within
moments, Abu Raja was talking with his brother, a concierge° in
Beirut. He didn't even have to raise his voice or shout to be heard.

19   If I hadn't seen it with my own two eyes and heard it with my
own two ears, I would not have believed it—and my friend Kameel
didn't. He was away that day watching his father's goats, and
when he came back to the village that evening, his cousin Habeeb
and I told him about the telephone and how Abu Raja had used it
to speak with his brother in Beirut. After he heard our report,
Kameel made the sign of the cross, kissed his thumbnail, and
warned us that lying was a bad sin and would surely land us in
purgatory. Kameel believed in Jesus and Mary, and wanted to be a
priest when he grew up. He always crossed himself when Habeeb,
who was irreverent, and I, who was Presbyterian, were around,
even when we were not bearing bad news.

20   And the telephone, as it turned out, was bad news. With its
coming, the face of the village began to change. One of the first
effects was the shifting of the village's center. Before the telephone's
arrival, the men of the village used to gather regularly at the house
of Im Kaleem, a short, middle-aged widow with jet-black hair and a
raspy voice that could be heard all over the village, even when she
was only whispering. She was a devout Catholic and also the village *shlikki*—whore. The men met at her house to argue about politics and drink coffee and play cards or backgammon. Im Kaleem
was not a true prostitute, however, because she did not charge for
her services—not even for the coffee and tea (and, occasionally, the

strong liquor called arrack) that she served the men. She did not
need the money; her son, who was overseas in Africa, sent her
money regularly. (I knew this because my father used to read her
son's letters to her and take down her replies, as Im Kaleem could
not read and write.) Im Kaleem was no slut either—unlike some
women in the village—because she loved all the men she entertained, and they loved her, every one of them. In a way, she was
married to all the men in the village. Everybody knew it—the wives
knew it; the itinerant° Catholic priest knew it; the Presbyterian minister knew it —but nobody objected. Actually, I suspect the women
(my mother included) did not mind their husbands' visits to Im
Kaleem. Oh, they wrung their hands and complained to one
another about their men's unfaithfulness, but secretly they were
relieved, because Im Kaleem took some of the pressure off them
and kept the men out of their hair while they attended to their endless chores. Im Kaleem was also a kind of confessor and trou-
bleshooter, talking sense to those men who were having family
problems, especially the younger ones.

Before the telephone came to Magdaluna, Im Kaleem's house   21
was bustling at just about any time of day, especially at night, when
its windows were brightly lit with three large oil lamps, and the
loud voices of the men talking, laughing, and arguing could be
heard in the street below—a reassuring, homey sound. Her house
was an island of comfort, an oasis for the weary village men,
exhausted from having so little to do.

But it wasn't long before many of those men—the younger   22
ones especially—started spending more of their days and
evenings at Abu Raja's *dikkan*. There, they would eat and drink
and talk and play checkers and backgammon, and then lean their
chairs back against the wall—the signal that they were ready to
toss back and forth, like a ball, the latest rumors going around the
village. And they were always looking up from their games and
drinks and talk to glance at the phone in the corner, as if expecting
it to ring any minute and bring news that would change their
lives and deliver them from their aimless existence. In the mean-
time, they smoked cheap, hand-rolled cigarettes, dug dirt out
from under their fingernails with big pocketknives, and drank
lukewarm sodas that they called Kacula, Seffen-Ub, and Bebsi.
Sometimes, especially when it was hot, the days dragged on so
slowly that the men turned on Abu Saeed, a confirmed bachelor
who practically lived in Abu Raja's *dikkan,* and teased him for
going around barefoot and unshaven since the Virgin had
appeared to him behind the olive press.

23   The telephone was also bad news for me personally. It took away my lucrative° business—a source of much-needed income. Before the telephone came to Magdaluna, I used to hang around Im Kaleem's courtyard and play marbles with the other kids, waiting for some man to call down from a window and ask me to run to the store for cigarettes or arrack, or to deliver a message to his wife, such as what he wanted for supper. There was always something in it for me: a ten- or even a twenty-five-piaster piece. On a good day, I ran nine or ten of those errands, which assured a steady supply of marbles that I usually lost to Sami or his cousin Hani, the basket weaver's boy. But as the days went by, fewer and fewer men came to Im Kaleem's, and more and more congregated at Abu Raja's to wait by the telephone. In the evenings, no light fell from her window onto the street below, and the laughter and noise of the men trailed off and finally stopped. Only Shukri, the retired Turkish-army drill sergeant, remained faithful to Im Kaleem after all the other men had deserted her; he was still seen going into or leaving her house from time to time. Early that winter, Im Kaleem's hair suddenly turned gray, and she got sick and old. Her legs started giving her trouble, making it hard for her to walk. By spring she hardly left her house anymore.

24   At Abu Raja's *dikkan*, the calls did eventually come, as expected, and men and women started leaving the village the way a hailstorm begins: first one, then two, then bunches. The army took them. Jobs in the cities lured them. And ships and airplanes carried them to such faraway places as Australia and Brazil and New Zealand. My friend Kameel, his cousin Habeeb, and their cousins and my cousins all went away to become ditch diggers and mechanics and butcher-shop boys and deli owners who wore dirty aprons sixteen hours a day, all looking for a better life than the one they had left behind. Within a year, only the sick, the old, and the maimed were left in the village. Magdaluna became a skeleton of its former self, desolate and forsaken, like the tombs, a place to get away from.

25   Finally, the telephone took my family away, too. My father got a call from an old army buddy who told him that an oil company in southern Lebanon was hiring interpreters and instructors. My father applied for a job and got it, and we moved to Sidon, where I went to a Presbyterian missionary school and graduated in 1962. Three years later, having won a scholarship, I left Lebanon for the United States. Like the others who left Magdaluna before me, I am still looking for that better life.

Words and Meanings

Paragraph

pestilences	disease epidemics	2
Big War	World War II	3
myopic	near-sighted	
incorporated	merged with, became part of	8
sinewy	lean, muscular	9
gendarme	police officer	13
concierge	hotel attendant	18
itinerant	moving from place to place, not resident	20
lucrative	profitable	23

Structure and Strategy

1. Does this essay focus primarily on cause or on effect? Of what?
2. This essay is divided into two parts: paragraphs 1 through 10 and 11 through 25. Summarize the content of the two halves of the piece.
3. What IRONY is there in paragraph 11, the turning point of the essay?
4. Identify two or three ANECDOTES in the essay that make it clear that the story is being told from the POINT OF VIEW of a child.
5. Identify three descriptive details in paragraph 1 that you think are particularly effective. How do these descriptive elements help support the topic of the paragraph?
6. The ILLUSTRATION developed in paragraphs 3 through 7 contains more dialogue than any other anecdote in the essay. What point is Accawi making here, and why do you think that he uses dialogue to support it?
7. Identify two SIMILES in paragraphs 13 and 17 that are specifically religious in meaning. Are they appropriate in an account of the introduction of technology into a village? Why or why not?
8. What are "Kacula, Seffen-Ub, and Bebsi" (paragraph 22)? Is Accawi's description of the villagers' pronunciation humorous? What is his attitude toward the speakers? How do details such as these influence the TONE of the essay?

Content and Purpose

1. According to Accawi, how did the villagers of Magdaluna mark time before the coming of the telephone? How did they "keep track of the hours, days, months, and years" (paragraph 1)?
2. Identify three memorable people among the villagers that Accawi describes. What descriptive and narrative details does

he provide to help you "know" each of these people? How do they come alive to you? How do you think the author feels about each of these characters?

3. Who works harder in Magdaluna, the women or the men? Support your answer with specific references to the essay.

4. The first effect of the telephone on the village community is told through the story of Im Kaleem, "the village *shlikki*" (paragraphs 20 through 22). What is this consequence, and why do you think Accawi chooses Im Kaleem's story to communicate it?

5. The effects of the telephone on two specific people are detailed in paragraph 23. Who are the people, and what happens to them?

6. In paragraph 24, we are told that the "calls did eventually come." What happens then? Where do people go? What happens to Magdaluna itself? Do you think that these effects are all due to the arrival of the telephone in the village?

7. In your own words, describe how Accawi feels about the changes that swept through his world. Refer to specific details from paragraphs 24 and 25.

Suggestions for Writing

1. How do technologies such as the Internet, computerized slot machines, cellphones, or video games change people and their environment? Write an essay describing the effects of a new technology on a person or place you know.

2. Write an essay describing a neighbourhood, town, or village that you know (perhaps one that you or your family came from). What has happened to this place over time? What caused the changes? Your essay should both describe the transformation and communicate your feelings about it.

Saving the Songs of Innocence

JOHN DIXON

A philosophy instructor at Capilano College, John Dixon (b. 1943) has been special policy adviser to the Minister of National Defence in Ottawa, senior policy adviser to the Attorney General of Canada, and president of the B.C. Civil Liberties Association. He is the author of numerous articles; *Catastrophic Rights* (1990); and co-author of *Kiddie Porn: Sexual Representation, Free Speech, and the Robin Sharpe Case* (2001), which won the Donner Prize for best Canadian book on public policy. In 2003,

Dixon was awarded an honorary doctorate in laws by Simon Fraser University.

W hen I was a little boy, we called them Blackfish. My father and I would sometimes see them when we strip-cast for coho° at the mouth of the Big Qualicum River. We never got very close to them in that shallow bay, and I don't remember much more than the big dorsal fins coming up and going down in the distance—except that the fishing always seemed to go off then. Dad said that it was because the salmon hugged the bottom, dodging the hunting sonar° of the killer-whale pack. I still don't know if that's true.   1

Last summer, with my own seven-year-old son, it was different. We were spinning for cutthroat° at the mouth of a stream that flows into Pryce Channel, in the Desolation Sound area of British Columbia. It was hot, the deer flies were getting very tough, and we were starting to think more fondly of swimming than catching big trout.   2

"Puuuff," it sounded far away. But loud enough that we stood still in our little aluminum boat, watching in the direction of the Brem River.   3

In less than a minute, the black fin of a killer slowly appeared about a quarter of a mile away. Edge on, it looked for all the world like a dock piling slowly wavering out of the water and then falling back in, except that pilings don't spout steamy breath. He was moving along the shore, coming out of Toba Inlet on a course that would bring him right up to us. His dorsal was so tall that its tip drooped over in the way that (we say) means it's a big bull. Excitement! I started our old Evinrude and began idling along the shore waiting for him to catch up.   4

The next time he surfaced he was beside us, about 30 feet away on the open water side. I speeded up a bit to match his pace, and we held our course, staying about 50 feet off the steep shore. With not a ripple of wind on the water, we could see all of him as he angled into us a bit, coming up 10 feet closer after his next shore dive.   5

To say what is seen then is easier than to say what is felt or known. He looked like a huge rubbery thing that had been molded out of six or seven elephants. And I say "thing" because on one level he didn't appear, deliberately swimming at such profound ease, to be alive. Beside the obvious matter of the scale being all wrong, there was none of the fuss or business we associate with life, even when it is quietly on the move. But on another level, you didn't have to know that he ate seals like buttered popcorn in order   6 to feel the near world humming with his predatory° purpose. And we were alone with him—primates on a tin half shell.

7   He went down again, shallow, and angled in another 10 feet. When he came up we saw his eye, and Matthew said, simply and emphatically: "I'm scared now." "Smart," I said to myself: "You've just been spotted by one who prefers dining as high up the food chain as possible." But out loud I did my father stuff: "We're okay. Let's just go along like this."

8   The tip of his dorsal slowly slid under again, and I watched it closely for any change of course. "Look!" Matthew yelled: "Look at the herring!" Under the boat I saw two things at once. We had shallowed up so much that I could see the ground about 20 feet down, and the boat was over a big school of herring packed against the shore. And then there was a different "Puuuuff!" as the killer surged up and dived, turning directly under the boat into the feed.

9   I saw white and black under us and hit the gas. We squirted away, and turned around to look just as, about 25 yards behind us, the whale erupted out of our wake. He came out completely, but so slowly that it was hard to believe, from about the point he was halfway, that he could possibly go any further. And when he fell back into the light smoke of our exhaust, it seemed to take as long as the collapse of a dynamited skyscraper.

10   I tend to think of Job° whenever I'm whacked over the head with a strong experience of nature. The story of his peek into God's wild portfolio and subsequent attitude-adjustment reminds us of one of the rudiments° of human wisdom: we are out of our depth in this world. In this respect, nothing has changed. What has changed, sadly and urgently, is the gap between our relatively unimproved powers of understanding and the monstrous development of our capacity to despoil. I cannot really know the oceans that Homer° called "the whale road," but I can effortlessly reach their deepest regions with a neoprene gumboot° that has a half-life of about a million years.

11   Looking that whale in the eye with Matthew has produced at least one point of clarity in me. I don't know how I made my children, but I know that—in a way that has nothing to do with possession—they are mine and I must try to find the strength and wisdom to care for them. Now we know that we have mixed ourselves so completely with the world that not even the mercury and cadmium-laced flesh of the whales has been spared our touch. We have made ourselves so thoroughly immanent° in the world that we have taken it away from nature and hence made it—if only through default—our own.

As is the case with God, when the wilderness no longer exists it 12
cannot be invented, no matter how appealing the idea or powerful
the human will to realize it. Because an invented God or an
invented wilderness lacks the autonomous power that is at the core
of its reality. Once innocence is lost, its songs can still be sung but it
can never be genuinely restored.

This means that the pious path of Job, leaving the running of 13
the world to some separate and autonomous competence such as
Spinoza°'s *deus sive natura* . . . God or nature, is now forever
closed to us. We never understood the significance of that path
(the next best thing to not getting kicked out of the Garden of
Eden in the first place) until it was too late, and now must search
out a future of which the only thing certainly known is that it will
require inestimably more from us than patient restraint. We face
responsibilities, and obstacles in the way of their being met, of
unfathomable° profundity°. The good news—and it didn't have
to turn out this way—is that when the world chooses to reveal
itself to us, as it does from time to time in Desolation Sound, we
continue to fall in love with it as deeply and inevitably as with
our children.

Words and Meanings

Paragraph

coho	salmon	1
sonar	underwater sound waves whales use to find fish	
spinning for cutthroat	fishing for trout	2
predatory	hunting for prey	6
Job	biblical figure who was severely tested by misfortune but adhered to his view of divine righteousness	10
rudiments	the basics	
Homer	legendary Greek poet traditionally credited with writing the classic *The Odyssey* and *The Iliad* in the 8th century B.C.E.	
neoprene gumboot	synthetic rubber boot	
immanent	indwelling; we have permeated the environment and all life forms with chemicals	11
Spinoza	seventeenth-century Dutch philosopher who believed that God and Nature were not two different things, but different aspects of one substance	13
unfathomable	so deep we cannot get to the bottom of it	
profundity	idea that is deep, complex, extremely difficult to understand	

Structure and Strategy

1. This essay combines all four RHETORICAL MODES. Identify passages that are primarily narrative, descriptive, expository, and persuasive in nature.
2. Identify five or six descriptive details involving the whale that you find particularly effective.
3. Paragraph 10 contains two ALLUSIONS (Job and Homer). Who were they? Why does Dixon include them to develop his THESIS?
4. How does the CONCLUSION contribute to the UNITY of the essay?

Content and Purpose

1. What is the connection between the brief narrative in paragraph 1 and that which begins in paragraph 2? What is the purpose of the contrast between these two stories?
2. What is Dixon's THESIS?
3. What does the author mean by "primates on a tin half shell" in paragraph 6?
4. Where in the essay does the author move from relating the experience to interpreting it? How does he interpret the encounter with the killer whale?
5. Summarize the point of paragraphs 10 and 11. What is the connection between "God's wild portfolio" and the "neoprene gumboot that has a half-life of about a million years" (paragraph 10)?
6. To what does Dixon compare the loss of the wilderness in paragraph 12? PARAPHRASE the meaning of the last sentence in this paragraph. What is the effect of this loss?
7. What human impulse does Dixon see as positive in its implications for the possible re-establishment of a healthy link between humankind and nature? (See paragraph 13.)

Suggestions for Writing

1. Write an essay recounting an experience you have had in nature (hiking, camping, fishing, kayaking, skiing, etc.) that had a profound effect on you. Using NARRATION, DESCRIPTION, and example to develop your THESIS, explain the causal relationship between your experience and its effects.
2. Write an essay exploring the causes or the effects of a particular kind of damage that you, your community, or an industry you are familiar with inflicts on the natural environment.

The Evolution of Evolution

HELENA CRONIN

A philosopher and natural scientist, Helena Cronin (b. 1942) is a co-director of the Centre for Philosophy of Natural and Social Science at the London School of Economics. She is the author of the award-winning *The Ant and the Peacock*, an account of the debates that have surrounded evolutionary theory since Darwin published *The Origin of Species*.

In one of my favorite cartoons, a hopeful patient asks his doctor, "Have you got something for the human condition?" One cannot but sympathize with the hapless physician. Or so I used to feel. Now my urge is to leap into action crying, "I'm a Darwinian°; perhaps I can help." For in the past decade or so evolutionary theory has yielded a mind-blowing discovery: it has pried open the neatly-arrayed toolbox that is our mind. Just as *Gray's Anatomy*° laid bare the human frame, so Darwinian scientists are beginning to write the owner-occupier's manual to that hitherto most recondite° of mysteries: human nature. Yes, human nature does exist and it is universal. Our minds and brains, just like our bodies, have been honed° by natural selection to solve the problems faced by our ancestors over the past two million years. Just as every normal human hand has a precision-engineered opposable thumb for plucking, so every normal human mind enters the world bristling with highly specialized problem-solving equipment. And these capacities come on stream during development as surely as the toddler's first faltering steps or the adolescent's acne and ecstasy.

This mind-and-body-building is orchestrated by genes. But we're not merely their slavish puppets. Certainly, genes can do their work single-mindedly. However, genes—responding to different environments—also underpin the flexibility and variety that typify human behavior. All this apparent design has come about without a designer. No purpose, no goals, no blueprints. Natural selection is simply about genes replicating° themselves down the generations. Genes that build bodies that do what's needed—seeing, running, digesting, mating—get replicated; and those that don't, don't. All the more wondrous, then, to discover what natural selection has achieved with human nature. The Darwinian exploration is still a fledgling science. But already it is yielding answers that we didn't even know had questions: What's the winning figure for ratio of waist to hips? Why are mother and fetus locked in irresolvable conflict? Why is fast food so addictive?

New though this science is, researchers are already pretty confident about some things. Fortunately, one of them is sex. Consider a

1

2

3

familiar sex difference that emerged in a study of American college students. Asked by a stranger for a date, 50% of both women and men agreed. But asked "Have sex with me tonight?" not one woman agreed—whereas men shot to 75%. And when students were asked "How long would you have to know someone before having sex?" the questionnaire had to be rescaled for males requiring only minutes or seconds. Not only are men willing to have sex with a perfect stranger; they're more than willing with an imperfect one too. Another American study found that, for brief encounters, men (but not women) were willing to drop their standards as low as their trousers, ready to dispense with intelligence, humor, charm, honesty and emotional stability.

4   Why this difference between men and women? When natural selection shaped male–female differences, it didn't stop at muscles and naughty bits. It also shaped differences in our psychologies. Evolution made men's and women's minds as unalike as it made their bodies. Why? Think of it this way. Give a man 50 wives and he could have children galore. But a woman with 50 husbands? Huh! Generation after generation, down evolutionary time, natural selection favored the men who strove most mightily for mates—the most competitive, risk-taking, opportunistic. We are all the descendants of those winners. Females, meanwhile, faced nine months hard labor, breast feeding, rearing. A woman had to be far more picky about whose genes ended up partnering hers. Faced with the prospect of highly dependent offspring, she'd be on the lookout for someone who was not only fit and healthy but also had access to resources. Nowadays a Rolex or designer trainers provide cues. But for our hunter-gatherer ancestors roving the Pleistocene° plains, what mattered were social resources—status, reputation, respect. Genes that built brains with tools for making these shrewd decisions were the ones that got themselves replicated.

5   Of course, natural selection doesn't download its strategic plans straight into our consciousness. Its instruments are emotions, priorities, desires. Behind each of these everyday human feelings are the calculations of natural selection, millions of careful years in the making. So, for example, men, without knowing it, tend to prefer women with a waist-to-hip ratio (WHR) of 0.7—a waist that is 70% of the hips. Twiggy's skeletal form and Rubens' hefty muses share a 0.7 WHR; so do dumpy Paleolithic "Venuses," figurines shaped by our ancestors 28 000 years ago. Why? It's an ingenious fertility-detection mechanism. Waists and hips are shaped by sex hormones, estrogen in particular. And the optimal hormonal mix for fertility also sculpts that desired ratio.

Both sexes have a predilection° for symmetry. A body with 6
matching right and left sides is an honest signal (because it is hard
to fake) that the genes that built it are robust against invading
pathogens°. As for women's breasts, the larger they are, the more
symmetrical they're likely to be. Why? Breast-building requires
estrogen; the larger the breasts the more the developing body must
have been awash with it. But estrogen suppresses immunity,
making the woman vulnerable to pathogens. So breasts that are
large and yet manage to be symmetrical signal that their owner's
immune system is reliably robust. Facial symmetry, too, is highly
attractive; beauty, far from being skin deep, is a Stone Age body
scan, brimming with information about health and fertility. It's no
surprise, then, that there's cross-cultural agreement on what consti-
tutes a beautiful face; even two-month old babies concur.

Sherlock Holmes° read the personal column "because it is 7
always instructive." Yes, the instructions come straight from the
Darwinian textbook. Turn to lonely hearts listings: man seeks
young, good-looking woman; woman seeks older, financially stable
man. Study sexual fantasies: men—anonymous multiple partners,
thoughts of bare skin; women—someone familiar, tender emotions.
Consider adultery (what Darwinians politely call "extra-pair copu-
lations"): males go for quantity; females, having established
resources within monogamy°, go for quality, particularly high-
quality genes. Across all its manifestations, human sexuality bears
the stamp of evolved sex differences: always preferences diverge°
and always predictably. But it's not just sexuality. A funny thing
happened on the way to divergent mating strategies. Natural selection created males and females so unalike that the differences don't
stop at how fast you'll jump into bed; they pervade our psychology,
shaping our interests, our values, our ambitions, our skills.

It's often said, for example, that men lack social skills. Don't 8
believe it. It's just that their skills are, all too understandably, not
what we call sociable. They are masters at status-seeking, face-
saving, assessing reputation, detecting slights, retaliating against
insults and showing off. They are more persistent and competitive
than females, more disposed to take risks. Who causes most road
accidents, climbs Everest, flies to the moon, commits suicide? Who
are the alcoholics, motor-bike riders, scientists, child-abusers,
CEOs, gamblers, smokers, bungee jumpers, murderers and computer nerds? Men, of course. Men outstrip women in deaths from
smoking, homicide and accidents. Social scientists view these
causes of death as "life-style" as opposed to "biology." But, in the
light of evolutionary theory, speeding to death in a flashy car is
enmeshed in men's biology.

9   Put males and females in the same environment and their evolved psychologies trigger hugely different responses. Boys thrive in competitive exams; girls could do without. Boys play competitive games, big on rules and winners; girls play co-operative games with consensual° endings. Men buy records to complete the set, women to enjoy the music. Rich, successful men go for ever-younger "trophy" wives; top women go for men even richer, more successful—and older—than themselves.

10   After the enlightenment of the personal column, Sherlock Holmes would turn dutifully to the criminal news. This, he felt, was not instructive. Darwinian detectives do better. Consider the family. Criminologists° are fond of remarking that it is the most dangerous place to be. If this were true, it would be a Darwinian scandal. Why? Remember that evolution is about genes getting themselves replicated. Sex is one way. Another is for genes to help copies of themselves in other bodies. One reliable way is to help kin—the closer the relationship, the more help is given. From this genetic reckoning, calculated by the blind forces of natural selection over millions of years, spring some of our most cherished human values. Whenever a mother braves hazards to save her child from drowning, whenever a brother donates a kidney for his sibling, "kin selection" is at work. We are evolved to lavish altruism on our kin, not to abuse or kill them. So it's no surprise to find that the criminologists are wrong.

11   Take murder. For a start, most family victims are spouses—not genetically related at all. But what about infanticide°? Children are cargoes of their parents' genes, 50% each, sallying forth into future generations. Infanticide is therefore a profound challenge to evolutionists—so profound that it sent intrepid Darwinians trawling through the statistics in Britain and North America to find out what proportion of murdered children died at the hands of their genetic parents. The researchers discovered that step-children are about 100 times more likely to be killed than genetic children. It's true what they say about Cinderella: having a step-parent puts a child at greater risk than any other known cause.

12   But where there is sharing, there also lies competition. When your children insist indignantly that your decision is not fair; when they squabble over a toy; when mother's keen to wean and baby resists—then bear in mind the following calculus of kin selection. A child's life is its sole bid for genetic immortality; and it values itself more than it values its brothers and sisters. Indeed, it is 100% related to itself but has only a 50% chance of sharing genes with siblings. But for a parent each child has the same value, a 50% relationship. The child will therefore always value itself, relative to its

siblings, more than its parents do. The result is conflict. A child is evolved to want more than parents are evolved to give.

Pregnancy puts its own peculiar twist on this conflict because, at this point in the child's life, even the parents' interests diverge. Indeed, the womb harbors strife between mother and father that would make a divorce court look peaceable. "He only wants me for my body," women have cried down the ages. Darwinian analysis is now revealing that this is even more true after conception than before it. Fifty per cent of a fetus' genes come from its father. Our species cannot boast a history of reliable monogamy; so genes from that father might never borrow that womb again. Therefore paternal genes in the fetus have evolved to exploit the mother's body more than is optimal for her. The battleground is the placenta°, an invasive network of plumbing that seizes control of the mother's blood supply, enabling the fetus to grab more than its (maternally calculated) fair share of nutrients. This has set off a maternal–fetal arms race, escalating wildly over evolutionary time. Occasionally, a mother succumbs to one of the typical illnesses of pregnancy, such as diabetes. Only in the light of Darwinian analysis have we at last been able to understand these recurrent pathologies; they are glitches in an irresolvable conflict. 13

Darwinian science is also beginning to discover how our ancient tool kit fares in the modern world. For 99% of human existence we lived as hunter-gatherers. Ten thousand years ago agriculture arrived. Our evolved bodies and minds were unchanged; but, placed in novel environments, triggered by cues they were not designed to cope with, how would they respond? For an inkling°, go no further than your local fast-food joint. It is a monument to ancient tastes, to our evolved preferences for sugar, fat and salt. In our past, these finds were so scarce that we couldn't eat too much. Now our instincts are misled, resulting in the first epidemic of obesity that humans have ever known. 14

And we are processing not only food but also information that we weren't designed to digest. We have initiated a huge inadvertent° experiment on human nature. Think of our devices for choosing mates—exquisitely fine-tuned but not, perhaps, to some of today's challenges. A recent study found that, when people were shown pictures of beautiful and high status people of the opposite sex, both women and men became more dissatisfied with their own partners. We were evolved to assess beauty and status, and to calibrate° our satisfaction against a few hundred people at most. Yet we are all now exposed daily to images of the world's most beautiful women and richest and most powerful men, more beguiling 15 than any our ancestors ever saw. Global communications amplify these invidious° messages across the world.

16   Our species has been faced with unprecedented inequalities ever since agriculture enabled us to hoard resources. But in recent years the game has increasingly become winner-take-all. From the world's chess champion to the leading libel lawyer, the few places at the top command almost all the status; and, as rewards rise, the gap between top and bottom grows. Caught in this game are males who are evolved to value status. What impact might these novel inequalities be making on them? Might it be significant that throughout the developed world, countries with the greatest inequalities in income have the poorest health and earliest death?

17   What of the future? It is often claimed that human evolution has ended because technology cushions us from disease and death; and, equally often, it is claimed that human evolution is accelerating because technology favors balloon brains on puny bodies. Neither is true. Natural selection's pace is slow; genes are plodding on with building bodies and minds in much the same way as they were for a million or so years, and that's how they'll continue for a long time to come. The adaptations that we bear tell us about long-lost worlds in which our ancestors dwelt. But those same adaptations tell us about our future. For it is not to human nature that we should look for change but to the intriguing new responses, the innovative behavior, that changing environments will elicit from that nature. And this enduring thread of humanity reminds us that, however novel our environments, their most salient° feature—for us and our descendants, as for our ancestors—is other human beings like ourselves, a meeting of evolved minds.

Words and Meanings

Paragraph

1   Darwinian
someone who supports the theory of natural selection originated by Charles Darwin (1809–82), which states that all species arise and develop through genetic variations that increase the individual's ability to survive and reproduce

Gray's Anatomy
medical text first published in 1858 and still in use today

recondite
profound, hidden

honed
shaped, perfected

2   replicating
reproducing, copying

Pleistocene	era that began about two million years ago	4
predilection	preference	6
pathogens	disease-carrying agents	
Sherlock Holmes	famous fictional detective, protagonist of Sir Arthur Conan Doyle's mystery novels	7
monogamy	practice of having only one mate at a time	
diverge	differ, go in different directions	
consensual	based on the agreement of all participants	9
criminologists	social scientists who study crime and criminals	10
infanticide	murder of a child	11
placenta	organ in womb connecting mother and fetus	13
inkling	hint or suggestion	14
inadvertent	unplanned, accidental	15
calibrate	measure	
invidious	causing resentment, ill will	
salient	noticeable, prominent	17

Structure and Strategy

1. What strategy does Cronin use in her INTRODUCTION? Does the essay focus primarily on causes or on effects?
2. In paragraph 1, Cronin introduces an ANALOGY, comparing the human mind to a toolbox. Where else in the essay does she use this same analogy? Can you find other instances where the author explains an ABSTRACT idea by comparing it to a CONCRETE example?
3. Paragraph 2 ends with three questions. Where are these questions answered in the essay? What three KEY IDEAS do these questions represent? Rephrase the last sentence of paragraph 2 as a traditional thesis statement.
4. What is the TOPIC SENTENCE of paragraph 3? What strategy does Cronin use to develop it?
5. Find three or four examples of Cronin's use of question-and-answer to develop her points (see, for instance, the first sentence of paragraph 4). Is this informal, conversational style effective, given the seriousness of Cronin's topic?
6. Why are Cronin's ALLUSIONS to the literary figure Sherlock Holmes (paragraphs 7 and 10) appropriate in a causal analysis essay?

Content and Purpose

1. Cronin proposes that human nature is genetically determined. According to paragraphs 1 and 2, how do "our minds and brains" come to share certain characteristics?
2. What fundamental difference between men and women is explored in paragraph 3? How does the theory of natural selection explain this difference (see paragraph 4)?
3. According to the author, what physical characteristic do both men and women find attractive in the opposite sex? How do Darwinians explain the attractiveness of this characteristic?
4. Sex is one way that genes produce copies of themselves. What is another way for genes to promote their survival? How does Darwinian theory alter our traditional notions of the family and of altruism? (See paragraph 10.)
5. Cronin states that criminologists are wrong in their thinking that the family "is the most dangerous place to be." How does she defend the Darwinian point of view against that of the criminologists? Who does Cronin say is most likely to be murdered within a family? Why?
6. According to evolutionary theory, what is the source of sibling rivalry?
7. In your own words, explain why Darwinians think mother and fetus are locked in "irresolvable conflict" (see paragraph 13).
8. According to Cronin, why do we like junk food? What effect is our taste for junk food having on us in a world where we no longer have to hunt to survive?
9. Cronin suggests that the media, like junk food, adversely affect us because they feed us "information that we weren't designed to digest" (paragraph 15). What two negative effects of global communication does Cronin cite to support her point?

Suggestions for Writing

1. Write an essay in which you argue that perception of beauty, sibling conflict, and addiction to fast food are culturally rather than genetically determined.
2. Write an essay that explains a possible evolutionary cause of some aspect of human nature not discussed in Cronin's essay: for example, our religious impulse, inherent curiosity, fear of the dark, consumerism, fondness for jokes, tendency to break promises, xenophobia.
3. Does the theory that humans are creatures of evolution, designed simply to "replicate genes" (in other words, to get our own personal genetic material into the gene pool) appeal to

you? Write an essay that details your response and argues either for or against the Darwinian point of view.

4. Read Natalie Angier's "The Cute Factor" on page 227 and/or Olivia Judson's "Why I'm Happy I Evolved" on page 261. Write an essay that explores two or three significant aspects of human behaviour as seen in the light of evolutionary biology. Use examples from the essays to support your THESIS.

Additional Suggestions for Writing: Causal Analysis

Choose one of the topics below and write a paper that explores its causes *or* effects. Write a clear thesis statement and plan the development of each KEY IDEA before you begin to write the paper.

1. sibling rivalry
2. cheating in school
3. the popularity of a current television show
4. online gambling
5. polygamy
6. compulsive shopping
7. the pressure on women to be thin
8. vegetarianism
9. peer pressure among adolescents
10. depression
11. obesity
12. the trend to postpone childbearing until a couple is in their thirties or even forties
13. a specific phobia that affects someone you know
14. the attraction of religious cults
15. marriage breakdown
16. lying
17. Internet shopping
18. the increasing demand among men for plastic surgery (or spa treatments, cosmetics, etc.)
19. shyness
20. our tendency to distrust or dislike people who are different from ourselves

UNIT 6

Definition

WHAT IS DEFINITION?

All communication depends on shared understanding. In writing, the writer and the reader must have a common understanding of what the words mean. Sometimes a definition is required to ensure this common understanding. Knowing when and how to define terms clearly is one of the most useful skills a writer can learn. Through definition, a writer creates shared meaning.

There are two basic ways to define terms: the short way and the long way. The short way is sometimes called **formal definition.** The writer explains in one sentence a word that may be unclear to the reader. In the model essay "Talking Pidgin," the second paragraph begins with a formal definition: "A pidgin is a simplified language that evolves between groups of people who have no language in common." A fuller, more elaborate definition of "pidgin languages" follows. The essay as a whole is an example of the long way of definition, known as **extended definition.** Extended definition is a form of expository writing in which the word or idea being defined is the topic of the essay. Extended definition is required when the nature of the thing to be defined is complex, and explaining *what it is* in detail is the writer's goal.

WHY DO WE WRITE DEFINITION?

Definition answers the lead-in question *what*. It is a key way to provide information about a topic. A short, formal definition is often used to introduce an unfamiliar word or technical term. It may also be used to explain an unusual meaning of a word that is normally understood in another way. For instance, in the first paragraph of "Altruism" on page 234, Lewis Thomas defines the word "survival" as follows: "Survival, in the cool economics of biology, means simply the persistence of one's own genes in the generations to follow." This unusual definition—and the shared understanding between writer and reader that it ensures—is crucial to the ideas Thomas presents in the essay.

An extended definition is useful to explain ABSTRACT ideas, as Lewis Thomas does in his essay on the meaning of altruism. In "Nature or Nurture—What's the Real Test of 'Home'?" on page 210, Ken Wiwa makes some poignant observations about his concept of "home" that will resonate with many people who have left their birthplace behind. In "The Cute Factor" on page 227, Natalie Angier first identifies the features that humans find "cute" as distinct from beautiful. Then she extends her definition by showing how and why our response to cuteness is hard-wired into our emotional make-up.

Sometimes a writer takes a new word and explains its origins and meaning. Curtis Gillespie's "Bling Bling" on page 213 is an example of this kind of definition. Sometimes a writer does the opposite. In "Blush, Cringe, Fidget" on page 217, Margaret Visser defines "embarrassment," a term for an experience with which most of us are all too familiar, but she does so in such a way that we learn new information about a common experience. Some definitions are designed to be fun as well as informative. Gillespie's essay takes a humorous approach to "bling," and Visser not only clarifies the meaning of "embarrassment" by providing the etymological origins of the word but also provides a number of funny examples.

Definition is not restricted to a purely informative or expository function but can involve argument or persuasion as well. In "I'm a Banana and Proud of It" on page 205, Wayson Choy appropriates the controversial term "banana" to pay respect to his Chinese immigrant forebears whose lives in Canada were almost unbearably difficult. Choy wants his readers not only to understand but also to value his cultural history. Denise Chong's essay on page 222 develops a definition of "Being Canadian" that people from diverse cultures can relate to. Lewis Thomas uses his definition of altruism as a platform from which he makes a passionate plea for us to understand that we are part of an indescribably complex web of life on this planet and to change our wasteful, destructive ways.

HOW DO WE WRITE DEFINITION?

There is no single rhetorical pattern that applies to extended definition. Its development relies instead on one or more of the other patterns explained in this text. In other words, depending on the topic and the AUDIENCE, an extended definition can employ any of a number of organizational patterns, or even a combination of strategies.

It is often helpful to begin your extended definition with a formal definition. To write a formal definition, first put the term you are defining into the general class of things to which it belongs; then identify the qualities that set it apart or distinguish it from the others in that class. Here are some examples of formal definitions:

TERM		CLASS	DISTINGUISHING FEATURES
A turtle	is	a shelled reptile	that lives in water.
A tortoise	is	a shelled reptile	that lives on land.
Misogyny	is	the hatred	of women.
Misanthropy	is	the hatred	of people in general.

Constructing a formal definition is a logical way to begin the task of definition. It prevents vague formulations such as "a turtle lives in water" (so does a tuna), or "misanthropy is when you don't like people."

Here are two pitfalls to avoid when writing definitions:

1. Do not begin your essay with a word-for-word definition copied from the dictionary. When you're staring at a piece of blank paper, it's hard to resist the temptation to resort to this strategy. But you should resist, because a dictionary definition is boring and often not directly relevant to your own topic.

2. Don't chase your own tail by using in your definition a form of the word you're defining. Stating that "adolescence is the state of being an adolescent" doesn't clarify anything for readers.

A good definition establishes clearly, logically, and precisely the boundaries of meaning. It communicates the meaning in an organizational pattern appropriate to the term and to the reader. To define is an act of creation, and defining terms clearly shows respect for both the ideas you're explaining and the readers you're addressing.

The following model essay—an extended definition of the term "pidgin language"—illustrates definition by example, etymology, and distinctive characteristics.

Talking Pidgin

Introduction (quotation and question to intrigue the reader) Thesis is a question Begins with formal definition and adds examples	*Pren, man bolong Rom, Wantok, harim nau. Mi kam tasol long plantim Kaesar. Mi noken beiten longen.* Can you translate these words? Not likely, unless you are familiar with Tok Pisin, a pidgin language spoken by about a million people in Papua New Guinea. What is a pidgin language?

A pidgin is a simplified language that evolves between groups of people who have no language in common. It is a new "hybrid" language made up of elements derived from its source languages: English and Chinese, for example, or Spanish and Tagalog. Most pidgin languages developed to permit groups to trade with each other. For example, when the Nootka and Chinook peoples living on the West Coast came in contact with French and English traders in the nineteenth century, they developed a pidgin language so they could talk and do business with each other. Like all pidgins, this language—Chinook Jargon—combined elements of its source languages: Nootka, Chinook, English, and French. From the 1830s to the 1920s, from California to Alaska, Chinook Jargon was spoken by people from widely varying language backgrounds who came together to hunt, log, or look for gold. Chinook Jargon expressions are still used on the West Coast today: *mucketymuck* is a slang term for an important person, and *saltchuck* means the sea.

Definition by example

There are hundreds, perhaps thousands, of pidgin languages around the world. Many are based on European languages such as Portuguese, Spanish, French, Dutch, and English, and they reflect the extent of European colonization over the past 500 years. Probably the best-known example is Pidgin English, the language used by British and Chinese traders in ports such as Canton. But pidgins can develop wherever different languages collide. Mogilian is a Choctaw-based pidgin formerly used by Amerindian tribes along the Gulf of Mexico. Pachuco, or "Spanglish," is an English–Spanish hybrid used in Latino communities in the United States. Bazaar Malay is a pidgin derived from Malaysian and Chinese that is widely used in Malaysia and Indonesia.

Definition by
etymology

Pidgins are so widespread and so multilingual in origin that linguists (scholars who study the nature of language) are not certain where the word *pidgin* comes from. Some suggest that it derives from the Portuguese word for business, *ocupacao;* others think the source is a Chinese-inflected pronunciation of the English word *business.* Some etymologists (linguists who specialize in word origins) theorize that the word comes from the Hebrew *pid yom,* which means *barter.*

Definition by
distinctive
characteristics

All pidgin languages are characterized by a small vocabulary (a few hundred or thousand words), a simplified grammatical structure, and a narrower range of use than the languages they are based on. Pidgins are unique in that they are the native languages of no one. Speakers use them for a few restricted purposes—usually work and trade—and they use their native tongues for more diverse and complex communications.

Conclusion
(highlights
significance
and provides
translation of
opening
quotation)

Pidgins cease to exist when the contact between the source-language groups diminishes, or when one group adopts the language of the other. In their adaptability and transience, pidgins are excellent examples of the processes of linguistic change. More than any other kind of verbal communication, pidgins demonstrate how resourceful and ingenious humans can be in adapting language to fit their needs.

So what does the opening quotation actually say? It is none other than Shakespeare's famous words from *Julius Caesar:* "Friends, Romans, countrymen, lend me your ears; I come to bury Caesar, not to praise him."

I'm a Banana and Proud of It

WAYSON CHOY

Wayson Choy (b. 1939) was born in Vancouver into a Chinese immigrant family. He attended the University of British Columbia and has spent much of his life teaching and writing. He was a faculty member at Toronto's Humber College until 2004. His works include the award-winning novel *The Jade Peony* (1994) and its sequel *All That Matters* (2004). In 2005, he was named a Member of the Order of Canada.

1   Because both my parents came from China, I look Chinese. But I cannot read or write Chinese and barely speak it. I love my North American citizenship. I don't mind being called a "banana," yellow on the outside and white inside: I'm proud I'm a banana.

2   After all, in Canada and the United States, native Indians are "apples" (red outside, white inside); blacks are "Oreo cookies" (black and white); and Chinese are "bananas." These metaphors assume, both rightly and wrongly, that the culture here has been primarily anglo-white. Cultural history made me a banana.

3   History: My father and mother arrived separately to the B.C. coast in the early part of the century. They came as unwanted "aliens." Better to be an alien here than to be dead of starvation in China. But after the Chinese Exclusion laws were passed in North America (late 1800s, early 1900s), no Chinese immigrants were granted citizenship in either Canada or the United States.

4   Like those Old China village men from *Toi San*° who, in the 1850s, laid down cliff-edge train tracks through the Rockies and the Sierras, or like those first women who came as mail-order wives or concubines and who as bond-slaves were turned into cheaper labourers or even prostitutes—like many of those men and women, my father and mother survived ugly, unjust times. In 1917, two hours after he got off the boat from Hong Kong, my father was called "chink" and told to go back to China. "Chink" is a hateful, racist term, stereotyping the shape of Asian eyes: "a chink in the armour," an undesirable slit. For the Elders, the past was humiliating. Eventually, the Second World War changed hostile attitudes against the Chinese.

5   During the war, Chinese men volunteered and lost their lives as members of the Canadian and American military. When hostilities ended, many more were proudly in uniform, waiting to go overseas. Record Chinatown dollars were raised to buy War Bonds. After 1945, challenged by such money and ultimate sacrifices, the Exclusion laws in both Canada and the United States were revoked. Chinatown residents claimed their citizenship and sent for their families.

6   By 1949, after the Communists took over China, those of us who arrived here as young children, or were born here, stayed. No longer "aliens," we became legal citizens of North America. Many of us also became "bananas."

7   Historically, "banana" is not a racist term. Although it clumsily stereotypes many of the children and grandchildren of the old Chinatowns, the term actually follows the old Chinese tendency to assign endearing nicknames to replace formal names, semicomic

names to keep one humble. Thus, "banana" describes the generations who assimilated so well into North American life.

In fact, our families encouraged members of my generation in   8
the 1950s and sixties to "get ahead," to get an English education, to
get a job with good pay and prestige. "Don't work like me,"
Chinatown parents said. "Work in an office!" The *lao wah-kiu* (the
Chinatown old-timers) also warned, "Never forget—you still be
Chinese!"

None of us ever forgot. The mirror never lied.   9

Many Chinatown teenagers felt we didn't quite belong in any   10
one world. We looked Chinese, but thought and behaved North
American. Impatient Chinatown parents wanted the best of both
worlds for us, but they bluntly labelled their children and grandchildren *"juk-sing"* or even *"mo no."* Not that we were totally
"shallow bamboo butt-ends" or entirely "no brain," but we had less
and less understanding of Old China traditions, and less and less
interest in their village histories. Father used to say we lacked
Taoist ritual, Taoist manners. We were, he said, *"mo li."*

This was true. Chinatown's younger brains, like everyone else's   11
of whatever race, were being colonized by "white bread" U.S.
family television programs. We began to feel Chinese home life was
inferior. We co-operated with English-language magazines that
showed us how to act and what to buy. Seductive Hollywood
movies made some of us secretly weep that we did not have movie-
star faces. American music made Chinese music sound like noise.

By the 1970s and eighties, many of us had consciously or   12
unconsciously distanced ourselves from our Chinatown histories.
We became bananas.

Finally, for me, in my 40s or 50s, with the death first of my   13
mother, then my father, I realized I did not belong anywhere unless
I could understand the past. I needed to find the foundation of my
Chinese-ness. I needed roots.

I spent my college holidays researching the past. I read   14
Chinatown oral histories, located documents, searched out early
articles. Those early citizens came back to life for me. Their long toil
and blood sacrifices, the proud record of their patient, legal challenges, gave us all our present rights as citizens. Canadian and
American Chinatowns set aside their family tongue differences and
encouraged each other to fight injustice. There were no borders.
"After all," they affirmed, *"Daaih ga tohng yahn* ... we are all
Chinese!"

In my book, *The Jade Peony*, I tried to recreate this past, to   15
explore the beginnings of the conflicts trapped within myself, the
struggle between being Chinese and being North American. I discovered a truth: these "between world" struggles are universal.

16   In every human being, there is "the Other"—something that makes each of us feel how different we are to everyone else, even to family members. Yet, ironically, we are all the same, wanting the same security and happiness. I know this now.

17   I think the early Chinese pioneers actually started "going bananas" from the moment they first settled upon the West Coast. They had no choice. They adapted. They initiated assimilation. If they had not, they and their family would have starved to death. I might even suggest that all surviving Chinatown citizens eventually became bananas. Only some, of course, were more ripe than others.

18   That's why I'm proudly a banana: I accept the paradox of being both Chinese and not Chinese.

19   Now, at last, whenever I look in the mirror or hear ghost voices shouting, "You still Chinese," I smile.

20   I know another truth: In immigrant North America, we are all Chinese.

Words and Meanings

Paragraph

4   *Toi San*   Most of the Chinese who came to the West Coast were from Guangdong Province (Canton delta region) and the four counties of Toi-san, Sun-wui, Hoi-ping, and Yin-pang

Structure and Strategy

1. What is the TOPIC SENTENCE of paragraph 1? How is it supported?
2. Where does Choy actually define the term "banana"?
3. The narrative parts of the essay use the first-person point of view, yet this changes from first-person plural "we" in paragraphs 8–12 to the singular "I" in paragraphs 14–17. Why do you think Choy makes this shift? What is the function of paragraph 13?
4. What is the THESIS of this essay? Is it implied or stated?
5. What are the foods (apples, Oreos, bananas) mentioned in paragraph 2 METAPHORS for? Does Choy think that these characterizations are racist? Do you?

Content and Purpose

1. When and where was the author born? Where did he grow up? How familiar was he with Chinese culture as he grew up?

2. Where did Choy's parents come from? Why did they leave? What was their life in Canada like?

3. What were the "Exclusion laws" (paragraph 3)? What historical event, according to Choy, led to the repeal of these laws?

4. Summarize the conflict between generations that Choy develops in paragraphs 8–12. How did it affect his own generation's view of themselves?

5. What caused Choy to begin to research his family's past? What was the outcome of this search?

6. What does Choy think about the tendency to assimilate that resulted in a generation of "bananas"? Does Choy's conclusion hold true for "apples" and "Oreos" too?

7. What do you think Choy means by the last sentence of his essay?

Suggestions for Writing

1. Are you an immigrant to Canada or the child of immigrants? Write an essay that identifies and explains the kinds of assimilation you and your family have undergone in Canada.

2. What elements of their home country culture (e.g., language, history, religion, values, customs) should immigrants to Canada teach their children? Are there any elements of the original culture that should not be taught? Write an essay identifying the cultural elements that should be transmitted from one generation to the next and suggest ways that parents can pass them on to their children.

3. Read Denise Chong's "Being Canadian," on page 222. Write an essay comparing Chong's view of her Chinese heritage in Canada with Wayson Choy's view in "I'm a Banana."

4. Read Michael Ignatieff's essay, "Immigration: The Hate Stops Here," on page 282. Write an essay contrasting Choy's and Ignatieff's views of the responsibilities of immigrants to this country.

Nature or Nurture—What's the Real Test of "Home"?

KEN WIWA

Journalist, documentarian, and activist Ken Wiwa (b. 1968) was born in Nigeria. His father, the internationally renowned playwright and human rights activist Ken Saro-Wiwa, was executed in 1995 after being imprisoned for 18 months by the Nigerian military dictatorship. In 2004, Wiwa founded the Ken Saro-Wiwa Foundation, an organization that plans to set up a secondary school in Ogoni, offer scholarships to Ogoni children, and maintain his father's gravesite. Ken Wiwa has written for newspapers and magazines around the world, including *The Globe and Mail*.

1   There's no place like home. Whenever I contemplate that phrase, I usually regard it with [ambivalence°], and over the past two weeks I've experienced both sides of its meaning. Watching six years of accumulated belongings from a family life in Canada being loaded into a shipping container would send a shiver of apprehension running through the most footloose nomad. It might be a truism, but it is only when you leave home that you really begin to appreciate it.

2   Without my knowing or suspecting it, Toronto, especially the cul-de-sac where I lived in the west end of the city, now sticks out in the collage of places that spring to mind whenever I think of "home." That street, which was my home base for six increasingly peripatetic° years, is one of those places where everyone really does know your name. It is odd, considering that I was one of its most transient residents, that I have so many memories of my Toronto street—my neighbours; children playing out on the road and running in between the gardens; the street parties; the cranks, loners and extroverts; the smell of skunks on a summer night; going for a run in High Park and lounging by Lake Ontario in summer—oh and er, shovelling snow in the winter.

3   Friends and neighbours: That's what has imprinted Ridley Gardens as home on my world's interior map. Like the sitcoms that take their names from the things that make us humane and sociable animals, the final episode of our Ridley Gardens life has ended, leaving a gaping hole. In Africa, we say it takes a village to raise a child. That was true in Toronto for my youngest son. He was born at home at Ridley Gardens and nurtured by the street. But as one of my neighbours succinctly put it while watching our sons play soccer one night, moving my family to the U.K. while I shuttle in and out of Africa will make my family life more coherent geographically.

4   For much of the past week, I have been homeless, living between my mother's place and my sister-in-law's house outside

London. We're not actually moving to our new place until the end of this month but this halfway house is good preparation for taking what for me is a leap of faith—living outside a big city. I thought I couldn't resist the lure of the big smoke, but darting in and out of London this week, I am surprised at how easily I seem to have let go of my addiction to metropolitan hustle. London is the place I have always regarded as my turf, having spent the longest stretch of my life there. Driving into a half-empty city on a recent Saturday morning was an eerie experience; I imagine it was the underlying caution in the aftermath of the terrorist attacks°. A few days later, I struggled for an hour to get across town on the underground train, trying not to think about who might be carrying a bomb. If nothing else, such thoughts expose you to your prejudices, so you adopt the *sang-froid°* that comes with the territory. Living in a big city like London is a skittish experience these days. You don't have to be mad—but it helps. . . .

I escaped to Africa . . . [and tomorrow] I head to the sanctuary   5
of my village. It will be a strange trip for me because the meaning of that home has changed since the last time I was there. When my grandfather passed away in April, he was the last of my grandparents; I have fewer compelling reasons to return to the village. Like anyone raised far away from their roots, the death of grandparents can cut you off. I guess you could call it the law of diminishing returns.

The thing about villages in Africa though is that most Africans,   6
like me, have a village, a specific place that is unequivocally° home. And to give up on that place is to abdicate the centre of our being. As the world turns on its economic wheels, the meaning of home for many of us spins with the dizzying pace of change. I like change, it keeps things fresh. But I also like to feel the ground beneath my feet. And I wonder, in all of this wandering: Is there no place like home any more?

Words and Meanings

Paragraph

ambivalence	experiencing two opposing attitudes or feelings at the same time	1
peripatetic	moving from place to place	2
terrorist attacks	the bombings of London's subway system in July 2005	4
sang-froid	cool, composed attitude	
unequivocally	unarguably; having only one interpretation	6

Structure and Strategy

1. How does the title prepare the reader for the topic Wiwa defines in this essay? Does Wiwa's essay fulfil the expectation that the title sets up in the reader?
2. The essay begins with a CLICHÉ that the author regards with "ambivalence. "What two contradictory meanings can you assign to the saying," There's no place like home"?
3. What TV situation comedy does Wiwa allude to in paragraph 2? Can you think of examples of "sitcoms that take their names from the things that make us humane and sociable animals" (paragraph 3)? Have any of these programs influenced your own definition of "home"?
4. Identify and explain the PUN with which the author concludes paragraph 5.

Content and Purpose

1. Explain the meaning of the title. What is the difference between "nature" and "nurture"?
2. Identify the three places Wiwa has called "home" so far. What connection is there between each place and the title of the essay?
3. In which "home" did Wiwa live longest? How does he feel about that place now? Why?
4. In which "home" did Wiwa and his family spend the previous six years? What about their life there will they miss?
5. How does Wiwa feel about his home in Africa? Why has the meaning of that home changed for him?
6. Explain what makes a place a "home," according to Wiwa. Do you agree with his definition? Has he missed any essential characteristics that you would include in your definition of "home"?

Suggestions for Writing

1. In how many "homes" have you lived? Define what "home" means to you.
2. Write an essay about the place where you grew up. Are you as connected to this place as an adult as you were as a child? How does this connection (or lack of connection) have an impact on your life?
3. Read Shandi Mitchell's "Baba and Me" on page 18. How are Baba's experiences of "home" different from Wiwa's? Write an essay contrasting the two views of "home." You might conclude

by suggesting some of the reasons for the differences between Baba's and Wiwa's attitudes to the changes they experienced in moving from one place to another.

Bling Bling

CURTIS GILLESPIE

Alberta-born Curtis Gillespie writes both fiction and non-fiction. He published a prize-winning collection of short stories, *The Progress of an Object in Motion*, in 1997, and the autobiographical *Playing Through: A Year of Life and Links Along the Scottish Coast* in 2004. Gillespie's articles have appeared in a variety of publications, including *Saturday Night*, *Toro*, and *Toronto Life*. He lives in Edmonton with his wife and two daughters.

There are few things more pathetic than a man shooting for hipness when it's so far beyond him he doesn't even remember that he never possessed it in the first place. One of the manifestations of this is utilizing the language of any street you don't personally walk down; a street, for instance, where I might strut with my bitch and show off my bling bling.

I was recently driving our sixteen-year-old babysitter home after my wife and I had had a nice, mellow dinner out, and I innocently asked our sitter what else she was getting up to for the rest of the weekend. She was wearing a t-shirt with some bad words on it, and a chunky necklace that had the word "Princess" laid out in diamonds (though I hoped they were fake, otherwise why were we paying her so much money to put our kids to bed and eat popcorn all night?). She told me that after I dropped her off she was going to meet some friends at a downtown hip-hop club, which was either a "rave" or her "fave." I didn't quite catch it all because my hearing is going, nor did I dare ask how she was planning on getting in to the club.

Naturally, I mentioned to her that I'd actually been to that club once or twice in my "other" life, trying to imply an interesting past. She curled up her lip and said, "Really? Wow, I never see old people there."

Feeling that I was getting less than the respect I deserved, but not wanting to lose a reliable sitter, I made up my own rap and recited it on the way home. I demanded street cred from the sitter, and told her that if next time she didn't pay respect I'd drop her off on the side of the street, "Wi' no ice, no ring, no Benz, no thing/'cept fitty cent for some s****y little bling bling."

5   Bling bling, of course, is the term rappers have been using since time began (about 1999) to denote flashy jewelry, expensive cars, furs, and so on, all the purely tangible consumer benefits made available through fabulous wealth. The term was first coined, so to speak, by the New Orleans rap family Cash Money Millionaires, and it was put into higher circulation by Cash Money rapper Baby Gangsta. BG's eponymous song "Bling Bling" was an ode to the simpler things in life, such as his Benz, the ice on his hoes, and jewelry so expensive "I got the price of a mansion 'round my neck and wrist."

6   The phrase likely reached its cultural apex when the Los Angeles Lakers won the 2000 NBA Championship and had their winner's rings engraved with the words "bling bling" carved straight into the gold below a sea of ice ... I mean, diamonds. Shaq was reported to have said he wanted the term on there because bling bling was the sound created when light bounces off an NBA Championship ring.

7   It didn't last long, though. Hiphopmusic.com reported in 2003 that the term was functionally dead as a culturally relevant term, given that the mainstream had begun to co-opt it in order to accrue, in time-honoured fashion, some second-hand cred. The online magazine was also one of the first to report that the phrase was about to gain entry into the *Oxford English Dictionary*. This is the surest sign that bling bling has shuffled off its linguistic coil. "We're going to draft an entry, which we'll probably publish soon," said . . . an editor with the OED. "We decide based on currency. In a case like bling bling, it's very widespread."

8   *Widespread* is the problem. The usage, and use, of bling bling by the mainstream is hardly unfamiliar to anyone wise in the ways of corporate advertising and culture. Irony has suffered the most from its being press-ganged into the work camps of the mainstream culture. There are so few advertisements and corporate messages today that don't give us a wink, that to find a direct message from anyone anywhere now inspires suspicion.

9   And in this way bling bling is now being used. CNN has put it and other hip-hop words on its scrolling graphics in a direct bid to stay "relevant, smarter and cooler" to a younger audience, as the station's general manager admitted in a recent interview. Even *The New York Times* is using it. [R]eporter Lynette Holloway, writing on Jennifer Lopez and her ubiquity°, noted that J-Lo's career handlers have recently begun to fear that she's becoming too mainstream. So they constructed the idiotic and utterly preposterous single "Jenny

from the Block," a song that lets her listeners know she's still a home girl and to not be "fooled by the rocks I got," a lyric Holloway termed "blingblinging."

Bling bling is one of those difficult phrases for the outsider to   10 use in any way, shape or form that doesn't immediately identify them as wannabes. The reasons for this are fairly clear, and most have to do with the transmission of neologisms°. Once created, words enter into colloquial usage fairly rapidly among their creative constituency. They gain credibility. But then they start to attain currency outside the constituency, which is what undermines that credibility. By the time a phrase like bling bling filters off the street and into the mainstream it's usually already been overtaken by the next trend or phase. This means, basically, that you're a double loser if you're a mainstreamer talking bling bling: first, because you're telling the world you are groping for some unearned cred, and second, because you are too far out of the loop to even know that its time has come and gone.

Jon Caramanica, writing in *GQ*, reported that the bling bling   11 era is over, that "the days of waving Rolexes side to side and racing model-filled speedboats around the islands now seems like a distant memory." What has replaced bling bling at hip-hop central is the *thug*, best represented by 50 Cent and his drug-dealing mother, teenage arrests, adventures in the crack trade, and real-life knife and bullet wounds.

Gangstas. Thugs. Charming.   12

Of course, by now, given the way that language and trends   13 work, the era of the *gangsta* is probably over where it matters—on the street of real experience. There has no doubt already been a new catch phrase created to supersede *gangsta* and *thug*. Whatever it is, I'm sure I'll hear about it in a year or two. At least then, we'll have a new babysitter I can try it out on.

Words and Meanings

		Paragraph
ubiquity	quality of being everywhere; high-profile popularity	9
neologisms	new words	10

Structure and Strategy

1. What kind of INTRODUCTION does Gillespie use in this essay?
2. Where does the author define the term "bling bling"?

3. For what AUDIENCE did Gillespie write this essay? Support your answer with reference to the media sources he cites and the language he uses, as well as his topic.
4. Identify some of the ALLUSIONS that are likely to be unfamiliar to people outside Gillespie's target audience. How do these terms and allusions affect you as a reader? Do they increase or decrease the effectiveness of the essay?
5. How would you describe the TONE of this essay?

Content and Purpose

1. What PURPOSE did the author have in mind when he wrote this essay?
2. What does Gillespie's babysitter look like? What is her attitude toward him? How do you know?
3. According to this essay, when was the term "bling bling" first used? Who used it? When did the term's usage reach its peak?
4. When did the term cease to be cool? Why?
5. What is the "wink" (paragraph 8) that Gillespie says we get from ads?
6. What terms does Gillespie claim replaced "bling" in the hip-hip world? Do you agree?
7. Gillespie wrote this piece in 2003. What are the current "in" words that have replaced "bling" and its immediate successors?

Suggestions for Writing

1. Choose a slang word or term from popular culture that is current among a small group of hip people. Write an essay, using examples, that defines the term.
2. Write an essay that explores teenagers' views of people in their parents' generation. Draw on some of the same topics, such as clothing, language, and cultural icons, that Gillespie employs in his essay.
3. Read "The World Is Phat" on page 114 and contrast Edlund's view of hip-hop culture with Gillespie's.

Blush, Cringe, Fidget

MARGARET VISSER

Margaret Visser (b. 1940) describes herself as "an anthropologer of everyday life." A former professor of classics at York University, she now devotes her time to writing and lecturing. Her books include *Much Depends on Dinner* (1986), *The Rituals of Dinner* (1991), *The Way We Are* (1994), *The Geometry of Love* (2001), and *Beyond Fate* (2002).

The reactions are physical all right: face turning red and some- 1
times white, voice switching to falsetto or to bass°, stuttering, throat contracting, inhibited breath, dry mouth, stomach contractions, blinking, lowered head and eyes, shaking, fumbling, fidgeting, plucking at the clothes, hands cold and twisting together or held behind the back, smile fixed, feet frozen. These are symptoms of embarrassment, or dis-ease. They are brought on by entirely social and mental conditions, and they constitute proof positive that the human body reacts directly to the mind, even without reference to willpower or design.

To be embarrassed is to be disclosed, in public. Both factors are 2
important: you must have something to hide first, and you must have an audience. Fall over your shoes as you get out of your solitary bed in the morning, and you may curse but you will not blush: embarrassment is about how you look in *other people's* eyes. (Extremely sensitive people might blush in private—but only when imagining that audience, which remains indispensable to the experience.)

The revelation of something we wanted to keep hidden 3
explains the fingering of our clothes: we touch, tighten, and arrange, reassuring ourselves that the shell is still in place. Clothes cover what society has decreed shall be concealed, and a good many embarrassing moments involve clothes: lacking them, popping out of them, or wearing the wrong ones.

What we would like to hide is most often the truth about our- 4
selves: the inexperience, incompetence, and ignorance that lie behind the bombastic° or slick facade°. To step forward before the expectant crowd with every sign of cool control, and then to fall flat on your face, is to produce embarrassment at nightmare level. The slip on the banana peel, the rug sliding out from under are concrete shorthand for the public fall from grandeur that everyone who is sane can recognize and remember. Failure to live up to expectations is another cause for embarrassment, both for you (provided you understand the extent of your inadequacy) and for everybody watching. . . .

5   The word *embarrass* is from the Spanish *embarazar*, "to hinder by placing a bar or impediment in the way." It creates confusion, as when the march of a column of ants is broken up by a sudden interference—someone "putting their foot in it," perhaps. (In dialects of French and Spanish the equivalents of this word are coarse terms for "to get someone pregnant [*embarazada*].") . . .

6   The specific meaning of *embarrassment* in English arrives fairly late in the language. The term once meant merely "not knowing what to do" in a specific situation, for instance when confronted by a dilemma (as in the French *embarras de choix*), or when there is a superfluity of good things (an *embarras de richesses*). The narrowing of the sense till we get "an inability to respond where a response is due," approaches the modern English meaning of the word. One can still feel "financially embarrassed," or unable to pay. The sense of inadequacy that having no money can arouse in the breasts of upright citizens was then further honed° and differentiated until we get the naming of the precise phenomenon we now call "embarrassment." It still includes occasions where we have to respond, but the role we must play is one we have not learned. Examples are finding yourself honoured by a surprise party, or having suddenly to dance in public (if you are not in the habit of dancing, of course).

7   If, on the other hand, what your image *requires* is a crowd of spectators, then, if no one takes any notice of you, that absence will constitute your shame. If you set yourself up to give a speech and no one comes, the lack will hurt as much as being howled down. But even here, embarrassment comes about only if there are *some* people around: the three members who make up the audience, or the idle ticket sellers who watch you arrive, are needed in order for you to cringe. (Cringing is making yourself small, which is why embarrassment causes the hanging of heads, the shrinking back: these physically express the belittlement you see in the eyes of others.)

8   There is often complicity° in the watching crowd; embarrassment is contagious. So when you step out on stage, or before the TV cameras, and start to sing, only to hear yourself warbling way out of tune, the audience will start to squirm and blush on your behalf. They imagine what it must be like to be you—and they can do it because somewhere in their lives they too have experienced your fate. It is far worse, of course, for members of the crowd who are your friends and relatives, for, as allies, their reputations are vested in° your behaving "properly."

9   The only way socially to pass muster° is to "fit in," as we say: to do what is proper, or "fitting." Impropriety°, then, is the very stuff of embarrassment. Once again the body comes into play: exposure that is deemed "indecent" evokes embarrassment, and so do flatulence,

snores, dribbles, burps, and sniffing. You should not be caught
talking to yourself either, or picking your nose, or being smelly. To
have committed such misdemeanours in public means the death of
your reputation—and it is important to remember that in such cases
whether you are to blame or not is of no significance. Your only hope
is that the crowd, who usually have an interest in not interrupting
the official agenda of the meeting and in not being contaminated by
an impropriety through drawing attention to it, will behave—at least
for the moment—as though nothing has happened.

Incompetence is what impropriety of the embarrassing kind   10
most often demonstrates. I once said to an important gentleman
who arrived to visit my French landlady, "*Madame est sur le
téléphone*," and he answered gravely, "*Cela ne doit pas être très confor-
table*." The stories travellers bring home from foreign countries often
concern the embarrassing results of not knowing the language well
enough, or not knowing what the social norms are: what you should
on no account do or say. You bumble ahead with the best intentions,
yet commit the offence—and the horror or the amusement you
evoke cannot subsequently be put back into the bottle.

Involuntary impropriety is, of course, most acutely embar-   11
rassing when you cannot explain away what you have done. What
you want more than anything else on earth is an escape from your
predicament, and there is none. You are caught and helpless (which
is why you wring or hide your hands in reaction to embarrassment).
You haven't the vocabulary in the foreign language; or your situation
is compromised° in such a way that no one would believe your
explanation if you gave it, the clues pointing so much more plau-
sibly° to what the audience believes they can see. Into this category
fall many of the cases of mistaken identity. You hug your husband,
whisper extremely private endearments into his ear, then discover to
your horror that you have made a mistake: this is not your husband
at all. And immediately you know exactly what this total stranger
must be thinking: sympathy is essential to embarrassment.

[Ironically,] the embarrassed reaction itself shows not that you   12
lack social adjustment but that you have it, in spades. You *care* what
society thinks, and really that is what it wants most. If we look at
who most often gets embarrassed, we see that it is sensitive people,
people who are trying hard to succeed, who are prepared to mend
their ways, who never forget the lesson learned—and what more
could society ask? On the whole, people who are never embarrassed (the "shameless") are the most antisocial of us, the least con-
siderate and most uncaring.

The most exquisite kind of embarrassment, and the one that   13
helps us see that the reaction need not merely mean a blind bowing

to the pressures of convention, is the horrible realization that you might have hurt someone without intending to do so, or that your own arrogance has made you behave condescendingly° where respect was due. Again you have demonstrated incompetence, but here the lesson learned has ethical implications.

14   Two women discuss, in Norwegian, the handicap of a man with one leg who is sitting opposite them on a Paris subway train. What would it be like to sleep with a one-legged man? The man gets up and says, in faultless Norwegian, "If you would care for a demonstration, Madam, I would be happy to oblige." . . .

15   My favourite example of this kind of embarrassment happened to John Fraser, the [former] editor of *Saturday Night* magazine. Visiting one of Jean Vanier's l'Arche° communities, he saw a man struggling with a carpentry chore, and spoke to him in a slow clear voice, with the nervously careful solicitude° that we all reserve for the mentally retarded. He discovered later that the man was a Sorbonne professor who had taken time off to care for and learn from the handicapped. The way John tells this story, all those listening imagine themselves in the same position, being kind. Then the punch line is delivered, to all of us. Embarrassment, when it is in working order, can produce enlightenment as well as shock.

16   Precisely because embarrassment often arises from unawareness of important factors in the social environment, and because it is a powerful aid to learning and never forgetting, it most commonly occurs in adolescence. Almost all the good embarrassment stories happened when we were young, and just discovering the mines and traps laid for those who want desperately to find a place among their peers. Very small children know fear and shyness, but they never blush because of social faux pas°.

17   Adults become surer and surer of themselves as well as less and less sensitive, largely through knowing the rules, and through practice and general wear and tear. It often requires decades of experience and self-assurance before the worst of our blunders can be told to people. Yet even then, what is laughing publicly at ourselves but further social complicity? We have found out not only that everybody else knows what it's like to look a fool, but that a very good way to defuse and rise above a crowd's contempt is to make an even larger crowd laugh *with* you, even if it's at yourself.

Words and Meanings

falsetto or bass	very high or very low	1
bombastic	pompous, inflated	4
facade	surface appearance	
honed	refined	6
complicity	participation, involvement	8
vested in	personally connected to	
pass muster	be found acceptable	9
impropriety	behaviour that is improper, not "fitting"	
compromised	made to look bad	11
plausibly	believably	
condescendingly	"talking down" to your audience	13
l'Arche	an international organization that helps people who have developmental disabilities to create communities and share life together	15
solicitude	concern	
faux pas	blunders, mistakes	16

Structure and Strategy

1. The title and long first sentence of this essay describe symptoms of the topic before telling the reader what the topic is. What, specifically, is being defined here? Do you think this indirect approach is an effective INTRODUCTION? Why or why not?
2. Which sentences in the introduction of this essay contain a broad statement of its THESIS?
3. What techniques does the author use in paragraphs 5 and 6 to define the word "embarrass"? How has the meaning of the word in English changed over time?
4. What strategy does Visser use to develop the topic of paragraph 9?
5. What contrast does Visser use in paragraph 12 to help develop her definition?

Content and Purpose

1. According to Visser, what two factors must be present for a person to suffer embarrassment?
2. Why do people sometimes feel uncomfortable, even cringe or fidget, when they watch someone else embarrass himself or herself? Where in the essay is this phenomenon described?

3. According to Visser, we are embarrassed by improprieties because they reveal our inexperience or incompetence, but "the most exquisite kind of embarrassment" (paragraph 13) has "ethical implications." What do you think she means by this, and how does she support the point? Do you agree or disagree? Why?

4. According to the author, at what age is a person most likely to suffer from embarrassment? Do you think people this age suffer from personal embarrassment only, or does their heightened sensitivity extend to include the "social faux pas" (paragraph 16) of other people? Why?

5. Visser suggests that suffering through an embarrassing incident can have a positive outcome. Where in the essay do you find this suggestion?

Suggestion for Writing

Tell the story of your most embarrassing moment. What happened? How did you feel? How did you deal with the situation? What did you learn from the incident?

Being Canadian

DENISE CHONG

Vancouver-born Denise Chong (b. 1953) trained as an economist and worked as an economic adviser to Pierre Elliott Trudeau before pursuing her interest in writing. She edited *The Penguin Book of Canadian Women's Short Stories* (1997) and is the author of a best-selling memoir, *The Concubine's Children* (1994), which chronicles the experiences of her family, especially her grandparents, who came to Canada from China. Her book, *The Girl in the Picture* (1999), is built around the horrific photograph—taken during the Vietnam War—of a severely burned Kim Phuc fleeing her napalmed village.

1   I ask myself what it means to be a Canadian. I was lucky enough to be born in Canada [, so] I look back at the price paid by those who made the choice that brought me such luck.

2   South China at the turn of the century became the spout of the teapot that was China. It poured out middle-class peasants like my grandfather, who couldn't earn a living at home. He left behind a wife and child. My grandfather was 36 when exclusion° came.

Lonely and living a penurious existence, he worked at a sawmill on the mud flats of the Fraser River, where the Chinese were third on the pay scale behind "Whites" and "Hindus." With the door to Chinese immigration slammed shut, men like him didn't dare even go home for a visit, for fear Canada might bar their re-entry. With neither savings enough to go home for good, nor the means once in China to put rice in the mouths of his wife and child there, my grandfather wondered when, if ever, he could return to the bosom of a family. He decided to purchase a concubine, a second wife, to join him in Canada.

The concubine, at age 17, got into Canada on a lie. She got around the exclusion law in the only way possible: she presented the authorities with a Canadian birth certificate. It had belonged to a woman born in Ladner, British Columbia, and a middleman sold it to my grandfather at many times the price of the old head tax. Some years later, the concubine and my grandfather went back to China with their two Vancouver-born daughters. They lived for a time under the same roof as my grandfather's first wife. The concubine became pregnant. Eight months into her pregnancy, she decided to brave the long sea voyage back so that her third child could be born in Canada. [Her] false Canadian birth certificate would get her in. Accompanied by only my grandfather, she left China. Three days after the boat docked, on the second floor of a tenement on a back alley in Vancouver's Chinatown, she gave birth to my mother.

Canada remained inhospitable. Yet my grandparents *chose* to keep Canada in their future. Both gambled a heritage and family ties to take what they thought were better odds in the lottery of life. . . .

My own sense, four generations on, of being Canadian is one of belonging. I belong to a family. I belong to a community of values. I didn't get to choose my ancestors, but I can try to leave the world a better place for the generations that follow. The life I lead begins before and lingers after my time.

I am now the mother of two young children. I want to pass on a sense of what it means to be a Canadian. But what worries me as a parent, and as a Canadian, is whether we can fashion an enduring concept of citizenship that will be the glue that holds us together as a society. Curiously, Canadian citizenship elicits the most heartfelt response outside Canada. Any Canadian who has lived or travelled abroad quickly discovers that Canadian citizenship is a coveted possession. In the eyes of the rest of the world, it stands for an enlightened and gentle society.

Can we find a strong concept of citizenship that could be shared by all Canadians when we stand on our own soil? Some would say it is unrealistic to expect a symbol to rise out of a rather pragmatic° past. We spilled no revolutionary blood, as did France—where the word *citoyen*° was brought into popular usage—or America. Some lament the absence of a founding myth; we don't have the equivalent of a Boston Tea Party. Others long for Canadian versions of heroes to compete with the likes of American images that occupy our living rooms and our playgrounds. The one Canadian symbol with universal recognition is the flag. But where does the maple leaf strike a chord? Outside Canada. On the back packs of Canadian travellers. . . .

8   Some say Canadian citizenship is devalued because it is too easy to come here. But what sets Canadian society apart from others is that ours is an inclusive society. Canada's citizenship act remains more progressive than [the immigration laws of] many countries. Canadians by immigration have equal status with Canadians by birth. In contrast, in western Europe, guest workers, even if they descended from those who originally came, can be sent "home" any time. In Japan, Koreans and Filipinos have no claim to the citizenship of their birth. The plight of the Palestinians in Kuwait after the Gulf War gave the lie to a "free Kuwait."

9   Canadian citizenship recognizes differences. It praises diversity. It is what we as Canadians *choose* to have in common with each other. It is a bridge between those who left something to make a new home here and those born here. What keeps the bridge strong is tolerance, fairness, understanding, and compassion. Citizenship has rights and responsibilities. I believe one responsibility of citizenship is to use that tolerance, fairness, understanding, and compassion to leaf through the Canadian family album together. . . .

10   How we tell our stories is the work of citizenship. The motive of the storyteller should be to put the story first. To speak with authenticity and veracity° is to choose narrative over commentary. It is not to glorify or sentimentalize the past. It is not to sanitize our differences. Nor [is it] to rail against or to seek compensation today for injustices of bygone times. In my opinion, to try to rewrite history leads to a sense of victimization. It marginalizes Canadians. It backs away from equality in our society, for which we have worked hard to find expression.

11   I believe our stories ultimately tell the story of Canada itself. In all our pasts are an immigrant beginning, a settler's accomplishments and setbacks, and the confidence of a common future. We all know the struggle for victory, the dreams and the lost hopes, the pride and the shame. When we tell our stories, we look in the mirror. I believe what we will see is that Canada is not lacking in heroes. Rather, the heroes are to be found within.

The work of citizenship is not something just for the week that 12
we celebrate citizenship every year. It is part of every breath we
take. It is the work of our lifetimes. . . .

If we do some of this work of citizenship, we will stand on 13
firmer ground. Sharing experience will help build strength of character. It will explain our differences, yet make them less divisive.
We will yell at each other less, and understand each other more. We
will find a sense of identity and a common purpose. We will have
something to hand down to the next generation.

My grandfather's act of immigration to the new world and the 14
determination of my grandmother, the girl who first came here as a
kay toi neu°, to chance a journey from China back to Canada so that
my mother could be born here, will stand as a gift to all future generations of my family. Knowing they came hoping for a better life
makes it easy to love both them and this country.

In the late 1980s, I [found] myself in China, on a two-year stint 15
living in Peking and working as a writer. In a letter to my mother
in Prince George, I confessed that, despite the predictions of
friends back in Canada, I was finding it difficult to feel any
"Chineseness." My mother wrote back: "You're Canadian, not
Chinese. Stop trying to feel anything." She was right. I stopped
such contrivances. I was Canadian; it was that which embodied
the values of my life.

Words and Meanings

		Paragraph
exclusion	the closing off of Chinese immigration to Canada	2
pragmatic	practical as opposed to idealistic	7
citoyen	citizen [French]	
authenticity and veracity	genuineness and truthfulness	10
kay toi neu	serving girl [Cantonese]	14

Structure and Strategy

1. Identify the METAPHOR at the beginning of paragraph 2. Is it an effective image or a CLICHÉ? Explain.
2. Paragraph 8 is developed mainly by use of examples. What are these examples, and what KEY IDEA do they support?
3. How does Chong support her definition of Canadian citizenship in paragraph 9?
4. What kind of CONCLUSION does the essay use? Is it effective? Why or why not?

Content and Purpose

1. Summarize the experience of the people whose story is told in paragraphs 2, 3, and 4. What is the relationship between them and the author? What is her attitude toward them?
2. What is the question that "worries" Chong as she defines what being Canadian means to her? (See paragraphs 6 through 8.)
3. According to Chong, how do people outside Canada view this country? Do you agree with her? Why or why not?
4. What are some of the obstacles Chong sees to a "concept of citizenship that could be shared by all Canadians" (paragraph 7)?
5. What are the "rights and responsibilities" (paragraph 9) of citizenship expressed in the essay?
6. Paragraph 10 discusses the role of narrative—"how we tell our stories"—as an important element of the "work of citizenship." How does Chong feel about stories that condemn past injustices as a way of demanding compensation? Do you agree with her? Why or why not?
7. According to the essay, how will all Canadians benefit from telling our stories as part of the "work of citizenship" (paragraph 13)?
8. In two or three sentences, summarize Chong's definition of "being Canadian." How does her definition compare with your own understanding of what it means to be Canadian?

Suggestions for Writing

1. Chong maintains, "How we tell our stories is the work of citizenship." Write an essay that tells the story of someone you know who has become a Canadian citizen.
2. Chong argues that seeking compensation for past injustice "leads to a sense of victimization [and] marginalizes Canadians." Do you agree? Why or why not?
3. Read Wayson Choy's "I'm a Banana and Proud of It" on page 205. Write an essay comparing Choy's view of his Chinese heritage in Canada with Chong's.

The Cute Factor

NATALIE ANGIER

Natalie Angier (b. 1958) attended Barnard College, where she combined English literature with physics and astronomy. She was on the staff of *Discover* magazine before she joined the staff of *The New York Times* in 1990, where she won a Pulitzer Prize for science writing. She published *Woman: An Intimate Biography* in 2000 and edited *The Best American Science and Nature Writing 2002*.

If the mere sight of Tai Shan, the roly-poly, goofily gamboling masked bandit of a panda cub on view at the National Zoo isn't enough to make you melt, then maybe the crush of his human onlookers, the furious flashing of their cameras and the heated gasps of their mass rapture will do the trick. 1

"Omigosh, look at him! He is too cute!" 2

"How adorable! I wish I could just reach in there and give him a big squeeze!" 3

"He's so fuzzy! I've never seen anything so cute in my life!" 4

A guard's sonorous voice rises above the burble. "OK, folks, five oohs and aahs per person, then it's time to let someone else step up front." 5

The 6-month-old, 25-pound Tai Shan—whose name is pronounced "tie-SHON" and means, for no obvious reason, "peaceful mountain"—is the first surviving giant panda cub ever born at the Smithsonian's zoo. And though the zoo's adult pandas have long been among Washington's top tourist attractions, the public debut of the baby in December [2005] has unleashed an almost bestial frenzy here. Some 13,000 timed tickets to see the cub were snapped up within two hours of being released, and almost immediately began trading on eBay for up to $200 a pair. 6

Panda mania is not the only reason that 2005 proved an exceptionally cute year. In the summer, a movie about another black-and-white charmer, the emperor penguin, became one of the highest-grossing documentaries of all time. Sales of petite, willfully cute cars like the Toyota Prius and the Mini Cooper soared, while those of noncute sport utility vehicles tanked. Women's fashions opted for the cute over the sensible or glamorous, with low-slung slacks and skirts and abbreviated blouses contriving to present a customer's midriff as an adorable preschool bulge. Even the too big could be too cute. King Kong's newly reissued face has a squashed baby-doll appeal, and his passion for Naomi Watts° ultimately feels like a serious case of puppy love—hopeless, heartbreaking, cute. 7

8   Scientists who study the evolution of visual signaling have identified a wide and still expanding assortment of features and behaviors that make something look cute: bright forward-facing eyes set low on a big round face, a pair of big round ears, floppy limbs and a side-to-side, teeter-totter gait, among many others.

9   Cute cues are those that indicate extreme youth, vulnerability, harmlessness and need, scientists say, and attending to them closely makes good Darwinian sense. As a species whose youngest members are so pathetically helpless they can't lift their heads to suckle without adult supervision, human beings must be wired to respond quickly and gamely to any and all signs of infantile desire. The human cuteness detector is set at such a low bar, researchers said, that it sweeps in and deems cute practically anything remotely resembling a human baby or a part thereof, and so ends up including the young of virtually every mammalian species, fuzzy-headed birds like Japanese cranes, woolly bear caterpillars, a bobbing balloon, a big round rock stacked on a smaller rock, a colon, a hyphen and a close parenthesis typed in succession. The greater the number of cute cues that an animal or object happens to possess, or the more exaggerated the signals may be, the louder and more italicized are the squeals provoked.

10   Cuteness is distinct from beauty, researchers say, emphasizing rounded over sculptured, soft over refined, clumsy over quick. Beauty attracts admiration and demands a pedestal; cuteness attracts affection and demands a lap. Beauty is rare and brutal, despoiled by a single pimple. Cuteness is commonplace and generous, content on occasion to [consort] with homeliness.

11   Observing that many Floridians have an enormous affection for the manatee, which looks like an overfertilized potato with a sock puppet's face, Roger L. Reep of the University of Florida said it shone by grace of contrast. "People live hectic lives, and they may be feeling overwhelmed, but then they watch this soft and slow-moving animal, this gentle giant, and they see it turn on its back to get its belly scratched," said Dr. Reep, author with Robert K. Bonde of "The Florida Manatee: Biology and Conservation." "That's very endearing," said Dr. Reep. "So even though a manatee is 3 times your size and 20 times your weight, you want to get into the water beside it."

12   Even as they say a cute tooth has rational roots, scientists admit they are just beginning to map its subtleties and source. New studies suggest that cute images stimulate the same pleasure centers of the brain aroused by sex, a good meal or psychoactive drugs like cocaine, which could explain why everybody in the panda house wore a big grin.

At the same time, said Denis Dutton, a philosopher of art at the   13
University of Canterbury in New Zealand, the rapidity and promis-
cuity of the cute response makes the impulse suspect, readily over-
ridden by the angry sense that one is being exploited or deceived.
"Cute cuts through all layers of meaning and says, Let's not worry
about complexities, just love me," said Dr. Dutton, who is writing a
book about Darwinian aesthetics. "That's where the sense of cheap-
ness can come from, and the feeling of being manipulated or taken
for a sucker that leads many to reject cuteness as low or shallow."

Quick and cheap make cute appealing to those who want to   14
catch the eye and please the crowd. Advertisers and product
designers are forever toying with cute cues to lend their merchan-
dise instant appeal, mixing and monkeying with the vocabulary of
cute to keep the message fresh and fetching. That market-driven
exercise in cultural evolution can yield bizarre if endearing results,
like the blatantly ugly Cabbage Patch dolls, Furbies, the figgy face
of E.T., the froggy one of Yoda. As though the original Volkswagen
Beetle wasn't considered cute enough, the updated edition was
made rounder and shinier still. "The new Beetle looks like a smiley
face," said Miles Orvell, professor of American studies at Temple
University in Philadelphia. "By this point its origins in Hitler's
regime, and its intended resemblance to a German helmet, is totally
forgotten."

Whatever needs pitching, cute can help. A recent study at the   15
Veterans Affairs Medical Center at the University of Michigan
showed that high school students were far more likely to believe
antismoking messages accompanied by cute cartoon characters like
a penguin in a red jacket or a smirking polar bear than when the
warnings were delivered unadorned. "It made a huge difference,"
said Sonia A. Duffy, the lead author of the report, which was published in *The Archives of Pediatrics and Adolescent Medicine*. "The kids
expressed more confidence in the cartoons than in the warnings
themselves."

Primal and widespread though the taste for cute may be,   16
researchers say it varies in strength and significance across cultures
and eras. They compare the cute response to the love of sugar:
everybody has sweetness receptors on the tongue, but some people,
and some countries, eat a lot more candy than others.

Experts point out that the cuteness craze is particularly acute in   17
Japan, where it goes by the name *kawaii* and has infiltrated the most
masculine of redoubts. Truck drivers display "Hello Kitty"-style
figurines on their dashboards. The police enliven safety billboards
and wanted posters with two perky mouselike mascots, Pipo kun
and Pipo chan. Behind the kawaii phenomenon, according to Brian

J. McVeigh, a scholar of East Asian studies at the University of Arizona, is the strongly hierarchical nature of Japanese culture. "Cuteness is used to soften up the vertical society," he said, "to soften power relations and present authority without being threatening."

18   In this country, the use of cute imagery is geared less toward blurring the line of command than toward celebrating America's favorite demographic: the young. Dr. Orvell traces contemporary cute chic to the 1960s, with its celebration of a perennial childhood, a refusal to dress in adult clothes, an inversion of adult values, a love of bright colors and bloopy, cartoony patterns, the Lava Lamp. Today, it's not enough for a company to use cute graphics in its advertisements. It must have a really cute name as well. "Companies like Google and Yahoo leave no question in your mind about the youthfulness of their founders," said Dr. Orvell.

19   Madison Avenue may adapt its strategies for maximal tweaking of our inherent baby radar, but babies themselves, evolutionary scientists say, did not really evolve to be cute. Instead, most of their salient qualities stem from the demands of human anatomy and the human brain, and became appealing to a potential caretaker's eye only because infants wouldn't survive otherwise. Human babies have unusually large heads because humans have unusually large brains. Their heads are round because their brains continue to grow throughout the first months of life, and the plates of the skull stay flexible and unfused to accommodate the development. Baby eyes and ears are situated comparatively far down the face and skull, and only later migrate upward in proportion to the development of bones in the cheek and jaw areas.

20   Baby eyes are also notably forward-facing, the binocular vision a likely legacy of our tree-dwelling ancestry, and all our favorite Disney characters also sport forward-facing eyes, including the ducks and mice, species that in reality have eyes on the sides of their heads. The cartilage tissue in an infant's nose is comparatively soft and undeveloped, which is why most babies have button noses. Baby skin sits relatively loose on the body, rather than being taut, the better to stretch for growth spurts to come, said Paul H. Morris, an evolutionary scientist at the University of Portsmouth in England; that lax packaging accentuates the overall roundness of form.

21   Baby movements are notably clumsy, an amusing combination of jerky and delayed, because learning to coordinate the body's many bilateral sets of large and fine muscle groups requires years of practice. On starting to walk, toddlers struggle continuously to balance themselves between left foot and right, and so the toddler

gait consists as much of lateral movement as of any forward momentum.

Researchers who study animals beloved by the public appreciate the human impulse to nurture anything even remotely baby-like, though they are at times taken aback by people's efforts to identify with their preferred species. Take penguins as an example. Some people are so wild for the creatures, said Michel Gauthier-Clerc, a penguin researcher in Arles, France, "they think penguins are mammals and not birds." They love the penguin's upright posture, its funny little tuxedo, the way it waddles as it walks. How like a child playing dress-up! Endearing as it is, Dr. Gauthier-Clerc explained that the apparent awkwardness of the penguin's march had nothing to do with clumsiness or uncertain balance. Instead, he said, penguins waddle to save energy. A side-to-side walk burns fewer calories than a straightforward stride, and for birds that fast for months and live in a frigid climate, every calorie counts. 22

As for the penguin's maestro° garb, the white front and black jacket suits its aquatic way of life. While submerged in water, the penguin's dark backside is difficult to see from above, camouflaging the penguin from potential predators of air or land. The white chest, by contrast, obscures it from below, protecting it against carnivores and allowing it to better sneak up on fish prey. 23

The giant panda offers another case study in accidental cuteness. Although it is a member of the bear family, a highly carnivorous clan, the giant panda specializes in eating bamboo. As it happens, many of the adaptations that allow it to get by on such a tough diet contribute to the panda's cute form, even in adulthood. Inside the bear's large, rounded head, said Lisa Stevens, assistant panda curator at the National Zoo, are the highly developed jaw muscles and the set of broad, grinding molars it needs to crush its way through some 40 pounds of fibrous bamboo plant a day. When it sits up against a tree and starts picking apart a bamboo stalk with its distinguishing pseudo-thumb, a panda looks like nothing so much as Huckleberry Finn shucking corn. Yet the humanesque posture and paws again are adaptations to its menu. The bear must have its "hands" free and able to shred the bamboo leaves from their stalks. 24

The panda's distinctive markings further add to its appeal: the black patches around the eyes make them seem winsomely low on its face, while the black ears pop out cutely against the white fur of its temples. As with the penguin's tuxedo, the panda's two-toned coat very likely serves a twofold purpose. On the one hand, it helps a feeding bear blend peacefully into the dappled backdrop of 25 bamboo. On the other, the sharp contrast between light and dark may serve as a social signal, helping the solitary bears locate each other when the time has come to find the perfect, too-cute mate.

Words and Meanings

7	Naomi Watts	film actor who played the love object in *King Kong* (2005)
23	maestro	orchestra conductor

Structure and Strategy

1. What kind of INTRODUCTION strategy does the essay use?
2. What is the TOPIC SENTENCE of paragraph 7? How does Angier develop her key idea?
3. In which paragraph does Angier first define "cute"? According to what criteria?
4. What is the basis of the contrast in paragraph 10?
5. Along with description, how does Angier support her point that the strange-looking manatee is widely seen as "cute" (paragraph 11)? Where else in the essay is this kind of development strategy used?
6. What ANALOGY is used in paragraph 16? What point does it develop?
7. What is the basis of the comparison in paragraph 18?
8. Consider the essay's CONCLUSION. How does it bring the essay full circle?

Content and Purpose

1. What visual features signal to human beings that someone or something is "cute"? What characteristics do those features signify to us?
2. Why does our affection for cuteness make "good Darwinian sense" (paragraph 9)?
3. What is a physiological theory for the human response to the cute factor? Why do we "melt" in the face of "cute"?
4. Angier, relying on the research of a philosopher of art, claims that our instant and undiscriminating response to cuteness is often followed by a sense of being manipulated (paragraph 13). Do you agree or disagree? Are there some images of cuteness that do not lead to this sense of exploitation?

5. What is the role of the cute factor in business and marketing? Identify three of the examples Angier uses to illustrate this phenomenon. Can you think of other examples?
6. According to one scholarly theory, why is "the cuteness craze ... particularly acute in Japan" (paragraph 17), even among macho types such as truck drivers? Do you agree or disagree? Why?
7. According to the author, North America's fondness for cute imagery is based on something quite different from Japan's. What is it? (See paragraph 18.) Do you agree or disagree? Why?
8. Identify three of the physiological features that encourage adults to see infants as cute and appealing. Why is it biologically essential that their caretakers see human babies as cute?
9. What physical characteristics of pandas and penguins do humans find "cute"? (See paragraphs 22–25.) What purpose do these characteristics serve in adapting these animals for survival?

Suggestions for Writing

1. Contrast two well-known celebrities (e.g., Jennifer Aniston vs. Angelina Jolie), products (e.g., Apple vs. PCs), art (Norman Rockwell vs. Vincent van Gogh), animals (not mentioned in the essay), or fashions (e.g., flip-flops vs. stilettos) in terms of overall cuteness. Who or what do we respond to more positively, and what is the relationship to the cute factor described in the essay?
2. Oddly, very young babies and very old adults share some physical features; for example, loose skin, soft (flabby) features, indeterminate gender, lack of hair and teeth, teeter-totter gait, occasional cantankerousness, and overall vulnerability. Why are babies seen as attractive whereas old people are often seen as unattractive? Write an essay contrasting our society's attitudes to the very young and the very old.
3. Read Jeffrey Moussaieff Masson's "Dear Dad" on page 80, and write an essay explaining why penguins are so fascinating to many people.
4. Read Helena Cronin's "The Evolution of Evolution" on page 191 and/or Olivia Judson's "Why I'm Happy I Evolved" on page 261. Write an essay that explores various aspects of human behaviour as seen in the light of evolutionary biology. Use examples from the essays to clarify your ideas.

Altruism

LEWIS THOMAS

Dr. Lewis Thomas (1913–1993) combined the careers of research scientist, physician, teacher, and writer. The recipient of many scientific and academic awards, he strove in his essays to humanize science and to remind us that medicine is an art. A recurring theme in books such as *The Lives of a Cell* (1974), *The Medusa and the Snail* (1979), and *The Youngest Science* (1983) is the interrelatedness of all life forms.

1   Altruism has always been one of biology's deep mysteries. Why should any animal, off on its own, specified and labeled by all sorts of signals as its individual self, choose to give up its life in aid of someone else? Nature, long viewed as a wild, chaotic battlefield swarmed across by more than ten million different species, comprising unnumbered billions of competing selves locked in endless combat, offers only one sure measure of success: survival. Survival, in the cool economics of biology, means simply the persistence of one's own genes in the generations to follow.

2   At first glance, it seems an unnatural act, a violation of nature, to give away one's life, or even one's possessions, to another. And yet, in the face of improbability, examples of altruism abound. When a worker bee, patrolling the frontiers of the hive, senses the nearness of a human intruder, the bee's attack is pure, unqualified suicide; the stinger is barbed, and in the act of pulling away the insect is fatally injured. Other varieties of social insects, most spectacularly the ants and higher termites, contain castes of soldiers for whom self-sacrifice is an everyday chore.

3   It is easy to dismiss the problem by saying that "altruism" is the wrong technical term for behavior of this kind. The word is a human word, pieced together to describe an unusual aspect of human behavior, and we should not be using it for the behavior of mindless automata°. A honeybee has no connection to creatures like us, no brain for figuring out the future, no way of predicting the inevitable outcome of that sting.

4   But the meditation of the 50,000 or so connected minds of a whole hive is not so easy to dismiss. A multitude of bees can tell the time of day, calculate the geometry of the sun's position, argue about the best location for the next swarm. Bees do a lot of close observing of other bees; maybe they know what follows stinging and do it anyway.

5   Altruism is not restricted to the social insects, in any case. Birds risk their lives, sometimes lose them, in efforts to distract the

attention of predators from the nest. Among baboons, zebras, moose, wildebeests, and wild dogs there are always stubbornly fated guardians, prepared to be done in first in order to buy time for the herd to escape.

It is genetically determined behavior, no doubt about it.   6
Animals have genes for altruism, and those genes have been selected in the evolution of many creatures because of the advantage they confer for the continuing survival of the species. It is, looked at in this way, not the emotion-laden problem that we feel when we try to put ourselves in the animal's place; it is just another plain fact of life, perhaps not as hard a fact as some others, something rather nice, in fact, to think about.

J. B. S. Haldane, the eminent British geneticist, summarized the   7
chilly arithmetic of the problem by announcing, "I would give up my life for two brothers or eight cousins." This calculates the requirement for ultimate self-interest: the preservation and survival of an individual's complement of genes. Trivers, Hamilton, and others have constructed mathematical models to account nicely for the altruistic behavior of social insects, quantifying the self-serving profit for the genes of the defending bee in the act of tearing its abdomen apart. The hive is filled with siblings, ready to carry the *persona* of the dying bee through all the hive's succeeding generations. Altruism is based on kinship; by preserving kin, one preserves one's self. In a sense.

Haldane's prediction has the sound of a beginning sequence: 8
two brothers, eight (presumably) first cousins, and then another series of much larger numbers of more distant relatives. Where does the influence tail off? At what point does the sharing of the putative° altruist's genes become so diluted as to be meaningless? Would the line on a graph charting altruism plummet to zero soon after those eight cousins, or is it a long, gradual slope? When the combat marine throws himself belly-down on the live grenade in order to preserve the rest of the platoon, is this the same sort of altruism, or is this an act without any technically biological meaning? Surely the marine's genes, most of them, will be blown away forever; the statistical likelihood of having two brothers or eight cousins in that platoon is extremely small. And yet there he is, belly-down as if by instinct, and the same kind of event has been recorded often enough in wartime to make it seem a natural human act, normal enough, even though rare, to warrant the stocking of medals by the armed services.

At what point do our genetic ties to each other become so   9
remote that we feel no instinctual urge to help? I can imagine an argument about this, with two sides, but it would be a highly

speculative discussion, not by any means pointless but still impossible to settle one way or the other. One side might assert, with total justification, that altruistic behavior among human beings has nothing at all to do with genetics, that there is no such thing as a gene for self-sacrifice, not even a gene for helpfulness, or concern, or even affection. These are attributes that must be learned from society, acquired by cultures, taught by example. The other side could maintain, with equal justification, since the facts are not known, precisely the opposite position: we get along together in human society because we are genetically designed to be social animals, and we are obliged, by instructions from our genes, to be useful to each other. This side would argue further that when we behave badly, killing or maiming or snatching, we are acting on misleading information learned from the wrong kinds of society we put together; if our cultures were not deformed, we would be better company, paying attention to what our genes are telling us.

10   For the purposes of the moment I shall take the side of the sociobiologists because I wish to carry their side of the argument a certain distance afield, beyond the human realm. I have no difficulty in imagining a close enough resemblance among the genomes° of all human beings, of all races and geographic origins, to warrant a biological mandate° for all of us to do whatever we can to keep the rest of us, the species, alive. I maintain, despite the moment's evidence against the claim, that we are born and grow up with a fondness for each other, and we have genes for that. We can be talked out of it, for the genetic message is like a distant music and some of us are hard-of-hearing. Societies are noisy affairs, drowning out the sound of ourselves and our connection. Hard-of-hearing, we go to war. Stone-deaf, we make thermonuclear missiles. Nonetheless, the music is there, waiting for more listeners.

11   But the matter does not end with our species. If we are to take seriously the notion that the sharing of similar genes imposes a responsibility on the sharers to sustain each other, and if I am right in guessing that even very distant cousins carry at least traces of this responsibility and will act on it whenever they can, then the whole world becomes something to be concerned about on solidly scientific, reductionist, genetic grounds. For we have cousins more than we can count, and they are all over the place, run by genes so similar to ours that the differences are minor technicalities. All of us, men, women, children, fish, sea grass, sandworms, dolphins, hamsters, and soil bacteria, everything alive on the planet, roll ourselves along through all our generations by replicating DNA° and RNA°, and although the alignments of nucleotides within these molecules are different in different species, the molecules them-

selves are fundamentally the same substance. We make our proteins in the same old way, and many of the enzymes most needed
for cellular life are everywhere identical.

This is, in fact, the way it should be. If cousins are defined by   12
common descent, the human family is only one small and very
recent addition to a much larger family in a tree extending back at
least 3.5 billion years. Our common ancestor was a single cell from
which all subsequent cells derived, most likely a cell resembling
one of today's bacteria in today's soil. For almost three-fourths of
the earth's life, cells of that first kind were the whole biosphere°. It
was less than a billion years ago that cells like ours appeared in the
first marine invertebrates, and these were somehow pieced together
by the joining up and fusion of the earlier primitive cells, retaining
the same blood lines. Some of the joiners, bacteria that had learned
how to use oxygen, are with us still, part of our flesh, lodged inside
the cells of all animals, all plants, moving us from place to place
and doing our breathing for us. Now there's a set of cousins!

Even if I try to discount the other genetic similarities linking   13
human beings to all other creatures by common descent, the existence of these beings in my cells is enough, in itself, to relate me to
the chestnut tree in my backyard and to the squirrel in that tree.

There ought to be a mathematics for connections like this   14
before claiming any kinship function, but the numbers are too big.
At the same time, even if we wanted to, we cannot think the sense
of obligation away. It is there, maybe in our genes for the recognition of cousins, or, if not, it ought to be there in our intellects for
having learned about the matter. Altruism, in its biological sense, is
required of us. We have an enormous family to look after, or perhaps that assumes too much, making us sound like official gar-
deners and zookeepers for the planet, responsibilities for which we
are probably not yet grown-up enough. We may need new technical
terms for concern, respect, affection, substitutes for altruism. But at
least we should acknowledge the family ties and, with them, the
obligations. If we do it wrong, scattering pollutants, clouding the
atmosphere with too much carbon dioxide, extinguishing the thin
carapace° of ozone, burning up the forests, dropping the bombs,
rampaging at large through nature as though we owned the place,
there will be a lot of paying back to do and, at the end, nothing to
pay back with.

Words and Meanings

Paragraph		
3	automata	unthinking, machine-like organisms
8	putative	supposed
10	genomes	chromosomal structures
	mandate	contract, requirement
11	DNA	deoxyribonucleic acid; the molecule that carries genetic information
	RNA	ribonucleic acid; the substance that transmits genetic information from the nucleus to the surrounding cellular material
12	biosphere	earth's zone of life—from crust to atmosphere—encompassing all living organisms
14	carapace	protective outer shell or covering

Structure and Strategy

1. What two ABSTRACT terms does Thomas define in his introductory paragraph? How does he do so?
2. The BODY of this essay can be divided into sections, as follows: paragraphs 2 through 5, 6 through 8, 9 and 10, and 11 through 13. Identify the KEY IDEA Thomas develops in each of these four sections, and list some of the expository techniques he uses in his development.
3. In paragraphs 1 through 8, Thomas writes in the third person. Why does he shift to the first person in paragraph 9 and continue in the first person until the end? To understand the different effects of the two POINTS OF VIEW, try rewriting some of the sentences in paragraph 14 in the third person.
4. In paragraph 10, Thomas introduces and develops a SIMILE to explain his faith in the "genetic message." Identify the simile and explain how it helps prepare the reader for the conclusion.
5. What concluding strategy does Thomas use in paragraph 14? How does his CONCLUSION contribute to the UNITY of the essay?

Content and Purpose

1. What is Thomas's THESIS? Summarize it in a single sentence.
2. In paragraph 1, Thomas introduces the fundamental IRONY on which this essay is based. Explain in your own words the ironic connection between altruism and survival.
3. Identify six or seven specific examples of animals that, according to Thomas, display altruistic behaviour. What

ILLUSTRATION does Thomas use to show the altruistic behaviour of human beings?
4. Explain in your own words Thomas's claim that altruism is not an "emotion-laden problem," but rather a behaviour that is based on self-interest. (See paragraph 7.)
5. In paragraph 9, Thomas identifies two opposing explanations for altruistic behaviour: the cultural and the sociobiological. Summarize these in your own words. Which side does Thomas take, and why? (See paragraphs 10 through 13.)

Suggestions for Writing

1. Write an extended definition of the term "parenthood." Explain the reasons why people choose to have children, an act that involves a considerable amount of self-sacrifice.
2. Define another ABSTRACT term such as "wisdom," "integrity," "freedom," "evil," or "success." Attempt to define this term as clearly and concretely as Thomas does "altruism."
3. Write an essay exploring how a particular word has changed in meaning over time. Words such as "gay," "cool," "black," or even "grammar" reveal interesting changes in denotation and connotation.
4. Why are are some people attracted to careers—such as fire-fighting and police work—in which they risk their lives for other people?

Additional Suggestions for Writing: Definition

Write an extended definition of one of the topics below.

1. Canadian humour
2. superstition
3. anxiety (or depression)
4. poverty
5. wisdom
6. terrorism
7. creativity
8. pop culture
9. biodiversity
10. success

Argument and Persuasion

WHAT ARE ARGUMENT AND PERSUASION?

In Unit 6, we pointed out that some words have specific meanings that are different from their generally accepted meanings. The word ARGUMENT is commonly defined as a disagreement or quarrel, while PERSUASION usually refers to the act of trying to convince someone of the validity of our opinion. In the context of writing, however, argument and persuasion refer to specific kinds of writing that have a special PURPOSE—one that is a bit different from the purpose of expository prose.

The introductions to Units 2 through 6 of this text have explained organizational patterns commonly found in EXPOSITION—writing intended primarily to explain. It is true that a number of the essays in these units contain strong elements of argument or persuasion: consider Jessica Mitford's indictment of embalming in Unit 2, for instance, or Lewis Thomas's plea for altruism in Unit 6. Nevertheless, the primary purpose of expository writing is to *inform* the reader—to explain a topic clearly.

Argument and persuasion have a different primary purpose. They attempt to lead the reader to share the writer's beliefs and perhaps even to act on these beliefs. For example, in "Immigration: The Hate Stops Here" (page 282), Michael Ignatieff attempts to convince readers that although Canadians like to think of their country as a haven of tolerance, it may actually be an incubator of ethnic hatred. On the lighter side, Emily Nussbaum wants to persuade us that online dating is a great innovation ("Net Gain," page 257). Of course, readers are not likely to be persuaded of anything without clear explanation, so there is nearly always some overlap between exposition and argument. Nonetheless, in this unit, we consider argument and persuasion as writing strategies intended mainly to *convince* the reader of an opinion, judgment, or course of action.

WHY DO WE WRITE ARGUMENT AND PERSUASION?

Argument and persuasion answer the lead-in question *why*. Why is this idea or action a good (or bad) idea? There are two fundamental ways to appeal to readers: through their minds and through their hearts. *Argument* is the term applied to the logical approach, convincing a person by way of the mind. "The Case for Marriage" (page 246), which uses statistics and logic to support the authors' pro-marriage thesis, is a clear example of argument. *Persuasion* is the term often applied to the emotional approach, convincing a person by way of the heart. Hal Niedzviecki's "Stupid Jobs Are Good to Relax With" (page 274) is a provocative piece of persuasion that appeals to the emotions—mostly resentment—of well-educated people in their twenties who are stuck in dead-end jobs. Often, writers use both strategies. For example, in "The Great Democracy Drop-Out" (page 265), Gregory Boyd Bell uses the techniques of logical argument as well as emotional appeals to encourage young Canadians to participate in the political process. We decide which approach to use—logical, emotional, or a combination of the two—depending on the issue we are discussing.

HOW DO WE WRITE ARGUMENT AND PERSUASION?

While exposition tends to focus on objective facts, argument and persuasion focus on issues. An **issue** is an opinion or belief that not all people agree on. It is always *controversial,* which literally means "having two sides." To begin to argue an issue, clearly and concisely state your opinion about it. This is your statement of THESIS. Here are three theses from essays in this unit:

> I like paying taxes. (Neil Brooks, "Why I Like to Pay My Taxes," page 252)

> Stupid jobs can be good for you. (Hal Niedzviecki, "Stupid Jobs Are Good to Relax With," page 274)

> The climate crisis is dangerous, but it also offers new opportunities. (Al Gore, "The Moment of Truth," page 287)

The test of a good thesis for an argument or persuasion paper is that someone could plausibly argue the opposite POINT OF VIEW: "I hate paying taxes"; "stupid jobs are depressing and demeaning."

Once your opinion about an issue is clearly stated, you need to identify reasons to support it. The lead-in question to ask is *why.* Why do you believe what you do about your issue? The reasons you identify are the KEY IDEAS you will explore and support in your essay.

Argument/persuasion papers can be structured in a number of ways. How you organize your essay depends on your target AUDIENCE. How much do your readers know about the topic? Are they likely to be biased in favour of or against your opinion? For example, how many people actually *like* to pay taxes? Most—not all—people probably think marriage is a good idea, but those who don't are probably strongly opposed.

Once you've analyzed your audience, you can decide how best to approach them: directly or indirectly. If your readers are likely to be sympathetic to your point of view on an issue, you can state your opinion up front, then outline your reasons for holding that opinion, and then provide the EVIDENCE that supports those reasons. This is the direct approach—basically, the same thesis statement-based organization you've become familiar with in the previous six units. For example, the model essay "Why Write?" is based on this pattern, as is "The Case for Marriage."

On the other hand, if you think your readers are not likely to support your opinion, you would do better to build your case indirectly, setting out definitions, examples, and other evidence before declaring where you stand on the issue. Readers who are confronted early with a statement with which they disagree often do not listen to an explanation of the opposite point of view. In "Why I'm Happy I Evolved"(page 261), for example, Olivia Judson recognizes that her opinions will be threatening to some people, so she begins by presenting upbeat examples of diverse, fascinating life forms—evidence that is bound to engage most readers. Judson resists maligning people whose religious beliefs may put them at odds with her scientific approach to how these diverse life forms came to be. Another example of a successful indirect approach is "Immigration: The Hate Stops Here," in which Ignatieff is careful to get his audience onside before he states strongly and clearly what Canada expects from immigrants to this country.

One structural pattern is common to both argument and persuasion: the "two sides of the story" approach. This technique is particularly useful when you are arguing a contentious issue that may provoke serious dispute. "Why I Like to Pay My Taxes" is a fully developed example of the "two sides" approach. Neil Brooks carefully considers and dismisses his opponents' anti-tax arguments after he has presented convincing reasons for his pro-tax position. In "The Case for Marriage," the authors acknowledge that arguments against marriage can be made: "Marriage, its detractors contend, can trap women and men in unhealthy relationships." By acknowledging your opponents' position and their arguments, you enhance the credibility of your own position on an issue.

Here are four guidelines for writing effective argument and persuasion:

1. Write a thesis statement that clearly states your opinion on an issue and, if appropriate, briefly previews your key ideas—your reasons for holding that opinion. (You may or may not include this statement in your final version, but it's a good idea to have it in front of you as you draft your essay.)

2. Think through your key ideas carefully and make sure that you can support them with appropriate and convincing details. It is a good idea to do some research to find supporting EVIDENCE.

3. Assemble accurate, relevant, and sufficient evidence to develop your key ideas.

4. Structure your argument in whatever pattern is most appropriate for your issue and your target audience. Usually, whether you choose to approach your topic directly or indirectly, you discuss your most compelling reason last.

Bringing readers over to our side through well-chosen words is a challenge. Argument and persuasion are probably the most formidable writing tasks that we undertake, yet they may also be the most important. Armed with logic, emotions, and words, we can persuade others to agree with us and even to act. Effective persuasion is an art that truly deserves to be called civilized.

The model essay that follows takes a light-hearted approach to an old but still timely argument.

Why Write?

Introduction challenges the view that writing skill has nothing to do with sex appeal

This may come as a surprise to you, but being able to write well contributes to your sex appeal. Even more surprising is the fact that not being able to write well decreases your attractiveness to prospective mates. Intrigued? Read on! Writing is an essential skill if you want to achieve three vital objectives: communicate effectively and memorably, obtain and hold satisfying employment, and attract worthy sex partners. Once you understand the influence good communication can have on your life, then you will see how skills such as faultless grammar, sound sentence structure, and an appealing style can transform you from road kill on the highway of life to a turbocharged powerhouse.

While spoken communication is, for most of us, easy, natural—almost automatic—it doesn't have the lasting power of written language. Even e-mail, the least permanent form of writing, can be re-read, forwarded, and redirected, attaining a kind of permanence that conversation cannot. Who wants to be the author of a message remembered for its unintended but hilarious grammatical flaws or syntactical blunders, such as a headline reading, "Judge to rule on nude beach"? Writing permits us to organize and present our thoughts effectively. Who hasn't mentally replayed a conversation over and over before finding, when it's too late, just the right comeback to a humiliating put-down? Writing allows the time to ensure that every sentence is precise, memorable, and devastating.

In business environments, good writing is a predictor of success. People who communicate well, do well. This fact is continually emphasized in executive surveys, recruitment panels, and employer polls. At one time, novices heading for a career on the corporate ladder held the attitude that writing was something secretaries did. In today's climate of instant and incessant electronic communication and networked industries, few people can rely on a subordinate to correct their errors or polish their style before their colleagues or clients see their work. Besides, many of those secretaries who could write well are now occupying executive suites themselves. It doesn't matter what career you choose: your effectiveness is going to be judged in part by how well you communicate. Whether you're a health-care worker who must keep comprehensive and accurate notes, an environmental technician who writes reports for both experts and laypeople, or a technologist who must defend her need for a budget increase, good writing enhances both the message and the messenger.

Key idea #3: the reason is developed by contrasting the survival skills required in prehistoric times with those required today

Note use of descriptive details

Topic is reinforced in a paraphrase

Conclusion emphasizes significance of the topic

Author answers the question "Why write?" with a carefully constructed sentence fragment designed to linger in the reader's mind

Throughout evolutionary history, men and women have sought mates with the skills and attributes that would enable them to thrive in the environment of the times. Eons ago, female survival depended on choosing a man with a concrete cranium and bulging biceps because he was most likely to repel predators and survive attacks. Prehistoric men selected women for their squat, sturdy bodies and thick fat layer because such females were more likely than their sinewy sisters to survive an Ice Age winter (and even provide warmth). Attraction between the sexes is based on attributes that suggest ability to survive, procreate, and provide. Skills such as spear-hurling and fire-tending are not in much demand anymore. Today's men and women are on the lookout for mates with updated thriving expertise. Your ability to communicate effectively is one of the skills that places you among the twenty-first-century elite, those who will rise to the top of the corporate food chain, claiming the most desirable mates as you ascend. Besides, the ability to write melting love letters or clever, affectionate e-mail is a far more effective turn-on these days than the ability to supply a slab of mastodon or a well-crafted loincloth. Go ahead—flex those writing muscles, flaunt that perfect style!

Why write? Because excellent communication skills are the single most important attribute you can bring to the table, whether you are negotiating for power, profession, prestige, or a partner.

The Case for Marriage

LINDA J. WAITE AND MAGGIE GALLAGHER

Linda J. Waite (b. 1947) is a professor of sociology at the University of Chicago whose research focuses on the family, divorce, and aging. She recently co-edited *Being Together, Working Apart: Dual-Career Families and the Work-Life Balance* (2005). Maggie Gallagher (b. 1960) is a journalist and commentator who is known as a strong social conservative. She gained notoriety in 2005 when it was reported that she had accepted contracts from U.S. government agencies to promote family policies advocated by the George W. Bush administration, a move that was seen by many people as a breach of journalistic ethics.

In the 1950s, the rules were clear: first love, next marriage, and only then the baby carriage. Who could have imagined the tsunami° ahead? In a rapid blur came the Pill, the sexual revolution, gay pride, feminism, the mass move of married mothers into the workplace, no-fault divorce, and an unexpected orgy of unmarried child-bearing. Without warning, the one firm understanding that marriage is a cornerstone of our society had all but disappeared. 1

Marriage, its detractors contend, can trap women and men in unhealthy relationships, pressuring them with irrational taboos to live in a way that does nobody any good. Preferences for marriage, special benefits for married couples—once viewed as commonsense supports for a vital social institution—are denounced as discriminatory. Some say marriage is financially unfair to men and frustrates their sexual needs. Others argue that it benefits men at the expense of women's independence, gratification, physical safety, and even sanity. Marriage "protects men from depression and makes women more vulnerable," [contends] Neil Jacobson, University of Washington psychologist and author of the 1998 book *When Men Batter Women.* . . . 2

From this perspective, divorce is perceived as a great social boon. And far from being cause for alarm and reform, the astonishing growth of births out of wedlock—from about five percent of total births in 1960 to a third of all births today—is seen as welcome proof of the emancipation of women from marital restrictions. 3

Even our language betrays the new attitudes toward marriage. A reluctance even to use the word seems to be sweeping the West. The Marriage Guidance Council of Australia recently changed its name to Relationships Australia. Britain's National Marriage Guidance Council metamorphosed into Relate. A popular sex education manual for children does not mention the M-word, although it acknowledges, vaguely, that "there are kids whose mothers and fathers live together." 4

But here is the great irony: if you ask the right questions, there is plenty of evidence suggesting that marriage is a vital part of overall well-being. Contrary to what many Americans now believe, getting and staying married is good for men, women, and children. Marriage, it turns out, is by far the best bet for ensuring a healthier, wealthier, and sexier life. 5

Imagine, for example, a group of men and women all 48 years old and as alike in background as social scientists can make them. 6

How many will be alive at age 65? According to a study we did, of those men who never married or are divorced, only 60 percent will still be around. By contrast, 90 percent of the married [men] will survive. Similarly, 90 percent of married women will reach 65, compared to 80 percent of single and divorced women.

7   It's not just a matter of mortality. Among men and women nearing retirement age, wives are almost 40 percent less likely than unmarried women to say their health is poor. Even in old age married women are less likely to become disabled, and married people of both sexes are much less likely to enter nursing homes.

8   How can a mere social contract have such far-reaching effects? For one thing, new research suggests that marriage might improve immune system functioning, as married people are shown to be less susceptible than singles to the common cold. For another, married people tend to pursue healthier lifestyles. The evidence is clear: spousal nagging works. A wife feels licensed to press her husband to get checkups or eat better. And a man responds to a wife's health consciousness in part because he knows that she depends on him as he depends on her. Statistics show that getting married leads to a dramatic reduction in smoking, drinking, and illegal drug use for both men and women, while just moving in together typically does not. And according to Justice Department data, wives are almost four times less likely than single women to fall victim to violent crime.

9   Then there's the question of domestic violence. Many commentators talk as if the institution of marriage itself is at fault. Two eminent scholars, for example, title their influential essay on rates of domestic violence "The Marriage License as Hitting License." And Jacobson declares flatly that "marriage as an institution is still structured in such a way as to institutionalize male dominance, and such dominance makes high rates of battering inevitable." Even the best researchers tend to use *wife abuse* and *domestic violence* interchangeably, strongly implying that getting married can put women at special risk.

10   But the truth is that women who live with men out of wedlock are in much greater danger. Cohabiting men are almost twice as likely as husbands to engage in domestic violence. To look at it another way, women who have never married are more than four times more likely than wives—and divorced women more than seven times more likely—to be the victims of intimate violence.

11   The kids' health can also benefit from marriage. Children are 50 percent more likely to develop health problems due to a parental separation, and those in female-headed single-parent homes are more likely to be hospitalized or to suffer chronic health conditions

such as asthma. And for babies marriage can mean the difference between life and death. Those born to single mothers are much more likely to die in the first year. Even among groups with the lowest risk of infant mortality, marriage makes a big difference: babies born to college-educated single mothers are 50 percent more likely to die than babies born to married couples. What's more, the health advantage of having married parents can be long-lasting.

If marriage can benefit health, how about its effect on the pocket-   12
book? Recent research suggests that getting and keeping a wife may be as important to a man's financial portfolio as getting a good education. Depending on which study you cite, husbands earn anywhere from 10 percent to 40 percent more than single men, and the longer men stay married, the greater the gap.

Like men, women get an earnings boost from marriage. But   13
children change the picture. One study finds that having a child reduces a woman's earnings by almost four percent and that two or more reduce her pay by almost 12 percent. Women get a marriage premium, but also pay a substantial motherhood penalty.

Still, there are countervailing benefits. Married couples manage   14
their money more wisely than singles and are less likely to report signs of economic hardship. And the longer they stay married, the more wealth they build. By retirement, the average married couple has accumulated assets worth about $410,000, compared to $167,000 for those never married and $154,000 for the divorced.

Arguably, marriage itself is a form of wealth. Because they can   15
share both the labor and the goods of life, husbands and wives produce more with less effort and cost. And having a partner who promises to care for you in good times and bad is also valuable—equal, according to one recent estimate, to a 12 percent increase in wealth for a 30-year-old spouse, and a whopping 33 percent for 75-year-old married people.

In theory, unmarried people who live together might enjoy the   16
same economies. In practice, however, things work out differently. In *American Couples*, Philip Blumstein and Pepper Schwartz describe how a typical cohabiting couple thinks about money. Jane is a pediatrician living with Morton, a lawyer. "Morton was not particularly thrilled when I took the bonus and traded in the Volvo for the Alfa. Well, too bad. I let him alone and I expect him to let me alone." Morton agrees, somewhat wistfully: "I would not always make the same decisions she does. I would save and invest more. But it's her money, and I don't dare interfere."

By contrast, Lisa, a homemaker married to machinist Al, has no   17
problems interfering with her husband's spending habits, because

the money he makes is not "his" but "theirs." "He doesn't control it," Lisa says of her husband's spending, "so we have to stop quite often and discuss our budget and where did all this money go to. Why are you broke? Where did it go to? If it went to good causes, I can find 10 dollars more," she says confidently—the money manager for both of them. "If it didn't, tough."

18   Some experts try to de-emphasize the apparent benefits of marriage as a cover for the "real" problems plaguing children of divorce: poverty, family conflict, and poor parenting. As scholar Arlene Skolnick put it in a recent family studies textbook, "Family structure—the number of parents in the home or the fact of divorce—is not in itself the critical factor in children's well-being. In both intact and other families, what children need most is a warm, concerned relationship with at least one parent."

19   But three decades of evidence have made it clear that divorce dramatically increases economic hardship and puts new stress on the parent–child bond, thus exacerbating° precisely the problems Skolnick decries. In the face of the hard data, it is almost impossible to argue that having married parents is not a critical factor in a child's well-being.

20   All right: so marriage trumps being single as far as health, wealth, and the kids' well-being goes. But surely the single person enjoys better sex? Wedding cake, in the old joke, is the best food to curb your sexual appetite. "What is it about marriage," wonders Dalma Heyn in *Marriage Shock*, "that so often puts desire at risk?"

21   Surprisingly, the truth is just the opposite: married people have better sex lives than singles. Indeed, married people are far more likely to have sex lives in the first place. Married people are about twice as likely as unmarried people to make love at least two or three times a week.

22   And that's not all: married sex is more fun. Certainly, at least, for men: forty-eight percent of husbands say sex with their partners is extremely satisfying, compared to just 37 percent of cohabiting men.

23   When it comes to creating a lasting sexual union, marriage implies at least a promise of permanence, which may be why cohabiting men are four times more likely to cheat, and cohabiting women eight times more likely, than husbands and wives.

24   That is doubtless one reason why married men and women, on average, tend to be emotionally and mentally healthier—less depressed and anxious or psychologically distressed than single, divorced, or widowed Americans. One study that followed 14,000 adults over a 10-year period found that marital status was one of the single most important predictors of personal happiness.

Marriage, we'd like to argue, is not just one of many kinds of 25
relationships that are all "equally valid"—equally likely to advance
health and happiness of men, women, and children. Of course we
don't suggest that people should be dragooned into marrying
against their will, or that some marriages should not end. But we
do say that what enables marriage to deliver its powerful life-
enhancing benefits is that it is not just a private lifestyle, an
arrangement whose success or failure concerns the lover alone.

Marriage creates powerful positive changes in couples' lives 26
because it is a public relationship, living proof that interdependence, faithfulness, obligation, responsibility, and union are more
fruitful over the long run than choices that may seem more immediately gratifying.

Helping people imagine that long run, then making it come 27
true, is what marriage still does best.

Words and Meanings

Paragraph

tsunami	a large, destructive ocean wave; also called a tidal wave	1
exacerbating	making worse	19

Structure and Strategy

1. Find the essay's thesis statement. What three KEY IDEAS does it contain? Identify the paragraphs that develop each key idea.
2. What strategy do the authors use in the INTRODUCTION? Is it effective? Why or why not?
3. What kind of development do the authors use as support for their ideas in paragraphs 6 through 7, 12 through 15, and 22 through 23? Is this development strategy effective? Convincing? Why or why not?
4. How are the topics of paragraphs 16 and 17 developed? Do you find this development strategy more or less convincing than the one used in the paragraphs identified in question 3? Explain.
5. What is the function of paragraph 20? How does it help the reader to follow the authors' ARGUMENT?
6. Which paragraphs make up the essay's CONCLUSION? What kind of concluding strategy is used? Why do you think the final paragraph is so short?

Content and Purpose

1. What is a tsunami? As a METAPHOR for the change that is the topic of paragraph 1, is it effective? Why or why not?
2. According to the authors, what are some of the factors that have changed our view of marriage over the last fifty years?
3. Identify three ARGUMENTS used by opponents of marriage. (See paragraphs 2 and 3.) Do you agree with any of these arguments? Why or why not?
4. According to the authors, you'll discover the benefits of marriage for men, women, and children "if you ask the right questions" (paragraph 5). What are the "right questions"?
5. What are three health benefits that the authors attribute to marriage?
6. After citing statistics to support their argument that married people are wealthier than unmarried people, the authors suggest that "marriage itself is a form of wealth" (paragraph 15). Explain this statement in your own words.
7. What is "one reason why married men and women, on average, tend to be emotionally and mentally healthier" (paragraph 24) than their unmarried counterparts? Do you find the authors' argument convincing? Why or why not?
8. How do married people benefit from the fact that marriage is a "public relationship" (paragraph 26)? Do you agree with the authors that marriage "creates powerful positive changes in couples' lives"? Why or why not?

Suggestions for Writing

1. Write an essay that either confirms or disproves the arguments presented in "The Case for Marriage." Draw on your own marriage, or that of someone you know, to support your argument.
2. Using some of Waite and Gallagher's argumentation techniques, write an essay in which you argue for or against having children.

Why I Like to Pay My Taxes

NEIL BROOKS

A professor of law at Osgoode Hall Law School in Toronto, Neil Brooks has taught tax law and policy for nearly 30 years. He has published extensively on tax issues and consulted widely for the Canadian and numerous other governments. He was awarded the Canadian Association of Law Teachers' Award for Academic Excellence in 2002.

Ilike paying taxes. Taxes allow us to pursue our aspirations collectively and thus greatly enrich the quality of life for the average Canadian family. Taxes have brought us high-quality public schools that remain our democratic treasure, low tuition at world-class universities, freedom from fear of crippling health bills, excellent medical services, public parks and libraries, and liveable cities. None of these things comes cheaply.

Taxes also assist us in spreading our incomes over our lifetimes to maximize our well being by, for example, transferring income from our high-income years to our retirement years, from times when we are supporting children to times when we are not, and from periods when we are well and able to take care of our own needs to periods when we are ill or suffering from a disability.

Just as importantly, the public goods and services that we purchase with taxes leave working people more secure, healthier, better educated, more economically secure and therefore better protected against business threats, and thus more able to win their fair share of the national income that we all collectively produce.

Taxes also allow us to discharge our moral obligations to one another. They enable us to establish democratically controlled public institutions that attempt to prevent exploitation in market exchanges and family relations; to ensure mutuality in our interdependence upon each other; to compensate those who are inevitably harmed through no fault of their own by the operation of a dynamic market economy that we all benefit from; to ensure a more socially acceptable distribution of income and wealth than that which results from market forces alone; to strive for gender and racial equality; and to provide full entitlement and open access to those services essential to human development. As a result, taxes buy us a relatively high level of social cohesion and social equality and therefore the benefits of community existence. What would any of us have without community?

In spite of the fact that they enable us to collectively provide our most valuable goods and services, no one likes paying taxes. There is a good deal of public misunderstanding about the role of taxes in modern democratic states. In large part, this misunderstanding has been fostered by business interests and others who would like to roll back the economic and social borders of the public sector so that they can exercise unhindered power in our society through private markets. Part of their deliberate and clever strategy has been to use language and concepts in discussing taxes that make it appear self-evident that, while citizens can afford more private goods and services, which businesses produce, they are deluding themselves and living beyond their means if they think they can afford more public goods and services produced by government. Examples of such misleading characterizations of taxes abound. Here are three:

6   **Increased taxes cannot be afforded.** This common and compelling-sounding refrain is patently nonsense. Many public goods provided by government and financed by taxes, such as health and education services, are necessities. Therefore, reducing the government supply of these services will not mean that people are no longer paying for them, it will simply mean that they are paying for them in the form of prices demanded by private providers instead of taxes paid to finance their provision through the public sector.

7   Similarly, when people say that we cannot afford to pay taxes to provide child and elderly care services, presumably they are not saying that we can no longer afford to look after our children or the elderly. What they must mean is that instead of spreading the cost of these services equitably, through the tax system, across the entire population, we should leave them to be borne by women, by and large, who provide these services unpaid in their own homes.

8   Thus, often when business interests assert that taxes should be reduced it is not because they think we can no longer afford the services that governments provide, but because they want to shift the cost of providing them from themselves and other high-income individuals to low-income families and women working in their homes at tasks that we all benefit from but for which they are not paid.

9   **Taxes are a burden.** This common description of taxes is equally misleading. Taxes are the price that we pay for goods and services produced in the public sector from which we all benefit. They are equivalent to amounts we pay as prices for goods and services produced in the private sector. Compounding the deception, at the same time as they speak of public goods as being financed by the "imposition of taxes," business interests often speak of private goods as being financed by "the dollar votes of consumers." Here rational understanding is stood on its head. The vote, which is the symbol of democracy, is assigned to a marketplace transaction, while taxes, which are democratically determined, are treated as being amounts people have no control over but that are imposed on them.

Taxes restrict freedom. This common objection to taxes subtly rein-   10
forces the idea that the public sector simply consumes whatever it
purchases with tax money, instead of using the money to deliver
goods and services that benefit citizens. Taxes, in fact, increase the
amount of freedom in society.

In a market economy, to have money is to have freedom. The   11
government transfers over 65 per cent of the taxes it receives to
families in need in the form of pensions, child allowances, social
assistance, and compensation for work-related injuries or loss of
employment. Thus, while it might be said that taxes restrict the
freedom of some, they greatly enlarge the freedom of others.

Taxes increase our freedoms in other ways, including for   12
example, the freedom to travel by using publicly financed roads
and other transportation systems, the freedom to learn and think
critically, freedom from concerns over crippling health bills, and the
freedom to enjoy public libraries, beaches and parks.

To promise, as some politicians are doing, that they are going to   13
cut taxes in order "to allow Canadians to keep more of their hard-
earned dollars" is simply a way of saying "forget about recognizing
your moral obligations to one another, to heck with pursuing your
most noble aspirations collectively and do not worry about securing
the blessings of real freedom." These people need a civics lesson. As
a famous U.S. jurist noted, taxes are the price we pay for civilization.

Ultimately, what is at stake is the question of who will exercise   14
power in our society. Will important sources of power be controlled
by a small number of people through private markets? Or will
important sources of power remain in the control of the majority of
Canadians through democratically elected institutions?

Structure and Strategy

1. Where does Brooks state the THESIS of this essay?
2. This essay is an example of the "two sides of the story"
   approach explained in the introduction to this unit. Which paragraphs develop the pro-taxes point of view and which paragraphs deal with the anti-tax view?
3. How does paragraph 5 contribute to the structure and development of the piece?
4. Who do you think is the intended AUDIENCE for this essay?
5. What CONCLUSION strategy does Brooks use?
6. Is Brooks' essay developed primarily by ARGUMENT or by PER-
   SUASION? Cite examples from the essay to support your opinion.

Content and Purpose

1. What are some examples of "public goods and services" (paragraph 3) that our tax money provides in Canada? Do you agree with the author that without taxes, we would not have "the benefits of community existence" (paragraph 4)?
2. Identify the three points that Brooks uses to explain why he likes paying taxes (paragraphs 2–4). Can you see a pattern in the arrangement of these points?
3. Why does Brooks think that there is a general misunderstanding about what taxes do in a modern democracy?
4. What does Brooks think of individuals and groups who would like to "roll back the economic and social borders of the public sector" (paragraph 5)?
5. What are the three "misleading characterizations of taxes" (paragraph 5), according to Brooks, and how does he counter each of them? Do you agree or disagree with him?
6. What is the relationship between voting and taxes? According to Brooks, which institution gives citizens more choice—democratic elections or the marketplace?
7. What does Brooks think that politicians who promise to cut taxes are really doing?

Suggestions for Writing

1. Do you agree or disagree with Brooks' essay? Write an essay that argues your point of view.
2. Free public education through high school is one of the public services that are financed by taxes. Should postsecondary education also be tuition-free? Write an essay that argues your position on this issue.
3. Brooks maintains that Canada provides "excellent medical services" (paragraph 1) through its publicly-financed health care system. However, there are waiting lists for many medical services, and many Canadians cannot find a family doctor. Write an essay that explores whether Canadians would be better or worse off if they had to pay for some of their medical care themselves.
4. Read Gregory Boyd Bell's "The Great Democracy Drop-Out" (page 265). Write an essay comparing and/or contrasting Brooks' and Boyd Bell's views of citizen responsibility in a democratic Canada, as well as their approaches to building an argument.

Net Gain: A Pollyanna-ish° View of Online Personals

EMILY NUSSBAUM

Emily Nussbaum is the former editor-in-chief of *Nerve.com*. Currently working as a freelance journalist, she writes regularly for *The New York Times* and *Slate*, among other publications.

When I first went to work at *Nerve.com*, the online sex and culture magazine, I knew very little about the "personals" side of the site. No, I was a big editorial snob, too busy soliciting personal essays on Canadian toplessness and begging Michael Chabon° for table scraps to pay much attention to the tech-heads to my left, who were beta-testing classified-ad databases. Little did I know about the real literary revolution taking place—that out of the inky duckling of the print personal ad was emerging this proud and freaky swan, the online profile.

The old-style personal ad was a solitary, faintly musty, two-line cry for help, delivered with haiku-length° concision. The language was as coy as that of a real-estate ad: Rubenesque meant fat, generous meant rich patsy, artistic meant broke. Two types of daters were assumed to use these ads: the extremely lonely and those with narrowly specific sexual kinks. Before a meeting, one likely knew very little about one's date, other than the fact that he or she would be sporting a glittery beret as a signal.

Online ads, in contrast, are more informative, more frank, and judging from anecdotal evidence, much more popular. Every single person I know has placed an ad—whether they've done so at self-consciously edgy *Spring Street Personals* (which fuels *Nerve*, the *Onion*, and *Salon*, among others); over in that big bus station of cow-eyed romance *Match.com*; at one-stop gay emporium *PlanetOut*; or at *JDate*, the Jewish singles site. If there's still any stigma attached to online dating, it's on its way out. Part of this is generational: Young People of Today don't view the Web as dorky (or dangerous) by nature. While everyone has heard scary stories about online romance (beware the pedophiles and married creeps!), the chiding articles, like anti-drug ads, may trigger more curiosity than caution. And then there's the sheer convenience: Where else can you make a romantic impulse buy at 3 a.m., other than the West Side Highway?

What's more, creating an online ad is in and of itself a weirdly satisfying creative experience—and most often not a solitary one. A newsprint personal is terse and permanent, something one whispers to a copy editor during work hours, hand cupped over the phone. In contrast, a personal ad online is a linked, living creature—it can be drunkenly altered at 2 a.m. or mass-edited by a squad of enthusiastic co-workers or critiqued snarkily via instant message. It can be hidden for six months then revved back to life like a discarded motorcycle.

5   Rather than seeing this technical innovation as the death of romance, or some kind of mechanized nightmare, I wonder if it isn't in fact a change for the better—and not necessarily because it creates better relationships. (As with most ways of meeting, the payoff rate for online personals is inevitably low, and the oh-well anecdote rate high.) Instead, online dating has social benefits that extend beyond the dinner-and-a-movie circuit. For starters, profiles turn good writing into a turn-on, rewarding wit, concision, and creativity. The best ads find new ways to brag: "I have been told that I am a phenomenal lover" (from a *Match* ad) is radically less convincing than "I eat the hot sauce with the warning labels" (from *Nerve*). While plenty of ads are stupid or depressing, sharp language gets you more play, and thus even the dullest profile-writers are forced to gaze at their own words with an editor's eye.

6   Lately, I've been nudging recently broken-up friends to place ads—because it allows them to start dating (mentally at least) without actually having to date. Besides, the placement of an online ad is a social bonding ritual. People not only edit one another's ads, they cherry-pick ads for their friends to answer, cheer for them if they make "Personal of the Day," and generally get so involved in their friend's dating lives that it's all, granted, a little frightening and occasionally adolescent. But this companionship makes dating less like grim tryouts for Noah's Ark and more like a game of Madlibs. Are guys who mention Henry Rollins° likely to be independent-minded or just narcissistically personality disordered? What about yoga: sign of limberness or soft-headed New Age beliefs? These are questions you need your friends' help in figuring out.

7   Certainly, online ads offer plenty of material to analyze: pictures of pets, lists of favourite movie sex scenes, accounts of geographic origins—in other words, stuff you'd never find in a print ad or even the richest description of a potential blind date. (Among the responses to *Nerve's* "most humbling moment" question: "having to wear a size XS athletic supporter in 7th grade gym" and "getting cancer at eighteen.") My editor for this piece claims she learned personal details from a friend's ad that she hadn't known about in their seven years of friendship. And unlike purely print ads, online profiles most often have photos. This has at least one major benefit: You can reject, or be rejected, for superficial reasons

before ever meeting—in fact, before exchanging a single line of correspondence. (What, it's better to go to the cafe and have an awkward conversation, and *then* be dumped for your double chin?) The first date itself is transformed by reams of preparatory dialogue: It's more like a real date than a blind one.

But perhaps the best part of the whole personals process is the   8
randomizing effect of diving into a database in the first place. One might imagine that being able to pick and choose hair color and geography would narrow the dating pool—that people would zero in on only someone who fit all their parameters. But in practice, most people are probably less picky in an anonymous database than they are in a social situation. In real life, flirting with strangers has all sorts of risks; online, one can take a cautious, well-researched risk. This is perhaps the most idealistic potential of Internet profiles: that they may knock people out of their established social circles. After all, in real life, few people meet cute. We date in the same way we get jobs: through connections. Friends of friends mean same schools, same professions, same ethnic group. This might guarantee compatibility, but it also maintains the social status quo. Paradoxically, by entering the rather rigid and literal-minded algorithms of a computer (as opposed to the two-degrees environment of a party), one is more likely to come across a genuine stranger. It's hardly a radical redistribution of social connections (sites like *JDate* still focus on like meets like), but it's a nudge outward.

Still, the greatest strength of the online dating sites is their play-   9
fulness—they're more like video games than premarital business spreadsheets. In a culture that seems to regard singleness as a problem to be solved, they turn the process of dating into something that can be turned on and off as easily as your computer. Some might call that trivializing. I call it progress.

Words and Meanings

Pollyanna-ish	cheerfully optimistic (the term derives from the name of the protagonist of a 1913 children's novel, whose sunny nature gladdens the hearts of people in the dispiriting little town to which she is sent after her parents' death)	Title
Michael Chabon	award-winning novelist, film writer, and journalist	Paragraph 1

| 2 | haiku-length | extremely short, though packed with meaning (Haiku is a Japanese verse form consisting of three unrhymed lines of five, seven, and five syllables) |
| 6 | Henry Rollins | American rock singer and songwriter; storyteller, actor, poet, and radio personality (b. 1961) |

Structure and Strategy

1. Do you think this essay is an example of ARGUMENT or PERSUASION—or both?
2. What is the THESIS of the essay? Is it stated or implied?
3. Paragraphs 1 and 4 both conclude with a FIGURE OF SPEECH. Identify them, then decide which one is more effective and why.
4. What two things are being contrasted in paragraphs 2, 3, and 4? Identify at least five images that you find effective in conveying this contrast.
5. Who is the target AUDIENCE for this article? How would you describe the article's TONE?

Content and Purpose

1. Where did the author work? (See paragraph 1.) What did she do there?
2. Identify three differences between a personal ad in a newspaper and an online personal profile.
3. What are the drawbacks of print personal ads? (See paragraph 3.)
4. Why does Nussbaum think online personals are preferable to print ones? (See paragraph 4.)
5. Does Nussbaum think that online dating leads to better relationships?
6. Do you agree or disagree with the author's opinion of online dating?

Suggestions for Writing

1. Have you ever dated someone you met online? How did you create your profile (or choose the person)? How did the date work out? Write an essay that explores the phenomenon of online dating based on your own experience.

2. What should a person look for in a potential spouse? How does someone find the right person to marry? Does a person's family need to be involved? Write an essay that convinces your reader that the process you describe is likely to lead to a happy marriage.
3. Read "Bonding Online: Websites as Substitute Communities" (page 142) or "The Pleasures of the Text" (page 270). Compare the view of online communication in one of those essays with Nussbaum's.

Why I'm Happy I Evolved

OLIVIA JUDSON

Evolutionary biologist and prize-winning journalist Olivia Judson (b. 1970 in England) is the author of the best-selling book *Dr. Tatiana's Sex Advice to All Creation: The Definitive Guide to the Evolutionary Biology of Sex* (2002). Written in the style of a sex-advice column to animals, the book details the variety of sexual practices in the natural world and provides the reader with an overview of the evolutionary biology of sex. Judson has given lectures and seminars at numerous institutions and recently has written science essays for *Prospect*, a British magazine, and *The New York Times*. Judson lives in London, England, where she is a research fellow at Imperial College.

I n 2005, [chimpanzees] joined humans, chickens and mosquitoes, as well as less famous occupants of the planet, on an exclusive but growing list: organisms whose complete genomes° have been sequenced. 1

What would they make of this news, I wonder? Perhaps they would resent the genetic evidence that they are related to us. Or perhaps they would, as I do, revel in being part of the immensity of nature and a product of evolution, the same process that gave rise to dinosaurs, bread molds and myriad organisms too wacky to invent. 2

Organisms like the sea slug Elysia chlorotica. This animal not only looks like a leaf, but it also acts like one, making energy from the sun. Its secret? When it eats algae, it extracts the chloroplasts, the tiny entities that plants and algae use to manufacture energy from sunlight, and shunts them into special cells beneath its skin. The chloroplasts continue to function; the slug thus becomes able to live on a diet composed only of sunbeams. 3

4   Still more fabulous is the bacterium Brocadia anammoxidans. It blithely makes a substance that to most organisms is a lethal poison—namely, hydrazine. That's rocket fuel.

5   And then there's the wasp Cotesia congregata. She injects her eggs into the bodies of caterpillars. As she does so, she also injects a virus that disables the caterpillar's immune system and prevents it from attacking the eggs. When the eggs hatch, the larvae eat the caterpillar alive.

6   It's hard not to have an insatiable° interest in organisms like these, to be enthralled by the strangeness, the complexity, the breathtaking variety of nature. Just think: the Indus River dolphin doesn't sleep as you or I do, or indeed as most mammals, for several hours at once. Instead, it takes microsleeps, naps that last for a few seconds, like a driver dozing at the wheel.

7   Or consider this: a few days after its conception, a pig embryo has become a filament that is about a yard long. Or: the single-celled parasite that causes malaria is descended from algae. We know this because it carries within itself the remnants of a chloroplast.

8   It's not that I have a fetish° for obscure facts. It's that small facts add up to big pictures. For although Mother Nature's infinite variety seems incomprehensible at first, it is not. The forces of nature are not random; often, they are strongly predictable. For example, if you were to discover a new species and you told me that the male is much bigger than the female, I would tell you what the mating system is likely to be: males fight each other for access to females. Or if you discover that the male's testicles make up a large part of his weight, I can tell you that the females in his species consort with several males at a time.

9   Suppose you find that a particular bacterium lives exclusively in the gullets of leeches and helps them digest blood. Then I can tell you how that bacterium's genome is likely to differ from those of its free-living cousins; among other changes, the genome will be smaller, and it will have lost sets of genes that are helpful for living free but useless for living inside another being.

10   Because a cell is a kind of factory that produces proteins, and because proteins can have a variety of components, some of which are cheaper to synthesize than others, you might expect that proteins that are mass produced are made from cheaper components than proteins that are constructed only occasionally. And you'd be right.

11   The patterns are everywhere. Mammals that feed on ants and termites have typically evolved long, thin noses and long, sticky tongues. A virus that is generally passed from mother to child will tend to make its host less sick than one that readily jumps from one host to another via a cough or a sneeze.

When I was in school, I learned none of this. Biology was a sub-   12
ject that seemed as exciting as a clump of cotton wool. It was a
dreary exercise in the memorization and regurgitation of apparently unconnected facts. Only later did I learn about evolution and
how it transforms biology from that mass of cotton wool into a
magnificent tapestry, a tapestry we can contemplate and begin to
understand.

Some people want to think of humans as the product of a special   13
creation, separate from other living things. I am not among them; I
am glad it is not so. I am proud to be part of the riot of nature, to
know that the same forces that produced me also produced bees,
giant ferns and microbes that live at the bottom of the sea.

For me, the knowledge that we evolved is a source of solace   14
and hope. I find it a relief that plagues and cancers and wasp larvae
that eat caterpillars alive are the result of the impartial—and com-
prehensible—forces of evolution rather than the caprices° of a deity.

More than that, I find that in viewing ourselves as one species   15
out of hundreds of millions, we become more remarkable, not less
so. No other animal that I have heard of can live so peaceably in
such close quarters with so many individuals that are unrelated. No
other animal routinely bothers to help the sick and the dying, or
tries to save those hurt in an earthquake or flood.

Which is not to say that we are all we might wish to be. But in   16
putting ourselves into our place in nature, in comparing ourselves
with other species, we have a real hope of reaching a better understanding, and appreciation, of ourselves.

Words and Meanings

Paragraph

genomes	all genes contained in one set of chromosomes	1
insatiable	incapable of being satisfied	6
fetish	an obsessive interest in something	8
caprices	impulses, whims	14

Structure and Strategy

1. Where does Judson state the THESIS of her essay?
2. Which paragraphs contain examples of the "myriad organisms too wacky to invent" that Judson refers to in paragraph 2?
3. What examples does Judson use to illustrate her point that "the forces of nature are not random; often, they are strongly pre-dictable" (paragraph 8)?

4. Identify two FIGURES OF SPEECH that Judson uses in paragraph 12 to reinforce the difference in her attitude to biology before and after she learned about evolution.
5. Paragraphs 3 and 16 begin with sentence fragments. We can assume that Judson used these fragments deliberately, not by accident. What effect do they achieve?

Content and Purpose

1. This essay uses examples to make its point, but what is its PURPOSE in terms of RHETORICAL MODE?
2. What has science discovered that chimpanzees share with humans, chickens, and mosquitoes?
3. Which organism as described by Judson exhibits characteristics common to both plants and animals? Which category is this creature actually in?
4. Which of the evolutionary examples that Judson describes can be applied to human biology?
5. What are Judson's reasons for being happy to consider herself part of the evolutionary process?
6. Why does Judson not agree with the view that "humans [are] the product of a special creation, separate from other living things"?
7. In Judson's view, how are humans unique among the millions of creatures on the planet? Why does she suggest that we think of ourselves in context, as one of the millions of species found in nature?

Suggestions for Writing

1. Do you agree or disagree with Judson's perspective on evolution? Write an essay that explains your opinion in a clear and persuasive way.
2. Read Lewis Thomas's "Altruism" (page 234). Write an essay that explores the similarities and/or differences between his and Olivia Judson's views of the human relationship with other species.
3. Read Helena Cronin's "The Evolution of Evolution" (page 191) and Natalie Angier's "The Cute Factor" (page 227). Write an essay that explores various aspects of human behaviour as seen in the light of evolutionary biology. Use examples from at least two of the readings to support your thesis.

The Great Democracy Drop-Out

GREGORY BOYD BELL

Writer and editor Gregory Boyd Bell (b. 1963) is an editor at *The Globe and Mail*. He has also been on the staff of *The Hamilton Spectator* and has written a column for *eye Weekly*, a Toronto arts and opinion magazine. Boyd Bell's essays on media, politics, and culture have appeared in such publications as *This Magazine* and *New York Newsday*.

When British Columbia's . . . new Liberal government took power [in 2001], one of its priorities was to undo the previous NDP government's work on treaty negotiations with First Nations. The crowbar of choice was a referendum that sought, through eight innuendo-laced° questions, to manufacture a popular mandate to damn legal precedent and revise the constitutional status of treaty rights to somewhere just below the inalienable right to go camping. 1

The B.C. referendum was a horrid bit of mobocracy. It asked voters, though of course not in quite so many words, if they'd like to gang up and turn all those claimed lands into provincial parks and tell the pesky Indians to take a long walk off a short pier. 2

In response, the Union of B.C. Indian Chiefs, supported by union groups and various social justice campaigners, called for an "active boycott" of the vote in which participants would send their mail-in ballots to First Nations governments for ritual burning. On June 10 the Hupacasath First Nation, which lost its attempt to persuade the B.C. Supreme Court to block the referendum, held a ballot-burning party for some of the nearly 13,000 voided ballots they [had] received. They planned to immolate° the rest in Victoria on July 3, when the results of the referendum were to be published. While there's no doubting the newsworthiness of the scheme, it sadly reflects how progressive political groups find themselves drawn to the margins, from the actual practice of power and influence to the mere performance of political theatre. 3

"Don't vote—it only encourages them!" This ancient bumper sticker joke is one of the slogans adopted by the Edible Ballot Society, a small Canadian group that follows the proud tradition of parodic critiques of establishment democracy. The familiar notion is that voting doesn't make a difference because the whole thing is rigged. Candidates only get to be on the ballot by selling out to The Man, so picking one tool over another is but an illusion of democracy. But whether you burn, eat, or quietly scrawl "burn in hell" on your ballot, you are making a statement. And the statement is: Please ignore me. 4

5   That statement can be made by organized groups, like the B.C. chiefs, or the edible ballotists, or by those who get their jollies from chucking rocks at riot cops. It is certainly being made by a much larger number of younger citizens who are simply withdrawing from politics, if indeed they were ever involved. When Canada's federal Liberals won their third straight majority government in November 2000, only 61% of eligible citizens cast a ballot. The abysmal turnout bumped Canada from its place among high-participation democracies—like Sweden, Germany, France, Italy, Uruguay, Chile, and Brazil—and relegated us to the slough° of apathy that prevails in places like Poland, Guatemala, Egypt and the United States. Post-election surveys confirmed that the sharp drop—down by six percent from the 1997 federal vote—was largely due to an even greater drop in voting by one demographic group: people born after 1970.

6   In recent studies of voter (and non-voter) behaviour, activist critiques of democracy do not register. What studies do show is that the number of people who do not vote is strongly correlated with the number who are clueless. In a 1990 survey carried out for the Royal Commission on Electoral Reform and Party Financing, a dismal five percent of Canadians could not name the prime minister. In 2000, the number in a similar survey was 11%. It gets worse. Since 1965, surveys of voters have been carried out by the Canadian Election Study. In the 1984 study, almost 90% could name their provincial premier. In 1997, it was 77%. The decline in knowledge was greatest among young adults.

7   Luring younger voters into the system is certainly a top priority for the . . . New Democratic Party, whose declining support through the 1990s follows the falling participation by younger voters like hangover follows the fifth martini. Yet the problem affects all Canadian political parties, and indeed most modern liberal democracies, which have seen declines in voter turnout of varying severity over the past decade. If this Great Democracy Drop-Out continues, we face being ruled by governments whose corroding legitimacy can only fuel a vicious circle of further alienation, still lower turnout, and a spiral into inherently unstable oligarchy°.

8   Of course, some younger citizens don't vote because they believe the words on another old bumper sticker: "If voting could change anything, it would be illegal." They're too smart to fall for the con. They've exchanged passive voting for an active quest for political or social change, usually within a patchwork of organizations that are often lumped together under the banner of anti-capitalism or anti-globalism.

Consider for a moment the key contention by activists that 9
meetings like the Summit of the Americas or the G-8 are "non-
democratic." The critique is rather undercut if the critics themselves
aren't participating in electoral politics, whether by running as candidates or infiltrating major parties.

The alternative to electoral participation is marginalization. 10
That's how democratic electoral politics works. All parties have
core supporters, but in order to win a majority they must extend
their support by appealing to other groups, usually on an issue-by-
issue basis. If one of your group's defining characteristics is that
you don't vote, won't vote, or just say screw the vote, then don't
look so surprised when vote-seekers demonstrate no sympathy or
concern for your priorities.

This isn't to dismiss valid concerns about Canadian democracy. 11
It's true that democracy needs to be more than an event that happens every few years in which you mark your X and go home and
bar the door. And it's hard to argue with the view that the government appears to be a revolving door of the same business interests
and party fat cats. But this criticism doesn't support abandoning
the system in order to save it. If you want to fix the government, it's
a bit odd to announce that your first step will be to avoid the government. This is like announcing you're going to fix your bicycle by
reassembling the toaster oven. If we agree that the baddies are
dehumanizing and anti-democratic, doesn't that mean we should
humanize democracy?

If you want big changes, there are only two approaches open: 12
revolution or peaceful takeover. For a revolution, you need lots of
people who aren't squeamish. Or you can make like the Ottawa
Committee of the World March of Women who . . . launched a
"Revolutionary Knitting Action in protest against corporate greed
and globalization" by inviting women of the community to knit or
crochet one-foot squares to be assembled into a "gigantic 'social
safety net' to symbolize a caring, compassionate and peaceful
society." The project hopes to create "a 'soft' barrier of knitted yarn as
a way to reclaim public spaces from the elite to the common good."

The knitting project, like lobbing teddy bears at riot cops, is 13
amusing and ingenious but not much of a basis for constitutional
government. In the event that the mass knitters of Ottawa fail to
bring global capitalism to its knees, that leaves the less socially
exciting option of actually trying to change the system. That
requires you to get involved in the practice of politics.

Today's younger activists could kick ass in mainstream political 14
parties. Do they realize how few votes it takes to nominate a candidate? Or perhaps they secretly fear that their commitment, or that

of their fellow travellers, is so shallow that it could be uprooted by a few executive meetings or, God forbid, taking a seat in the Commons.

15   It's vital for the future of Canada, and all Western liberal democracies, to reintegrate those who are turning or simply falling away from electoral politics. Activists need to lead their peers, not like sheep back into the fold of electoral politics, but as a powerful block of voters and policy makers. The alternative is further declines in voter turnout and more noisy but marginal activism, leading to an oligarchy in which a narrowing electorate selects a largely permanent government. If this seems an exaggeration, consider that in both Canadian and American elections, the lower the turnout, the better the odds that the incumbent will win. Or that the next leadership vote for the Liberal Party of Canada, which is restricted to paid-up members, will have more impact on Canada's federal government than the last two general elections combined.

16   Burning and eating ballots—organized nonparticipation—is a waste of effort that might go into actual reform of actual politics. The better course is to persuade people that, if they fail to exercise their franchise°, it will get flabby—and it may not be up to much when they really need it. This kind of mass persuasion is something that many younger activists are very good at. For example, one project that needs help is the push for some form of proportional representation°, which just happens to be a great way to raise voter turnout because people get a better sense that their individual vote matters.

17   Activists who stay to the outside are unlikely to get much more than a few headlines unless they dirty their hands with boring dusty old electoral politics. Taking part in protests like those in Quebec City or Calgary is, of course, a healthy outdoor activity that gives young people a chance to make new friends and learn about the value of co-operation. But it's not going to fix the system.

18   No matter whether it's apathy or misguided activism, dropping out of mainstream politics is an excellent way to ensure that young life is circumscribed by a bunch of aging white guys whose primary ambitions are to pay off their pals, leave their name on a building and die in the arms of someone less than half their age.

19   Before you go drop out, remember that democracy is a lot of things, many of them untidy, some of them embarrassing. But it's not supposed to be the solution; it's just a process by which we try to grant a government a public mandate. Mainstream politics is a nasty, dirty, smelly, noisy sort of monkey house. You can stand on the outside and throw peanuts through the bars. But if you really want change, you have to go inside and get dirty.

Words and Meanings

Paragraph

innuendo-laced	biased	1
immolate	burn	3
slough	swamp	5
oligarchy	government by a small group of people who govern for their own purposes	7
franchise	the right to vote	16
proportional representation	an electoral system in which a political party is represented in the legislature in direct proportion to the number of votes it receives	

Structure and Strategy

1. Summarize the details of the political narrative presented in the INTRODUCTION (paragraphs 1 through 3). Why do you think Boyd Bell begins the essay with this narrative? What is his opinion of the action taken by the Union of B.C. Indian Chiefs?
2. What is the example Boyd Bell uses in paragraph 4? What does "parodic" mean?
3. Who is the target AUDIENCE for this essay? Identify four or five examples of DICTION and supporting EVIDENCE Boyd Bell uses to appeal to this audience.
4. Identify the SIMILES in paragraphs 7 and 11. How does each one reinforce the point Boyd Bell is making?
5. Describe the STYLE of the essay. What is the effect of the author's dramatic shifts from formal to informal? (Compare, for example, paragraphs 15 and 18.)
6. What METAPHOR does Boyd Bell use in paragraph 19? Is it an effective way to conclude the essay? Why or why not?

Content and Purpose

1. According to the essay, what demographic group most consistently ignores or refuses to participate in electoral politics? Why? How does the "clueless" (paragraph 6) factor contribute to this behaviour?
2. Define in your own words the term "oligarchy" (paragraphs 7 and 15). Why does Boyd Bell see oligarchy as a possible result of what he calls the "Great Democracy Drop-Out"?
3. According to Boyd Bell, for people who "want big changes" (paragraph 12), what is the alternative to electoral participation? Why does he include the Revolutionary Knitting Action as an example in this CONTEXT?

4. Do you agree with Boyd Bell that "younger activists could kick ass in mainstream political parties" (paragraph 14)? Why or why not?
5. Summarize Bell's ARGUMENT. Do you find it convincing? Why or why not?
6. Do you follow electoral politics? Belong to a political party? Vote? Why or why not?

Suggestions for Writing

1. Why do many Canadians choose not to vote? What are the consequences of low voter turnout? Write an essay explaining the causes and/or effects of voter apathy.
2. Imagine that you are running for a government office (e.g., school trustee, member of Parliament, mayor). What issues do you think would be of special interest to younger voters? What strategies would you use to get them to vote for you?
3. Read Neil Brooks' "Why I Like to Pay My Taxes" (page 252). Write an essay comparing Brooks' and Gregory Boyd Bell's content, their views on citizen responsibility in a democratic Canada, and their approaches to building an argument.

The Pleasures of the Text

CHARLES MCGRATH

Charles McGrath is the former editor of *The New York Times Book Review* and *The New Yorker* and contributes frequently to the *New York Times Magazine*, *Golf Digest*, and other publications.

1   There used to be an ad on subway cars, next to the ones for bail bondsmen and hemorrhoid creams, that said: "if u cn rd ths u cn gt a gd job & mo pa." The ad was promoting a kind of stenography° training that is now extinct, presumably. Who uses stenographers anymore? But the notion that there might be value in easily understood shorthand has proved to be prescient°. If u cn rd these days, and, just as important, if your thumbs are nimble enough so that u cn als snd, you can conduct your entire emotional life just by transmitting and receiving messages on the screen of your cellphone. You can flirt there, arrange a date, break up and—in Malaysia at least—even get a divorce.

Shorthand contractions, along with letter–number homophones   2
("gr8" and "2moro," for example), emoticons (like the tiresome
colon-and-parenthesis smiley face) and acronyms (like the ubiquitous "lol," for "laughing out loud"), constitute the language of text-
messaging—or txt msg, to use the term that txt msgrs prefer.
Text-messaging is a refinement of computer instant-messaging,
which came into vogue five or six years ago. But because the typical
cellphone screen can accommodate no more than 160 characters,
and because the phone touchpad is far less versatile than the computer keyboard, text-messaging puts an even greater premium on
concision. Here, for example, is a text-messaging version of *Paradise
Lost*° disseminated by some scholars in England: "Devl kikd outa
hevn coz jelus of jesus&strts war. pd'off wiv god so corupts man
(md by god) wiv apel. devl stays serpnt 4hole life&man ruind. Woe
un2mnkind."

As such messages go, that one is fairly straightforward and   3
unadorned. There is also an entire code book of acronyms and
abbreviations, ranging from CWOT (complete waste of time) to
DLTBBB (don't let the bedbugs bite). And emoticonography has
progressed way beyond the smiley-face stage, and now includes
hieroglyphics to indicate drooling, for example (:-) . . .), as well as
secrecy (:X), Hitler (/.#( ) and the rose (@};—). Keep these in mind;
we'll need them later.

As with any language, efficiency isn't everything. There's also   4
the issue of style. Among inventive users, and younger ones especially, text-messaging has taken on many of the characteristics of
hip-hop, with so much of which it conveniently overlaps—in the
substitution of "z" for "s," for example, "a," for "er" and "d" for
"th." Like hip-hop, text-messaging is what the scholars call "performative"; it's writing that aspires to the condition of speech. And
sometimes when it makes abundant use of emoticons, it strives not
for clarity so much as a kind of rebus°-like cleverness, in which
showing off is part of the point. A text-message version of *Paradise
Lost*—or of the prologue, anyway—that tries for a little more
shnizzle might go like this: "Sing hvnly mewz dat on d :X mtntp
inspyrd dat shephrd hu 1st tot d chozen seed in d begnin hw d hvn
n erth @};— outa chaos."

Not that there is much call for Miltonic messaging these days.   5
To use the scholarly jargon again, text-messaging is "lateral"° rather
than "penetrative,"° and the medium encourages blandness and
even mindlessness. On the Internet there are several Web sites that
function as virtual Hallmark stores and offer ready-made text messages of breathtaking banality. There are even ready-made Dear
John letters, enabling you to dump someone without actually

speaking to him or her. Far from being considered rude, in Britain this has proved to be a particularly popular way of ending a relationship—a little more thoughtful than leaving an e-mail message but not nearly as messy as breaking up in person—and it's also catching on over here.

6   Compared with the rest of the world, Americans are actually laggards when it comes to text-messaging. This is partly for technical reasons. Because we don't have a single, national phone company, there are several competing and incompatible wireless technologies in use, and at the same time actual voice calls are far cheaper here than in most places, so there is less incentive for texting. But in many developing countries, mobile-phone technology has so far outstripped land-line availability that cellphones are the preferred, and sometimes the only, means of communication, and text messages are cheaper than voice ones. The most avid text-messagers are clustered in Southeastern Asia, particularly in Singapore and the Philippines.

7   There are also cultural reasons for the spread of text-messaging elsewhere. The Chinese language is particularly well-suited to the telephone key pad, because in Mandarin the names of the numbers are also close to the sounds of certain words; to say "I love you," for example, all you have to do is press 520. (For "drop dead," it's 748.) In China, moreover, many people believe that to leave voice mail is rude and it's a loss of face to make a call to someone important and have it answered by an underling. Text messages preserve everyone's dignity by eliminating the human voice.

8   This may be the universal attraction of text-messaging, in fact: it's a kind of avoidance mechanism that preserves the feeling of communication—the immediacy—without, for the most part, the burden of actual intimacy or substance. The great majority of text messages are of the "Hey, how are you, whassup?" variety, and they're sent sometimes when messenger and recipient are within speaking distance of each other—across classrooms, say, or from one row of a stadium to another. They're little electronic waves and nods that, just like real waves and nods, aren't meant to do much more than establish a connection—or disconnection, as the case may be—without getting into specifics.

9   "We're all wired together" is the collective message, and we'll signal again in a couple of minutes, not to say anything, probably, but just to make sure the lines are still working. The most depressing thing about the communications revolution is that when at last we have succeeded in making it possible for anyone to reach anyone else anywhere and at any time, it turns out that we really don't have much we want to say.

Words and Meanings

Paragraph

stenography	the obsolete practice of recording speech in shorthand	1
prescient	forward-looking; being able to predict future trends	
Paradise Lost	formal epic poem in 12 books published in the 17th century by John Milton; the epic is elaborate, heroic, and richly worded; in diction, syntax, and theme, it stands at one end of the prose continuum while text messaging sits at the other	2
rebus	text that uses letters, numbers, or pictures to represent words (examples range from ancient Egyptian hieroglyphics through 18th-century puzzles, to modern word games)	4
lateral	superficial message (see the discussion of surface reading in the Introduction, on page xxi)	5
penetrative	complex message with layers of meaning (see the discussion of deep reading in the Introduction, on p. xxi)	

Structure and Strategy

1. What kind of INTRODUCTION strategy does McGrath use in this essay?
2. What is the TOPIC SENTENCE of paragraph 3? How is it developed?
3. What is the topic sentence of paragraph 5? How is it developed?
4. What CONTRAST is developed in paragraph 6? Does it apply to Canada as well as the United States?
5. The THESIS is stated in the final sentence of the essay, which McGrath leads into with what has gone before. Has he provided enough support for his opinion? Do you agree or disagree?
6. How would you describe the TONE of this essay?

Content and Purpose

1. Why do you think the old subway ads in paragraph 1 are described as being "next to the ones for bail bondsmen and hemorrhoid creams"?
2. What is a "letter–number homophone" (paragraph 2)? Can you provide examples of others?

3. Why do you think McGrath uses text-message versions of Milton's *Paradise Lost* (paragraphs 2 and 4) as part of his argument?
4. What does text-messaging demand more of than computer instant-messaging? Why? (See paragraph 2.)
5. According to McGrath, what kind of "style" (paragraph 4) is often adopted by creative young text-messagers? What does it mean that this style is "performative"?
6. What is a "Dear John" letter (paragraph 5)? How would you feel about sending or receiving one of these via text-messaging?
7. Why is the Chinese language especially suited to text-messaging?
8. According to McGrath, what kind of communication is text-messaging actually encouraging? Do you use text-messaging? If u do, he rite o wrng?

Suggestions for Writing

1. Write an essay that argues for or against the idea that text- and instant-messaging make us better communicators.
2. Read "Bonding Online: Websites as Substitute Communities" (page 142) or "Net Gain" (page 257). Compare the view of online communication in one of these readings with that expressed in McGrath's essay.
3. Read Carol Shields' "The Case for Curling up with a Book" (page 359) and/or Mario Vargas Llosa's "With Pens Drawn" (page 361). What do you think one (or both) of these writers would think of text-messaging? Write an essay supporting your opinion with references to the reading(s).
4. Do you think the increasing popularity of text-messaging is influencing your generation's interest in reading or their ability to read? If so, is that influence positive or negative? Support your opinion with reference to two or more sources.

Stupid Jobs Are Good to Relax With°

HAL NIEDZVIECKI

Hal Niedzviecki (b. 1971) is a writer, editor, and cultural commentator. He is the author of six books, including a portrait of contemporary culture, *Hello, I'm Special: How Individuality Became the New Conformity* (2004), and a novel, *The Program* (2005). He is the founder, publisher, and current fiction editor of *Broken Pencil*, a periodical about 'zines (an abbreviation of the word *magazines*) and other independent arts. Niedzviecki's articles about culture have appeared in newspapers and magazines across North America, including *Utne Magazine*, *The Globe and Mail*, *Walrus*, *Saturday Night*, and *This Magazine*. In 1999, he won the Alexander Ross Award, which is given annually to the country's best new magazine journalist. He has been described as the "guru of independent/alternative action" by the *Toronto Star*. For more information about his work, visit www.smellit.ca.

Springsteen kicked off his world tour at Toronto's Massey Hall   1
a while back. Along with record company execs and those who could afford the exorbitant° prices scalpers wanted for tickets, I was in attendance. As Bruce rambled on about the plight of the itinerant Mexican workers, I lolled° in the back, my job, as always, to make myself as unapproachable as possible—no easy feat, trapped as I was in paisley vest and bow-tie combo. Nonetheless, the concert was of such soporific° proportions and the crowd so dulled into pseudo-reverence, I was able to achieve the ultimate in ushering—a drooping catatonia° as close as you can get to being asleep while on your feet at a rock concert.

But this ushering nirvana° wouldn't last long. For an usher,   2
danger takes many forms, including vomiting teens and the usher's nemesis°: the disruptive patron. And yes, to my semi-conscious horror, there she was: well-dressed, blond, drunk and doped up, swaying in her seat and . . . clapping. Clapping. In the middle of Springsteen's solo dirge about Pancho or Pedro or Luisa, she was clapping.

Sweat beaded on my forehead. The worst was happening. She   3
was in my section. Her clapping echoed through the hall, renowned for its acoustics. The Boss glared from the stage, his finger-picking folksiness no match for the drunken rhythm of this fan. Then, miracle of miracles, the song ended. The woman slumped back into her seat. Bruce muttered something about how he didn't need a rhythm section. Placated° by the adoring silence of the well-to-do, he launched into an even quieter song about an even more desperate migrant worker.

I lurked in the shadows, relaxed the grip I had on my flashlight   4
(the usher's only weapon). Springsteen crooned. His guitar twanged. It was so quiet you could hear the rats squirrelling around the ushers' subterranean change rooms. The woman roused herself from her slumber. She leaned forward in her seat, as if suddenly appreciating the import of her hero's message. I wiped the sweat off my brow, relieved. But slowly, almost imperceptibly, she brought her arms up above her head. I stared, disbelieving. Her hands waved around in the air until . . . boom! Another song

ruined, New York record execs and L.A. journalists distracted from their calculations of Bruce's net worth, the faint cry of someone calling, "Usher! Do something!"

5   For several years now, I have relied on stupid jobs to pay my way through the world. This isn't because I am a stupid person. On the contrary, stupid jobs are a way to avoid the brain-numbing idiocy of full-time employment. They are the next best thing to having no job at all. They will keep you sane, and smart.

6   I'm lazy sometimes. I don't always feel like working. On the stupid job, you're allowed to be lazy. All you have to do is show up. Hey, that's as much of an imposition on° my life as I'm ready to accept. Does The Boss go to work every day? I don't think so. He's The Boss.

7   Understanding the stupid job is the key to wading your way through the muck of the working week and dealing with such portentous° concepts as The Youth Unemployment Crisis and The Transformation of the Workplace. So sit back and let me explain. Or, as I used to say behind the scowl of my shining grin: "Hi, how are you this evening? Please follow me and I will show you to your seat."

8   "Out of Work: Is There Hope for Canada's Youth?" blurted the October 1997 issue of *Canadian Living*. My answer? There is more hope than ever. I'm not talking about ineffectual governments and their well-intentioned "partners," the beneficent corporations, all banding together to "create" jobs. After all, what kind of jobs do you think these corporations are going to create? Jobs that are interesting, challenging and resplendent° with possibilities? Hardly. These are going to be stupid jobs. Bring me your college graduates, your aspiring business mavens°, your literature lovers and we will find them rote° employment where servility° and docility° are the best things they could have learned at university.

9   But hope, hope is something altogether different. Hope is the process whereby entire generations learn to undervalue their work, squirm out of the trap of meaningless employment, work less, consume less and actually figure out how to enjoy life.

10   I hope I'm right about this, because the reality of the underemployed, overeducated young people of Canada is that the stupid job is their future. As the middle-aged population continues to occupy all the "real" jobs, as the universities continue to hike tuition prices (forcing students to work and study part time), as the government continues to shore up employment numbers with make-work and "retraining," there will be more stupid jobs than ever. And these stupid jobs won't be reserved for the uneducated and poor. The fer-

tile growth of the stupid job is already reaping a crop of middle-class youngsters whose education and upbringing have, somehow, given way to (supposedly) stalled° prospects and uncertain incomes.

These are your grandchildren, your children, your sisters, your   11
cousins, your neighbours. Hey, that might very well be a multi-coloured bow-tie wrapped around your neck.

I took a few tenuous° steps down the aisle. All around me, luxurious   12
people hissed in annoyance and extended their claws. Clapping woman was bouncing in her seat. She was smiling. Her face was flushed and joyous. The sound of her hands coming together was deafening. I longed for the floor captain, the front-of-house manager, the head of security, somebody to come and take this problem away from me. I hit her with a burst of flashlight. Taking advantage of her momentary blindness, I leaned in: "Excuse me Miss," I said. "You can't do that." "What?" she said. "That clapping," I said. "Listen," she slurred. "I paid $300 to see this. I can do what I want."

My flashlight hand wavered. Correctly interpreting my silence   13
for defeat, she resumed her clapping. Springsteen strummed louder, unsuccessful in his attempt to drown out the beat of luxury, the truth of indulgence. I faded away, the darkness swallowing me up. For a blissful moment, I was invisible.

A lot of young people think their stupid jobs are only temporary.   14
Most of them are right, in a way. Many will move on from being, as I have been, an usher, a security guard, a delivery boy, a data co-ordinator, a publishing intern. They will get marginally better jobs, but what they have learned from their stupid jobs will stay with them forever. Hopefully.

If I'm right, they will learn that the stupid job—and by exten-   15
sion, all jobs—must be approached with willing stupidity. Set your mind free. It isn't necessary, and it can be an impediment°. While your body runs the maze and finds the cheese, let your mind go where it will.

Look at it this way: you're trading material wealth and luxury   16
for freedom and creativity. To simplify this is to say that while you may have less money to buy things, you will have a lot more time to think up ways to achieve your goals without buying things. It is remarkable how quickly one comes to value time to just sit and think. Oddly, many of us seem quite proud of having absolutely no time to think about anything. The words "I'm so busy" are chanted over and over again like a mantra°, an incantation° against some horrible moment when we realize we're not so busy. In the stupid job universe, time isn't quantifiable. You're making so many dollars

an hour, but the on-job perks include daydreams, poems scribbled on napkins, novels read in utility closets and long conversations about the sexual stamina of Barney Rubble. How much is an idea worth? An image? A moment of tranquillity? A bad joke? The key here is to embrace the culture of anti-work.

17   Sometime after the Springsteen debacle°, I was on a delivery job dropping off newspapers at various locales. I started arguing with my co-worker, the van driver, about work ethic. I suggested we skip a drop-off or two, claiming that no one would notice and even if they did, we could deny it and no one would care. He responded by telling me that no matter what job he was doing, if he accepted the work, he was compelled to do it right. I disagreed. Cut corners, I argued. Do less for the same amount of pay. That's what they expect us to do, I said. Why else would they pay us so little? Not that day, but some weeks later, he came to see things my way.

18   What am I trying to tell you? To be lazy? To set fire to the corporation?

19   Maybe. Our options might be limited, but they are still options. Somewhere in the bowels of Massey Hall it has probably been noted in my permanent record that I have a bad attitude. That was a mistake. I wasn't trying to have a bad attitude. I was trying to have no attitude. . . .

20   What I should have told my friend in the delivery van was that when working the stupid job, passivity° is the difference between near slavery and partial freedom. It's a mental distinction. Your body is still in the same place for the same amount of time (unless you're unsupervised), but your mind is figuring things out. Figuring out how many days you need to work to afford things like hard-to-get tickets to concerts by famous American icons. Or figuring out why it is that at the end of the week, most people are too busy or too tired to do anything other than spend their hard-earned dollars on fleeting moments of cotton candy ecstasy as ephemeral° as lunch hour. Personally, I'd take low-level servitude over a promotion that means I'll be working late the rest of my life. You want me to work weekends? You better give me the rest of the week off. . . .

21   Montreal has one of the highest unemployment rates of any city in Canada. Young people in that city are as likely to have full-time jobs as they are to spend their nights arguing about Quebec separation. Not coincidentally, some of the best Canadian writers, comic artists and underground periodicals are from that city. We're talking about the spoken-word capital of North America here. Creativity plus unemployment equals art.

The burgeoning° stupid job aesthetic° is well documented in   22
another youth culture phenomenon, the vaunted 'zine (photo-
copied periodicals published by individuals for fun, not money).
Again, it doesn't take a genius to make the connection between the
youth culture of stupid jobs and the urgency and creativity 'zine
publishers display when writing about their lives. "So why was I
dishonest and subversive?" asks Brendan Bartholomew in an article
in the popular Wisconsin 'zine *Temp Slave*. "Well, I've been sabo-
taging employers for so long, it's become second nature. It's in my
blood. I couldn't stop if I wanted to."

Slacking off, doing as little as possible, relishing my lack of   23
responsibility, this is what the workplace has taught me to do. This
is the stupid job mantra. It isn't about being poor. The stupid job
aesthetic is not about going hungry. Canada is a country of excess.
You cannot have a stupid job culture when people are genuinely,
truly, worried that they are going to starve in the streets.

Nevertheless, the tenets° of the stupid job revolution are uni-   24
versal: work is mainly pointless; if you can think of something
better to do, you shouldn't have to work; it's better to have a low-
paying job and freedom than a high-paying job and a 60-hour
workweek. It was Bruce's drunken fan who highlighted the most
important aspect of what will one day be known as the stupid job
revolution: with money, you think you can do whatever you want,
but you rarely can; without money, you can be like Bartholomew—
a postmodern rat, a stowaway writing his diaries from the comfort
of his berth at the bottom of the sinking ship.

My father's plight is a familiar one. He started his working life at 13   25
in Montreal. He's 55 now. His employer of 12 years forced him to
take early retirement. The terms were great, and if he didn't own so
much stuff (and want more stuff) he could live comfortably without
ever working again. But he feels used, meaningless, rejected.

On his last day, I helped him clean out his office. The sight of   26
him stealing staplers, blank disks and Post-it note pads was something I'll never forget. It was a memo he was writing to his own
soul (note: they owe me).

But the acquisition° of more stuff is not what he needs to put a   27
life of hard work behind him. I wish that he could look back on his
years of labour and think fondly of all the hours he decided not to
work, those hours he spent reading a good book behind the closed
door of his office, or skipping off early to take the piano lessons he
never got around to. Instead of stealing office supplies, he should
have given his boss the finger as he walked out the door. Ha ha. I
don't care what you think of me. And by the way, I never did.

28   Despite his decades of labour and my years of being barely employed (and the five degrees we have between us), we have both ended up at the same place. He feels cheated. I don't.

Words and Meanings

Title		an echo of the title of Susan Swan's 1996 short story collection, *Stupid Boys Are Good to Relax With*
Paragraph		
1	exorbitant	grossly excessive
	lolled	lazily stood or leaned
	soporific	causing sleep
	catatonia	state of semiconsciousness in which one is unable to move
2	nirvana	blissful state
	nemesis	someone who is fated to do you harm
3	placated	soothed
6	imposition on	restriction on, interference with
7	portentous	of tremendous importance or significance (here, ironic)
8	resplendent	bright, shining
	aspiring mavens	ambitious would-be experts
	rote	routine, repetitive
	servility	slavishly doing what you're told
	docility	dutiful obedience, willingness to learn
10	stalled	at a standstill; halted with no hope of advancement
12	tenuous	hesitant
15	impediment	obstacle; something blocking your path to achievement
16	mantra	frequently repeated sound, word, or phrase, often sacred (see also paragraph 23)
	incantation	verbal charm or spell whose purpose is to produce magic effect
17	debacle	disaster
20	passivity	patient acceptance, not resisting
	ephemeral	lasting only a short time

burgeoning	fast-growing	22
aesthetic	theory of what is valid, worthwhile, or beautiful	
tenets	beliefs, principles	24
acquisition	accumulation, piling up	27

Structure and Strategy

1. Identify the paragraphs that tell the story of the author's ushering at a Springsteen concert. What is the point of the paragraphs that he inserts into the middle of the narrative? Why do you think he interrupts his story in this way?
2. What does Niedzviecki's DICTION tell us about his attitude toward the people in the audience, the music, and his job as an usher? See, for example, paragraphs 1, 3, 4, and 12.
3. Which paragraph states the THESIS of the essay?
4. What strategy does the author use in his CONCLUSION (see paragraphs 25 through 28)? Do you think it's effective? Why or why not?
5. Why is the author's use of IRONY appropriate in this essay, given his topic? Identify two or three examples of both verbal and situational irony and explain why you find them effective.
6. What were your expectations of the author when you read the title of the essay? Were you surprised to find words such as "exorbitant," "soporific," and "catatonia" in the first paragraph? What other elements of STYLE and structure tell us that the author is far from "stupid"?
7. Is this essay primarily ARGUMENT or PERSUASION?

Content and Purpose

1. According to Niedzviecki, what kinds of jobs are college graduates most likely to get in the coming years? (See paragraphs 8 through 11.) Why? Even if the author's pessimistic view proves to be correct, do you agree that "servility and docility are the best things [students can learn] at university"?
2. At several points in the essay, the author refers to rats—some literal, some figurative. (See, for example, paragraphs 4, 15, and 24.) What point is he making?
3. Explain what Niedzviecki means by "the culture of anti-work" (paragraph 16). What advantages does he see in being underemployed?
4. What is the basis of the author's argument with the van driver as they're dropping off newspapers? (See paragraphs 17

through 20.) Whom do you agree with? Who has the right attitude toward the job?

5. What proof does Niedzviecki offer to support his point that art and creativity are likely to flourish among people who are unemployed or have "stupid jobs"?

6. What is Niedzviecki's attitude toward consumerism? Does he think we buy too much or not enough? Where in the essay is his attitude most clearly revealed? Do you agree with him? Why or why not?

Suggestions for Writing

1. Most of us have worked in what Niedzviecki calls a "stupid job." Did you learn anything from the experience? Write an essay that details your own experience in a low-paying, routine job in which intelligence and creativity were neither required nor encouraged.

2. Write an essay that argues for or against the "do it right" work ethic: that we should work hard at any or all jobs we do.

3. What should a postsecondary education prepare us for? Do people go to college or university to prepare for work, learn about the world, or pursue personal interests? What reasonable expectations might graduates have after completing their education?

4. Read Christopher DeWolf's "Hit the Brakes" (page 311). Compare his views of life and work with those of Niedzviecki.

Immigration: The Hate Stops Here

MICHAEL IGNATIEFF

Michael Ignatieff (b. 1947) is a scholar, writer, and journalist who was born and raised in Toronto, the son of a Russian émigré diplomat and a Canadian mother. He holds degrees from or has taught at a number of distinguished universities, including the University of Toronto, Oxford, and Harvard. Ignatieff is considered to be one of the world's leading experts on democracy, human rights, and international affairs. Along with his scholarly work and broadcasting, he is an important writer of both fiction and nonfiction. His latest work is *The Lesser Evil: Political Ethics in an Age of Terror* (2004). In February 2006, Ignatieff was elected as the Member of Parliament for the Toronto riding of Etobicoke Lakeshore.

C anadians tell the story of immigration to our country in   1
terms of two myths: that we are a welcoming people, and
that we are welcoming because those we welcome are only
too happy to leave their hatreds behind. When the two myths are
put together, they allow us to imagine Canada as a haven, a place
where people abandon their own hatreds and escape the hatreds
that drove them from their homes. This double myth is both self-
congratulatory and self-deprecating. A safe haven is not necessarily
a very exciting place—but better to be dull than dangerous. Most
newcomers have lived our dullness as deliverance.

But now we must ask two other questions. Were we ever as   2
welcoming as the myth made us out to be? And now, in a world
transfigured by terror, are we sure that newcomers are leaving their
hatreds behind?

A multicultural Canada is a great idea in principle, but in   3
reality it is more like a tacit contract of mutual indifference.
Communities share political and geographical space, but not necessarily religious, social or moral space. We have little Hong Kongs,
little Kabuls, little Jaffnas, just as we once had little Berdichevs,
little Pescaras, little Lisbons. But what must we know about each
other in order to be citizens together?

In 1999, a moderate Tamil intellectual I greatly admired was   4
blown to pieces by a car bomb in Colombo by an extremist Tamil
group. His offence: seeking a peaceful solution to the Sri Lankan
catastrophe through negotiations with the Sinhalese government.
After I went to Colombo to denounce the act of terror that had
claimed his life, I began receiving Tamil magazines arguing that
anyone from the Tamil community who sought non-violent solutions to political problems was a stooge or a fool.

The French call this strategy *la politique du pire*°: endorsing   5
strategies to make things worse so that they cannot possibly get
better. I came away from these Tamil magazines feeling that I could
say nothing to the persons who had written them. The punch line
of my story is that the postmarks were Canadian; they had been
printed and published on my native soil.

The point of the story is not to turn on the Tamil community;   6
most members despise the sort of rhetoric that I, too, despise. The
point is that we need to rethink larger Canadian myths about the
passage to Canada as a passage from hatred to civility. Is it true
now? Was it ever true?

In the 1840s, the Irish brought their hatreds with them on the   7
emigrant ships. Emigrants from the Balkans did not forget or for-
give the oppression that caused them to flee. After the Second
World War, emigrants from territories under Soviet tyranny came to

this country with all their hatreds still alive. It is an innocent, liberal assumption to suppose that hatred is always bad. It's a necessity to hate oppression. I think, for example, of the Baltic Canadians who, whenever the Soviet Bolshoi Ballet toured Canada, held up signs outside the theatre protesting Soviet tyranny. These people now seem more morally aware than those, and they included me, who thought it was time to acquiesce in the facts of life, i.e. the permanent Soviet occupation of Eastern Europe.

8   It is not always right for exile and emigration to be accompanied by political forgetting. Remembering a conquered or oppressed home is one of the duties of emigrants. The problem is that exile can freeze conviction at the moment of departure. Once in exile, groups fail to evolve; they return, once their countries are free, speaking and behaving as if it were still 1945. A case in point: Croatian exiles, who escaped to Canada in the 1940s to flee Josip Broz Tito's° imposition of Communist rule over Yugoslavia, remained more nationalistic than they would have in Tito's post-war Croatia. In exile, few could bear to learn that the country they had lost was also guilty of atrocities against Jews, Serbs, Roma and other minorities. Facing up to the reality of Ante Pavelic's° wartime regime was hard enough in Zagreb; it was harder in Toronto. Indeed, it was often said in Zagreb that the chief support for the most intransigent and aggressive Croatian nationalism after independence was to be found, not in Zagreb, but in Toronto.

9   Dual allegiances are complex: A newly-minted Canadian citizen who would not dream of assassinating a fellow citizen from some oppressor group does not hesitate to fund assassinations in the old country. Sometimes emigration is accompanied by the guilt of departure. This guilt makes diaspora groups° more violent and more extreme than those that live in the country where the oppression is taking place. Diaspora nationalism is a dangerous phenomenon because it is easier to hate from a distance: You don't have to live with the consequences—or the reprisals.

10   Canadians, new and old, need to think about what role their diasporas play in fanning and financing the hatreds of the outside world. The disturbing possibility is that Canada is not an asylum from hatred but an incubator of hatred. Are we so sure that acts of terror in Kashmir do not originate in apparently innocent funding of charitable and philanthropic appeals in Canadian cities? Are we certain that the financing of a car bomb in Jerusalem did not begin in a Canadian community? Do we know that when people die in Colombo, or Jaffna, there's no Canadian connection?

I don't have answers to these questions and it would be inflam-   11
matory to make allegations without evidence. My point is only to
ask us to rethink our myths of immigration, particularly that innocent one that portrays us as a refuge from hatred. It is clear that this
was never entirely true: Many immigrant groups that make their
lives here have not been extinguishing, but rather fanning, the
hatreds they brought with them.

It would be a good idea to get the rules for a multicultural   12
Canada clear to all. Canada means many things—and in the debate
about what it means, new voices are as valuable as older ones—but
one meaning is indisputable. We are a political community that has
outlawed the practice and advocacy of violence as an instrument of
political expression. We have outlawed it within, and we need to
outlaw it without. Just as we have laws against racial incitement or
the promulgation of ethnic hatred in order to protect our new citizens from bigotry, abuse and violence, so we must have laws for
the prosecution of anyone in Canada who aids, abets, encourages
or incites acts of terror. There may be political causes that justify
armed resistance, but there are none that justify terrorizing and
murdering civilians.

The distinction between freedom fighters and terrorists is not   13
the relativist° quagmire°. There are laws of war governing armed
resistance to oppression, as there are laws of war governing the
conduct of hostilities between states. Those who break these laws
are barbarians, whatever cause they serve. Those who target civilians to cause death and create fear are terrorists, no matter how just
their armed struggle may be. States that use terror against civilians
are as culpable as armed insurgents.

Coming to Canada is not the passage from hatred to civility   14
that we have supposed. And frankly, some hatred—of oppression,
cruelty, and racial discrimination—is wanted on the voyage. But
Canada must keep to one simple rule of the road: We are not a
political community that aids, abets, harbours or cultivates terror.

So it is appropriate to say to newcomers: You do not have to   15
embrace all our supposed civilities. You can and should keep the
memory of the injustice you have left firmly in your heart. But the
law is the law. You will have to leave your murderous fantasies of
revenge behind.

Paragraph

Words and Meanings

5	*la politique du pire*	literally, "the worst kind of politics"
8	Josip Broz Tito	Communist dictator of Yugoslavia, 1945 to 1980
	Ante Pavelic	the Croatian "Butcher of the Balkans," responsible for the deaths of some 1 million Serbs, Jews, and Roma during and after World War II
9	diaspora groups	ethnic or religious communities who have left—or been exiled from—their homeland and have established settlements elsewhere
13	relativist	relativism is a theory that considers values (e.g., truth, morality) as "relative" rather than absolute; i.e., there is no black or white—right or wrong—only shades of grey.
	quagmire	swampy ground where one cannot find sure footing; a metaphor for the relativists' view of values being conditional rather than absolute. In a quagmire, one is neither in water nor on solid ground

Structure and Strategy

1. With what introductory strategy does Ignatieff begin this essay? Read the first paragraph aloud. Identify some of the stylistic features that capture attention and make it memorable.
2. What are the functions of paragraphs 2 and 6? How do they move the ARGUMENT forward?
3. What is the TOPIC SENTENCE of paragraph 7? What kind of development is used to support it?
4. What AUDIENCE did Ignatieff have in mind for this essay? How do you know?
5. How would you describe Ignatieff's TONE?
6. With what concluding strategy does Ignatieff end his essay? Is his CONCLUSION effective? Why?
7. Is this essay primarily an argument or a persuasive piece?

Content and Purpose

1. What are the two "myths" that Canadians believe about immigration to this country? Why does Ignatieff think that they are more myth than reality?
2. It's often said that immigrants to the United States enter a "melting pot" whereas immigrants to Canada become part of a

"mosaic." How would you explain the difference? In which paragraphs does Ignatieff allude to this supposed Canadian model?
3. What is the IRONY that underlies the personal ANECDOTE Ignatieff recounts about the tragic death of a moderate Tamil intellectual?
4. Do you think that Ignatieff believes that, once they arrive here, immigrants from strife-torn nations should somehow forget the politics that may have driven them to Canada?
5. What is "diaspora nationalism" (paragraph 9), and what does Ignatieff think of it?
6. Ignatieff's proposals for dealing with ethnic hatred in a multicultural Canada are presented in paragraph 12. Summarize them in your own words.
7. What does Ignatieff see as the difference between freedom fighters and terrorists? Do you agree or disagree?

Suggestions for Writing

1. Do you agree or disagree with Ignatieff's argument that the "rules for a multicultural Canada" must be made clear to all (paragraph 9)? Write an essay explaining your opinion.
2. Read Denise Chong's "Being Canadian" (page 222) or Wayson Choy's "I'm a Banana and Proud of It" (page 205). Compare Chong's or Choy's view of what should be maintained—or left behind—from one's original culture with Ignatieff's view.
3. When people are forced to flee a country in which they have been oppressed, what behaviours and attitudes should they adopt to help them ease the transition from one culture to another? Write an essay exploring the complex phenomenon of cultural adaptation.

The Moment of Truth

AL GORE

Al Gore (b. 1948) served both in the U.S. Congress and as vice president under Bill Clinton (1993 to 2001). He ran as the Democratic Party's candidate for president in 2000 and won the popular vote. However, he was defeated in the Electoral College by Republican George W. Bush after a recount of votes in Florida took the election decision to the Supreme Court. He has always been a proponent for the environment. He published *Earth in the Balance* in 1993 and *An Inconvenient Truth*, which was the basis for the Academy Award-winning documentary film, in 2006. In recognition of his environmental advocacy, Gore was awarded the Nobel Peace Prize in 2007.

1   Clichés are, by definition, over used. But here is a rare exception—a certifiable cliché that warrants more exposure, because it carries meaning deeply relevant to the biggest challenge our civilization has ever confronted. The Chinese expression for "crisis" consists of two characters: 危機. The first is a symbol for "danger"; the second is a symbol for "opportunity."

2   The rapid accumulation of global-warming pollution in the Earth's atmosphere is now confronting human civilization with a crisis like no other we have ever encountered. This climate crisis is, indeed, extremely dangerous, but it also presents unprecedented opportunities. Before we can get to the opportunities, however, it is crucial to define the danger, and to discuss how it is that we in the United States seem to be having such difficulty perceiving that danger.

危

3   The climate crisis may at times appear to be happening slowly, but in fact it is a true planetary emergency. The voluminous evidence suggests strongly that, unless we act boldly and quickly to deal with the causes of global warming, our world will likely experience a string of catastrophes, including deadlier Hurricane Katrinas° in both the Atlantic and Pacific.

4   We are melting virtually all of the mountain glaciers in the world—including those in the Rockies, the Sierras, the Andes, and the Alps—and, more ominously, the massive ice field on the roof of the world, on the enormous Tibetan Plateau, which has 100 times more ice than the Alps, and which supplies up to half of the drinking water of 40 percent of the world's people, through seven river systems that all originate there: the Indus, the Ganges, the Brahmaputra, the Salween, the Mekong, the Yangtze and the Yellow.

5   Even more important, we are rapidly melting the vast, but relatively thin, floating ice cap that covers the Arctic Ocean. For the first time, scientists are finding significant numbers of polar bears that have died by drowning, as the distance from the shores of the Arctic to the edge of the ice cap has stretched in places to 60 kilometers or more. At present, the North Polar cap helps to cool the planet by reflecting the vast majority of the sunlight that hits the Arctic during six months of the year. It is like a gigantic mirror larger than the entire United States. But the growing areas of open water left as the ice cap melts are absorbing the vast majority of the energy coming from the Sun, raising temperatures at the top of our planet far more rapidly than anywhere else.

6   We are beginning to melt—and possibly de-stabilize—the enormous, 10,000-foot-thick mound of ice on top of Greenland and the

equally enormous mass of ice of West Antarctica, which is propped up precariously against the tops of islands, poised to slip into the sea. Either of these massive, land-based ice sheets would, if it melted or broke up and slid into the ocean, raise the sea level worldwide by more than 20 feet. The largest ice mass of all on the planet—East Antarctica—was long thought to be still growing. Until recently, that is, when a new, in-depth scientific survey showed that it, too, may be beginning to melt.

Since the entire climate system of Earth is formed by the plan- 7 etwide pattern of wind and ocean currents, which redistribute heat from the tropics to the poles, there is growing concern that the relatively stable pattern that has persisted for 11,000 years—since the last ice age and before the first appearance of cities—may now be on the verge of radical and disruptive changes. The Gulf Stream, the monsoon cycle in the Indian Ocean, the El Niño/La Niña cycle in the Eastern Pacific, and the jet streams, among the other circulatory phenomena, are all at risk of being pushed into new and unfamiliar patterns.

Global warming, together with the cutting and burning of 8 forests and the destruction of other critical habitats, is causing the loss of living species at a rate comparable to that of the extinction of dinosaurs 65 million years ago. Most scientists theorize that that event, by the way, was caused by a giant asteroid colliding with the Earth. This time it is not an asteroid wreaking havoc; it is us. We are recklessly dumping so much carbon dioxide into the Earth's atmosphere that we have literally changed the relationship between the Earth and the Sun, altering the balance of energy between our planet and the rest of the universe, so the buildup of heat energy that should be re-radiated by the Earth is beginning to wilt, melt, dry out, and parch delicate components of the planet's living systems.

More than 70 percent of the planet's surface is covered by 9 ocean, and a series of new, comprehensive studies show that the amount of CO_2 being absorbed into the oceans is about one-third of what we have put into the environment with the burning of fossil fuels. As a result, the oceans of the world are becoming more acid, and the total amount of carbonic acid—even though it is a relatively weak acid—is beginning to change the mix of carbonate and bicarbonate ions in the oceans. This interferes with the ability of corals to form their calcium-carbonate skeletons, which constitute the base of many food chains in the oceans. Even more ominously, the amounts of carbonic acid we are continuing to sink into the oceans will, if we don't change the current reckless pattern, make it more difficult for many ocean creatures, large and tiny, to make shells, because the shells would instantly dissolve in the newly acid ocean water, the way chalk (also calcium carbonate) dissolves in vinegar. Continuing on our current path will return the oceans to a chemical pH balance that last existed 300 million years ago—when the Earth was a very different planet from the one that gave birth to and nurtured the human species.

10   All of this, incredibly, could be set in motion in the lifetime of the children already living—unless we act boldly and quickly. Even more incredibly, some of the leading scientific experts are now telling us that without dramatic changes we are in grave danger of crossing a point of no return within the next ten years! So the message is unmistakable. This crisis means danger!

11   But in order to move through the danger to seize the opportunity, we have first to recognize that we are in fact facing a crisis. So why is it that our leaders seem not to hear such clarion° warnings? Are they resisting the truth because they know that the moment they acknowledge it they will face a moral imperative to act? Is it simply more convenient to ignore the warnings? Perhaps, but inconvenient truths do not go away just because they are not seen. Indeed, when they are not responded to, their significance doesn't diminish; it grows.

12   For example, the Bush administration was warned on August 6, 2001, of an attack by al-Qaeda: "Bin Ladin Determined to Strike in US," said the intelligence community in a message so important that it was the headline of the president's daily briefing that day, five weeks before the attacks of September 11. Didn't he see that clear warning? Why were no questions asked, meetings called, evidence marshaled, clarifications sought?

13   The Bible says, "Where there is no vision, the people perish."

14   Four Augusts later, as Hurricane Katrina was roaring across the unusually warm water of the Gulf of Mexico and growing into a deadly monster that was less than two days away from slamming into New Orleans, the administration received another clear warning: the levees—which had been built to protect the city against smaller, less powerful hurricanes—were in grave danger. But once again an urgent warning was ignored. The videotapes of one session make clear that the president heard the warnings but, again, asked not a single question.

15   This is not a partisan analysis. A recent report by Republicans in the House of Representatives called the White House reaction a "blinding lack of situational awareness." Republican representative Tom Davis of Virginia, the chairman of the House Committee on Government Reform, which produced the report, added, "The White House failed to act on the massive amounts of information at its disposal." Coupled with "disjointed decision making," the

report continued, the president's failure to see the danger "need-lessly compounded and prolonged Katrina's horror."

Where there is a blinding lack of situational awareness, the people perish. 16

Nearly 70 years ago, when a horrible and unprecedented storm of another kind was gathering in Europe, British prime minister Neville Chamberlain° found it inconvenient to see the truth about the nature of the evil threat posed by the Nazis. In criticizing his government's blinding lack of awareness, Winston Churchill° said, "So they go on in strange paradox, decided only to be undecided, resolved to be irresolute, adamant for drift, solid for fluidity, all-powerful to be impotent." After the appeasement° at Munich, Churchill said, "This is only the first sip, the first foretaste, of a bitter cup which will be proffered to us year by year—unless by supreme recovery of moral health and martial vigor we rise again and take our stand for freedom." Then he warned prophetically that "the era of procrastination, of half measures, of soothing and baffling expedients, of delays, is coming to a close. In its place, we are entering a period of consequences." 17

Today, there are dire warnings that the worst catastrophe in the history of human civilization is bearing down on us, gathering strength as it comes. And these warnings have also been met with a blinding lack of awareness, by the Congress as well as by the administration. 18

After the tragedy of Hurricane Katrina, many Americans now believe that we have entered a period of consequences—that Katrina, as horrible as it was, may have been the first sip of a bitter cup which will be proffered to us over and over again until we act on the truth we have wished would go away. And they are begin-ning to demand that the administration open its eyes and look at the truth, no matter how inconvenient it might be for all of us—not least for the special interests that want us to ignore global warming. 19

As Abraham Lincoln° said during our time of greatest trial, "We must disenthrall° ourselves, and then we shall save our country." America is beginning to awaken. And now we will save our planet. 20

機

So it is time for the good news: we can solve this crisis, and as we finally do accept the truth of our situation and turn to boldly face down the danger that is stalking us, we will find that it is also bringing us unprecedented opportunity. I'm not referring just to new jobs and new profits, though there will be plenty of both. Today we have all the technologies we need to start the fight against global warming. We can build clean engines. We can harness 21 the sun and wind. We can stop wasting energy. We can use the Earth's plentiful coal resources without heating the planet.

22   The procrastinators and deniers would have us believe that this will be painful and impossibly expensive. But in recent years dozens of companies have cut emissions of heat-trapping gases and saved money. Some of the world's largest companies are moving aggressively to capture the enormous economic opportunities in a clean-energy future.

23   But there's something far more precious than the economic gains that will be made. This crisis is bringing us an opportunity to experience what few generations in history ever have had the privilege of knowing: a generational mission; the exhilaration of a compelling moral purpose; a shared and unifying cause; the thrill of being forced by circumstances to put aside the pettiness and conflict that so often stifle the restless human need for transcendence; the opportunity to rise.

24   When we do rise, it will fill our spirits and bind us together. Those who are now suffocating in cynicism and despair will be able to breathe freely. Those who are now suffering from a loss of meaning in their lives will find hope. When we rise, we will experience an epiphany as we discover that this crisis is not really about politics at all. It is a moral and spiritual challenge.

25   What is at stake is the survival of our civilization and the habitability of the Earth. Or as one eminent scientist put it, the pending question is whether an opposable thumb and a neocortex° are a viable combination on this planet.

26   The new understanding we will gain—about who we really are—will give us the moral capacity to comprehend the true nature of other, related challenges that are also desperately in need of being defined as moral imperatives with practical solutions: HIV/AIDS and other pandemics that are ravaging large parts of humankind, global poverty, the ongoing redistribution of the world's wealth from the poor to the rich, the ongoing genocide in Darfur, famines in other parts of Africa, chronic civil wars, the destruction of ocean fisheries, families that don't function, communities that don't commune, the erosion of democracy in America, and the re-feudalization of the public forum.

27   Consider once again what happened during the crisis of global Fascism°. When England and then America and our allies ultimately did rise to meet the threat, we won two wars simultaneously, in Europe and in the Pacific. And by the end of those terrible wars, the Allies had gained the moral authority and vision to create the Marshall Plan°—and persuade the taxpayers to pay for it! They had gained the spiritual capacity and wisdom to rebuild Japan and

Europe and launch the renewal of the very nations they had just defeated in the war. In the process, they laid the foundation for 50 years of peace and prosperity. One of their commanders, General Omar Bradley, said at the end of World War II, "It is time we steered by the stars and not by the lights of each passing ship."

And now so must we. For this, too, is a critical moment. Ultimately, it is not about any scientific discussion or political dialogue; it is about who we are as human beings. It is about our capacity to transcend our limitations, to rise to this new occasion. To see with our hearts, as well as our heads, the response that is now called for. This is a moral, ethical, and spiritual challenge. 28

Just as we can no longer ignore this challenge, neither should we fear it. Instead, we should welcome it. Both the danger and the opportunity. And then we will meet it because we must. We have accepted and met other great challenges in the past. We declared our liberty and then won it. We designed a new form of government. We freed the slaves. We gave women the right to vote. We took on Jim Crow° and segregation. We cured polio and helped eradicate smallpox, we landed on the moon, we brought down Communism, and we helped end apartheid. We even solved a global environmental crisis—the hole in the stratospheric ozone layer—because Republicans and Democrats, rich nations and poor nations, businessmen and scientists, all came together to shape a solution. 29

And now we face a crisis with unprecedented danger that also presents an opportunity like no other. As we rise to meet this historic challenge, it promises us prosperity, common purpose, and the renewal of our moral authority. 30

We should not wait. We cannot wait. We must not wait. 31

The only thing missing is political will. But in our democracy, political will is a renewable resource. 32

Words and Meanings

Paragraph

Hurricane Katrina	major storm that devastated New Orleans and the Gulf Coast in August 2005	3
clarion	loud and clear	11
Neville Chamberlain	British prime minister from 1937–40, known for his policy of appeasement toward the Nazis	17
Winston Churchill	British prime minister who led England through WWII (1939–45) to defeat the Nazis	
appeasement	giving in or giving concessions to an enemy to avoid war	

20	Abraham Lincoln	American president during the U.S. Civil War (1861–65)
	disenthrall	set free
25	opposable thumb and neocortex	an allusion to the human capacity for tool-making and high-level thinking
27	global Fascism	the Nazi regimes in Germany, Italy, and Japan
	Marshall Plan	reconstruction plan for Europe after World War II
29	Jim Crow	discriminatory laws in parts of the United States that segregated public facilities according to race (1876–1964)

Structure and Strategy

1. Why does Gore begin his essay with what he acknowledges is a cliché?
2. Which paragraphs deal with the dangers that Gore thinks are the result of global warming? Which paragraphs deal with the opportunities that he thinks can result from global warming?
3. What kind of evidence does Gore use for support in paragraph 4?
4. Identify three quotations that Gore uses to support his points. Do you think they are effective? Why or why not?
5. What is the major point of transition in the essay?
6. Paragraphs 17 and 27 create an analogy between the crisis of global warming and what historical event? Do you think the analogy is a good one? Why or why not?
7. Identify the parallelism in paragraphs 24 and 31.
8. Is this essay an example of argument or persuasion? (See the Introduction to Unit 7, pages 241–44.)

Content and Purpose

1. What is the crisis that Gore describes as a "true planetary emergency" (paragraph 3)?
2. Paragraphs 4 through 9 deal with at least seven different dangerous results of global warming. Identify five of them. How many of them did you already know about? Which do you feel are most dangerous?
3. What does Gore argue is the political barrier to solving the problem of global warming (paragraphs 11–17)? What other events does he see as examples of the same political barrier? Do you think Gore himself may have political reasons for arguing this position? (See the biographical note.)
4. Identify the economic opportunities that Gore argues will result from the political decision to solve the crisis of global warming.

5. Beyond the economic gains that Gore says will come with the resolution of global warming, he maintains that a sense of "generational mission" (paragraph 23) will offer people a variety of rewards. What are they? Do you agree or disagree? Why?
6. What other problems will the "moral capacity" to reverse global warming enable human beings to resolve? (See paragraph 26.)
7. Identify the categorical statements about the global warming crisis in paragraphs 18 and 25. ("Categorical" means unambiguously explicit, direct.) Do you agree with Gore or do you think that he's engaging in rhetorical overstatement? Why?
8. What kind of encouragement does Gore offer in paragraph 29? In other words, why does he remain an optimist about a crisis that he sees as threatening life on the planet?

Suggestions for Writing

1. Do you agree with Gore's thesis that global warming presents a crisis situation? Do some focused research and then write an essay that argues either for or against the ideas in "The Moment of Truth."
2. Read Wade Davis's "The End of the Wild" (page 48), John Dixon's "Saving the Songs of Innocence" (page 186), or Lewis Thomas's "Altruism" (page 234). Write an essay that compares or contrasts "The Moment of Truth" with one of these essays in terms of form (structure) and content.

Additional Suggestions for Writing: Argument and Persuasion

Choose one of the topics below and write an essay based on it. Think through your position carefully, formulate your opinion, and identify logical reasons for holding that opinion. Construct a clear thesis statement before you begin to write the paper.

1. Violence against an established government is (or is not) justified in certain circumstances.
2. Racial profiling is (or is not) necessary for the police to protect society against criminals.
3. Genetically modified food should (or should not) be banned.
4. Canada should (or should not) adopt the U.S. dollar.
5. The government of Canada should (or should not) decriminalize the use of marijuana.

6. Same-sex marriage strengthens (or weakens) civil society.
7. Males and females should (or should not) play on the same sports teams.
8. Parents should (or should not) be legally responsible for property damage (e.g., vandalism, theft) caused by their underage children.
9. Children should (or should not) be responsible for the care of their elderly parents.
10. Private religious schools should (or should not) receive government subsidies.
11. Critically ill patients should (or should not) be permitted to end their lives if and when they choose.
12. A teacher should (or should not) aim most of the course work at the weakest students in the class.
13. Online pornography is (or is not) harmful to the social fabric.
14. Dishonesty is sometimes (or is never) the best policy.
15. Argue for or against the following statement: "One thing is certain: offering employment—the steady kind, with benefits, holiday pay, a measure of security, and maybe even union representation—has fallen out of economic fashion." (Naomi Klein)

UNIT 8

Potluck

INTRODUCTION

"Potluck" is a time-honoured Canadian tradition at school meetings, team parties, religious gatherings, Scout and Guide celebrations, card parties, and many other social occasions featuring a meal. Everybody brings a favourite dish to share with everyone else. The resulting lunch or dinner could, of course, end up being all desserts or all salads; however, for some reason, perhaps having to do with Canadian courtesy and variety, this never happens. Potluck meals are usually a culinary treat as well as a social delight.

In Unit 8, we provide a selection of essays that range as widely in content and style as does a potluck buffet. Our offerings are not presented in any particular order: we encourage you to sample each one and decide for yourself if it's a literary appetizer, entrée, salad, dessert—or something else entirely. Bon appétit!

*In the first of our potluck dishes, Christine Pountney raises
provocative issues about the rituals of bullfighting and our
squeamish relationship to the animals we eat. Caution: there
is some exceedingly graphic description here. Not for the faint
of heart!*

The Blood on Their Hands

CHRISTINE POUNTNEY

1   Three months ago, I was sitting in the Las Ventas stadium in
Madrid, waiting for a bullfight to begin. It was a Sunday
evening and I was sipping a whiskey and water that I had
bought off a vendor who called it "weekie" and had a grey han-
dlebar moustache. My arm was in a sling—I had broken it two
weeks earlier. When the matadors walked out to parade the bullring
and salute el presidente, they too wore what appeared to be slings,
but were in fact their capes folded intricately around their cocked
right arms. They doffed their black braided caps and bowed. The
shining trumpets signalled from a patch of land on the opposite side
of the stadium, the sound at once jaunty and portentous.

2   I had been to a bullfight the summer before in Pamplona and
appreciated the blatant honesty of the proceedings—not a
euphemistic turning away, but the acknowledgment of blood lust
as an aspect of the human psyche. A matador had been gored. One
of his testicles was caught on camera flying through the air above
him. It was terrible and compelling. A friend said it was the last
time she would go to a bullfight, while I simply felt more intrigued
by the whole sport.

3   By and large, the bulls do not stand a chance against the
onslaught of picadors, banderillos and, finally, the matador himself.
However, none of these roles is without risk. I once saw a picador
trapped underneath his horse after it was knocked over by a bull
that was bearing down on it, horns jabbed and locked into the
quilted mattress around the horse's ribs. He was pinned for several
minutes.

4   I remember thinking how the spectacle was a healthy reminder
that killing is a part of eating meat. The bulls have a good life until
they enter the ring—downright pampered. After their deaths, they
are slaughtered immediately and every last bit of them is trucked
out of the stadium to restaurants around the city.

5   A few days earlier I had ordered bull's tail at a restaurant on
the Plaza Santa Ana. The waiters were fussing over a man at a table
next to ours. The man was small, elegant and light-footed as a
heron. "He's a famous matador," my friend said. "He comes from a
poor family in the Basque country, but he's a celebrity in Madrid."

When the bulls are killed, four high-spirited mules drag them 6
to an abattoir located on the premises. During a bathroom break
between bullfights, I found myself watching a butcher sling a bull
up by the tail with an industrial-sized hook. The bull rose up like
the Titanic on a slow hydraulic winch. The butcher sawed the head
off and slung it across the floor to be tagged and labelled, along
with the innards: heart and liver. Then he peeled the hide off like a
heavy canvas sail. The butcher used a power saw, knives and axes.
In under eight minutes, the bull had been reduced to manageable
blocks of wet, red meat.

What a lesson. I had never seen an animal that size butchered. I 7
was standing on a trail of bull's blood beside a father and his two
young sons. This was a good lesson for them to learn, too, I
thought. It showed the source, the impressive bulk and hot life still
steaming up from the ground. The boys' solemn quietude gave me
hope that a kind of respect was being learned, some atavistic value
system reinforced. Look, boys, this is what we live off. It all comes
from the earth. It was one life offered up for another: a sacrifice.
And watching it seemed like paying homage, because you couldn't
help but be impressed.

Between bullfights a man in a red blazer and navy pants with a 8
red stripe down the outside seam would come out like a circus
ringmaster to announce the stats on the next bull: its pedigree, its
weight, its name. He held these facts aloft on a board fastened to a
pole. He reminded me of the bikini-clad ladies between fights at a
boxing ring. At one point, another man came out to re-chalk the
inner circle drawn onto the sandy floor of the bullring. It made me
think of a baseball diamond and how different things are in
America. I wondered if there wasn't some kind of analogy here: the
matador as the pitcher, the bull as the lone batter—the individual
against the mob. Only in baseball, nobody gets hurt.

North Americans: the stadium was littered with them. Tourists 9
like myself. If they weren't too outraged to attend in the first place,
they were here for the catharsis of a real blood sport, something we
don't have much of in North America. With the exception, perhaps,
of professional boxing and the fights that have become standard
fare at an ice hockey game, we don't approve of brutality. Not in a
public, ritualized performance, and certainly not involving animals.
Because animals are innocent—though we still consume their flesh
at an astonishing rate.

How squeamish North American culture has become and yet 10
how violent it still is. I can't help but feel a certain hypocrisy at
work. It's almost as if, influenced by the idealism of the puritans,
we would like to appear better than we are. But is there a connec-

tion between this bombastic piety and the quiet proliferation of our worst tendencies? And what purpose could a bona fide blood sport like bullfighting serve?

11   What I find so refreshing about bullfighting is how a blunt truth is at work. There is blood and there is death. Nobody is trying to convince you otherwise. And the whole spectacle provides you with an opportunity to analyze your own relationship to those two things.

12   To be honest, I felt excitement at the matador's risk. I felt a primal desire to see more gore, and when I did, as in the case of the matador who lost a testicle, it was wonderful and awful at the same time. I felt the urge to witness the matador's pain at the same time as my chagrin at having that desire. I didn't really, in the end, wish that pain on him. But whatever impulse I may have to witness the pain of another human being was stimulated, examined and deflated in a vicarious way. This is the purpose of catharsis. The ancient Greeks understood the benefit of this exercise.

13   The death of the bull is always tragic. You see how blameless the bull is, how innocent and, in this respect, how superior to the human being. Its behaviour at times is heartbreaking. How did I get here, you see the bull ask himself. All he knows is that he must protect himself.

14   When the matador has done his work, the other bullfighters come out to assist in the bull's demise, like inverted paramedics. They flash their fuchsia capes to make the bull wag its head from side to side, thus tricking the animal into shredding its own innards with the sword shoved to the hilt between its shoulder blades. The matador serves the death blow with a small knife, severing the nerves at the base of the skull. When the bull finally slumps lifeless to the ground, it is the end of something big. It is momentous. It has resonance. It is both literal and metaphoric.

15   However, the new Spanish generation is becoming squeamish, too. They would prefer to disavow their own brutal traditions. The bullfight in Madrid was badly attended.

16   I feel sorry for the matadors, seeking their glory at such high expense to a dwindling crowd of mainly old people. Their way of life is dying out, but the youth of Spain no longer want to be associated with an outmoded blood sport. They, too, have entered the age in which it is not okay to club a seal, but it is okay to bomb Iraq. But these are not brave politics; they are the politics of squeamishness. And squeamishness has so much more in common with sentimentality than it does with compassion.

Novelist Christine Pountney was born in Vancouver in 1971. She spent six years in London but is now living in Toronto, where she teaches creative writing at the University of Toronto and writes for a variety of publications. Her novels include *Last Chance Texaco* (2000) and *The Best Way You Know How* (2006).

The article that follows is more than an account of one man's experience in what Hal Niedzviecki would call a "stupid job." Strolling through the city with a high-definition television screen attached to his head, the author is literally a walking advertisement. Shaughnessy Bishop-Stall's objective is to make us aware of some of the myriad ways in which consumers are manipulated in our market-driven society. Only recently has "product placement" come to the attention of the public as a possible concern. Wait until you find out about "roaches"!

I, Pixman

SHAUGHNESSY BISHOP-STALL

DAY 1

When a friend you haven't seen for a long time tells you he's got a job for you as a high-definition television, you assume he's leaving something out. But apparently my old pal Max Lenderman, in a rare moment of simplicity, was being straightforward.

It's 7 A.M. when I get to the rendezvous point. There are six of us in the parking lot. A spiky-haired guy introduces himself as Joe, our captain, then opens the back of a van. And there, like a half-dozen alien hostages, are the Pixmen.

A Pixman comprises a screen, speakers and a heavy, hard-cased bag containing a small car battery and a portable DVD player. The bag fits onto your back like a backpack. From the top of it, an adjustable metal bar that looks like the Canadarm bends forward to support the high-definition television screen that hovers above your head. While a looped image plays in rotation, the accompanying dialogue and soundtrack blast out from the speakers built into the bag on your back. The whole apparatus weighs about 20 kilograms, and the screen leaves you constantly off balance. It is all very awkward. There is no word for those of us who carry the Pixman, so we are Pixmen, too.

We hoist the bags onto each other's backs. We press a button on the screen and it flashes to life as the speakers kick in. We tighten the straps across our waists and chests, nod once to each other, and head down the street, staring straight ahead like soldiers. I'm about to spend every day this week as a walking TV in downtown Toronto.

5   It doesn't take long for my back to start aching. We are advertising a television show. Because of the confidentiality agreement I signed, I'll call it *The Summy Dummy Show*. Not everyone is happy to see us. Some people stop and laugh. Some gaze up at the screen as though they're at home on the couch, watching TV. At a particularly low point, two young ladies inform me, in French, that I am making them sad. Strangest of all, however, is that most people just glance at the clip of *The Summy Dummy Show* and carry on—as if this isn't strange at all.

6   When my first day is over, I meet Max for a bottle of beer. "What the hell's going on out there?" I say, and collapse into a chair. My feet hurt.

7   "I told you you wouldn't like it," says Max. "I am a marketer now."

8   "Meaning?"

9   "Companies hire me to go into places where they have no inroads, in ways they don't know how. I have guerrillas on the streets in every major city."

10   "What's a guerrilla?"

11   "That's what you are."

12   "I thought I was a Pixman."

13   "First and foremost you're a guerrilla."

14   According to Max, marketing guerrillas are not that different from military ones. They're mobile and adaptable. They know the terrain, know the people and use the element of surprise. They strike fast and hard, then get the hell out. "You just gotta keep your head up," says Max, "and watch out for the cops and the culture jammers."

15   The jammers are like bizarro marketers: anti-corporate, anti-globalization, anti-media. They stage grassroots movements against various large corporations by using marketers' own tactics against them. And although the jammers see Max as the enemy, he has nothing but respect for them. He describes them as organized, committed, smart, daring and disciplined—"a basically good bunch of guys."

16   They consider a man like Max the worst offender, because he can infiltrate places that are usually reserved for non-marketing purposes. For the jammers, that's the final invasion by the corporate structure. Max explains that we are living in an oligarchical system now, with power in the hands of "the Merchants of Cool"— seven companies: Viacom, News Corp., Bertelsmann, Time Warner, Vivendi Universal, Sony and Walt Disney. The only thing they don't

control is personal interaction. That is the last bastion of power, and they're all fighting to get control of it. "And that's where I come in," says Max, "because I can get it for them."

"But doesn't that make you a tool of the merchants, or the oli- 17
garchy, or whatever?"

"Not if I can co-opt that power. In the face of mass marketing, 18
the individual's ability to spend money on what they truly want is the only thing left to fight for."

"What does this have to do with me being a TV?" 19

"That's just one campaign among many, but it's an important 20
one—it's the first time anyone's ever combined the Pixmen with the roaches."

The Pixmen, apparently, act as a sort of diversion. While we're 21
walking the streets, adding our message to the rest of the white noise, the roaches are working the angles—spreading the message like a virus. In any café or bar, any movie lineup or subway car, the roaches could be there. They are young and outgoing, and they're talking to each other about *The Summy Dummy Show*. They've got sample scripts, but don't have to follow them. They just talk about the show so that people can overhear them.

"Do people know about this?" 22

"They know some of it. *The New York Times* published an 23
exposé on roach marketing, for example. Then there are the screw-ups. Sony Ericsson blew a perfectly good guerrilla campaign for their new cellphone camera by going public with it. They got people all riled up about roaching. But even that might have been a bit of marketing jiujitsu, when you look at the press they got."

"Marketing jiujitsu?" 24

Max developed the theory of marketing jiujitsu—which refers 25
to the martial art in which one turns the weight and strength of an attacker against him—when he overheard two teens talking about a T-shirt that read "Satan Inside." One of the kids didn't get it, and the other explained that it's a takeoff on the "Intel Inside," and that Intel has Pentium chips in almost every computer, dominating the market, something consumer groups might not approve of. Max realized that the kid was giving a perfect marketing pitch, and that now his buddy would know that Intel's chips are omnipresent. Hence marketing jiujitsu: taking negative corporate brand percep-tion and making it into a de facto brand enhancer.

DAY 2

The six of us spend most of the day in the suburbs, walking around 26
malls and parking lots. We try to hold our heads high—as though we have some noble purpose—but it's impossible. We feel like

304 UNIT EIGHT • POTLUCK

idiots, and I'm not the only one with a sore back. My fellow Pixmen are a tae kwon do champion, a struggling actor, an ultimate fighter, a street kid who writes for a skateboard magazine and a self-proclaimed neo-hippie. Like me, they have no idea what we're doing. We lean against garbage cans to take some of the weight off, then walk. I wonder how the hell I ended up here.

27   I met Maxim Lenderman years ago, when I responded to a cryptic newspaper ad calling for "brave young writers." He suggested that we meet in a bar, and when I asked how I'd know him, he said, "I'll be the funny-looking guy with the big ears."

28   What I found was an imposing mix of Tommy Lee, Rasputin and—when he took off his black leather cowboy hat and grinned—Alfred E. Neuman on acid. He ordered us Jack Daniel's and we became the best of friends. He'd just come to Canada from the States and was starting up a web magazine, but had no interest in talking business. We talked about everything else instead. And although we were already both too old to think we could change the world, we decided to do it anyway. The first piece I wrote for him he rejected and told me to send [it] to a real magazine . . . . That's how I became a professional writer.

29   So it is with Max; people follow his advice and good things happen. He's big and amorphous and walks into the most powerful boardrooms as long-haired renegade rocker, or mohawked punk, or bespectacled revolutionary artist. He sits down, grins at the money men and starts talking. And then, in the middle of his spiel, he rolls up his sleeves. It's always the same: they see his tattoos and start to slobber. The most elusive thing for these guys, after all, is authenticity, and suddenly they imagine they've got it. They cut him a cheque and send him out to do his baddest.

30   At first, the idea was simple—you take them for small things now, and later for the things that change the world. In 2001, I remember Max saying, "OK, what would be fun? Nice cars and girls and some toys to play with." Two weeks later we were driving to frosh weeks at campuses across Canada, leading a convoy of everything he'd asked for. The models were to be auctioned off for dates to frat boys using Fido's new text-messaging system. The cars were to be spray-painted, and the school that did it best would win their car for their drive-safe program. The toys were life-sized renditions of Jenga—giant blocks that the engineering students would turn into towers.

31   It worked well and was fun—until the morning of September 11, 2001, when it all came crashing down. By the time we pulled the plug on the campaign, the spray paint on the cars read, "Burn, Babylon, Burn," and the world was changing.

Max's official biography merely hints at the life he led: "He graduated with a BA in international relations and a minor in Russian existentialism from Tufts University. He studied economics at UCL in London, England, then joined the U.S. Peace Corps, where he drilled water wells in Chad. He began his journalism career as a writer for such New York-based publications as *The Wall Street Journal, Beverage World, IMPACT, Wine Spectator* and *Cigar Aficionado*. He contributed frequently to youth lifestyle magazines such as *High Times, POPsmear* and *The Hemperor*, when not playing in a punk band called Mud Farm." 32

As long as I've known him, Max has been torn between his desire to do good and artful things and his unique ability to sell ideas for money. After 9/11, however, these parts became consolidated by passion and purpose. He brought together a small team of communications experts, artists and writers who he hoped could help him do the impossible—create independent, truthful media for the world that would be left when the dust had settled. It's not that we were naïve. We went along with it based on empirical evidence: no idea of Max's had ever failed. 33

Those were tricky days, and not long after the project fell apart Max and I went our separate ways. I lived in a Toronto shantytown with no electricity and little access to the outside world, planning to write a book. According to Max, he too went underground. But we're above ground now, and together again, and I still don't understand a thing. 34

DAY 3

Despite ourselves, we have all memorized *The Summy Dummy Show* trailer word for word and beat for beat. It is always there, like a taunt from the cable gods as we stumble around on this confusing earth. Our screens get caught in tree branches, bang into street signs. We lose our balance and get tossed into traffic like unwanted action figures. 35

Some people find us cool and futuristic, as if we're wearing jetpacks or *Ghostbusters* outfits. We try to pick up girls. "I can get you on the big screen," says Jeff, the ultimate fighter. Or, "You know what they say about guys with high definition." But then, inevitably, some punk says, "Don't you feel stupid with a TV on your head?" 36

In the winter of 2001, Max designed the first roach campaign in Canada. Based on an idea that had worked in New York—whereby attractive young club patrons ask someone closer to the bar to order a new brand of cooler for them—Max's company marketed a new 37 cigarette deodorant. In every major Canadian city, the roaches joined smoking circles outside office buildings and ostentatiously sprayed themselves before re-entering the building. Invariably, someone would ask about it and the roach would respond, "I don't want to smell like smoke when I walk into my interview." Everyone wanted to be sprayed.

38   This kind of subterfuge, says Max, also known as viral or buzz marketing, is a direct reaction to, even the antithesis of, traditional advertising. It's based on the pretext that consumers are now so marketing-savvy that they block out an ad campaign faster than you can say "sponsored by." The only way that you can reach them is to rise above the clutter, or to go where they don't expect you.

39   Max believes that roaching worked in part because of September 11. Not only did companies have to find less blatant ways of marketing, he explains, but after the attacks people were suddenly open to conversations with strangers. This new social interaction helped open the door for street-level marketing. "I know it sounds opportunistic, but it wasn't conscious on our parts. It just happened to make it work. It made it more acceptable. There's a part of me that wishes people would call me on it—get mad that I'm influencing them without their consent, just so I could find a way to harness that indignation and point it toward their TVs and radios and newspapers, and blast away."

40   "Because you don't have as much power as corporate media, that makes your tactics more acceptable? Why don't you just let people know what you're doing?"

41   "I don't need them to know right now. I'm still experimenting with methods. But I'm quickly realizing that roaching is imperfect. At the end of the day," says Max, refilling our glasses, "the paradigm of deceptive marketing is pretty much obsolete. Look, I used to hate the fact that I was pushing brands. I did it because I had to pay the bills. But now I know that marketing is the only thing that can really affect things. I tried to write, I tried to find water in Africa, I tried to create new ideas. None of that works in this world."

42   According to Max, mass marketing is the greatest form of mind control, because it makes you think you're believing in yourself: the power at your fingertips, the fastest processor, the choice of a new generation. The moment you Just Do It is the moment you've been tricked into believing in yourself for no discernable reason—the blindest faith of all.

43   Max's cellphone is ringing. "Just a minute," he says, "I gotta get this." His phone rings all the time, and when he chooses to answer you can bet it's worth listening in. "Max here. We just need some,

um, happy people dancing and being, um, happy…. No, for that we need the hug squads. Like that thing for the lotion company, the girls massaging people's hands on the streets. … No, they're just going to go up and hug people…. No, it's not assault—it's just hugging! Look, I gotta go." He clicks the phone closed. "Where were we?"

"Hug squads?" I ask, all innocent wonder, tinged with disdain. 44 "Happy people doing happy things? You haven't really become a rat, have you?"

"I'm the same as I ever was," he says, flashing a smile. "I'm a 45 pirate."

DAY 4

It appears everyone in this city has been brainwashed into thinking 46 they are uniquely funny: "Hey, man, switch it to the golf channel!" "Put on the porn, dude." People find it hilarious to ask if we know there's a TV on our head. At least one of us invariably loves it, and today it's Jimmy, the skateboarder.

"Yes, ma'am, I do know there's a TV on my head. How could I 47 not know? Tell you what—why don't *you* put this thing on and we'll see how cute it is then…. No, really, take it! Take it! Come back here!"

"This isn't good publicity," says our captain. But I think of it as 48 marketing jiujitsu, this woman telling everyone that she was chased by *The Summy Dummy Show*. Even if we warned people how awful the show is, we'd still be getting the word out.

One of the tenets of guerrilla warfare, as Max has explained, is 49 mobility. That doesn't just refer to physical action. Word of mouth can be moved, too. When I asked him about this, he started quoting Mao—"concentrating powerful forces speedily at strategic points…."

"OK, Max," I say at day's end. "I give up! Explain it to me." I 50 kick off my shoes and listen.

Capitalism is a colonial world, he explains, and the key natural 51 resource is the mind of the western consumer, aged 18 to 34. The different empires all have their maps and their merchant ships. But the mind of the new consumer resists traditional advertising. The merchants need someone who can work outside the confines of empire. "And that'd be me," says Max. "I sail up to the merchants of cool, and they hand me the booty."

"So it's all about the money now?" This is one of the confusing 52 things about Max—it's never about the money. He's always been overly generous and non-materialistic.

53   He laughs. "Money is cannonballs. Money is a fast ship. Money is a good crew and lots of rum. And do you know what I can do with those things? I can find the places that the merchants can't find."

54   Those hidden places, however, are a lot less romantic than they sound. Instead of underwater caves and uncharted islands, it turns out that the most sought-after commodity of all is the pimply pre-teen, or tween—the logic being that if you can find a way to the 13-year-old who has grown up so saturated with marketing that he knows every angle, but is still full of rebellion, then you've found a route to the future. "And if you can actually tap into his suspicions," says Max, "and show him that, yes, it's really just an illusion, a cultural swindle, then we've got a bit of leverage."

55   "Leverage for what?"

56   "Inevitably there is going to be some sort of social breakdown. We make it break down faster. You could start it like a flash mob."

57   "A flash mob?"

58   It goes like this: some guy sends out 50 e-mails with very specific instructions, and the next day there are thousands of people squawking like birds in Central Park. Just for the hell of it. People love the absurdity of it, the sheer capacity for it to happen. Max's plan, it seems, is to direct the absurdity. In a meaningless society, he insists, you work with meaninglessness: thousands of people gathering outside a clothing outlet, say, to demand a refund on shoes they bought 10 years ago, a different outlet every day, until the company implodes. "People would do it," says Max. "Because it's something to do. And because they've got no faith."

59   I rub my sore feet. "Do you have faith, Max?"

60   Max takes a long sip of his beer. "I believe in marketing," he says. "I would like to believe in art and culture, but Kurt Cobain killed himself and Picasso became a prostitute and we keep selling both of them. If you could go back to the Dark Ages and tell people that in the future someone, just by wearing a certain symbol on his chest, could influence people everywhere to buy that symbol, you know what they would say: 'What kind of magical power does that prince have? Has he slain any dragons lately?' Nobody slays anything anymore."

61   "Do you believe in God, Max?"

62   "I believe that Jesus' apostles were the first great marketers. The Bible is great word of mouth. I believe in karma. But you know what else?"

63   "What?"

64   "I believe you've almost got it. But you're still asking me more questions."

"Jesus, Max, I'm sick of being a television. And I'm sick of all   65
this Yoda crap."

"Good that is," says Max. "Sick you must be, to make healthy   66
the world."

DAY 5

You'd think we would have learned by now. The six of us took an   67
elevator down from the rooftop parking lot of a mall, and for some
reason we turned the Pixmen on before we got in. The echoing
hype of *The Summy Dummy Show* was so extreme that when we
reached the main concourse we were stumbling out in all directions, trying to flee from our own deafening message. Being a
Pixman is like a punishment from the Middle Ages—like being the
criminal in stocks in the town square. And yet we are also the town
crier, and the fool who—though he seems mad—sees things
nobody else can.

There are ads on banners in the sky. There are ads on vomit   68
bags and toilet paper. There are ads on eggs. Skyscrapers are
wrapped to look like bottles of Pepsi. There are ads on people's
heads. Everywhere is the new medium. The world is white noise
and clutter, and we have to rise above it for our message to be
heard. To control what people buy is to control people—not for any
other purpose, just to control what they buy. We carry the revolution on our backs, but not like a cross. I have spent all day in the
Eaton Centre, carrying the commercial on my back like a monkey,
and finally I have *the* question.

"What do we buy, Max?"   69

"We?"   70

"We. You and I."   71

He leans back in his chair. "I'm glad you asked. I buy very   72
specifically, and every time from somewhere different, because I
refuse to be sold to. But you—you're that rare thing. You *can't* be
sold to. What do you spend your money on? Chicken for dinner, a
bottle of whiskey. You spend it on traveling and poker. And you
always will. And that's our only salvation."

A while ago Max designed a campaign for a cosmetics com-   73
pany. He went to the hottest nightclubs to see if guys who wanted
to be *so* cool would—against all their gender conditioning and
social mores—get a facial, just because a marketing team and some
big-breasted woman said they should. The lineups were longer
than at the bar. That's when Max knew it—the temporal fantasy
had overtaken the greater yearning, and now it's survival of the
least materialistic: if you actually give a damn about something

other than the immediate dream of making your face prettier, you might still have a chance.

74   "It's up to us," says Max, with a sad laugh. "Those of us who don't need to buy any of it—we're the ones who'll be left. Then maybe we'll get the chance to create something new."

DAY 6

75   The six of us are standing at one of the city's busiest intersections. High above our own screens, giant TVs beam down from the tops of buildings, blocking out the sky. Today is our last day as Pixmen, and we are supposed to stick together. As we start across the street, however, I turn abruptly and head the other way. I zigzag through traffic, duck into an alley, head down a side street. People stare at me, the pack digs into my back, and my feet are hurting, but I keep moving. I make my way steadily south, down to the harbour, out along the boardwalk.

76   I get to the beach and cross the sand to the water's edge. A ribbon of scruffy foam lies along the shoreline. The sun is shining bright. I look up at the open sky, then down at my reflection in the lake. As the screen hovers there in the water, like Frankenstein's head, I decide to take the money I've earned as a Pixman and buy some new shoes.

Born in Montreal (1974), Bishop-Stall grew up in Vancouver. After hitch-hiking from Canada to Costa Rica at age 18, he picked olives in Spain, painted villas in Italy, hopped freight trains in Arizona, taught English in Mexico, and used scrap lumber to build a shack on the edge of Lake Ontario. Along the way, he earned degrees in Honours English and creative writing from Concordia University in Montreal. His first book, *Down to This* (2004), an account of the year he spent living in "a big-city shantytown," was short-listed for several awards. In 2005, he won the Knowlton Nash Journalism Fellowship at Massey College in Toronto. His non-fiction has appeared in *Saturday Night*, *Utne Magazine*, the *National Post*, and *The Globe and Mail*. Currently, Bishop-Stall is working on a screenplay based on *Down to This* for Shaftsbury Films, and on a novel.

"Hey, everybody, slow down"—that's the plea of a loosely associated group of people around the world who call themselves the "Slow Movement." As Christopher DeWolf asserts, they think that most of us jeopardize our health, relationships, families, and communities by living in the fast lane— moving too fast and working too hard to appreciate what we have and savour our lives.

Hit the Brakes

CHRISTOPHER DeWOLF

It's a gorgeous spring afternoon in Montreal and I'm sitting on my back balcony, sipping a beer and watching the alley life below. A long-haired cyclist passes by on a big city bicycle; a sneaky-eyed black cat darts up the stairs into the apartment next door. Little kids kick around a soccer ball. It's an enviable position, sitting around like this on a weekday, but student life affords such luxuries. Eventually, this will all come to an end. I'll have to grow some whiskers and scurry into the proverbial rat race like everyone else. 1

Right? 2

Not necessarily, and certainly not if I can help it. I want to work less and enjoy life more—and I'm not alone. There's a whole movement afoot with the same goal in mind. A Slow movement that, ironically enough, is quickly working its way into mainstream thought. Last year, a London-based journalist named Carl Honoré explored the philosophy in his book *In Praise of Slow: How a Worldwide Movement Is Challenging the Cult of Speed*. Examining the push to take it easy, from the Italian-born Slow Food and Slow Cities movements to the increasing acceptance of alternative health practices such as Traditional Chinese Medicine, Honoré insists that a slower way of life is a better way of life for anyone determined enough to hit the brakes. 3

It helps to define what exactly is meant by the word "slow." Honoré sums it up in his introduction: "Fast is busy, controlling, aggressive, hurried, analytical, stressed, superficial, impatient, active, quantity-over-quality. Slow is the opposite: calm, careful, receptive, still, intuitive, unhurried, patient, reflective, quality-over-quantity." He continues: "The Slow philosophy can be summed up in a single word: balance. Be fast when it makes sense to be fast, and be slow when slowness is called for. Seek to live at what musicians call the *tempo giusto*—the right speed." 4

Tempo giusto is nice-sounding, kind of sultry, but so what? Why slow down? What's the advantage to you, me and everyone else in the world? In a word, sustainability: economic, social and environ- 5 mental. Working too much gives you stress and sucks away the time you can spend doing the things you love. Anybody who has ever had a workaholic parent or partner knows what pain that can cause. There are broader implications too. Endless industrial growth, fuelled by ever-increasing workloads, wreaks ecological and social havoc around the world. Yet our whole society is geared toward working harder and faster. The evidence is everywhere. Earlier this year, the *Globe and Mail* ran a cloyingly upbeat story on an elite class of overachievers who drag themselves out of bed in the middle of the night to get a jump start on their workday. Every year, Canada's average workweek grows longer; up to a third of people in some cities, such as Edmonton, work more than fifty hours a week.

6   For a Montrealer like myself, that's a scary number. Only seven percent of us work that much, and there's a reason for that: most of us really, really don't want to. It's an attitude that has its share of devotees. In 2003, while I was working on a newspaper story about talented English-Canadians moving here after decades of brain drain, many of the people I interviewed pointed to Montreal's relaxed lifestyle as one of its biggest draws. Their feelings were reflected two years ago by a study that found that Montrealers spend an average of eight hours per week sitting on their 1.2 million apartment balconies—that's eight hours to read, watch the street, to relax and let your mind wander.

7   It's the kind of thing that would make the Work Less Party very happy. Last May, during British Columbia's provincial election campaign, I stumbled across a newspaper article that described how the fringe party was livening up an otherwise uneventful month. "Workers of the World—Relax!" is the Work Less Party's rallying cry, which only hints at the cheekiness of the events it has organized: road-hockey tournaments on major streets, "sleep-ins" at the provincial legislature (where, incredibly, it's illegal to take a nap) and a downtown race in which contestants dressed up as rats navigate a nightmarish corporate labyrinth, only to die when retirement is in sight.

8   I was intrigued, so I rang up Conrad Schmidt, the party's founder. For years, he tells me, "I was working the crazy lifestyle. Then I decided to slow down. I switched to a four-day workweek and found myself able to do all sorts of things like volunteering. So I decided to start a political party." The party's other candidates offer similar testimonials: one, an accountant, negotiated a thirty-two hour, four-day workweek with her employer. She now devotes her extra free time to organizing a community garden, sewing her own clothes, singing in community choirs and choreographing theatrical pieces for the Work Less Party. Another volunteers for a

variety of community organizations, is currently conducting an environmental audit of a Vancouver college and sits on the grant review board for the environment fund of Mountain Equipment Coop, an outdoor gear co-operative with locations across Canada.

The Work Less people sound like quite the bunch of ambitious overachievers, but there's nothing strange about that. The Slow movement isn't about slacking off, it's about doing things smarter and more efficiently. One of the most effective ways of accomplishing this is by reducing your workload. Mary Dean Lee, professor of management at McGill University, recently completed a six-year, North America-wide study on professionals who negotiated reduced workweeks with their employers. Her research team found that the subject gained, on average, an extra seventeen hours of free time per week without sacrificing much of their career success. Over half of the people studied earned promotions or switched to better jobs at other companies over the six years. The best thing about reducing your workload, Lee explained to me, in the faintest of Southern drawls, is that you get to choose what to do with your extra hours. What would you do with seventeen extra hours? 9

The answer for many is to get involved in the community—and there's no one more involved than Owen Rose, a Montreal interning architect who is one of the founding members of Mont-Royal Avenue Verte, a group dedicated to transforming the main street of the Plateau, one of Montreal's trendiest areas, into a car-free haven for pedestrians, cyclists and public transit. Rose sat down with me one afternoon in his airy Plateau office. "[Avenue Verte] fits right into the Slow movement," he began. "Our guiding philosophy is really quality of life, urban ecology and local participative democracy. When you empower people through democracy, they then start to get involved in [their community]." Public reaction to Avenue Verte has been overwhelmingly positive, with tens of thousands of Montrealers turning out to sign a petition demanding a public hearing on making the Plateau more ped[estrian]-friendly. 10

All of Avenue Verte's members are volunteers, driven to action by concern for their neighbourhood. It would be hard to see such local activism emerge in a hastily-built bedroom community whose residents spend most of their time at work or in their cars. What makes the Plateau worth fighting for are some of the very same things Honoré promotes in his book: environmentally friendly living (nearly a quarter of Plateau residents walk to work, and most of the rest take public transit), neighbourhood interaction (the Plateau has more street festivals than any other part of Montreal) and a quality built space (human-scaled streets, squares and parks that encourage street life are hallmarks of the neighbourhood). It's 11 certainly busier and more fast-paced than your average suburb, but in many ways it is a richer, more intimate environment. . . .

12   Being Slow, when you really get down to the bare bones of it, can only be achieved through personal effort. Small steps are important, and if that means cutting your working hours to fifty per week from the eighty that are the norm in your profession—as one of Mary Dean Lee's subjects did—so be it. Increasingly, it seems that slowing down is essential. Pollution, poor health, suburban sprawl: these seemingly disparate issues can all be blamed on the unrelenting, ever-faster treadmill we've created for ourselves. "Persuading people of the merits of slowing down is only the beginning," concludes Carl Honoré in *In Praise of Slow.* "Decelerating will be a struggle until we rewrite the rules that govern almost every sphere of life—the economy, the workplace, urban design, education, medicine."

13   Sitting on my balcony, legs propped up on the railing, Honoré makes perfect sense to me. Maybe that's just the product of a naïve young mind. But I'm optimistic there will be many more sunny afternoons spent on this very balcony.

Christopher DeWolf (b. 1984) is a freelance writer, photographer, and recovering Canadian Studies student who lives in Montreal. Raised in Calgary, DeWolf developed an interest in cities at an early age, nurtured first by playing endless bouts of SimCity and later by the words and wisdom of Jane Jacobs. His passion for cities has led him down some interesting paths. When he's not taking photos of back lanes and busy streets, DeWolf writes on topics as diverse as *dépanneurs* (Montreal's iconic corner stores) and the Indian diaspora in Hong Kong. Currently, DeWolf writes a biweekly urban issues column for *Maisonneuve* magazine and maintains a photoblog: urbanphoto.net.

"Look and See" is one of the essays in Ian Brown's book **What I Meant to Say: The Private Lives of Men** *(2005), a collection of essays about men, written by men, for women. Their purpose is to explain the mysteries of the male psyche to women and to discover more about themselves in the process. Brown's essay speaks intimately about two intensely private matters: the enjoyment a happily married man gets from watching and talking to strippers, and the experience of being the father of a severely disabled child. Through these two illustrations, Brown explores the difference between "looking" and "seeing."*

Look and See

IAN BROWN

A t three points in my life, I wanted to watch naked women   1
more or less incessantly. I don't mean to say there have been
other stretches when I haven't. But in those three phases,
the desire built into a compulsion.

I was a new young man, the first time, with a job for the first   2
time, and hence for the first time with enough money to get into a
strip club. Phase One lasted six months. I had a girlfriend, but she
came with strict conditions, whereas naked strippers did not. What
made me suddenly want to run, not walk, to the peeler bar was
simply the opportunity. It was a chance to see what I had never
been able to see enough of (naked female bodies) and to be, for
however short a time, without apology, what I was—a young man
interested in being near naked women.

Not touching. Near was enough.   3

The place was on the verge of downtown Toronto, which meant   4
I could slip over from work, at lunch. The girls danced in a miniature boxing ring, 10 feet square. If you sat next to the rope, you
could tuck a few dollars into a garter or a bra, which in turn might
win you a more private glimpse from the dancer. I had no spare
dollars and was too shy to do anything that venturesome, so I sat
halfway back and watched.

It was a jaunty, good-natured place, not at all like the darkened   5
cattle yards out in the suburbs, where mobsters lived, or the soul-
less airport strip, where everyone did his and her best not to feel
anything. It was more like a well-intentioned community centre for
young men, a place we could work off our primitive tendencies
without threatening society at large. There was no such thing then
as MTV, where female nakedness is just a channel away, and there
was certainly no such thing as lap dancing—girls weren't even
allowed to take off their panties at that point in the history of the
degradation of women.

6   The dancers had names like Suzie and Deeana, bright, extro-
verted gleams of names. I could watch five dancers, and then I had
to exit the premises—whether because it was too arousing, or too
frustrating, or too embarrassing, I am still not sure. (It could easily
have been all three.) I often ordered a meal—the burger was excellent—and sometimes I read the newspaper. I was a free man: I
could experience lust, and admit to it, on my lunch hour.

7   "To be surrounded by beautiful, curious, breathing, laughing
flesh is enough . . ." Walt Whitman wrote in *I Sing the Body Electric*.
"I do not ask any more delight, I swim in it, as in a sea."

8   That was my philosophy, too. If the business of girls taking
their clothes off for men was invented to democratize human
impulses—and that was what I believed—then shame was
invented to regulate that levelling. I wanted to be an enemy of
shame.

9   Then, one day, there was an accident at the bar. An old guy,
who liked to sit by the corner of the dancing ring and look up into
the girls' darknesses, was in his regular spot when a dancer took
pity on him. As I heard the story, she squatted down in his corner
with her back to him, and pushed her buttocks through the ropes at
his face. The experience was apparently too much: Overcome with
desire, he thrust his entire face into the cleft of her backside, much
to her surprise and very much against the rules of the club, which
forbade all touching.

10   The bouncers, two big square guys shaped like fridges, threw
the old guy out the door—but with such force that they killed him.

11   I seem to recall it made the papers. I stopped going after that,
and some time thereafter, the club closed. It's a café now, the kind
that sells large muffins and the healthy lifestyle. That was the first
time I realized that my desire to see a girl take off her clothes was
not as simple as I wanted it to be. Even looking has consequences.

12   "Tell me honestly," my wife says, standing in front of the bathroom
mirror. "Am I too fat to wear this?"

13   She's looking at her reflection. I'm looking at her, looking at her
own reflection. Her eyes are hard, appraising. She could be buying
a car.

14   "Am I? Why won't you answer me?"

15   Do you know this nightmare? It's a nightmare for a man
because *there's no acceptable answer*. It doesn't matter that she's a
well-dressed woman, my wife—slim, fashionable, a clever shopper
(Loehmann's, mostly). She wants me to tell her she looks great—

16   "You look great, honey."

17   —but she wants to feel that my answer is believable—

"Don't just say it because I want you to say it!"   18

—so it has to be discerning as well: 19

"I'm not. Turn around? Right around. Are you going to wear   20
those shoes?"

"Do you like these others better?" Whatever I say, the problem   21
has to be fixable.

"Yeah, the second ones."   22

She's pleased now. She has an answer, she believes I have been   23
straight and truthful. One more reassurance, and she will be done.

"You didn't used to think I was too fat."   24

"I don't think you're fat."   25

Etc.   26

This is another reason I have gone to strip clubs from time to   27
time: Because no one ever says, "Do I look fat in this?"—even if
they do. Because at a strip club it is very hard for a man to come up
with the wrong answer.

Fifteen years later, I was married and living in Los Angeles, and the   28
second phase of my addiction began. My wife had a demanding
job, and was pregnant, which left me even more on my own than I
was already.

The Star Strip wasn't far from our apartment—a heavy door up   29
the street from a lingerie store, in an otherwise residential neighbourhood. I went every couple of months, mostly between October
and February when it rained, mostly when my wife was away, in
that first, lonely year there.

The girls were astonishing, Hollywood pretty: I remember a   30
slim brunette with a face so beautiful she made the breath rush out
of my chest whenever she walked through the club. I liked the
gentle, unforced way her body seemed to follow her mind around
the room. (As opposed to another kind of woman, whose mind follows her body—equally charming.) I had the impression, looking at
her, that she would not defeat me sexually, and that I would not
defeat her.

I didn't keep my visits a secret from my wife: I was writing a   31
book about manhood, and she knew going to a strip club was a reliable way for me to see men at their most unfiltered.

In a strip bar, you can see what attracts you and what doesn't. I   32
find I need to be reminded occasionally. Men are often strangers to
themselves, in my experience, but in a strip club, in a room full of
naked girls, a man can see who he is and isn't, because men often
define themselves by what and whom we want.

Sometimes after I'd spent an evening happily watching TV   33
with my wife, after I'd been sufficiently domestic, the urge to see a

naked female stranger was like a small, sharp hunger in my stomach. I didn't need more than a snack: There was no cover charge at the Star Strip, and you could pop in and out as you would at a Starbucks for a creamy latté.

34   In any event, the club was no threat to my marriage. I loved my wife endlessly, the way you do in the early days of a marriage, and she loved me—especially in that strange and remarkable city, where we were on our own and everything was new and hilarious to us. There were celebrities buying tofu in the supermarkets, and riots, and earthquakes—details we still remember as undeniable evidence that we lived, saw these things, knew the world, in a way no one else could, because we were there in each other's company.

35   I never had loved and may never love a woman quite as properly as I did my wife in that lucky stretch of years away—and none of that was changed by my slip-outs to the peeler bar where I just needed to take the burr off the edge of physical longing that rasps a man, to see what I was missing and remind myself why I didn't mind missing it; to feel the headlong lurch of the need for friction, and see the scrap pile where the ride always ends. Going to a strip club was like enrolling in an evening sociology course: Alternative Ways of Male Being. It was as much adventure as I could handle, as much temptation as I could turn down.

36   Surely it is not so much of a sin for a man to remind himself, in the end, how lucky he is. Anyway, I came home calmer.

37 Soon thereafter, we had a baby, a little girl, and I didn't need to see naked women for a while.

38   A few years after that, we had another child, a boy. He surprised us: He was born with an impossibly rare syndrome, something almost no one had heard of. He can't speak, or reason, or walk too well, protect himself, or eat without a tube in his belly.

39   At 9, he has the body of a four-year-old and the mind of an infant. He has no eyebrows, or eyelashes; what he does have is patulous lips and thin but wildly curly hair, and low ears the way retarded people often do.

40   He is what doctors call an FLK, "a funny-looking kid," but that is putting it medically. He hits his head with his fists, often brutally, and is often in pain; but sometimes he has enormous bursts of happiness, great gusts of glee that are capable of charming anyone.

41   So he, too, is something to look at, though I have never been ashamed of him. To calm him down, I take him for marathon rides in his stroller for hours at a time. I like to talk to him as I walk: I'm not sure he understands, but sometimes he finds it amusing.

In any case, people look at us, often can't help themselves.   42
Some people peek and glance away; others make an effort to meet
my eye and smile, to convince me they accept us both. Others are
too shocked to do anything but goggle. Children stare blatantly,
and some parents don't even tell them not to.

Sometimes, pregnant women—or youngish women who have   43
begun to experience the lust to have a child of their own—come
upon my boy and me clattering down the street, and a look of
alarm passes over their faces: What if they have such a child? It's a
reasonable enough fear.

Then they seek my face out, to see what I look like, to see if   44
there is some hint in me that I could be the father of such a being—
because if there is something to spot in me, I can see them clearly
thinking, they will be able to spot it in their own men, and thus
avoid the terror of a deviant baby. But I am quite normal-looking,
even fairly robust genetically speaking—and so the look of fear on
their young, smooth faces often turns to terror. Then they look
away.

The worst offenders are 13-year-old girls, to whom appearance   45
is so paramount, who cannot stop wishing or fearing that the entire
world is gazing upon them in rapture. In some ways, they are the
exact opposite of strippers.

A few springs ago, at the opening of the baseball season, I took   46
my son—his name is Walker—to see a Toronto Blue Jays game. His
entire school, populated exclusively by disabled children, went
along—30 bent and broken bodies, beeping and whooping and
squawking in wheelchairs and cars, travelling in single file along
the sidewalk for 20 blocks through the centre of the city: Now, *that*
people watched. But we broke up when we arrived at the stadium,
and I walked my Walkie through the crowd.

It was School Day at the stadium, or Bat Day, or some unthink-   47
able combination of the two, and the place was overrun with rau-
cous teenagers. Again and again the same thing happened: Tall,
good-looking 14-year-old girls in pink or blue pop tops and white
miniskirts and flip-flops, the leaders of tiny gangs of three shorter
girls dressed exactly the same way, would spot Walker and me
coming at them—Quasimodo and his handler.

Then, when they thought I was not looking, they would lean   48
over and whisper to their cronies.

Then they would all look, and put their hands over their   49
mouths.

Then they would pretend to hide what they were doing.   50

So while I may be a man who goes to strip clubs and objectifies   51
women who are willing to take their clothes off, I, too, know what it

is like to be an object, of fear and pity and even scorn. And I guarantee this: Unless you are up there on the stage, or pushing that carriage, being looked at, naked—and Walker and I are psychologically stripped when we walk down the street—it probably doesn't feel like you think it does. It's not depressing, for starters. Sometimes it's the opposite—stark, but clear and clean, even slightly belligerent. I never feel a need to apologize. (That's a rare feeling for a man these days.)

52   I don't even mind the looks, most of the time: I figure you need to see us, the way a stripper figures a man needs to see her.

53   At least, when you are looking at me with Walker, or I am looking at a naked woman, by the act of looking we each declare our desire to see something true. I want to see her, unadorned. And I know you want to look at him, at my boy; you want to know what his darkness is, and why the light comes off him, too. I am no different.

54   Then one day two years ago, a woman from the government called: After seven years of worry and despair and sleeplessness, after seven years of counting the unspeakable cost of one broken child's life to himself and those around him, an agency found a home for my son. Suddenly, after nearly a decade, Walker had another place to live, a place where children like him live together, a place he could go home to and come home from. My broken boy was going away.

55   I didn't know which was worse—the fact that I had to give him up, or that part of me wanted to.

56   It took a long time to work out the details. And it was in that awful, grey time, after we knew Walker would be leaving but before he actually left, that I began to visit strip clubs again. This time the urges were more impatient, but shorter-lasting. At least it wasn't Internet porn, that sterile, repetitive motion machine. At least these women were living flesh and real.

57   The club was 10 minutes from our house by car, on the way home from our nanny's apartment. It was a rambling, three-storey place, always busy. Downstairs was cheaper, more crowded, younger guys; upstairs, where I went, had pretensions to sophistication: Upstairs you sometimes saw businessmen banging away on their BlackBerrys. The music was uniformly terrible.

58   For a nominal fee (the price of a drink), you could watch the "featured dancer" on stage take her clothes off. For a less nominal sum ($20 a dance, which made time with a girl more expensive than a night of cocaine), it was possible to have a girl take her clothes off and writhe naked on your lap and in your arms in the

cushioned booths that lined the perimeter of the room. The club advertised 160 exotic dancers.

I didn't want the girls to sit on my lap, and mostly asked them 59
not to, though I was nervous they'd be offended. I seldom touched them; it felt too intimate, and undeserved. It felt daring just to talk to them, and they were interesting—realistic, articulate, financially acute (I was never charged for fewer dances than I watched) and sometimes hilariously manipulative, as when they walked up and sat down, in their peignoirs and bikinis, on your lap, and asked why you were still alone, and pouted when you said you preferred it that way. They appreciated honesty, if it saved them time they could more profitably spend on other clients.

Still, it was nice to chat with a naked, pretty girl. The last thing 60
it felt was middle-class and ordinary, even if it was.

I suppose I was trying to fill the gap in my head where my boy 61
had lived.

I didn't feel much connection to the majority of the dancers in 62
the club, the vibe that men feel in the company of a woman they relate to, for whatever obscure reasons. It's the same democratic longing, the search for an unpredictable adventure, that makes almost every man walk down the street and privately scrutinize every woman he passes, no matter how young or old or big or small she is, and silently ask himself the famous, private male question: *Would I sleep with her?*

Not *could* I, or *should* I, or *do I want to* (especially not *do I want* 63
to, so agonizingly complicated). Just: *Would I? And if I would, what does that make me? What would happen to us? Where would that adventure lead? To a kitchen filled with children and bread? Or just to bed, and then nowhere?*

Cheryl was different, though. She was more intriguing—thin, 64
and tall, and by her own admission bisexual. (She wanted me to bring my wife. I said I thought that was unlikely.) Her breasts had been surgically augmented, and up close were almost absurdly out of proportion to her slim body; but they looked bombshell from 10 feet away, the distance at which she made most of her money. The first time I met her, she tried to sit down on my lap, but I told her it was too much, and after that we started to talk.

Like every other dancer in the room, she said she was 26 years 65
old. She said she rarely got turned on by the men she danced for. She said the majority of men for whom she lap-danced never climaxed. She said she was working on her master's degree.

One evening as Cheryl was sitting semi-clothed on a chair next 66
to me, drinking Perrier, I tried to explain why it was that only certain dancers appealed to me—how some women made me think

they would hurt me, sexually, while others didn't. Cheryl didn't, for instance.

67   "Sure," she said: "Men have control issues."

68   "What do you mean?"

69   "It makes sense. A man's never sure a woman's baby is his. Whereas the woman knows it's hers, no matter who the father is."

70   Two days later in *The New York Times* I read the same theory, espoused by a famous anthropologist. I felt like I'd had the winner of the Nobel prize for physics sitting next to me with her top off.

71   Every six weeks or so, generally on a Tuesday night, as my week at work geared up, I felt the urge to slip by the club. I didn't always go, and I didn't always stay; I just wanted to see some flesh, to calm the lurching in my head. It was like taking an Aspirin. I would walk into the club and dozens of semi-naked women would waft by in a wake of perfume, and sometimes even that was too intimate, enough to make me leave, and therefore instructive: The lesson was *slow down*.

72   I was always wrestling with myself in that place. I usually went on slow nights, early in the week; it was less intimidating. Sometimes the girls would say, "Hi, baby," or, "You gonna take that overcoat off?" before I was even in the door. It didn't matter that I knew this was a come-on to make money: I still managed to feel flattered. Flattery from a woman is such a rare thing in most men's lives—there's always something we tend to do wrong—that we'll take even the blatantly insincere variety.

73   Mostly, I liked watching it all. I liked to see the way the girls dressed, to see what they had discovered was sexy to men: It was remarkably uniform, geared to a guy's instinct, not to the eye of women. There was a lot of red, for instance. There were a lot of bottle blondes with huge breasts crammed into fluorescent yellow and pink bikinis. Some girls were heavy in places you wouldn't expect it, and that seemed to work for them too, though less reliably. Some traded on youth, some on tits, some on their eyes.

74   Sometimes I felt sorry for the girls who couldn't find a customer. I most liked the girls who didn't put on airs, who had some enthusiasm for whatever bodies they had, who weren't embarrassed but who didn't have to be hard or tough about not being embarrassed, either.

75   But whatever else it was—calculated, transactional, efficient—I knew the strip club was a fantasy too. It was the fantasy that sexual desire could be simple, that some woman somewhere might incite a desire that would simply overwhelm me, that I would never have to work at or be responsible for, that would work the way desire operated in Flaubert's novels, for instance. A woman who would

make my flickering, wandering, inconstant male desire blameless, unashamed, unavoidable—something that simply washed up like the sea.

Less romantically, I went to the club to bring lust into a more honourable place in my life, to normalize desire, to make it less of a big deal. And not just my sexual desire, but (by inference) all my desires—to be a man, but to be human; to be a good father, but to be a man; to be a husband, but not the sole foundation of a woman's existence. To be what I was, and nothing that I couldn't be. 76

Maybe that was why I found Cheryl sexy—because she was realistic. I never went home longing for her; she was a stripper, after all. Instead, back in bed at home, I dreamed I could fly. Being superficial at night made me more serious by day: It was during this stretch of looking that I took up gardening; that I took up painting again; that I began to try to find a road to satisfaction that didn't lead through a strip club. 77

But I couldn't have avoided it. Because a man learns a lot by looking—the difference between what he wants, and what he can have; or between what he thinks he wants, is supposed to want, and what he actually needs. My boy taught me that, and so did the strippers, albeit from a different direction. 78

[The morning] my son visited his new home for the first time, . . . I rode to work on my bicycle and burst into tears. It took me by surprise. I'd sob for a couple of blocks, settle down, collapse again. But eventually I got back to something like normal—struggling not to stare at the girls on the sidewalk, feeling the morning sun on my arms, trying to work up a less tumultuous feeling than grief. 79

I even thought about Cheryl. I'd run into her the night before, on my way out of the cave of nudes. 80

"Fancy seeing you here," she said, with a big smile, and that great way she had of standing with her body to the fore, as if her hips were asking a question. 81

"Yes," I said, "fancy that. But I'm on my way out." 82

In the end, I used her. She helped me back to a better place in myself. True, I paid her. But she showed me money isn't everything, and neither, alas, is love. 83

Born in Quebec (1954), Ian Brown earned a B.A. from the University of Toronto and a diploma from Harvard University. He has worked as a business writer at *Maclean's* and the *Financial Post*, as a roving feature reporter for *The Globe and Mail*, as the host of both *Later the Same Day* and *Sunday Morning* on CBC Radio, and as a freelance journalist for *Saturday Night* and many other magazines. His reporting and writing have won six gold National Magazine Awards and a National Newspaper Award. Brown is now the host of CBC Radio's *Talking Books* and the anchor of

Canada's premier documentary television series *Human Edge* and the Gemini Award-winning program *The View from Here*. He is the author of *Freewheeling* (1989), which won a National Business Book Award, and *Man Overboard: True Adventures with North American Men* (1993).

"Dads" draws an intimate portrait of Erika Ritter's parents, their earlier lives, and her own childhood. She presents a disturbing yet poignant picture of the life of her father, a man with whom she had a difficult relationship and from whom she was ultimately estranged.

Dads

ERIKA RITTER

1   I have only one memory of my mother's father, on the sole occasion he came to visit from the Coast, when I was seven. I recall a big, balding, bespectacled man, too large for our subdivision bungalow, looming over my brother and me with the bluff formality of someone uncomfortable with offspring, even his own daughter's.

2   In fact, he didn't seem all that comfortable with his daughter. He called our mother Margaret, instead of Marg, the way everybody else did. And took a polite but somewhat distant interest in what she tried to tell him about us, her house, her life, herself.

3   For her part, my mother appeared uncomfortable, too[: d]eferential and anxious to please in a self-justifying way uncharacteristic of her. Certainly, the day her father departed our house, there was a collective sigh of relief he may well have seconded.

4   Before his visit, our mother's father had already figured large in her stories about her childhood "back East"—Southwestern Ontario, actually. Her own mother had been something of a flapper, with a booze belt and a beaded cloche hat, and a restless, incandescent manner utterly at odds with the formal, bookish man she married.

5   When my mother was only four, her mother ran off with another man. Dismayed at the prospect of solo parenthood, her father enlisted relatives to raise his little girl. For the next decade or so, she shuttled between her two sets of grandparents, in London and Stratford.

6   It was not, she told us, such a bad arrangement. Both sets of grandparents were doting in their different ways, and, in addition,

one of the households—I forget which—boasted my mother's Great-Aunt Mary, a warm, tender-hearted maiden lady who called my mother "little lover" and petted her, coddled her, and spoiled her—just as our mother would my brother and me.

Sadly, this idyllic interlude in her life came to an abrupt end in early adolescence with the reappearance of her father, suddenly determined to reclaim her. 7

It was always at this point in the narrative that our mother would begin to cry, as she described to us the parting from her grandparents—and Aunt Mary!—in the company of the stranger her father had become. My brother and I would wail along as she reached the part where she clung to Aunt Mary at the curbside, until she was physically pried from the old lady's arms and forced into her father's car for the long, long trek west. 8

It also always seemed to be at this point in the story that the sound of the metal garage door could be heard to clang shut, heralding our own father's return from work. 9

"He's home!" Abruptly, our mother would remove me or my brother from her lap, in order to reach into her skirt pocket for a Kleenex. "Don't tell your father," she'd beg, wiping her eyes. "Don't tell your father." 10

Don't tell him *what*? I was never quite sure whether it was her crying in front of us that our dad would condemn, or the mere act of discussing her tragic past. Whatever she intended by it, my mother's injunction had the effect on me of intermingling events: her father's unannounced arrival from the West became forever confused with my father's return home to shut down her story. Dads, it seemed, had this way of showing up to spoil things. 11

As I got older, I began to appreciate more and more some of the awful complexity inherent in my mother's relationship with my Grandpa Cody. That trip across the country, for instance, must have been hellish. A shy, sheltered young girl, confined for days on end in a hot car on a hot journey over the mostly gravel TransCanada Highway of the time, with her sweating, fat, and forbidding father. 12

What on earth did they talk about over those hundreds and hundreds of miles? Where did they stay along the way, and in what proximity? Was my grandfather on hand to hear my mother crying in the night—as she must have cried—at the memory of her Great-Aunt Mary holding her close at the curb? And if he did overhear, how must he have reacted, in order to prompt her, years down the line, to keep her old sorrows secret from her husband, and to petition her children to do the same? 13

Their miserable trek led to an even more miserable destination. Compared to the leafy, chestnut-lined streets and genteel red brick 14 of Stratford and London, Regina was raw, ragged, almost physically painful to her in its wood-and-stucco ugliness. Worst of all was the discovery of a lady friend in her father's adopted world.

15   It wasn't until the final years of her life that my mother confessed to me the sense of rage and usurpation she had felt about Florence. She was earthy, unlettered—"common," to use my mother's most damning term. What could a diffident and almost pathologically unsociable man like Max Cody see in such a creature?

16   Sex. As a shy teenager, it must have shaken my mother to the core to face the fact of her father's sexual side. She barely knew the man, after all. Had made no perceptible progress in gaining his understanding or approval. And now she was faced with a rival who'd clearly already won. It was bad enough that her father had made an initial unsuitable match—later resulting in her own rejection and abandonment. Here he was, poised once more on the brink of choosing for a wife a woman whose ways were all wrong for him.

17   Once, late in her life and after a bit too much to drink, my mother recounted to me how she'd dared to dress down her father for the mistake he was about to make. Her anger, as she described it so many decades after the fact, was shockingly out of character. Whether she actually had shown that side to her father on the subject of Florence I can't be certain. But the marriage most assuredly went ahead. Children followed. My mother, barely anybody's daughter at any point in her life, was now relegated permanently to stepchild.

18   Yet something warmer must have rippled beneath the surface of what lay between her father and her. As the managing editor of the Regina *Leader-Post*, he made way for the writing and artwork of teenagers—including my mother's—in the pages of the paper. And on his frequent, impulsive solo travels by coach around North America, he'd send her postcards with brief but enthusiastic news of the people he'd met and the presents he planned to bring home.

19   I wonder if those gifts ever did appear, or were merely part of his mythology of himself as *paterfamilias*. An image perhaps more easily cultivated out on the open road, far from his second wife and uneasily assembled family. My mother would describe him returning refreshed from one of those bus trips, full of stories of strange passengers and stranger interludes, and animated by a raw curiosity about the human condition. Utterly unlike that large, looming, unfriendly grandfather I dimly recall from my own childhood, who more closely resembled my dad and all the other dark, forbidding dads in the neighbourhood.

20   Fathers of the 1950s were famously remote from their families. They acted as emissaries from the outside world of Work, showing

up at the end of the day to hear how things had gone on the home front. Or—in my father's case—to hear nothing revealing from any of us, in accordance with the "don't tell your father" ethic my mother impressed upon her children from an early age.

Yet, there was the occasional dad who did things differently. I remember my friend Judy's father as a sweet, sunny man with a tidy little moustache, who teased us girls with good-natured warmth, and—in the fall—pressed us into service to help him put up pickles. 21

I couldn't get over the novelty of a father who would laugh and joke as he directed his daughter and her friends to stuff sprigs of dill into the jars before sealing the lids. It felt unreal somehow, like watching *Father Knows Best*, where Robert Young addressed his girls as "Kitten" and "Princess," and never came storming into the house like an honest-to-God father to demand whose toys those were left out on the lawn. 22

An even earlier friend named Paula had a wistful, somewhat whimsical father, badly crippled by polio, who could recite to us entire Sherlock Holmes stories by heart, even "A Study in Scarlet," which was long and complicated and wholly unnerving. It was Paula's father, rather than her mother, who presided over what he called "dunging out" Paula and her sister's bedroom, overrun, like mine, with a menagerie of stuffed animals. 23

Astonishingly, Paula's father knew the names of all the individual bears and camels and cats who made up his daughters' collections. He remembered which coats and hats and blankets pertained to each particular bear or dog, especially those that belonged to Paula's oldest teddy, "Tiggy," whose garments were all in a shade described by every member of the family—including her father—as "Tiggy Blue." 24

Imagine having a father like Paula's or Judy's, I thought. But I couldn't. Fathers like mine weren't on-site to tease or entertain or enter into the realm of our imaginations. Fathers like mine were there to criticize, to judge, to hold their approval in abeyance. 25

The price that fathers like mine paid for their authority, however, was high. In a good mood, my dad would banter with my friends, but badly. In a dark mood, he ignored them, or upbraided me for my failings as if they weren't there. In none of that was he different from most of the other dads I knew: autocratic strangers in their own homes. 26

Occasionally, our dad seemed to sense his exclusion, and would react to my mother and brother and me with irritated bafflement, like a bear rousted unceremoniously from a campsite and sent shuffling back into the woods, bewildered and still hungry. At those times, he'd retreat behind the barrier of his evening paper, or into contemplation of his tired salesman's feet. 27

28   "Oh, my aching dogs," he'd groan, Willy Loman-like, in an unintended reproach to those of us whose day consisted of far less unremitting toil.

29   Yet he took a peculiar pride in his work. It was evident whenever we children got the chance to stop in with our mother at the men's store where he worked for a ride home at closing time. Ware's Limited was serious clothes only—suits, slacks, sports jackets, and coats. No shirts, no socks, nothing in the line dismissed by my father as "haberdashery." The store was a long, old-fashioned, heavily panelled place with big round wooden racks of suits and an endless linoleum floor, kept swept and shone by the caretaker, Mr. Murdoch. . . .

30   [T]he store was a man's world entirely. A sober world of dull-coloured, apparently identical suits, rack upon rack, and a silent tailor kneeling with a mouthful of pins to mark an alteration to a pantcuff or seam. As well as the small band of salesmen—Mr. Lipsett, Mr. Hoskins, and my father—hovering attendance on the customer with an air of quiet purpose appropriate to the gravity of such an important purchase.

31   With particularly favoured clients, my father would exhibit a heartiness and a joviality in marked contrast to the weary self he dragged home each night. Smoothing a shoulder line, or pinching a lapel between his fingers, he seemed another man, utterly in his mercantile element.

32   It was, in some ways, a lie. A kind of fiction of professional status that my dad felt forced to invent for himself after all his youthful ambitions had collapsed. A bright student—brilliant, perhaps—he'd graduated from the local college with a B.A. at age eighteen. Then dreamed of taking up a scholarship offered by Fordham University in New York—New York!—to study law.

33   The Drought, however, reigned over the West, and the Great Depression had the entire Western world in its grip. There simply was no money to cover his expenses. Therefore, at what must have been roughly the same moment that my mother was arriving by car to face the dust-blown Prairies, my father was facing the hard truth that he'd likely never leave them behind.

34   Shelving the dream of a career in the law, he found a job—when jobs were few—driving a paint truck for five dollars a week. His meagre salary was doled out among his out-of-work father, a raft of younger siblings, and a mother whose reason had snapped under the weight of financial woe. Not for nothing, it seemed to me as a child listening to this oft-told story, was that period recalled as The Great Depression.

Unlike my mother, my father told the tale of his early life 35
openly at the dinner table. A cautionary tale, designed to warn us
from a tender age about the tricks that Life could play, even on—
especially on—the clever and the deserving. No point in expecting
things to turn out for the best, our father seemed to be saying. Not
when Life had such a knack for putting you in your place, cutting
off your aspirations at the knees, arranging for a fall to follow your
pride, however justifiable. . . .

It was impossible to calculate the depth of my father's losses. 36
Ambition, optimism, any genuine capacity for joy—losses that only
deepened with the passage of years. In my childhood, he feigned
success in his role as a menswear store manager, and bragged about
the status of the customers he waited on. But as I got older, the bitterness of his lot became more obvious. The more his "dogs" ached,
the more frequently he referred to the once-revered customers as
"pigs," and railed against their boorishness, their stupidity, their
lack of class. By the time I was well into high school, he had begun
drinking rye with his morning orange juice to ease the pain of his
job's servility, as well as his agonized discovery that my mother
had been having an affair.

Later, once I'd reached the end of Grade Twelve, and had won a 37
scholarship to McGill, my father's reaction was more petulant than
pleased. He mused aloud that I'd be better off living at home, perhaps forgoing university altogether, and parlaying my summer job
writing TV ad copy into a full-time career. At first, I couldn't
believe I'd heard him correctly. Only that September, on the train
heading east, did it occur to me I was embarking upon the very
journey once denied to him.

If my father realized it too, he did not acknowledge the parallel. 38
If he had, we'd both have been better off. But facing the fact that, at
some level, he secretly begrudged me admission to a wider world
might have been too hurtful for him. Certainly, after his initial discouragement of my university career, he did what he could do to
support it—in the form of a five-dollar postal order, filled out in his
own rigidly upright printing, and mailed to me in residence once a
week. Not much money in the mid-1960s, five dollars a week, but it
was all he could spare, and I knew it. And counted myself lucky
not to have to support a large family on it, as he had once done.

In the months that I was away for the school term, some of the 39
rawness between us got a chance to heal. Our letters and occasional
phone calls were cordial, even warm. But from the moment I arrived
home for Christmas, or to search for a summer job, some collision
would inevitably occur, and set the tone for the rest of my stay.

40   On the Christmas break especially it got to a point where, from the instant I came through the door, my father would turn suddenly ill and betake himself to bed for the duration of my visit. Emerging only for meals, unshaven, in his pajamas and sullenly silent. Then, on the morning of my departure, he would stumble still pyjama-clad and stubbly into his overcoat to drive me to the airport, despite my mother's insistence that she could take me herself.

41   "Now, don't you go and make me feel worse than I do," my dad would snap at her as he shuffled queasily down the walk, car keys in hand. "It's the flu and I can't help it if I've gone and spoiled her stay, can I? Least I can do is see her off."

42   Angry at being discussed in the third person, affronted by his behaviour over the course of my visit, and embarrassed by his unkempt, rheumy-eyed appearance out in public, I'd snap in return. "Dad, the point is, I make you sick. Literally. Don't you see that? The very sight of me turns your stomach, and an hour after I leave you'll start feeling better. Now, why can't you just come out and admit that?"

43   "Bullshit!" Looking sicker than ever, my dad would set his jaw, hunch behind the steering wheel and ignore me and my mother studiously the rest of the way to the airport.

44   But I wasn't wrong in my diagnosis. After arriving back in Montreal, I'd phone home to let my mother know the plane hadn't crashed. "How's Dad feeling?"

45   "Oh, much better. Started to perk up right after we dropped you off, naturally. Sweetheart, please don't take it personally. The man's cracked, that's all. Simply cracked."

46   Well, maybe. Still, throughout the course of my college career, either he or I would sporadically make some attempt at *rapprochement*. Inevitably, however, something would intervene to screw it up. At first, when I told him I was studying *Death of a Salesman* in my Modern Drama class, he waxed enthusiastic. "Terrific play. That Arthur Miller, he really understood how even a top-notch salesman can fall apart, once the world of retail turns to crap the way it has."

47   "No, no, Dad," I informed him loftily. "Willy Loman has the wrong dreams. He's never been cut out for that work. It's always been crap. It's just that he was seduced by the fantasy of noble salesmanship that never actually existed. That's Miller's point."

48   My father's lips hardened into a narrow, Teutonic line and his face closed against me. "Aw, what the hell would you know about selling and about dreams? What the hell would *you* know?"

49   Being in the know in a world of know-nothings was profoundly important to him. So much so that it was a constitutional requirement for him to be the person with the information, the

person who dispensed opinions, pointed out landmarks, and took charge of explaining the fine print. It didn't matter whether someone else in the room might have more up-to-date information, or an equally legitimate yet opposing opinion, or closer knowledge of the locality in question, or greater claim to expertise in any particular area. My dad was the one who knew, even when the only source he could cite with authority was *Time* magazine. Questions answered by anyone else diminished him. Points of view out of sync with his were abhorrent, and any admission of ignorance or confusion was utterly out of the question.

Bursting with the callow pride of the recently educated, I was, in my way, no less insufferable. Somewhere inside, I understood that my father was filled with frustration at his lost opportunities. Yet I couldn't bring myself to cut him any slack. For his part, he must have understood it was not competition I was after, but commendation. And yet, he was congenitally incapable of offering me anything but argument. As incapable as I was of proffering him compassion.

And so we were rivals, my father and I. It was only toward the end of his life that I truly understood that, and it was only gradually that I came to appreciate why. Each of us believed that the other was bent on obtaining exclusive rights to my mother.

This competition over my mother had begun back in my mid-teens. Because my brother was away at university when my mother's infidelity came to light, it was I who was compelled to protect her from my father's jealous wrath. Later on, after I'd moved away from home, I made clear it was only my mother I wanted to come and visit me. On the rare occasions I flew home to see my parents, I would conspicuously contrive to get time in her company, away from my father.

Eventually, after my mother had become old and ill and increasingly addled, the struggle over her only intensified. Ailing himself, my father strove to hide the nature of her illness from my brother and me, for fear of losing her to our care. Whenever I'd turn up to visit, he'd treat me with hostility, like some intrusive stranger sent from an aid agency to perform an unwelcome intervention.

"What's that woman want?" he'd demand of my mother, indicating me with an impatient gesture. Physically unable to speak, my mother would shrug, big-eyed and childlike, as if suddenly unsure herself of my identity and purpose.

Before the true extent of her affliction became known to me, I would routinely beg my father, by phone or in person, to let me take my mother on a holiday, in New York or even Toronto—any place in her beloved "back East" that would allow her the pleasure of galleries and city streets denied to her in the small town they'd retired to. Anything to give us some time together, the two girls on the go that we'd always gloried in being together.

56   "Don't you worry," my dad would assure me bitterly. "I'll be dead soon. After that, you and your mother can have all the time you like with each other."

57   By that point, any vestige of civility that had ever existed between us was long since evaporated. "Oh, but you aren't going to die first," I'd tell him, with equal bitterness. "She will. And God, will I ever make you sorry for being such a bastard!"

58   My mother did die first. As I left my parents' condo after the funeral, I knew that I'd never see my father again. Not because I intended to make good my threat to make him sorry, but because I knew there was no way, for what was left of his life, my presence could ever be a comfort to him—or his to me.

59   The last recollections I have of him are vile, scorching messages left on my answering machine at odd hours. Curses against me for not being there when he called, angry accusations that I wanted nothing from him but his money.

60   Truth to tell, I didn't much want his money, either. What I'd wanted from him—back when I might arguably have wanted any-thing—was absolution from the guilt of having been born, evi-dently, to occupy the space he'd longed to occupy himself, the ability to pursue the dreams he'd been denied, and the opportunity to share with my mother the confidences she'd kept closed off from him.

61   Only once can I recall an unencumbered adventure shared with my father. We travelled together by train, just the two of us, from Regina to Edmonton to pick up a second-hand sports car my uncle had found for him in a classified ad. I was just sixteen; I'd never been on a train before, much less behind the wheel of a sports car.

62   On the way home from Edmonton, my dad let me drive. Not for long and not too fast, but long and fast enough to make me giddy with delight. Then—seeming genuinely happy for once—my dad drove the rest of the way. Very fast, and with the top down, so that the wind tore our hair, dried our smiling lips against our teeth, and ripped from our mouths whatever words we might have traded, back over our shoulders, to join the plume of exhaust trailing behind. . . .

63   That we never, thereafter, managed to replicate the simple plea-sure of that interlude goes to show how bred in the bone was our mutual mistrust. Yet the fact that we found any measure of happi-ness, however brief, out there together on the open road at least hints at something that might have been. I wonder whether—looking back on her own life with her own father—my mother could have claimed even that much.

Erika Ritter was born in Regina, Saskatchewan, and educated at McGill University in Montreal and the University of Toronto. She is a playwright, novelist, short-fiction writer, and radio broadcaster/interviewer/host. Her works include *Urban Scrawl* (1984), *Automatic Pilot* (1990), *The Hidden Life of Humans* (1997), and *The Great Big Book of Guys* (2004), from which this selection is taken.

In this selection, Eva Hoffman describes the difficult transition that people make when they change languages, in her case moving from Polish to English as a young teenager. She explores some of the cultural adaptations that are part of the transition and admits that at some points she felt simply empty, devoid of the most defining aspect of a human being: a living language.

Lost in Translation

EVA HOFFMAN

Every day I learn new words, new expressions. I pick them up 1 from school exercises, from conversations, from the books I take out of Vancouver's well-lit, cheerful public library. There are some turns of phrase to which I develop strange allergies. "You're welcome," for example, strikes me as a gaucherie, and I can hardly bring myself to say it—I suppose because it implies that there's something to be thanked for, which in Polish would be impolite. The very places where the language is at its most conventional, where it should be most taken for granted, are the places where I feel the prick of artifice.

Then there are words to which I take an equally irrational 2 liking, for their sound, or just because I'm pleased to have deduced their meaning. Mainly they're words I learn from books, like "enigmatic" or "insolent"—words that have only a literary value, that exist only as signs on the page.

But mostly, the problem is that the signifier has become severed 3 from the signified. The words I learn now don't stand for things in the same unquestioned way they did in my native tongue. "River" in Polish was a vital sound, energized with the essence of riverhood, of my rivers, of my being immersed in rivers. "River" in English is cold—a word without an aura. It has no accumulated associations for me, and it does not give off the radiating haze of connotation. It does not evoke.

4   The process, alas, works in reverse as well. When I see a river now, it is not shaped, assimilated by the word that accommodates it to the psyche—a word that makes a body of water a river rather than an uncontained element. The river before me remains a thing, absolutely other, absolutely unbending to the grasp of my mind.

5   When my friend Penny tells me that she's envious, or happy, or disappointed, I try laboriously to translate not from English to Polish but from the word back to its source, to the feeling from which it springs. Already, in that moment of strain, spontaneity of response is lost. And anyway, the translation doesn't work. I don't know how Penny feels when she talks about envy. The word hangs in a Platonic stratosphere, a vague prototype of all envy, so large, so all-encompassing that it might crush me—as might disappointment or happiness.

6   I am becoming a living avatar of structuralist wisdom; I cannot help knowing that words are just themselves. But it's a terrible knowledge, without any of the consolations that wisdom usually brings. It does not mean that I'm free to play with words at my wont; anyway, words in their naked state are surely among the least satisfactory play objects. No, this radical disjoining between word and thing is a desiccating alchemy, draining the world not only of significance but of its colors, striations, nuances—its very existence. It is the loss of a living connection.

7   The worst losses come at night. As I lie down in a strange bed in a strange house—my mother is a sort of housekeeper here, to the aging Jewish man who has taken us in in return for her services—I wait for that spontaneous flow of inner language which used to be my nighttime talk with myself, my way of informing the ego where the id had been. Nothing comes. Polish, in a short time, has atrophied, shriveled from sheer uselessness. Its words don't apply to my new experiences; they're not coeval with any of the objects, or faces, or the very air I breathe in the daytime. In English, words have not penetrated to those layers of my psyche from which a private conversation could proceed. This interval before sleep used to be the time when my mind became both receptive and alert, when images and words rose up to consciousness, reiterating what had happened during the day, adding the day's experiences to those already stored there, spinning out the thread of my personal story.

8   Now, this picture-and-word show is gone; the thread has been snapped. I have no interior language, and without it, interior images—those images through which we assimilate the external world, through which we take it in, love it, make it our own—become blurred too. My mother and I met a Canadian family who

live down the block today. They were working in their garden and engaged us in a conversation of the "Nice weather we're having, isn't it?" variety, which culminated in their inviting us into their house. They sat stiffly on their couch, smiled in the long pauses between the conversation, and seemed at a loss for what to ask. Now my mind gropes for some description of them, but nothing fits. They're a different species from anyone I've met in Poland, and Polish words slip off them without sticking. English words don't hook on to anything. I try, deliberately, to come up with a few. Are these people pleasant or dull? Kindly or silly? The words float in an uncertain space. They come up from a part of my brain in which labels may be manufactured but which has no connection to my instincts, quick reactions, knowledge. Even the simplest adjectives sow confusion in my mind; English kindliness has a whole system of morality behind it, a system that makes "kindness" an entirely positive virtue. Polish kindness has the tiniest element of irony. Besides, I'm beginning to feel the tug of prohibition, in English, against uncharitable words. In Polish, you can call someone an idiot without particularly harsh feelings and with the zest of a strong judgment. Yes, in Polish these people might tend toward "silly" and "dull"—but I force myself toward "kindly" and "pleasant." The cultural unconscious is beginning to exercise its subliminal influence.

The verbal blur covers these people's faces, their gestures with a sort of fog. I can't translate them into my mind's eye. The small event, instead of being added to the mosaic of consciousness and memory, falls through some black hole, and I fall with it. What has happened to me in this new world? I don't know. I don't see what I've seen, don't comprehend what's in front of me. I'm not filled with language anymore, and I have only a memory of fullness to anguish me with the knowledge that, in this dark and empty state, I don't really exist. . . .

My voice is doing funny things. It does not seem to emerge from the same parts of my body as before. It comes out from somewhere in my throat, tight, thin, and mat—a voice without the modulations, dips, and rises that it had before, when it went from my stomach all the way through my head. There is, of course, the constraint and the self-consciousness of an accent that I hear but cannot control. Some of my high school peers accuse me of putting it on in order to appear more "interesting." In fact, I'd do anything to get rid of it, and when I'm alone, I practice sounds for which my speech organs have no intuitions, such as "th" (I do this by putting my tongue between my teeth) and "a," which is longer and more

336 UNIT EIGHT • POTLUCK

open in Polish (by shaping my mouth into a sort of arrested grin). It is simple words like "cat" or "tap" that give me the most trouble, because they have no context of other syllables, and so people often misunderstand them. Whenever I can, I do awkward little swerves to avoid them, or pause and try to say them very clearly. Still, when people—like salesladies—hear me speak without being prepared to listen carefully, they often don't understand me the first time around. "Girls' shoes," I say, and the "girls" comes out as a sort of scramble. "Girls' shoes," I repeat, willing the syllable to form itself properly, and the saleslady usually smiles nicely, and sends my mother and me to the right part of the store. I say "Thank you" with a sweet smile, feeling as if I'm both claiming an unfair special privilege and being unfairly patronized.

11   It's as important to me to speak well as to play a piece of music without mistakes. Hearing English distorted grates on me like chalk screeching on a blackboard, like all things botched and badly done, like all forms of gracelessness. The odd thing is that I know what is correct, fluent, good, long before I can execute it. The English spoken by our Polish acquaintances strikes me as jagged and thick, and I know that I shouldn't imitate it. I'm turned off by the intonations I hear on the TV sitcoms—by the expectation of laughter, like a dog's tail wagging in supplication, built into the actors' pauses, and by the curtailed, cutoff rhythms. I like the way Penny speaks, with an easy flow and a pleasure in giving words a fleshly fullness; I like what I hear in some movies; and once the Old Vic comes to Vancouver to perform *Macbeth*, and though I can hardly understand the particular words, I am riveted by the tones of sureness and command that mold the actors' speech into such majestic periods.

12   Sociolinguists might say that I receive these language messages as class signals, that I associate the sounds of correctness with the social status of the speaker. In part, this is undoubtedly true. The class-linked notion that I transfer wholesale from Poland is that belonging to a "better" class of people is absolutely dependent on speaking a "better" language. And in my situation especially, I know that language will be a crucial instrument, that I can overcome the stigma of my marginality, the weight of presumption against me, only if the reassuringly right sounds come out of my mouth.

13   Yes, speech is a class signifier. But I think that in hearing these varieties of speech around me, I'm sensitized to something else as well—something that is a matter of aesthetics, and even of psychological health. Apparently, skilled chefs can tell whether a dish from some foreign cuisine is well cooked even if they have never tasted it and don't know the genre of cooking it belongs to. There seem to be

some deep-structure qualities—consistency, proportions of ingredients, smoothness of blending—that indicate culinary achievement to these educated eaters' taste buds. So each language has its own distinctive music, and even if one doesn't know its separate components, one can pretty quickly recognize the propriety of the patterns in which the components are put together, their harmonies and discords. Perhaps the crucial element that strikes the ear in listening to living speech is the degree of the speaker's self-assurance and control.

As I listen to people speaking that foreign tongue, English, I 14 can hear when they stumble or repeat the same phrases too many times, when their sentences trail off aimlessly—or, on the contrary, when their phrases have vigor and roundness, when they have the space and the breath to give a flourish at the end of a sentence, or make just the right pause before coming to a dramatic point. I can tell, in other words, the degree of their ease or dis-ease, the extent of authority that shapes the rhythms of their speech. That authority—in whatever dialect, in whatever variant of the mainstream language—seems to me to be something we all desire. It's not that we all want to speak the King's English, but whether we speak Appalachian or Harlem English, or Cockney, or Jamaican Creole, we want to be at home in our tongue. We want to be able to give voice accurately and fully to ourselves and our sense of the world. John Fowles, in one of his stories in *The Ebony Tower*, has a young man cruelly violate an elderly writer and his manuscripts because the legacy of language has not been passed on to the youthful vandal properly. This seems to me an entirely credible premise. Linguistic dispossession is a sufficient motive for violence, for it is close to the dispossession of one's self. Blind rage, helpless rage is rage that has no words—rage that overwhelms one with darkness. And if one is perpetually without words, if one exists in the entropy of inarticulateness, that condition itself is bound to be an enraging frustration. In my New York apartment, I listen almost nightly to fights that erupt like brush-fire on the street below—and in their escalating fury of repetitious phrases ("Don't do this to me, man, you fucking bastard, I'll fucking kill you"), I hear not the pleasures of macho toughness but an infuriated beating against wordlessness, against the incapacity to make oneself understood, seen. Anger can be borne—it can even be satisfying—if it can gather into words and explode in a storm, or a rapier-sharp attack. But without this means of ventilation, it only turns back inward, building and swirling like a head of steam—building to an impotent, murderous rage. If all therapy is speaking therapy—a talking cure—then perhaps all neurosis is a speech disease.

Born in Cracow, Poland, in 1945 to Jewish survivors of the Holocaust, Eva Hoffman immigrated to Canada at the age of 13. She lived in Vancouver, then moved to the United States where she completed her Ph.D. in English at Harvard. She taught literature at several universities including Columbia and Tufts, and also worked as an editor and writer at *The New York Times* from 1979–1990. She is the author of a number of books, including *Lost in Translation: A Life in a New Language* and *After Such Knowledge: Memory, History, and the Legacy of the Holocaust*. She currently lives in London but is also a visiting professor at MIT, near Boston.

This selection narrates two stories: one disturbing and one exhilarating, although both are permeated with Laura Robinson's passion for sport and physical challenge. First is the author's own love affair with cycling as a young girl and the obstacles she encountered in the men's world of competitive cycling. Second is an inspiring look at the Native youth whom she challenges to participate in a sacred run, finding an important piece of themselves as well as their culture.

An Athlete's Lament

LAURA ROBINSON

PART ONE: FASTEST, HIGHEST, GROSSEST

1   When I was in grade eight and living in a Toronto suburb, some of the boys in my class rode their bicycles over to my house for a visit. It was an April evening in 1972, the air warm and calm, but alive with the promise of summer. I looked out the front door and saw a line of ten-speeds propped against our house. Glistening under the sun room lights, they seemed to be speed itself.

2   That was it. I was smitten. My body and mind were acting together. Probably my soul was involved too. I *had* to have a ten-speed. My coaster bike had never intimated anything about speed. I went to find the person who made all the big decisions in my life.

3   She wasn't buying me any new bike, my mother told me, when my sister's old one was perfectly capable of getting me to school. If I wanted a new one that bad, I'd have to start saving my baby-sitting money, and quit spending so much on clothes.

4   Fair enough. By the end of June, I had my ten-speed. I was really lucky, too, because my brother, David, who was just eighteen months younger than I, also yearned for a new bike. He'd been saving his paper route money.

That summer, we passed from being kids to another magical   5
age—no longer children and not yet adults—and we took the first
real step away from home. Even my mother changed her tune.
Initially, she wanted to know why on earth we needed ten-speeds
when one speed had been just fine up to now. But once we had
them, she suggested we join the Mississauga Cycling Club. My
mother, the chain smoker, who would drive three blocks for
another carton of cigarettes. My mother, the queen of "do as I say,
not as I do," was recruiting us into a club where a cigarette would
never touch our teen-age lips. Though the irony was lost on us, we
signed up, and on a Tuesday evening in June, headed out to our
first cycling competition.

A couple of kilometres from our front door at the first stoplight,   6
two other cyclists, older guys, lined up with us while we waited for
the light to change. My brother sized the bikes up. They were way
better than ours, and one guy had an Italian accent, a sure give-
away that he was a real cyclist.

I learned quickly, after the first encounter, to look at the lines of   7
the bike frame and the way the derailleurs and brakes sit on it. The
angles, the wheel base, the gear ratios on the rear hub and, of
course, the name of the bike signaled in an instant that this was the
genuine article. But if the rider on it didn't have the legs—smooth,
tanned, ropey, layered muscles, twitching until the light changed, it
didn't matter how good the bike was: the person on it was not a
real cyclist.

My brother had bought his bike out of a Consumer's Distribut-   8
ing catalogue. Mine came from the hardware store. It cost me
eighty-eight dollars. For us, that was very expensive, but on the
grand scale of bicycles as finely crafted works of art, our bikes
didn't even register. They were anchors. Mine had a gear ratio on
the rear hub the size of a pie plate—unacceptable in this aerody-
namic world. My brother had toe clips, but I didn't. Just regular
pedals with reflectors on them. And, of course, my bicycle was
much too big for me; in 1972 you couldn't buy a ten-speed from a
hardware store, or anywhere else, that wasn't made for a man at
least six feet tall.

But all this was immaterial to us at the time. My brother and I   9
were riding to our first bike race with two grown-up cyclists. When
the light changed and we took off, I felt as if I had just opened a big
door to a new life.

On that summer evening I started to learn that sport wasn't   10
what was on television or what I read about in newspapers. All that
hype about yards gained and lost, all those guys screaming into
microphones about great saves and incredible catches and phenomenal touchdowns—that wasn't sport. It was some sort of malignant

male mutation. After all, men were virtually the only athletes who ever appeared on TV, and they didn't have any real connection to me—or to anyone else. They disappeared if you turned the TV off or threw out the paper. They didn't care about their fans; they cared about getting paid. How can you relate to nebulous images that don't know, or care, if you exist in the first place?

11   I was to learn that sport is about staying power. About a place where your body meets your soul and spirit. Sport is lonely and friendly all at once. Even when you're riding elbow to elbow in a pack, you can still feel alone. There are thousands of physical journeys to be made while cycling, but it's the human journey taking place in the subconscious that defines the experience.

12   Sport is about living from the inside out. It isn't about sitting in the seats of a stadium separated from the action—it *is* the action. So if you want to be a good athlete, you have to climb inside yourself and see what you're made of. Do you have what it takes? Are you going to find something very deep that will keep you going when your legs, your lungs, and your heart urge you to stop?

13   In the twenty-five years I've been riding, my bicycles have transported me to a world where anything seemed possible if I was willing to sweat enough. I'd find myself looking at a hill, thinking I can't possibly make it up, but I would, and I'd sail down the other side, leaning into corners and flying around curves. For a kid with endless energy, the first couple of years were magical. But the faster I got and the higher I rose in competitive sport, the more I realized the terrible price women had to pay to make it to the top level. For us, it was a hostile place where doing our best didn't necessarily count. Some days the pain and pressure of being female at a competition where only men mattered were overwhelming. Though I stuck it out for nearly twenty years, it wasn't until I quit that I regained the spiritual joys of those early years. But all of this—both lovely and terrible—stretched far ahead as I rode to my first time trial on that lovely summer evening.

14   A time trial is a race against the clock. Cyclists go off one at a time, usually a minute apart. The rider ahead of you is called your minuteman, and if you can see her, you can use her as a rabbit you try to catch. But really, you race against yourself, and once everyone's time has been tabulated, you find out who was the fastest.

15   This time trial was ten miles long. It was a perfect square, ending where it began, on the farm roads west of Mississauga. At the start line the riders were held up on their bikes by someone who grasped the back of the saddle while they got comfortable in their toe clips. Since I didn't have toe clips, I just waited, perched

on my bike, while a man straddled the back wheel, and held onto my saddle. "Don't be nervous," he said in a tony British accent. "Keep your head down, and go like stink."

The timer counted down from ten and I was off. I don't   16
remember much. I know I got chased by a dog and outsprinted him. The course didn't feel like ten miles; before I knew it, the finish line was coming up. I pedaled as hard as I could, and it was over.

There were a few boys from Scouts there[:] a father and son   17
who had French accents, real cycling shorts, and really good bikes; the two men my brother and I rode over with, whose names were Angelo and Duanne; and probably some other boys and men I can't remember. Through all these years in sport, there were always clusters of boys and men. They became generic guys to me.

When the timer had recorded our speeds, Angelo had the   18
fastest time for men, and much to the surprise of everyone, one of the new boys had the fastest time for the teenagers. The timer walked over to me and told me I had beaten all the other boys. Part of me said, "Wow, I'm faster than those guys," but in my gut I felt sick. Once again, I had been mistaken for a boy.

Today, I can hardly remember what the girly-girl culture I'd left   19
behind was like, except that girls weren't supposed to know much or do much besides agree with the boys. I'm forever grateful that I didn't have to grow up like most girls—on the sidelines.

At the time, I looked at the girls in my school who were in high   20
demand. They had beautiful clothes, wore make-up, and laughed when boys said something that was supposed to be funny.

I wondered how a bike helmet or ski toque could fit over their   21
hairdos. In gym class they had to run around the track in baggy blue one-piece rompers just like the rest of us. But their faces turned into splotchy red and white maps before they'd even completed one lap; mascara mixed with sweat, formed rivers and tributaries that ran from their eyes. Nothing moved in their legs. It was as if someone had stolen their strength and their muscles. They dropped out of phys ed as soon as it was no longer compulsory, and watched their boyfriends on the football team for the rest of their high-school years. Looking back, I wonder if they were ever able to make a friend of their own body.

If this was the alternative to feeling at home in your sweat, I   22
wanted no part of it. Yet I never once imagined myself anything but female. How could riding a bike possibly change your sex? Nonetheless, if I was going to continue to ride, I'd have to join the world of boys and men. . . .

Once I started racing for real—going beyond local time trials,   23
so I could see just how far and fast I could go—things changed.

Many of the men involved in cycling thought the presence of women contaminated their sacred sport. . . .

24   The only way women seemed to be accepted was if we were sleeping with the decision makers. I watched other young women pair off with much older men—important men who chose the team or coached it. I don't think they all did it to make the team. Some were so good, they couldn't have helped but make it. No, it had something to do with being a female without a man in a man's world. Men could open a door for you or they could slam it in your face. They knew I didn't like what they were doing to the other girls. I didn't sit beside them on the long trips to the races or during meals. I didn't want to get within an arm's length of those men. They accused me of not being a team player.

25   Just as boys didn't need to be told that sport was for them, girls weren't told specifically to have sex with older men, but we certainly got the message. We needed a man to help us onto the medal podium. We weren't capable of doing it ourselves.

26   Questions were asked about the girls who didn't find a nice older man to guide them. I was made to feel uncomfortable and uneasy, but there was no language to explain why. Girls who went out with boys our own age or girls our own age—there was no language for that either—started to look abnormal.

27   I feel so lucky to have escaped from sport without having been broken by these men. The women they got to will bear the scars for the rest of their lives. A trust was betrayed—the trust between coach and athlete—at a time when girls were trying to become women. Many survivors have eating disorders. Their coach-lover wanted them to remain as girl-like as possible. As they matured into women, their natural and beautiful shape was picked to pieces. Their weight was announced at dinner to the whole team while they tried vainly to eat. I know so many women athletes who did everything from starving to changing into frilly clothes right after the race, in an attempt to satisfy their coach-lovers. But their emaciated bodies were a metaphor for what was happening to their minds and spirits. The damage was often permanent.

28   These predators, the ones who called themselves coaches, controlled their girls as surely as pimps control street walkers. They had the power to stave off womanhood in maturing bodies and control the desire for sex. Their girls would never desire another man as long as they could be kept emotionally hungry for the coach-lover. When the coach-lover used one athlete up—when she either smartened up and left him or lost out to a new protégé—he soon had another human being to dominate.

But those private relationships were only one way men tried to 29 break us. There was a public fight too. Sometimes race organizers refused to hold events for women at all. They'd tell us to leave the race site, that we were trespassing, even though the course was on city streets. When we fought for equal prize money, they mounted a smear campaign against us. In 1989, the women's Tour of Niagara was three stages long and offered $1,500 in prize money. When we arrived for the first eighty-kilometre race, there were no washrooms, and no water. We used the fields for washrooms and filled our water bottles from a farmer's hose. We paid for our food, travel and accommodation. Much as I like riding in the country, it's not conducive to crowds and fans. No one watched us race. The men's equivalent was the Tour du Canada—a week-long stage race that offered $50,000. The organizers paid for travel and meals; the races were held in both country and city. The last stage ended before the crowds at the Canadian National Exhibition in Toronto.

The men who ran the Ontario Cycling Association swore they 30 wouldn't allow equal prize money. When I protested they told me I hadn't contributed anything to cycling. Why did I expect women to have equality? We hadn't earned it. In meetings, their faces turned red and the veins on their necks bulged. Once a man's wife had to restrain him from taking a swing at me. Even my own brother, the one I rode to my first bike race with, told me I was a step away from being burned at the stake as far as the other guys were concerned. The Toronto city councillor who supported us in our fight received two letters threatening rape and a death threat in the final days of the battle. I stopped riding home by myself after bike races. I stopped feeling safe.

Only lesbians would make such selfish demands, many male 31 cyclists told me. And yet, if any men agreed with us, obviously we had slept with them. Whether our struggle was private or public, the physicality of women athletes was defined sexually. It was as if it didn't matter how fast we were—our speed didn't satisfy the men in charge. If anything, it frightened them. They wanted to capture our bodies. They wouldn't allow sport—the place we felt so much freedom—to free us. But what they didn't realize was how strong they made us. Each time they put up a barrier, we cleared it. With each delay in the equality they said we'd have to earn, we developed a patience as strong as steel. We should thank them for the inner resolve they inadvertently built in us during those horrible times. . . .

Ironically, I was also spending more time competing on the 32 fierce circuit in the United States. Just as with everything else for Canadians, if you want to see if you've got what it takes, you have to go south. Once I passed that test, I realized just how far away I was from those quiet Mississauga roads I started out on. Once after a race in Nutley, New Jersey, I was trying to wash the dirt off my legs, but it wouldn't come off. The roads were layered with automobile emissions, so when we rode and whipped the grime up off the street, it caked on our sweaty legs. Later I stood on the sidewalk waiting for the men's race to start. All kinds of candy bar wrappers, popcorn bags and cigarette butts came floating down the gutter. What did all this crap have to do with the freedom I had originally found in cycling? When I started, I was gulping fresh air, pedaling under the shade of gracious old trees. I raced birds as they flew beside me. But all I could see around me now was a grimy American eastern seaboard town.

33   It took several more years, but I came to realize that competitive sport was not good for my health. After all the years, all the fights, the name calling and the tears, I decided I didn't have to race. It was probably on one of those lovely long rides that the thought hit me. Why not just ride? In the spring of 1991 I left bike racing behind. It would have been nice to race that season so I'd have a full twenty years behind me, but I had no interest in start lines any more. . . .

34   But when I quit, I started to feel again how exquisite riding a bike could be. I wasn't just free from the unhappy and unfriendly people in the sport; I was free from nervous sessions in the washroom before the race, free from weekends tied up with competition and travel, and finally free from the ride-till-you-die syndrome.

PART TWO: PATHFINDERS

35   Today, I have the best of all worlds. In the spring . . . I teach bike safety to kids. . . . Maybe some of them will have the kind of magical years I had when I was their age and started really cycling. In the winter, I teach kids how to cross-country ski. I like teaching in the far north—that way, I can ski early in the season and I get to meet kids I would never otherwise encounter. I work at a ski camp in LaRonge, Saskatchewan, with about fifteen other instructors. Once we're finished teaching for the day, we have our own little races that are by no means uncompetitive. They're just the right
36   kind of challenge. . . .

In the north, time has a different rhythm from the time in the city. It takes longer. There are only a couple of generations between the people who lived with the land and the kids I'm teaching. The Dene children come from a tradition of following the caribou that lasted until the fifties, when white people forced their great-grandparents to settle in hamlets. Many of the children—Cree and Dene—still have a strong connection to the way the earth lives and breathes. Everyone who knows anything about the north knows there are certain times of the year when everything closes and everyone goes hunting.

So for these kids, moving through the woods swiftly and gracefully just might mean a little more than it would to, say, someone from Toronto who goes to a crowded ski trail that's impossible to get lost on. There's a journey through the woods for everyone, but people who live in urban areas may not be able to make it. They don't know how to listen to the trees, or the wind, or watch for changes in the snow. There is no heartbeat for them. They're lost.

Most white people don't think of themselves as part of nature—that the way their bodies run is like the pulse of each season. Nature is separate from their being. The [descendants] of the Europeans who "settled" North America don't go to the woods. For most, the rhythm of nature is lost. They destroyed it. So great is their alienation, they don't even like living in their own bodies, let alone the wilderness. Yet there is a sense of identity in the woods, something that makes you feel in tune, especially if you come from a people whose existence, until quite recently, was intrinsically tied to the land. I think the kids in LaRonge can maintain that tie, so for me the sport of nordic skiing is not just a way of moving physically, but culturally and spiritually on a journey into the land and into your soul.

I once asked a school ski coach what he wanted the kids to take with them from being on his team. He replied, "I want them to feel what it's like to be larger than life. I want them to have worked all day long on the glide phase of the offset skate and then have something magical happen as they start to glide."

That, too, is what I want for kids in sport. I want them to glide, and soar, and ski curves and corners they never imagined they could get around. I want them to test themselves—see how much faster, higher and farther they can go.

But do I want them to enter the winning-is-the-only-thing system I endured? These kids can't afford their own skis, let alone compete in a sport where a winter's worth of wax, traveling and racing equipment costs thousands. And that's only the beginning. Am I naïve enough to believe lecherous coaches don't exist anymore? That native kids won't be discriminated against? That the white, competitive culture they'll have to perform in will do no harm to their spirit?

So do you give kids the opportunity to learn about what's in their hearts—whether it's skiing, dancing, music or painting—and not tell them about that other world where they can push their limits to the fullest? What if they have to trade their souls for that world? I still can't answer that question. It's a pity the traffic is going in the wrong direction. White people should be spending more time finding out how First Nations live a life in sport.

43   As a journalist, I have covered Aboriginal sport since 1990, and I've never been to an event that didn't include drumming, the recognition of elders, and a prayer for the athletes and their families. Willy Littlechild, who was the first Aboriginal person in Canada to obtain a physical education degree and for several years was the MP for Wetaskiwin, Alberta, says that for Cree people, dancing and running are very similar. "You celebrate thanksgiving to the Great Spirit, by dance or by running. They are a very spiritual part of our existence, and important in the development of our pride. The ceremonial run and the powwow dance are almost the same for us in giving thanks."

44   I got to experience that first-hand in the fall of 1992. I was covering a sacred run from Wasauksing to Neyaashiinigmiing—from the east side of Georgian Bay to "a place almost surrounded by water" on the west shore—for CBC Radio Sports. The organizers were short of runners, and invited me to join in. Seven runners—four adults and three kids—were to cover two hundred and sixty kilometres. Before we left, elders from Wasauksing folded up messages they wanted the runners to read when they reached Neyaashiinigmiing and placed them inside a staff. It wasn't much larger than a relay baton, but it contained a sacred bundle that we weren't to open and it was wrapped in the four colours of humanity: red, black, white and yellow. The elders did a sweetgrass smudging ceremony for the runners, and we were off.

45   The ceremonial or sacred run is a long distance event many people take part in. Much like a relay team, they pass the staff to one another, but instead of running a set distance, they go as far as they can, often surprising themselves with their endurance. Traditional runners spend years learning from elders and teachers about the responsibilities of being a First Nations person, of being an athlete and a carrier of culture and messages. Alcohol is forbidden, not just on the runs, but in life. So are drugs.

46   The roots of the run are buried so deeply in ritual and tradition that no amount of assimilation could destroy them. Spiritual runners would go from nation to nation, passing messages about powwows, councils and war, often covering hundreds of kilometres. Their footprints are in the earth forever and that's why they are still with us.

47   Meanwhile, I was running the best leg of the journey. I'd already gone twelve kilometres before night settled in and my next turn rolled around at midnight. I received the staff and continued to run

through the lakes district. The moon shone back from the water. At times I could see my shadow. It was like running through velvet.

A van and a small car followed the runners. About 1:00 a.m., I handed the staff to another runner, folded myself up in the back of the car, and fell asleep. It was my turn again just before dawn, but when I tried to stretch out of the back seat, all I felt was pain. I should have known better. Twenty-two kilometres worth of lactic acid (the enemy of all athletes) had settled into my muscles. Every injury I had ever sustained came back for a visit. 48

Now the run wasn't so romantic. It was hard. We had a sunrise sweetgrass ceremony at which we asked for help. Two runners from Christian Island joined us, only to misunderstand the rules and run eighteen kilometres without the staff. This distance couldn't be counted; we had to honour the runners of the past and that meant *with* the staff. Our youngest runner, Lester Taboboneung, was only eleven. It was his first run, and like the rest of the kids, he was worn out and limping. 49

"Who cares if they didn't carry the staff?" I told the chief runner. "It's not as if they had cars and cellular telephones, but we're using them. Let's just get where we're supposed to go as fast as we can. I'm injured and the kids are injured; they just won't tell you." 50

"Our ancestors must have had injuries and they kept running. We're supposed to understand what they felt like," he replied. 51

We retraced these eighteen kilometres, but our pace was decidedly slower. All I wanted was a shower and a place big enough to stretch and sleep. I was hungry, sweaty, smelly, cramped, stiff and sore. We forced ourselves to keep going. Yet whenever we came to roadkill, everything stopped. An off-duty runner would get out of the car and gently pull the animal off the road. "Why do you do that?" I asked. "He is our brother," the chief runner replied, looking at me oddly as if I should have figured it out for myself. "We can't leave him there." 52

Eventually, I started to understand. Everything I'd done in sport was about getting to the finish line the fastest way I could. Never mind roadkill, if I had heard a crash behind me in a bike race, I immediately turned on the speed to try to get a jump on those caught behind the crash. I wouldn't have stopped and helped anyone back up on her bike. It wasn't my fault she didn't know how to ride a straight line. If you don't finish first, I was taught, examine every detail of your preparation to figure out what you did wrong. 53

But this sacred run was about finishing as much as any race I'd ever been in. It was also as difficult as any race I'd ever been in. The 54 difference—and, for me, much of the difficulty—was that time didn't matter. What we did between the start and the finish mattered.

55   With sixty kilometres to go, we were met by five runners with fresh legs. Someone had used that sacred cellular phone to call ahead for help. From this point, everything moved swiftly. With five kilometres to go, the kids, who could barely walk earlier in the day, piled out of the car and started running. Lester was handed the staff as we ran down a graceful hill that led into the park where the gathering at Neyaashiinigmiing waited. The drums were stronger and stronger as we neared the cedar encampment. One thousand people cheered. The runners read the elders' messages, which were about such contemporary concerns as land claims, staying clear of drugs and alcohol, and being proud to be First Nations.

56   Watching the kids made me feel as if I'd completed a circle. I'd started out like them—young and excited. Now I was feeling the way Duanne and Angelo must have felt when they took my brother and me cycling and skiing—really happy to see kids figure out they can go farther than they imagined.

57   You can have the World Series. I'll take the feeling you get when you watch an eleven-year-old run when he thinks he can't, then sprint into an encampment and deliver the staff he and many others have carried for the past twenty-seven hours. Then this shy little guy finds it in himself to speak to one thousand people, mainly adults, about land claims and other important matters. He speaks in Ojibway and English.

58   During our time together on the run, I wondered what might be going on in Lester's mind. At such a young age, he had been honoured by the elders and allowed to carry their messages. He ran through the day and night, as his people had millennia before, when it was so hard to keep pushing one foot ahead of the other and his body kept begging him to stop.

59   There is a very small fraction of time when a runner has neither foot on the ground. It's a time when he flies, when he runs free of gravity. And so, I wondered, did Lester hear the seemingly endless road that stretched ahead of him whisper as he ran? Did he hear it say there would be unbearable times when he would have to run on the painful and parched path that stretched into the future? But also that at other times it would whisper to him and say, Lester Taboboneung, you will have the strength and the spirit to become the wind.

Laura Robinson was a nationally competitive cyclist and rower who now pursues a career as a writer and journalist, focusing mainly on sports issues, particularly those that affect women. Her books include *She Shoots, She Scores: Canadian Perspectives on Women in Sports*; *Crossing the Line: Violence and Sexual Assault in Canada's National*

Sport; Black Tights: Women, Sport, and Sexuality; and *Great Girls: Profiles of Awesome Canadian Athletes.* Robinson has written for a number of Canadian newspapers and magazines, and for the CBC and the National Film Board. She coaches First Nations' youths in mountain biking and cross-country skiing. Robinson has also served as a writer-in-residence at several colleges and universities.

Can you tell a dog by its spots? Can you predict its behaviour from its breed? Malcolm Gladwell asks some provocative questions about ethnic and racial profiling based on the canine stereotyping that prompted Ontario's controversial ban on pit bulls in 2006.

Troublemakers: What Pit Bulls Can Teach Us About Profiling

MALCOLM GLADWELL

One afternoon last February [2005], Guy Clairoux picked up his two-and-a half-year-old son, Jayden, from day care and walked him back to their house in the west end of Ottawa, Ontario. They were almost home. Jayden was straggling behind, and, as his father's back was turned, a pit bull jumped over a backyard fence and lunged at Jayden. "The dog had his head in its mouth and started to do this shake," Clairoux's wife, JoAnn Hartley, said later. As she watched in horror, two more pit bulls jumped over the fence, joining in the assault. She and Clairoux came running, and he punched the first of the dogs in the head, until it dropped Jayden, and then he threw the boy toward his mother. Hartley fell on her son, protecting him with her body. "JoAnn!" Clairoux cried out, as all three dogs descended on his wife. "Cover your neck, cover your neck." A neighbor, sitting by her window, screamed for help. Her partner and a friend, Mario Gauthier, ran outside. A neighborhood boy grabbed his hockey stick and threw it to Gauthier. He began hitting one of the dogs over the head, until the stick broke. "They wouldn't stop," Gauthier said. "As soon as you'd stop, they'd attack again. I've never seen a dog go so crazy. They were like Tasmanian devils." The police came. The dogs were pulled away, and the Clairouxes and one of the rescuers were taken to the hospital. Five days later, the Ontario legislature banned the ownership of pit bulls. . . .

2   Pit bulls, descendants of the bulldogs used in the nineteenth century for bull baiting and dogfighting, have been bred for "gameness," and thus a lowered inhibition to aggression. Most dogs fight as a last resort, when staring and growling fail. A pit bull is willing to fight with little or no provocation. Pit bulls seem to have a high tolerance for pain, making it possible for them to fight to the point of exhaustion. Whereas guard dogs like German shepherds usually attempt to restrain those they perceive to be threats by biting and holding, pit bulls try to inflict the maximum amount of damage on an opponent. They bite, hold, shake, and tear. They don't growl or assume an aggressive facial expression as warning. They just attack. . . . In epidemiological studies of dog bites, the pit bull is overrepresented among dogs known to have seriously injured or killed human beings, and, as a result, pit bulls have been banned or restricted in several Western European countries, China, and numerous cities and municipalities across North America. Pit bulls are dangerous.

3   Of course, not all pit bulls are dangerous. Most don't bite anyone. Meanwhile, Dobermans and Great Danes and German shepherds and Rottweilers are frequent biters as well, and the dog that recently mauled a Frenchwoman so badly that she was given the world's first face transplant was, of all things, a Labrador retriever. When we say that pit bulls are dangerous, we are making a generalization, just as insurance companies use generalizations when they charge young men more for car insurance than the rest of us (even though many young men are perfectly good drivers), and doctors use generalizations when they tell overweight middle-aged men to get their cholesterol checked (even though many overweight middle-aged men won't experience heart trouble). Because we don't know which dog will bite someone or who will have a heart attack or which drivers will get in an accident, we can make predictions only by generalizing. . . .

4   Another word for generalization, though, is "stereotype," and stereotypes are usually not considered desirable dimensions for our decision-making lives. The process of moving from the specific to the general is both necessary and perilous. A doctor could, with some statistical support, generalize about men of a certain age and weight. But what if generalizing from other traits—such as high blood pressure, family history, and smoking—saved more lives? Behind each generalization is a choice of what factors to leave in and what factors to leave out, and those choices can prove surprisingly complicated. After the attack on Jayden Clairoux, the Ontario government chose to make a generalization about pit bulls. But it could also have chosen to generalize about powerful dogs, or about

the kinds of people who own powerful dogs, or about small children, or about back-yard fences—or, indeed, about any number of other things to do with dogs and people and places. How do we know when we've made the right generalization?

In July [2005], following the transit bombings in London, the New York City Police Department announced that it would send officers into the subways to conduct random searches of passengers' bags. On the face of it, doing random searches in the hunt for terrorists—as opposed to being guided by generalizations—seems like a silly idea. As a columnist in *New York* wrote at the time, "Not just 'most' but nearly every jihadi who has attacked a Western European or American target is a young Arab or Pakistani man. In other words, you can predict with a fair degree of certainty what an Al Qaeda terrorist looks like. Just as we have always known what Mafiosi look like—even as we understand that only an infinitesimal fraction of Italian-Americans are members of the mob."

But wait: do we really know what mafiosi look like? In "The Godfather," where most of us get our knowledge of the Mafia, the male members of the Corleone family were played by Marlon Brando, who was of Irish and French ancestry, James Caan, who is Jewish, and two Italian-Americans, Al Pacino and John Cazale. To go by "The Godfather," mafiosi look like white men of European descent, which, as generalizations go, isn't terribly helpful. Figuring out what an Islamic terrorist looks like isn't any easier. Muslims are not like the Amish: they don't come dressed in identifiable costumes. And they don't look like basketball players; they don't come in predictable shapes and sizes. Islam is a religion that spans the globe.

"We have a policy against racial profiling," Raymond Kelly, New York City's police commissioner, told me. "I put it in here in March of the first year I was here. It's the wrong thing to do, and it's also ineffective. If you look at the London bombings, you have three British citizens of Pakistani descent. You have Germaine Lindsay, who is Jamaican. You have the next crew, on July 21st, who are East African. You have a Chechen woman in Moscow in early 2004 who blows herself up in the subway station. So whom do you profile? Look at New York City. Forty per cent of New Yorkers are born outside the country. Look at the diversity here. Who am I supposed to profile?"

Kelly was pointing out what might be called profiling's "category problem." Generalizations involve matching a category of people to a behavior or trait—overweight middle-aged men to heart-attack risk, young men to bad driving. But, for that process to work, you have to be able both to define and to identify the category you are generalizing about. "You think that terrorists aren't aware of how easy it is to be characterized by ethnicity?" Kelly went on. "Look at the 9/11 hijackers. They came here. They shaved. They went to topless bars. They wanted to blend in. They wanted to look like they were part of the American dream. These are not dumb people. Could a terrorist dress up as a Hasidic Jew and walk into the subway, and not be profiled? Yes. I think profiling is just nuts."

9   Pit-bull bans involve a category problem, too, because pit bulls, as it happens, aren't a single breed. The name refers to dogs belonging to a number of related breeds, such as the American Staffordshire terrier, the Staffordshire bull terrier, and the American pit bull terrier—all of which share a square and muscular body, a short snout, and a sleek, short-haired coat. Thus the Ontario ban prohibits not only these three breeds but any "dog that has an appearance and physical characteristics that are substantially similar" to theirs; the term of art is "pit bull-type" dogs. But what does that mean? Is a cross between an American pit bull terrier and a golden retriever a pit bull-type dog or a golden retriever-type dog? If thinking about muscular terriers as pit bulls is a generalization, then thinking about dangerous dogs as anything substantially similar to a pit bull is a generalization about a generalization. . . .

10   The goal of a pit-bull ban, obviously, isn't to prohibit dogs that look like pit bulls. The pit-bull appearance is a proxy for the pit-bull temperament—for some trait that these dogs share. But "pit bull-ness" turns out to be elusive as well. The supposedly troublesome characteristics of the pit-bull type—its gameness, its determination, its insensitivity to pain—are chiefly directed toward other dogs. Pit bulls were not bred to fight humans. On the contrary: a dog that went after spectators, or its handler, or the trainer, or any of the other people involved in making a dogfighting dog a good dog-fighter was usually put down. (The rule in the pit-bull world was "Man-eaters die.")

11   A Georgia-based group called the American Temperament Test Society [ATTS] has put twenty-five thousand dogs through a ten-part standardized drill designed to assess a dog's stability, shyness, aggressiveness, and friendliness in the company of people. A handler takes a dog on a six-foot lead and judges its reaction to stimuli such as gunshots, an umbrella opening, and a weirdly dressed stranger approaching in a threatening way. Eighty-four per cent of the pit bulls that have been given the test have passed, which ranks pit bulls ahead of beagles, Airedales, bearded collies, and all but one variety of dachshund. . . . It can even be argued that the same traits that make the pit bull so aggressive toward other dogs are

what make it so nice to humans. "There are a lot of pit bulls these days who are licensed therapy dogs," the writer Vicki Hearne points out. "Their stability and resoluteness make them excellent for work with people who might not like a more bouncy, flibberti-gibbet sort of dog. When pit bulls set out to provide comfort, they are as resolute as they are when they fight, but what they are res-olute about is being gentle. And, because they are fearless, they can be gentle with anybody."

Then which are the pit bulls that get into trouble? "The ones   12 that the legislation is geared toward have aggressive tendencies that are either bred in by the breeder, trained in by the trainer, or reinforced in by the owner," [ATTS president Carl] Herkstroeter says. A mean pit bull is a dog that has been turned mean, by selec-tive breeding, by being cross-bred with a bigger, human-aggressive breed like German shepherds or Rottweilers, or by being condi-tioned in such a way that it begins to express hostility to human beings. A pit pull is dangerous to people, then, not to the extent that it expresses its essential pit bullness but to the extent that it deviates from it. A pit-bull is a generalization about a generalization about a trait that is not, in fact, general. That's a category problem.

One of the puzzling things about New York City is that, after the   13 enormous and well-publicized reductions in crime in the mid-nine-teen-nineties, the crime rate has continued to fall. In the past two years, for instance, murder in New York has declined by almost ten per cent, rape by twelve per cent, and burglary by more than eigh-teen per cent. Just in the last year, auto theft went down 11.8 per cent. On a list of two hundred and forty cities in the United States with a population of a hundred thousand or more, New York City now ranks two hundred-and-twenty-second in crime, down near the bottom with Fontana, California, and Port St. Lucie, Florida. In the nineteen-nineties, the crime decrease was attributed to big obvious changes in city life and government—the decline of the drug trade, the gentrification of Brooklyn, the successful implemen-tation of "broken windows" policing. But all those big changes hap-pened a decade ago. Why is crime *still* falling?

The explanation may have to do with a shift in police tactics.   14 The N.Y.P.D. has a computerized map showing, in real time, pre-cisely where serious crimes are being reported, and at any moment the map typically shows a few dozen constantly shifting high-crime hot spots, some as small as two or three blocks square. What the N.Y.P.D. has done, under Commissioner Kelly, is to use the map to establish "impact zones," and to direct newly graduated officers—who used to be distributed proportionally to precincts across the city—to these zones, in some cases doubling the number of officers in the immediate neighborhood. . . .

15   For years, experts have maintained that the incidence of violent crime is "inelastic" relative to police presence—that people commit serious crimes because of poverty and psychopathology and cultural dysfunction, along with spontaneous motives and opportunities. The presence of a few extra officers down the block, it was thought, wouldn't make much difference. But the N.Y.P.D. experience suggests otherwise. More police means that some crimes are prevented, others are more easily solved, and still others are displaced—pushed out of the troubled neighborhood—which Kelly says is a good thing, because it disrupts the patterns and practices and social networks that serve as the basis for lawbreaking. In other words, the relation between New York City (a category) and criminality (a trait) is unstable, and this kind of instability is another way in which our generalizations can be derailed.

16   Why, for instance, is it a useful rule of thumb that Kenyans are good distance runners? It's not just that it's statistically supportable today. It's that it has been true for almost half a century, and that in Kenya the tradition of distance running is sufficiently rooted that something cataclysmic would have to happen to dislodge it. By contrast, the generalization that New York City is a crime-ridden place was once true and now, manifestly, isn't. People who moved to sunny retirement communities like Port St. Lucie because they thought they were much safer than New York are suddenly in the position of having made the wrong bet.

17   The instability issue is a problem for profiling in law enforcement as well. The law professor David Cole once tallied up some of the traits that Drug Enforcement Administration [D.E.A.] agents have used over the years in making generalizations about suspected smugglers. Here is a sample:

18   Arrived late at night; arrived early in the morning; arrived in afternoon; one of the first to deplane; one of the last to deplane; deplaned in the middle; purchased ticket at the airport; made reservation on short notice; bought coach ticket; bought first-class ticket; used one-way ticket; used round-trip ticket; paid for ticket with cash; paid for ticket with small denomination currency; paid for ticket with large denomination currency; made local telephone calls after deplaning; made long distance telephone call after deplaning; pretended to make telephone call; traveled from New York to Los Angeles; traveled to Houston; carried no luggage; carried brand-new luggage; carried a small bag; carried a medium-sized bag; carried two bulky garment bags; carried two heavy suitcases; carried four

pieces of luggage; overly protective of luggage; disassociated self from luggage; traveled alone; traveled with a companion; acted too nervous; acted too calm; made eye contact with officer; avoided making eye contact with officer; wore expensive clothing and jewelry; dressed casually; went to restroom after deplaning; walked rapidly through airport; walked slowly through airport; walked aimlessly through airport; left airport by taxi; left airport by limousine; left airport by private car; left airport by hotel courtesy van.

Some of these reasons for suspicion are plainly absurd, suggesting   19 that there's no particular rationale to the generalizations used by D.E.A. agents in stopping suspected drug smugglers. A way of making sense of the list, though, is to think of it as a catalogue of unstable traits. Smugglers may once have tended to buy one-way tickets in cash and carry two bulky suitcases. But they don't have to. They can easily switch to round-trip tickets bought with a credit card, or a single carry-on bag, without losing their capacity to smuggle. There's a second kind of instability here as well. Maybe the reason some of them switched from one-way tickets and two bulky suitcases was that law enforcement got wise to those habits, so the smugglers did the equivalent of what the jihadis seemed to have done in London, when they switched to East Africans because the scrutiny of young Arab and Pakistani men grew too intense. It doesn't work to generalize about a relationship between a category and a trait when that relationship isn't stable—or when the act of generalizing may itself change the basis of the generalization.

Before Kelly became the New York police commissioner, he   20 served as the head of the U.S. Customs Service, and while he was there he overhauled the criteria that border-control officers use to identify and search suspected smugglers. There had been a list of forty-three suspicious traits. He replaced it with a list of six broad criteria. Is there something suspicious about their physical appearance? Are they nervous? Is there specific intelligence targeting this person? Does the drug-sniffing dog raise an alarm? Is there something amiss in their paperwork or explanations? Has contraband been found that implicates this person?

You'll find nothing here about race or gender or ethnicity, and   21 nothing here about expensive jewelry or deplaning at the middle or the end, or walking briskly or walking aimlessly. Kelly removed all the unstable generalizations, forcing customs officers to make generalizations about things that don't change from one day or one month to the next. Some percentage of smugglers will *always* be nervous, will *always* get their story wrong, and will *always* be caught by the dogs. That's why those kinds of inferences are more reliable than the ones based on whether smugglers are white or black, or carry one bag or two. After Kelly's reforms, the number of searches conducted by the Customs Service dropped by about seventy-five per cent, but the number of successful seizures improved by twenty-five per cent. The officers went from making fairly lousy decisions about smugglers to making pretty good ones. . . .

22   Does the notion of a pit-bull menace rest on a stable or an unstable generalization? The best data we have on breed dangerousness are fatal dog bites, which serve as a useful indicator of just how much havoc certain kinds of dogs are causing. Between the late nineteen-seventies and the late nineteen-nineties, more than twenty-five breeds were involved in fatal attacks in the United States. Pit-bull breeds led the pack, but the variability from year to year is considerable. For instance, in the period from 1981 to 1982 fatalities were caused by five pit bulls, three mixed breeds, two St. Bernards, two German-shepherd mixes, a pure-bred German shepherd, a husky type, a Doberman, a Chow Chow, a Great Dane, a wolf-dog hybrid, a husky mix, and a pit-bull mix—but no Rottweilers. In 1995 and 1996, the list included ten Rottweilers, four pit bulls, two German shepherds, two huskies, two Chow Chows, two wolf-dog hybrids, two shepherd mixes, a Rottweiler mix, a mixed breed, a Chow Chow mix, and a Great Dane. The kinds of dogs that kill people change over time, because the popularity of certain breeds changes over time. The one thing that doesn't change is the total number of the people killed by dogs. When we have more problems with pit bulls, it's not necessarily a sign that pit bulls are more dangerous than other dogs. It could just be a sign that pit bulls have become more numerous. . . .

23   There is no shortage of more stable generalizations about dangerous dogs, though. A 1991 study in Denver, for example, compared a hundred and seventy-eight dogs with a history of biting people with a random sample of a hundred and seventy-eight dogs with no history of biting. The breeds were scattered: German shepherds, Akitas, and Chow Chows were among those most heavily represented. (There were no pit bulls among the biting dogs in the study, because Denver banned pit bulls in 1989.) But a number of other, more stable factors stand out. The biters were 6.2 times as likely to be male than female, and 2.6 times as likely to be intact than neutered. The Denver study also found that biters were 2.8 times as likely to be chained as unchained. . . .

24   In many cases, vicious dogs are hungry or in need of medical attention. Often, the dogs had a history of aggressive incidents, and, overwhelmingly, dog-bite victims were children (particularly

small boys) who were physically vulnerable to attack and may also have unwittingly done things to provoke the dog, like teasing it, or bothering it while it was eating. The strongest connection of all, though, is between the trait of dog viciousness and certain kinds of dog owners. In about a quarter of fatal dog-bite cases, the dog owners were previously involved in illegal fighting. The dogs that bit people are, in many cases, socially isolated because their owners are socially isolated, and they are vicious because they have owners who want a vicious dog. The junk-yard German shepherd—which looks as if it would rip your throat out—and the German-shepherd guide dog are the same breed. But they are not the same dog, because they have owners with different intentions.

"A fatal dog attack is not just a dog bite by a big or aggressive   25
dog," [Randall] Lockwood [senior vice president of the A.S.P.C.A. and one of the country's leading dog experts] went on. "It is usually a perfect storm of bad human–canine interactions—the wrong dog, the wrong background, the wrong history in the hands of the wrong person in the wrong environmental situation. I've been involved in many legal cases involving fatal dog attacks, and, certainly, it's my impression that these are generally cases where everyone is to blame. You've got the unsupervised three-year-old child wandering in the neighborhood killed by a starved, abused dog owned by the dogfighting boyfriend of some woman who doesn't know where her child is. It's not old Shep sleeping by the fire who suddenly goes bonkers. Usually there are all kinds of other warning signs."

Jayden Clairoux was attacked by Jada, a pit-bull terrier, and her   26
two pit-bull–bullmastiff puppies, Agua and Akasha. The dogs were owned by a twenty-one-year-old man named Shridev Café, who worked in construction and did odd jobs. Five weeks before the Clairoux attack, Café's three dogs got loose and attacked a sixteen-year-old boy and his four-year-old half brother while they were ice skating. The boys beat back the animals with a snow shovel and escaped into a neighbor's house. Café was fined, and he moved the dogs to his seventeen-year-old girlfriend's house. This was not the first time that he ran into trouble; a few months later, he was charged with domestic assault, and, in another incident, involving a street brawl, with aggravated assault. . . . Agua and Akasha were now about seven months old. The court order in the wake of the first attack required that they be muzzled when they were outside the home and kept in an enclosed yard. But Café did not muzzle them, because, he said later, he couldn't afford muzzles, and apparently no one from the city ever came by to force him to comply. A

few times, he talked about taking his dogs to obedience classes, but never did. The subject of neutering them also came up—particularly Agua, the male—but neutering cost a hundred dollars, which he evidently thought was too much money, and when the city temporarily confiscated his animals after the first attack it did not neuter them, either, because Ottawa does not have a policy of pre-emptively neutering dogs that bite people.

27   On the day of the second attack, according to some accounts, a visitor came by the house of Café's girlfriend, and the dogs got wound up. They were put outside, where the snowbanks were high enough so that the back-yard fence could be readily jumped. Jayden Clairoux stopped and stared at the dogs, saying, "Puppies, puppies." His mother called out to his father. His father came running, which is the kind of thing that will rile up an aggressive dog. The dogs jumped the fence, and Agua took Jayden's head in his mouth and started to shake. It was a textbook dog-biting case: unneutered, ill-trained, charged-up dogs, with a history of aggression and an irresponsible owner, somehow get loose, and set upon a small child. The dogs had already passed through the animal bureaucracy of Ottawa, and the city could easily have prevented the second attack with the right kind of generalization—a generalization based not on breed but on the known and meaningful connection between dangerous dogs and negligent owners. But that would have required someone to track down Shridev Café, and check to see whether he had bought muzzles, and someone to send the dogs to be neutered after the first attack, and an animal-control law that insured that those whose dogs attack small children forfeit their right to have a dog. It would have required, that is, a more exacting set of generalizations to be more exactingly applied. It's always easier just to ban the breed.

Malcolm Gladwell (b. 1963) was born in England and grew up in Canada, where he graduated with a degree in history from the University of Toronto. He has been a staff writer for *The New Yorker* since 1996. Gladwell draws on sociology, psychology, politics, technology, and consumer behaviour in his articles. He has written two books: *The Tipping Point: How Little Things Can Make a Big Difference* (2000) and *Blink: The Power of Thinking Without Thinking* (2005). Gladwell often focuses on the unexpected implications of sociological and psychological research in our lives, as "Troublemakers" illustrates.

Tired of TV? Bored with your PlayStation? Even fed up with
your iPod? Novelist Carol Shields suggests a revolutionary—
if somewhat old-fashioned—medium for entertaining yourself
and nourishing your spirit: curl up with a good book.

The Case for Curling Up with a Book

CAROL SHIELDS

Some years ago a Canadian politician, one of our more admirable   1
figures, announced that he was cutting back on his public life
because it interfered with his reading. *His reading*—notice the
possessive pronoun, like saying his arm or his leg—and notice too,
the assumption that human beings carry, like a kind of cerebral brief
case, this built-in commitment to time and energy[:] *their reading*.

I'm told that people no longer know how to curl up with a   2
book. The body has forgotten how to curl. Either we snack on
paperbacks while waiting for the bus or we hunch over our books
with a yellow underliner in hand. Or, more and more, we sit before
a screen and "interact."

Curling up with a book can be accomplished in a variety of   3
ways: in bed for instance, with a towel on a sunlit beach, or from an
armchair parked next to a good reading lamp. What it absolutely
requires is a block of uninterrupted time, solitary time and our
society sometimes looks with pity on the solitary, that woman alone
at the movies, that poor man sitting by himself at his restaurant
table. Our hearts go out to them, but reading, by definition, can
only be done alone. I would like to make the case today for solitary
time, for a life with space enough to curl up with a book.

Reading, at least since human beings learned to read silently   4
(and what a cognitive shift that was!) requires an extraordinary
effort at paying attention, at remaining alert. The object of our
attention matters less, in a sense, than the purity of our awareness.
As the American writer Sven Birkerts says, it is better, better in
terms of touching the self within us, that we move from a state of
half-distraction to one of full attention. When we read with attention, an inner circuit of the brain is satisfyingly completed. We feel
our perceptions sharpen and acquire edge. Reading, as many of
you have discovered, is one of the very few things you can do only
by shining your full awareness on the task. We can make love,
cook, listen to music, shop for groceries, add up columns of figures
all with our brain, our self that is, divided and distracted. But print
on the page demands all of us. It is so complex, its cognitive cir-
cuitry so demanding; the black strokes on the white page must be
apprehended and translated into ideas, and ideas fitted into

patterns, the patterns then shifted and analyzed. The eye travels backward for a moment; this in itself is a technical marvel, rereading a sentence or a paragraph, extracting the sense, the intention, the essence of what is offered.

5   And ironically, this singleness of focus delivers a doubleness of perception. You are invited into a moment sheathed in nothing but itself. Reading a novel, *curled up* with a novel, you are simultaneously in your armchair and in, for instance, the garden of Virginia Woolf in the year 1927, or a shabby Manitoba farmhouse conjured by Margaret Laurence, . . . participating fully in another world while remaining conscious of the core of your self, that self that may be hardwired into our bodies or else developed slowly, created over the long distance of our lives.

6   We are connected through our work, through our familial chain and, by way of the Internet, to virtually everyone in the world. So what of the private self which comes tantalizingly alive under the circle of the reading lamp, that self that we only occasionally touch and then with trepidation. We use the expression "being lost in a book," but we are really closer to a state of being found. Curled up with a novel about an East Indian family for instance, we are not so much escaping our own splintered and decentred world as we are enlarging our sense of self, our multiplying possibilities and expanded experience. People are, after all, tragically limited: we can live in only so many places, work at a small number of jobs or professions; we can love only a finite number of people. Reading, and particularly the reading of fiction . . . lets us be other, to touch and taste the other, to sense the shock and satisfaction of otherness. A novel lets us be ourselves and yet enter another person's boundaried world, to share in a private gaze between reader and writer. *Your* reading, and here comes the possessive pronoun again, can be part of your life and there will be times when it may be the best part. . . .

7   [A] written text, as opposed to electronic information, has formal order, tone, voice, irony, persuasion. We can inhabit a book; we can possess it and be possessed by it. The critic and scholar Martha Nussbaum believes that attentive readers of serious fiction cannot help but be compassionate and ethical citizens. The rhythms of prose train the empathetic imagination and the rational emotions. . . .

8   Almost all of [us are] plugged into the electronic world in one way or another, reliant on it for its millions of bytes of information. But a factoid, a nugget of pure information, or even the ever-widening web of information, while enabling us to perform, does relatively little to nourish us. A computer connects facts but cannot reflect upon them. There is no depth, no embeddedness. It is, liter-

ally, software, plaintext, language prefabricated and sorted into byte sizes. It does not, in short, aspire; it rarely sings. Enemies of the book want to see information freed from the prison of the printed page, putting faith instead in free floating information and this would be fine if we weren't human beings, historical beings, thinking beings with a hunger for diversion, for narrative, for consolation, for exhortation.

We need literature on the page because it allows us to experi-   9
ence more fully, to imagine more deeply, enabling us to live more freely. Reading, [we] are in touch with [our best selves], and I think, too, that reading shortens the distance we must travel to discover that our most private perceptions are, in fact, universally felt. *Your* reading will intersect with the axis of *my* reading and of his reading and of her reading. Reading, then, offers us the ultimate website, where attention, awareness, reflection, understanding, clarity, and civility come together in a transformative experience.

Novelist, poet, and playwright Carol Shields was born in Oak Park, Illinois, in 1935. She was the winner of a Pulitzer Prize, the Governor General's Award, the Orange Prize, the Charles Taylor Prize, and the National Book Critics Circle Award. Her later works included a biography of Jane Austen and the novel *Unless*. Shields lived in Victoria, British Columbia, and died there in 2003.

In this essay, one of the world's great writers tackles the question: Does fiction matter? Mario Vargas Llosa contrasts the impact of stories told in print with stories told through images (television, movies) and argues that one form of story-telling encourages us to confront and resolve personal and political problems, while the other encourages us to ignore or hide from them. Is he right? Is fiction dying?

With Pens Drawn

MARIO VARGAS LLOSA

My vocation as a writer grew out of the idea that literature   1
does not exist in a closed artistic sphere but embraces a larger moral and civic universe. This is what has motivated everything I have written. It is also, alas, now turning me into a dinosaur in trousers, surrounded by computers.

Statistics tell us that never before have so many books been   2
sold. The trouble is that hardly anybody I come across believes any

longer that literature serves any great purpose beyond alleviating boredom on the bus or the underground, or has any higher ambition beyond being transformed into television or movie scripts. Literature has gone light. That's why critics such as George Steiner have come to believe literature is already dead, and why novelists such as V. S. Naipaul have come to proclaim that they will not write another novel because the genre now fills them with disgust.

3   But amid this pessimism about literature, we should remember that many people still fear the writer. Look at the criminal clique that governs Nigeria and executed Ogoni author and activist Ken Saro-Wiwa after a trumped-up murder charge; at the imams who declared a *fatwa* on novelist Salman Rushdie for criticizing Islamic practices in *The Satanic Verses*; at the Muslim fundamentalists in Algeria who have cut the throats of dozens of journalists, writers, and thespians; and at all those regimes in North Korea, Cuba, China, Laos, Burma, and elsewhere where censorship prevails and prisons are full of writers.

4   So in countries that are supposed to be cultivated—and are the most free and democratic—literature is becoming a hobby without real value, while in countries where freedom is restricted, literature is considered dangerous, the vehicle of subversive ideas. Novelists and poets in free countries, who view their profession with disillusionment, should open their eyes to this vast part of the globe that is not yet free. It might give them courage.

5   I have an old-fashioned view: I believe that literature must address itself to the problems of its time. Authors must write with the conviction that what they are writing can help others become more free, more sensitive, more clear-sighted; yet without the self-righteous illusion of many intellectuals that their work helps contain violence, reduce injustice, and promote liberty. I have erred too often myself, and I have seen too many writers I admired err—even put their talents at the service of ideological lies and state crimes—to delude myself. But without ceasing to be entertaining, literature should immerse itself in the life of the streets, in the unraveling of history, as it did in the best of times. This is the only way in which writers can help their contemporaries and save literature from the flimsy state to which it sometimes seems condemned.

6   If the only point of literature is to entertain, then it cannot compete with the fictions pouring out of screens, large or small. An illusion made of words requires the reader's active participation, an effort of the imagination and sometimes, in modern literature, complex feats of memory, association, and creativity. Television and cinema audiences are exempt from all this by virtue of the images. This makes them lazy and increasingly allergic to intellectually challenging entertainment.

Screen fiction is intense on account of its immediacy and   7
ephemeral in terms of effect: it captivates us and then releases us
almost instantly. Literary fiction holds us captive for life. To say that
the works of authors such as Dostoevsky, Tolstoy, and Proust are
entertaining would be to insult them. For, while they are usually
read in a state of high excitement, the most important effect of a
good book is in the aftermath, its ability to fire memory over time.
The afterglow is still alive within me because without the books I
have read, I would not be who I am, for better or worse, nor would
I believe what I believe, with all the doubts and certainties that
keep me going. Those books shaped me, changed me, made me.
And they continue changing me, in step with the life I measure
them against. In those books I learned that the world is in bad
shape and that it will always be so—which is no reason to refrain
from doing whatever we can to keep it from getting worse. They
taught me that in all our diversity of culture, races, and beliefs, as
fellow actors in the human comedy, we deserve equal respect. They
also taught me why we so rarely get it. There is nothing like good
literature to help us detect the roots of the cruelty human beings
can unleash.

Without a committed literature it will become even more diffi-   8
cult to contain all those outbreaks of war, genocide, ethnic and religious strife, refugee displacement, and terrorist activity that
threaten to multiply and that have already smashed the hopes
raised by the collapse of the Berlin Wall. Removing blindfolds,
expressing indignation in the face of injustice, and demonstrating
that there is room for hope under the most trying circumstances are
all things literature has been good at, even though it has occasionally been mistaken in its targets and defended the indefensible.

The written word has a special responsibility to do these things   9
because it is better at telling the truth than audiovisual media,
which are by their nature condemned to skate over the surface of
things and are much more constrained in their freedom of expression. The phenomenal sophistication with which news bulletins can
nowadays transport us to the epicenter of events on every continent
has turned us all into voyeurs and the whole world into one vast
theater, or more precisely into a movie. Audiovisual information—
so transient, so striking, and so superficial—makes us see history as
fiction, distancing us by concealing the causes and context behind
the sequence of events that are so vividly portrayed. This con-
demns us to a state of passive acceptance, moral insensibility, and
psychological inertia similar to that inspired by television fiction
and other programs whose only purpose is to entertain.

10   We all like to escape from reality; indeed, that is one of the functions of literature. But making the present unreal, turning actual history into fiction, has the effect of demobilizing citizens, making them feel exempt from civic responsibility, encouraging the conviction that it is beyond anyone's reach to intervene in a history whose screenplay is already written. Along this path we may well slide into a world where there are no citizens, only spectators, a world where, although formal democracy may be preserved, we will be resigned to the kind of lethargy dictatorships aspire to establish.

Novelist and critic Mario Vargas Llosa was born in Peru in 1936. Always politically outspoken, Vargas Llosa served as the first Latin American president of PEN, an international group that champions the rights of writers, and was a presidential candidate in Peru's 1990 elections. After a close race, Alberto Fujimora was elected, and Vargas Llosa began his travels, living for a time in Spain, London, and Washington, DC, before returning to Lima. Some of his best-known works are *Death in the Andes* (1993), *Notebooks of Don Rigoberto* (1998), and *The Feast of the Goat* (2000). His most recent novel, the critically acclaimed *Travesuras de la niña mala*, was published in 2006.

What is meant by "one"? Mark Kingwell returns to his philosophical roots to define the meaning of "1": as a numeral, a mathematical concept, and as a social and cultural idea. In typical Socratic fashion, after posing significant questions and hinting at possible answers to those questions, Kingwell leaves the reader with even more questions to ponder.

1

MARK KINGWELL

1   In [the] hit comedy *Wedding Crashers*, the slick motor-mouth Jeremy, played by Vince Vaughn, effectively seduces a young woman by riffing on the "metaphysical awareness" he acquired in a moment of crisis, seeing a friend in danger. (He burnishes it with a reference to "the 19th-century German philosopher Schopenhauer," which he pronounces "Shoppen-hower.")

2   What is the awareness? "That we are all one," Jeremy croons to the girl, "that separateness is an illusion, that I'm one with everyone." Before suggesting his cheek might perhaps be one with hers, Jeremy offers a superbly demented catalogue of people with

whom he, in particular, is one—among them the Olsen Twins, Natalie Portman, Jay-Z, the guy who wrote *Catcher in the Rye*, Nat King Cole, Harry Potter (if he existed), Carrot Top, and the whore on the street corner.

This surely ranks as the sole line of dialogue, past or future, to link Jay-Z and Nat Cole; but its comedy runs deeper than a garbage list of popmental clutter. Jeremy may be nuts but he's no dummy. Indeed, his cynicism neatly dices up that common saw of cheap compassion, the oneness of us all. This "we are all one" speech is just one dart in a quiver full of cheesy lines guaranteed to make wedding-softened lovelies fall for him. . . .   3

Are we all one? Is there a power of one? What is the meaning of one, anyway? Bryce Courtenay's novel, *The Power of One*, implies an individual has the ability to make a difference. There is also the power of being number one, as when the University of Texas football team won the Rose Bowl. (This claim is ubiquitous, everywhere symbolized by the oversized novelty finger with team logo stencilled on foam—the ultimate positional good.)   4

In a less attractive recent usage, there is the killing power of a single soldier as lauded by a U.S. Army recruitment campaign—conveniently overlooking the essence of all military hierarchy, which is to suppress individual decision in order to exploit individual courage.   5

One may be (as the Harry Nilsson song goes) the loneliest number you'll ever do, but it is a happy king of the mathematical world: one half of the binary code bit, the stuff of the universe; the value signifying certainty in the world of probability theory. Statisticians are familiar with Benford's Law, which shows that around 30 percent of the numbers in any collection of data—from stock market prices to the heat capacities of chemicals—will begin with the digit 1. Two follows at about 18 per cent, and so on down to nine at about 4.5 per cent. Nobody is quite sure why.   6

You can see why the metaphysical-oneness line might be effective—if only in the overheated male fantasyland of the movies. It is, after all, something we wish to be true, one of those standard bromides of the age. It is invoked equally as a panacea for racism (beneath the skin, we're all human!) and a solution to ideological disagreement (beyond the debate, creationists are people too!).   7

In a romantic context, the oneness thesis is piggybacked to—or maybe even underwrites—the widespread notion that love is a fusion of souls, an overcoming of separateness. Indeed, generalized oneness is widely supposed to transcend every imaginable difference and all manner of conflict, such that, if we only had eyes to see,   8 we would appreciate our essential brother- and sisterhood—only some of which, presumably, would involve later physical oneness.

9   That is nonsense in both the strict and loose senses. In the loose sense, it is sentimental eyewash, often enough in the service of the current arrangement. As the French critic and philosopher Roland Barthes points out in his essay *The Great Family of Man*, claims for universal humanity are almost invariably conservative in tendency. They ignore history, and so work to leave everything as it is. Barthes calls this ideology of essential sameness "Adamism."

10   Here, "we are held back at the surface of an identity, prevented precisely by sentimentality from penetrating into this ulterior zone of human behaviour where historical alienation introduces some 'differences,' which we shall here quite simply call 'injustices.'" The "wisdom" and the "lyricism" of oneness are mere gestures that defuse, via cheap emotion, the truths of difference. French president Jacques Chirac may claim that all French citizens are one, but riots in *les banlieues* give his words the lie.

11   Even the inescapable fact of death is not shared in this banal great-family sense, despite the frequent allusions by the rich and powerful that they, too, will someday die. Such existential mugging should always remind us of Anatole France's tart assessment of "equality before the law," namely that it forbids rich and poor alike to steal firewood or to sleep under bridges.

12   The oneness of us all is also nonsense in the strict sense, which is to say that it has no truth-value at all, being neither true nor false. This may be one reason it is so often invoked as loose nonsense, since sentiments without truth-value cannot be denied. We cannot be all one without ceasing to be us. If that were so, there would be no us for us all to be one of. To be one would mean there was no non-one, rendering the category meaninglessly wide. The idea that we-are-all-one is, as the 18th-century German philosopher Georg Wilhelm Friedrich Hegel said, the night in which all cows are black.

13   We can push the thought of oneness still further. If the concept of "one" means a whole, somehow indivisible or coherent, it must possess limit: One cannot be merely undifferentiated stuff.

14   But that which has a limit establishes the region beyond itself as not-it. One thus immediately implies, at least, two: that which is one, and everything else. For the Pythagoreans, among others, there could not be one one, there had to be two; and if there were two, there had to be more. Hence, among other things, numbers are revealed as a divine expression of the cosmos. Later, on the basis of similar logic, Hegel could even claim, in apparent violation of the law of non-contradiction, that "A" is equivalent to "not-A" because both necessitate the other.

I agree that this rarely comes up in daily life. A more pressing 15
and practical question is what makes for oneness anywhere at all?
A recent dinner-table dispute in my family involved the issue of
what counted as "one chocolate." Did that mean one chunk of con-
fection taken from the passing box, or (my own view) the contents
of one miniature paper cup, which sometimes included more than
one piece? Like Democritus in the ancient world and Niels Bohr in
the modern, we seek the truth of the atom; but when is the piece
not the whole? The rival parties both understood the notion of oneness perfectly well; they just didn't apply it at the same point,
meaning that there was, as it were, no longer any such thing as
"one chocolate." Let us call this Burdick's Paradox, after the brand
of chocolates in question.

Most of the time, we have no trouble distinguishing one unit 16
from another, seeing this or that thing as not something else. I take
an apple, you take an apple. If there is just one, we cut it in pieces—
perhaps applying a neat dinner-table version of distributive justice
to do so by having the cutter taking the last piece. Sometimes a unit
is a function of a system of exchange, as with one dollar or one
metre, and without substance; sometimes it is a token issued from a
type, as with a reproduced song or postcard. We nimbly negotiate
these everyday ones and manys without difficulty, avoiding both
reduction to sameness, on the one hand, and creeping Platonism of
master-types, on the other.

But consider an ancient problem once more occupying the 17
attention of many professional philosophers: When does one
become many? One grain of sand is not a heap. Neither is two. On
the other hand, we all know a heap when we see it. So at what
point—with the addition of which new grain—does the non-heap
become the heap?

Heaps of sand may not interest you, but many important con- 18
cepts are also subject to these problems of vagueness between one
and many. The idea of one person is one of them. How many limbs
or organs can I lose before I cease to be myself? How many brain
cells or memories or intellectual capacities? We recognize each
other as one pretty reliably, but at the margins—where vagueness
rules—things are not so clear. My identity may seem reliably to
belong to me, but to what degree is it dependent on your seeing me
as me? Not the oneness of everything, but the fragility of one's personal oneness in the face of everything.

Integrity is a notion found in both ethics and materials science, but 19
it derives a more basic meaning from mathematics. Integer is the
name we give to a whole number, something entire and complete;

and thus, by metaphorical extension, to something sound or good. One good thing, there (*teger* being the Latin for "touch") for the touching. Tangible oneness.

20   Four centuries into the modern era, we are well aware of the limitations inherent in what political philosophers call "atomic individualism." Everybody counts for one, in votes and in claims on the state we share; legitimacy begins and ends here. But if we come to view individuals as fundamentally self-interested and separate, at war with their neighbours, alienation and conflict loom. What starts as a great victory for the self declines swiftly into pathology: not deliberation between friends but bargaining among strangers.

21   The truth is that there are duties, both ethical and civic, that make no sense without a prior commitment to a web of care, which, however tenuously, connects one person to another. We are not alone, because we cannot be who we are in the first place without the others for whom we act, and from whom we seek recognition.

22   But that doesn't mean we are all part of one great family. The power of oneness as integrity lies not in us all being one, but in our each being so. Not later in death, and not under the skin; but now, as we are—and aren't—the same. Call this recognition "justice," or anyway its beginning.

23   Just one person's view, of course. And don't get me started on zero.

A professor of philosophy at the University of Toronto, Mark Kingwell (b. 1963) specializes in political and cultural theory, citizenship and justice theory, and the philosophy of architecture and design. He was educated at the   and Yale. Kingwell is the author of nine books on philosophy and cultural theory, including *Better Living: In Pursuit of Happiness from Plato to Prozac* (1998), *Nothing for Granted* (2005), and *Nearest Thing to Heaven* (2006). His articles and reviews have appeared in numerous academic journals and more than 40 mainstream publications, including *Harper's*, *Utne Magazine*, *The New York Times Magazine*, and *The Globe and Mail*. He has been a television columnist for *Saturday Night*, a political columnist for *Adbusters*, and a comment-page columnist for the *National Post*. He also writes a column on cocktails for *Toro*.

GLOSSARY

ABSTRACT and **CONCRETE** are terms used to describe two kinds of nouns. **Abstract nouns** name ideas, terms, feelings, qualities, measurements—concepts we understand through our minds. For example, *idea, term, feeling, quality,* and *measurement* are all abstract words. **Concrete nouns**, on the other hand, name things we perceive through our senses: we can see, hear, touch, taste, or smell what they stand for. *Author, rhythm, penguin, apple,* and *smoke* are all concrete nouns.

An **ALLUSION** is a reference to something—a person, a concept, a quotation, or a character—from literature, history, mythology, politics, or any other field familiar to your readers. For instance, if you were to describe one of your friends as "another Bubbles" (referring to a character in the TV show *Trailer Park Boys*), the reader might picture a bespectacled, cat-loving, foul-mouthed but lovable character who isn't too bright but represents the voice of reason and conscience in your group.

There are two guidelines for the effective use of allusions. First, allude to events, books, people, or quotations that are known to your readers. If your readers have never seen *Trailer Park Boys*, they will have no mental image of Bubbles, so they will be no better informed; worse, they may feel frustrated because they are "missing something." Detailed knowledge of your intended audience and their cultural frames of reference will help you choose appropriate allusions.

Second, be sure your allusions are clear and unambiguous. A reference to "King" could mean Mackenzie King, B.B. King, Stephen King, or Martin Luther King, Jr. Who knows? Imagine the confusion if the reader has the wrong King in mind.

AMBIGUITY: An ambiguous statement is one that has two or more meanings. An ambiguous action is one that can be interpreted in more than one way. When used deliberately and carefully, ambiguity can add richness of meaning to your writing; however, most of the time ambiguity is not planned and leads to confusion. For instance, the statement "He never has enough money" could mean that he is always broke, or that he is never satisfied no matter how much money he has. As a general rule, it is wise to avoid ambiguity in your writing.

An **ANALOGY** is a comparison. Writers explain complicated or unfamiliar concepts by comparing them to simple or familiar ones. For instance, one could draw an analogy between life's experiences and a race: the stages of life—infancy, childhood, adolescence, maturity, old age—become the laps of the race, and the problems or crises of life become the hurdles of an obstacle course. If we "trip and fall," we've encountered a crisis; if we "get up and continue the race," we refuse to let the crisis defeat us. See Jeffrey Moussaieff Masson's "Dear Dad" (page 80) for an extended analogy between penguins and humans. Analogies are often used for stylistic or dramatic effect, as well as to explain or illustrate a point.

ANALYSIS means looking at the parts of something individually and considering how they contribute to the whole. In essay writing, the common kinds of analysis are **process analysis** and **causal analysis**. See the introductions to Unit 2, Process Analysis (page 61), and Unit 5, Causal Analysis (page 161), for more detailed explanations.

An **ANECDOTE** is a short account of an event or incident, often humorous, that is used to catch the reader's interest and illustrate a point. Writers frequently use this technique to introduce an essay. See paragraph 1 of Brent Staples' "Just Walk On By" (page 173) and paragraphs 2 and 3 of Curtis Gillespie's "Bling Bling" (page 213) for examples of effective anecdotes.

ARGUMENT/PERSUASION: See RHETORICAL MODES.

The **AUDIENCE** is the writer's intended reader or readers. Knowing their level of understanding, their interests, and their expectations of what they are reading is critically important to the writer. TONE, level of vocabulary, the amount of detail included, even the organizational structure, will all be influenced by the needs of the audience.

When you speak to children, you instinctively use simple, direct language and short sentences. You adapt your speaking style to suit your listeners. Similarly, good writers adapt their prose to suit their readers. Before you begin to write, think about your readers' knowledge of your topic, their educational background, and their probable age level. These factors will influence their interests and, consequently, their initial attitude to your paper. Will they approach it with interest? Or will they pick it up with a yawn? (If the latter is the case, you will have to work harder.) Never talk down to your readers, but don't talk over their heads, either, or they will stop reading.

For example, suppose you are preparing an article on the appeal of sports cars to the public. For a popular women's magazine, you would probably stress reliability, style, and comfort, and you would support your thesis with examples of stylish women who love the sports cars they drive. You would not include much technical automotive jargon. If you were writing about the same topic for a general-audience magazine, however, you would include more specifics about base price, family-friendly options, ease and cost of maintenance, fuel consumption, and reliability under various weather and road conditions. You would probably include easy-to-read statistical tables comparing several popular makes. And if you were writing for a publication such as *Popular Mechanics* or *Road and Track,* you would include detailed statistics on performance, handling under high speed or unusual road conditions, and the ease or difficulty with which owners could maintain their cars themselves.

The **BODY** of any piece of writing is the part that comes between the INTRODUCTION and the CONCLUSION. In a PARAGRAPH, the body consists of sentences supporting and developing the TOPIC SENTENCE, which identifies the paragraph's KEY IDEA. In an essay, the BODY consists of paragraphs that explain, discuss, or prove the essay's THESIS.

CHRONOLOGICAL ORDER means time order. Items or ideas that are introduced chronologically are discussed in order of *time sequence*. Historical accounts are usually presented chronologically. In a chronological arrangement of KEY IDEAS, TRANSITIONS such as *first, second, third, next, then, after that,* and *finally* help to keep your reader on track. See the introduction to Unit 2, Process Analysis (page 61), for further details.

A **CLICHÉ** is a phrase or expression that has been used so often that it no longer conveys much meaning. Any phrase that you can automatically complete after reading the first two or three words is a cliché. Consider, for example, the expressions *better late than* _____, *easier said than* _____, and *as stubborn as a* _____. The endings are so predictable that readers can (and do) skip over them.

CLIMACTIC ORDER is the arrangement of points in order of importance. Writers usually arrange their KEY IDEAS so that the most important or strongest idea comes last. Thus, the paper builds up to a climax.

COHERENCE is the continuous logical connection between the KEY IDEAS of a piece of writing. In a coherent paper, one paragraph leads logically to the next. Ideas are clearly sequenced within a paragraph and between paragraphs. The topic is consistent throughout; and the writer has supplied carefully chosen and logical TRANSITIONS such as *also, however, nevertheless, on the other hand, first, second,* and *thus*. If a paper is coherent, it is probably unified as well. (See UNITY.)

COLLOQUIALISM: Colloquial language is the language we speak. Expressions such as *guys, okay, a lot,* and *kids* are acceptable in informal speech but are not appropriate in essays, research papers, or reports. Contractions (such as *they're, isn't, it's,* and *let's*) and abbreviations (such as *TV, ads,* and *photos*) that are often used in speech are appropriate in writing only if the writer is consciously trying to achieve a casual, informal effect.

CONCLUSION: The conclusion of any piece of writing is what will stay with your reader; therefore, it should be both logical and memorable. A good conclusion contributes to the overall UNITY of the piece, so a conclusion is no place to throw in a new point you just thought of, or a few leftover details. Your conclusion should reinforce your THESIS, but it should not simply restate it or repeat it word for word (boring). Here are five strategies you can choose from to create an effective conclusion:

1. *Refer back to your introduction.* "Refer" does not mean "repeat." It means alluding to the content of your introduction and, if the connection is not obvious, clarifying the link for your readers. Good examples of this strategy include "Dispatches from the Poverty Line" (page 33), "What I Have Lived For" (page 122), "The Dimensions of a Complete Life" (page 124), and "The Cute Factor" (page 227).

2. *Ask a rhetorical question*—one that is intended to emphasize a point, not to elicit an answer. See the concluding paragraph of "Listen Up" (page 105).

3. *Issue a challenge.* See the conclusion of "She Said, He Said" (page 136).

4. *Highlight the value or significance of your topic.* See the last paragraph of "Why Write?" (page 244).

5. *Conclude with a relevant, thought-provoking quotation.*

There are several other techniques you can use to conclude effectively: provide a suggestion for change, offer a solution, make a prediction, or end with an ANECDOTE that illustrates your THESIS. Whatever strategy you choose, you should leave your reader with a sense that you have completed your discussion of your thesis, not that your paper has "just stopped."

CONCRETE: See ABSTRACT/CONCRETE.

CONNOTATION and **DENOTATION:** The **denotation** of a word is its literal or dictionary meaning. **Connotation** refers to the emotional overtones the word has in the reader's mind. Some words have only a few connotations, while others have many. For instance, "house" is a word whose denotative meaning is familiar to all; it has few connotations. "Home," on the other hand, is also denotatively familiar, but this word has rich connotative meanings that differ from reader to reader. (See, for example, the essay by Ken Wiwa on page 210.)

To take another example, the word "prison" is denotatively a "place of confinement for lawbreakers convicted of serious crimes." But the connotations of the word are much deeper and broader: when we hear or read the word "prison," we think of colours like grey and black; we hear sounds of clanging doors or wailing sirens; and we associate emotions like anger, fear, despair, or loneliness with the word. A careful writer will not use this word lightly: it would be inappropriate, and therefore bad style, to refer to your workplace as a "prison" simply because you don't like the location or the length of the lunch break.

CONTEXT is the verbal background of a word or phrase—the words that come before and after it and determine its meaning. For example, the word "period," which has many different meanings, refers to a particular kind of sentence structure in Eva Hoffman's "Lost in Translation" (page 333).

When a word or phrase is taken *out of context,* it is often difficult to determine what it originally meant. Therefore, when you are quoting from another writer, be sure to include enough of the context so that the meaning is clear to your reader.

DEDUCTION is the logical process of applying a general statement to a specific instance and reasoning through to a conclusion about that instance. See also INDUCTION.

DESCRIPTION: See RHETORICAL MODES.

DICTION refers to the choice and arrangement of words in a written work. Effective diction is that which is suited to the topic, the AUDIENCE, and the PURPOSE of the piece. Good writers do not carelessly mix formal with colloquial language, Standard English with dialect or slang, or informal vocabulary with technical JARGON or archaisms (outmoded, antique phrases). Writing for a general audience about the closing of a neighbourhood grocery store, a careful writer would not say, "The local retail establishment for the purveyance of essential foods and beverages has shut its portals for the last time." This statement is pretentious nonsense (see GOBBLEDYGOOK). A careful writer would say, "The corner store has been closed." This statement conveys the same meaning, but it states the message concisely and appropriately.

EMPHASIS: A writer can highlight important points in several ways: through *placement* (the essay's first and last sections are the most prominent positions); *repetition;* or *phrasing.* Careful phrasing can call attention to a particular point. Parallel structure, a very short sentence or paragraph, even a deliberate sentence fragment are all emphatic devices. A writer can also add emphasis by developing an idea at greater length; by directly calling attention to its significance; or by inserting expressions such as "significantly" or "most important." TONE, particularly IRONY or even sarcasm, can be used to add emphasis. Finally, diction can be used as an emphatic device. See Danny Irvine's "A Tree-Planting Primer" (page 85) and Curtis Gillespie's "Bling Bling" (page 213) for good examples of distinctive diction.

EVIDENCE in a piece of writing functions the same way it does in a court of law: it proves the point. Evidence can consist of facts, statistical data, examples, expert opinions, surveys, illustrations, quotations or PARAPHRASES. Charts, graphs, and maps are also forms of evidence and are well suited to particular kinds of reports.

A point cannot be effectively explained, let alone proved, without evidence. For instance, it is not enough to say that computers are displacing many workers. You need to find specific examples of companies, jobs, and statistics to prove the connection. After all, the number of dogs in Canada has increased almost as much as the number of computers. Does that prove that dogs breed computers? What makes a paper credible and convincing is the evidence presented and the COHERENCE with which it is presented. See Wade Davis's "The End of the Wild" (page 48) for an example of effective use of several kinds of evidence.

EXPOSITION: See RHETORICAL MODES.

FIGURES OF SPEECH are words or phrases that mean something more than the literal meanings of the individual words or phrases. Writers choose to use figurative language when they want the reader to associate one thing with another. Some of the more common figures of speech include SIMILES, METAPHORS, IRONY, PERSONIFICATIONS, and PUNS.

GENERAL and **SPECIFIC: General words** refer to classes or groups of things. "Bird" is a general word; so is "fruit." **Specific words** refer to individual members of a class or group; e.g., "penguin" or "lemon." Good writing is a careful blend of general and specific language. (See also ABSTRACT/CONCRETE.)

GOBBLEDYGOOK is a type of JARGON characterized by wordy, pretentious language. Writing that has chains of vague, abstract words and long, complicated sentences—sound without meaning—is gobbledygook. See the example included under DICTION.

ILLUSTRATION: See the introduction to Unit 1, in the "Example" section.

INDUCTION is the logical process of looking at a number of specific instances and reasoning through to a general conclusion about them. See also DEDUCTION.

INTRODUCTION: The introduction to any piece of writing is crucial to its success. A good introduction catches the reader's attention, identifies the THESIS of the piece, and establishes the TONE. It "hooks" the reader, making him or her curious to see what you have to say. Here are five different attention-getters you can use:

1. *Begin with a story related to your topic.* The story could be an ANECDOTE (a factual, often humorous account of an incident) or a scenario (an account of an imagined situation). See the first four paragraphs of Curtis Gillespie's "Bling Bling" (page 213) for an example of a good anecdotal introduction.

2. *Begin with a striking fact or startling statistic.* See the first paragraph of "Listen Up" (page 105).

3. *Set up a comparison or contrast to hook your reader.* See the introduction to Jeffrey Moussaieff Masson's "Dear Dad" (page 80) for a comparison and the introduction to Thane Rosenbaum's "Yeah, But the Book Is Better" (page 155) for a contrast.

4. *Begin by stating a common opinion that you intend to challenge.* See "Why Write?" (page 244).

5. *Begin with a question or series of questions.* See the introduction to "The Trouble with Readers" (page 163).

Other strategies you might want to experiment with include beginning with a relevant quotation, offering a definition (yours, not the dictionary's), or even telling a joke. You know how important first impressions are when you meet someone. Treat your introductory paragraph with the same care you take when you want to make a good first impression on a person. If you bait the hook attractively, your reader will want to read on.

IRONY is a way of saying one thing while meaning something else, often the opposite of what the words themselves signify. To call a hopelessly ugly painting a masterpiece is an example of verbal irony. For an extended example of verbal irony, see Danny Irvine's "A Tree-Planting Primer" (page 85). Situations can also be ironic: in Dennis Bodanis's "Toothpaste" (page 110), we learn that a health-and-beauty product is concocted from disgusting ingredients; in Anwar F. Accawi's "The Telephone" (page 178), the instrument that was supposed to enhance the life of a village in fact destroys it.

Irony is an effective technique because it forces readers to think about the relationship between seemingly incompatible things or ideas. Jessica Mitford's "Behind the Formaldehyde Curtain" (page 92) is a well-known piece of extended irony. Although she seems on the surface to be enthusiastic about the processes of embalming and restoration, Mitford forces her readers to consider the possibility that these practices are unnatural, even barbaric.

JARGON is the specialized language used within a particular trade, discipline, or profession. Among members of that trade or profession, jargon is an efficient, timesaving means of communication. Outside the context of the trade or profession, however, jargon is inappropriate because it inhibits rather than promotes the listener's or reader's understanding. Another meaning of jargon—the meaning usually intended when the word is used in this text—is pretentious language or GOBBLEDYGOOK, which means using words in a misguided attempt to impress readers rather than to convey meaning.

KEY IDEAS are the main points into which the development of a THESIS is divided. (See also PARAGRAPH.)

A **METAPHOR** is a figurative rather than a literal comparison. An effective metaphor is one that draws a fresh, imaginative connection between two dissimilar things. Dennis Dermody, for example, writes that a movie theatre is "a jungle . . . filled with a lot of really stupid animals" ("Sit Down and Shut Up or Don't Sit by Me," page 107). An apt, unusual metaphor makes the writer's idea memorable.

NARRATION: See RHETORICAL MODES.

ORDER refers to the arrangement of information (KEY IDEAS) in a paper. While you are still in the planning stage, choose the order most appropriate to your THESIS. There are four arrangements to choose from:

1. *Chronological order* means in order of time, from first to last.
2. *Climactic order* means arranging your points so that the strongest one comes last (the climax). Present your second-strongest point first, then tuck in your not-so-strong point(s) where it will attract least attention, and conclude with your clincher.

3. *Causal* or *logical order* refers to the arrangement of key ideas that are logically/causally linked. One point must be explained before the next can be understood. In process and causal analysis, where there is a direct and logical connection between one point and the next, this arrangement of key ideas is the obvious one to choose.

4. *Random order* is a shopping-list kind of arrangement: the points can be presented in any order without loss of effectiveness. Random order is appropriate only when your key points are all equal in significance and not logically or causally linked.

A **PARAGRAPH** is a unit of prose made up of a group of sentences (usually between 5 and 12) all dealing with one point or KEY IDEA. In an essay, you argue or explain your THESIS in a number of key ideas. Each key idea is developed in one or more paragraphs.

Most paragraphs have a TOPIC SENTENCE—a sentence that states the point of the paragraph and is often (but not always) the first or second sentence. The sentences that follow develop the point using one or more supporting strategies: examples, specific details, definition, quotation or paraphrase, comparison and/or contrast. All sentences in the paragraph should be clearly related to its key idea.

Each paragraph should be COHERENT and UNIFIED and should lead the reader smoothly to the next (see TRANSITION). The essays of Bertrand Russell (page 122) and Wade Davis (page 48) deserve careful analysis: their paragraphs are models of form.

PARALLELISM describes a series of words, phrases, clauses, or sentences that are all expressed in the same grammatical construction. In a parallel sentence, for example, the items in a series would be written as single words, phrases, or clauses. Julius Caesar's famous pronouncement, "I came, I saw, I conquered," is a classic example of parallelism.

Parallelism creates symmetry that is pleasing to the reader. Lack of parallelism, on the other hand, can be jarring: "His favourite sports are skiing, skating, and he particularly loves to sail." Such potholes in your prose should be fixed up before you hand in a paper. For example, "What Carol says, she means; and she delivers what she promises, too" would be much more effective if rewritten in parallel form: "What Carol says, she means; what she promises, she delivers."

Because the human mind responds favourably to the repetition of rhythm, parallelism is an effective device for adding EMPHASIS. "The Dimensions of a Complete Life" by Martin Luther King, Jr., contains numerous examples of parallelism in DICTION, SYNTAX, and PARAGRAPH structure.

To **PARAPHRASE** is to put another writer's ideas into your own words. You must acknowledge the original writer as the source of the idea. If you don't, you are guilty of plagiarism.

Paraphrasing is essential when you are writing a research paper. Once you have gathered the information you need from various sources and organized your ideas into an appropriate order, you write the paper, drawing on your sources for supporting evidence but expressing the sources' ideas in your own words.

A paraphrase should reflect both the meaning and the general TONE of the original. It may be the same length or shorter than the original (but it is not a PRÉCIS). For more information on paraphrasing, including instructions and examples, see our Web site: www.cancon6e.nelson.com.

PERSONIFICATION is a figure of speech in which the writer gives human qualities to an inanimate object or an abstract idea. For instance, if you write, "The brakes screeched when I hit them," you are comparing the sound of the car's brakes to a human voice. Strive for original and insightful personifications; otherwise, you will be trapped by CLICHÉS such as "The solution to the problem was staring me in the face."

PERSUASION: See RHETORICAL MODES and the introduction to Unit 7, Argument and Persuasion.

POINT OF VIEW, in EXPOSITION, means the narrative angle of the essay: who's telling the story? (In PERSUASION and ARGUMENT, point of view can also mean the writer's opinion in the essay.)

If the writer identifies himself as "I," the essay is written from the first-person point of view. In this case, we expect to encounter the writer's own opinions and first-hand experiences. All of the essays in Unit 1 are written in the first person.

If the writer is not grammatically "present," the essay is written from the third-person point of view. Most of the essays in Units 2 through 8 are written primarily in the third person. The writer uses "one," "he," "she," and "they," and the result is more formal than an essay written in the first person.

A careful writer maintains point of view consistently throughout an essay; if a shift occurs, it should be for a good reason, with a particular effect in mind. Careless shifts in point of view confuse the reader. See Lewis Thomas's "Altruism" (page 234) for an example of a purposeful change in point of view. Paragraphs 1 through 8, which explain altruistic behaviour among animals, are written in the third person. In paragraph 9, Thomas shifts focus and deliberately changes to the first-person plural point of view to reinforce his discussion of altruism among humans.

A **PRÉCIS** is a condensed SUMMARY of an article or essay. It is one-quarter to one-third the length of the original. The examples and ILLUSTRATIONS are omitted, and the prose is tightened up as much as possible. All the KEY IDEAS are included; most of the development is not.

A **PUN** is a word or phrase that brings to the reader's mind two meanings at one time. Max Eastman, in his book *Enjoyment of Laughter*, classifies puns into three sorts: atrocious, witty, and poetic. The person who wrote, "How does Dolly Parton stack up against Mae West?" was guilty of an atrocious pun. Martin Edlund's title "The World Is Phat" (page 114) contains a witty pun, as do Trina Rys's "The Slender Trap" (page 165) and Emily Nussbaum's "Net Gain: A Pollyanna-ish View of Online Personals" (page 257). Poetic puns go beyond the merely humorous double meaning and offer the reader a concise, original comparison of two entities, qualities, or ideas.

PURPOSE means the writer's intent: to inform, to persuade, or to amuse, or a combination of these. See RHETORICAL MODES.

RHETORICAL MODES: The word "rhetoric" means the art of using language effectively. There are four classic modes, or kinds, of writing: exposition, narration, description, and argument/persuasion. The writer's choice of mode is determined by his or her PURPOSE.

EXPOSITION is writing intended to inform or explain. Expository writing can be personal or impersonal, serious or light-hearted. The various methods of exposition (such as definition, comparison, process analysis, and the rest) are sometimes called *rhetorical patterns*.

NARRATION tells a story. Examples of narrative writing are often found in ANECDOTES or ILLUSTRATIONS within expository prose. Michael Ignatieff's "Deficits" (page 41) and Shandi Mitchell's "Baba and Me" (page 18) are good examples of the use of narration to develop a THESIS.

DESCRIPTION is writing that appeals to our senses: it makes us see, hear, taste, smell, or feel whatever is being described. Descriptive writing is often used to help develop KEY IDEAS in a piece of EXPOSITION or ARGUMENT. In addition to the essays in Unit 1, see the essays by David Bodanis (page 110), Germaine Greer (page 137), and Anwar F. Accawi (page 178) for examples of effective description.

ARGUMENT, sometimes called PERSUASION, is writing that sets out not only to explain something but also to convince the reader of the validity of the writer's opinion on an issue. Sometimes its purpose goes even further, and the writer attempts to motivate the reader to act in some way. Like exposition, argument conveys information to the reader, but not solely for the purpose of making a topic clear. Argument seeks to reinforce or to change a reader's opinion about an issue.

SATIRE is a form of humour, sometimes light-hearted, sometimes biting, in which the writer deliberately attacks and ridicules something: a person, a political decision, an event, an institution, a philosophy, or a system. The satirist uses exaggeration, ridicule, and IRONY to achieve his or her effect. There is often a social purpose in satire: the writer points to the difference between the ideal—a world based on common sense and moral standards—and the real, which may be silly, vicious, alienating, or immoral, depending on the object of the satirist's attack. Many of the authors of the selections in this book employ satire in the development of one or more of their KEY IDEAS: for example, "Put What Where?" (page 69), "The Pleasures of the Text" (page 270), "Stupid Jobs Are Good to Relax With" (page 274), and "I, Pixman" (page 301). Jessica Mitford's "Behind the Formaldehyde Curtain" (page 92) is an example of an extended satire.

A **SIMILE** is a stated or explicit comparison between two things. Most similes are introduced by *like* or *as*. In the following sentence, Douglas Coupland uses two similes to describe the raw beauty of the Yukon landscape: "Glaciers drape like mink over feldspar ridges like broken backs" ("The Yukon," page 22).

SPECIFIC: See GENERAL/SPECIFIC.

A **STEREOTYPE** is a fixed idea that a person holds about another person or group of people, an idea based on prejudice rather than reality. Stereotypes are based on generalizations: broad conclusions about whole classes of people. For example: women are poor drivers; truck drivers are illiterate; teenagers are boors. Stereotypical notions about races and nationalities are particularly objectionable: think of the well-known "Newfie" jokes, for example.

A careful writer avoids stereotypes, unless he or she is using them for satiric purposes. Unthinking acceptance of others' assumptions is a sure sign of a lazy mind. See Pat Capponi's "Dispatches from the Poverty Line" (page 33) and Wayson Choy's "I'm a Banana and Proud of It" (page 205) for two quite different explorations of stereotypes.

STYLE is the distinctive way a person writes. When two writers approach the same topic, even if they share many of the same ideas, the resulting works will be different. The difference is a product of the writers' personal styles. DICTION, sentence structure, paragraph length, TONE, and level of formality all contribute to style. For different stylistic treatments of similar topics, compare Mario Vargas Llosa's "With Pens Drawn" (page 361) and Carol Shields' "The Case for Curling Up with a Book" (page 359).

Good writers adapt their style to their AUDIENCE and PURPOSE. Academic writers and business writers do not write the same way because they are not writing for the same readers or for the same reasons. Similarly, good writers adapt their style to suit their topic. This stylistic adjustment is almost instinctive: you would not write an informal and humorous account of a teenage suicide, nor would you use a highly formal style in a promotional piece on new toys for the holiday season.

A **SUMMARY** is a brief statement, in sentence or paragraph form, of the KEY IDEAS of an article or essay. Compare PRÉCIS and PARAPHRASE. For instructions and examples, see www.cancon6e.nelson.com.

SYNTAX means the arrangement of words in a sentence. Good syntax means not only grammatical correctness, but also effective word order and variety of sentence patterns. Good writers use short sentences and long ones, simple sentences and complex ones, and natural-order sentences and inverted-order ones. The choice depends on the meaning and EMPHASIS the writer wants to communicate. See "Sentences: Kinds and Parts," www.cancon6e.nelson.com.

A **THESIS** is the particular approach to or point about a topic that the writer wants to communicate to the reader in an essay. It is often expressed in a *thesis statement*. (See "How to Write to Be Understood," page xxvii of the Introduction.) Sometimes professional writers do not include an identifiable thesis statement in their essay or article. Inexperienced writers would do well *not* to follow their example. A clearly stated thesis—one that expresses the central idea that everything in the essay is designed to support and explain—is the best guide you can provide for your reader. Equally important, it helps the writer to stay focused.

TONE reflects the writer's attitude to the topic and to his or her intended AUDIENCE. For instance, a writer who is looking back with longing to the past will use a nostalgic tone. An angry writer might use an indignant, outraged tone, or an understated, ironic tone—depending on the topic and purpose of the piece.

Through DICTION, POINT OF VIEW, sentence structure, PARAGRAPH development, and STYLE, a writer modulates his or her message to suit the knowledge, attitude, and expectations of the target audience. Contrast the bossy, dictatorial tone of Dennis Dermody's "Sit Down and Shut Up or Don't Sit by Me" (page 107) with the less aggressive, more reasoned, and appreciative tone of Rick Groen's "The Magic of Moviegoing" (page 65). Other examples of superb control of tone are Jessica Mitford's scathing "Behind the Formaldehyde Curtain" (page 92), Michael Ignatieff's sympathetic "Deficits" (page 41), Paul Quarrington's humorously informative "Home Brew" (page 72), and Mark Kingwell's playfully philosophic exploration of the meaning of "1" (page 356).

A **TOPIC SENTENCE** is a sentence that identifies the main point or KEY IDEA developed in a paragraph. The topic sentence is usually found at or near the beginning of the paragraph.

TRANSITIONS are linking words or phrases. They help connect a writer's sentences and paragraphs so that the whole piece flows smoothly and logically. Here are some of the most common transitions used to show relationships between ideas:

1. *To show a time relation:* first, second, third, next, before, during, after, now, then, finally, last

2. *To add an idea or example:* in addition, also, another, furthermore, similarly, for example, for instance

3. *To show contrast:* although, but, however, instead, nevertheless, on the other hand, in contrast, on the contrary

4. *To show a cause–effect relationship:* as a result, consequently, because, since, therefore, thus

   See also COHERENCE.

UNITY: A piece of writing has unity if all of its parts work together to contribute to the ultimate effect. A unified piece (paragraph, essay, article, report) develops one topic in one tone. Unity is an important quality of any piece of prose: each sentence of a paragraph must relate to and develop the KEY IDEA expressed in the TOPIC SENTENCE; each paragraph must relate to and develop the THESIS of the paper.

COPYRIGHT ACKNOWLEDGMENTS

Introduction, page xlii: "Cycling in the 1890s," by Katherine Murtha, in *Canadian Woman Studies*, vol. 21, no. 3 (Winter 2001/Spring 2002), pp. 119–121. (Revised, 2006)

Unit 1, page 8: "A Cultural Exchange," by Brian Green; **10:** "Escape to Paradise," by Armin Kumarshellah. Reprinted with permission from the author; **13:** "Finding a Flatmate," by Hilary Doyle. *Maisonneuve Magazine*, 14 November 2005. Reprinted with permission from the author; **18:** "Baba and Me," by Shandi Mitchell, 2001. Published originally in *Confluences*. Reprinted by permission of the author; **22:** "The Yukon," from *Souvenir of Canada,* by Douglas Coupland. Copyright © 2002 by Douglas Coupland. Published by Douglas & McIntyre Ltd. Reprinted by permission of the publisher; **25:** "My Life as a Cleaner," by Noreen Shanahan. *Toronto Life*, March 2005. Reprinted with permission from the author. Noreen Shanahan's forthcoming book is entitled *Dirt: A Writer's Survival Guide*; **33:** Excerpt from *Dispatches from the Poverty Line,* by Pat Capponi. Copyright © 1997 by Pat Capponi. Reprinted with permission of the author and Slopen Literary Agency; **41:** "Deficits," from *Scar Tissue,* by Michael Ignatieff. Copyright © 1989 by Michael Ignatieff. Reprinted with permission; **48:** "The End of the Wild," by Wade Davis, from *The Clouded Leopard,* by Wade Davis. Copyright © 1998 by Wade Davis. Published by Douglas & McIntyre. Reprinted by permission of the publisher.

Unit 2, page 63: "Metamorphosis," by Sarah Norton; **65:** "The Magic of Moviegoing," by Rick Groen, *The Globe and Mail*, 4 January 2002. Reprinted with permission from *The Globe and Mail;* **69:** "Put What Where? 2,000 Years of Bizarre Sex Advice," by John Naish. *The Times Online*, 1 October 2005. Reprinted with permission; **72:** "Home Brew," by Paul Quarrington. Reprinted with permission from The Saint Agency/Paul Quarrington; **80:** "Dear Dad," by Jeffrey Moussaieff Masson, from THE EVOLUTION OF FATHERHOOD by Jeffrey Moussaieff Masson. Copyright © 1999 by Jeffrey Masson. Used by permission of Ballantine Books, a division of Random House; **85:** "A Tree-Planting Primer," by Danny Irvine. Reprinted with permission of the author; **92:** "Behind the Formaldehyde

Curtain," by Jessica Mitford. Copyright © 1963, 1978 by Jessica Mitford. All rights reserved. Reprinted with permission of the Estate of Jessica Mitford.

Unit 3, page 105: "Listen Up," by Nell Waldman; **107:** "Sit Down and Shut Up or Don't Sit by Me," by Dennis Dermody, from *Paper*. Copyright © 1993. Reprinted with the permission of the author; **110:** "Toothpaste," from *The Secret House,* by David Bodanis. Copyright © 1986 by David Bodanis. Reprinted with the permission of Carol Mann Agency; **114:** "The World is Phat," by Martin Edlund, *Slate*, 25 May 2005. *Slate.com* and *Washingtonpost. Newsweek Interactive.* All rights reserved. **118:** "Principled Uncertainty," from *The Pleasure of Finding Things Out,* by Richard Feynman. Copyright © 1999 by Michelle Feynman and Carl Feynman. Reprinted by permission of Perseus Books Publishers, a member of Perseus Books, L.L.C.; **122:** "What I Have Lived For," by Bertrand Russell, from *Why I Am Not a Christian.* Copyright © 2004, Taylor & Francis. Reproduced by permission of Taylor & Francis Books U.K.; **124:** "The Dimensions of a Complete Life," by Martin Luther King. Copyright © 1959 by Martin Luther King, Jr.; copyright renewed 1987 by Coretta Scott King. Reprinted by arrangement with the Estate of Martin Luther King, Jr., c/o Writers House as agent for the proprietor, New York, NY.

Unit 4, page 136: "She Said, He Said," by Eva Tihanyi; **137:** "Ottawa vs. New York," by Germaine Greer, *Times Literary Supplement*, 27 August 1999, p. 17. Reprinted with permission of the author; **142:** "Bonding Online: Websites as Substitute Communities," by David Brooks. Copyright © 2006 by The New York Times Co. Reprinted with permission; **145:** "For Minorities, Timing Is Everything," by Olive Skene Johnson. Reprinted with permission from the author; **149:** "Shorter, Slower, Weaker: And That's a Good Thing," by Jay Teitel, *Saturday Night*, August 1997. Reprinted with permission from the author; **155:** "Yeah, But the Book Is Better," by Thane Rosenbaum, *The Forward*, 23 December 2005. Reprinted with permission from the author.

Unit 5, page 163: "The Trouble with Readers," by Eva Tihanyi; **165:** "The Slender Trap," by Trina Rys. Reprinted with permission from the author; **169:** "Scaring Us Senseless," by Nassim Nicholas Taleb, from *The New York Times*, 24 July 2005. Reprinted with permission; **173:** "Just Walk On By: A Black Man Ponders His Power to Alter Public Space," by Brent Staples. Copyright © 1986. Reprinted with permission of the author; **178:** "The Telephone," from *Boy from the Tower of the Moon,* by Anwar F. Accawi, © 1999 by Anwar F. Accawi. Reprinted by permission of Beacon Press, Boston; **186:** "Saving the Songs of Innocence," by John Dixon. Copyright © John Dixon. Reprinted with permission of the author; **191:** "The Evolution of Evolution," by Dr. Helena Cronin, originally published in *Time* magazine, Winter 1997–98. Reprinted with permission of the author.

Unit 6, page 204: "Talking Pidgin," by Nell Waldman; **205:** "I'm a Banana and Proud of It," by Wayson Choy. Copyright © 1997 by Wayson Choy.

AUTHOR INDEX